Essential Words You Need to Know!

1800

주제별 필수
토플
VOCA

1800 주제별 필수 토플 VOCA

지은이 조상익
펴낸이 정규도
펴낸곳 (주)다락원

초판 1쇄 인쇄 2009년 8월 28일
초판 10쇄 발행 2023년 11월 24일

책임편집 이동호·황준
디자인 윤지영·박소연

다락원 경기도 파주시 문발로 211
내용문의 (02)736-2031 내선 550
구입문의 (02)736-2031 내선 250~252
Fax (02)732-2037
출판등록 1977년 9월 16일 제 406-2008-000007호

ISBN 978-89-5995-857-3   13740

http://www.darakwon.co.kr

다락원 홈페이지를 방문하시면 상세한 출판정보와 함께 동영상강좌, MP3자료 등 다양한 어학 정보를 얻으실 수 있습니다.

Essential Words You Need to Know!

1800

주제별 필수
토플
VOCA

DARAKWON

머리말

 TOEFL은 영어 공인 인증 시험의 하나로서 그 명성과 전통을 유지하기 위해 PBT에서 CBT로, 다시 iBT로 다양한 형태를 보이며 진화해 왔다. 하지만 그 다양한 변화에도 불구하고, TOEFL 대비 어휘 학습에 대한 중요성은 결코 변하지 않고 있으며, 오히려 더욱 강조되는 경향을 보이고 있다.

 어느 시험에서나 어휘는 많이 알고 있을수록 좋은 결과 혹은 높은 성적과 직결된다는 식으로 생각되고 있는 듯 하다. 그러나 수험생 입장에서는 시간적 제약이라는 한계와 자신의 실력 수준이라는 제약이 존재하기 때문에, 시험에 나오는 모든 어휘를 학습한 상태로 시험에 임하기는 사실상 불가능하다. 또한 TOEFL Reading 영역은 결코 상식 시험이 아니며, 더욱이 전공 시험도 아니다. 주어진 정보를 어느 정도 이해하고 있는지에 대한, 엄연한 독해 시험이기 때문에, 모든 어휘를 다 알고 있을 필요도 없다.

 그러나 시중의 TOEFL 어휘 교재들을 보면, 주먹구구식 구성으로 이루어진 교재들이 다수이며, 난이도를 너무 높게, 혹은 너무 낮게 책정하여 수험생들을 곤혹스럽게 하는 경우가 많다. 특히 한 교재를 어느 정도 학습한 수험생들이 실제 시험에서는 어휘 때문에 낭패를 보는 경우가 종종 있다는 점은 현 교재들의 한계라고 할 수 있을 것이다. 그렇다면 TOEFL 어휘 학습을 어떻게 해야 할 것인가. 답은 비교적 간단하다. 지문 이해에 필수적인 단어들을 광범위하고도 집중적으로, 그리고 자신의 수준에 맞게 단계별로 학습하는 것이 하나의 답이 될 것이며, 본 교재도 이와 같은 목적 하에 집필되었다.

 어휘 학습은 TOEFL 준비의 출발이자 기반이다. 이를 바탕으로 수험생들이 – 조금이나마 – 자신의 목표에 도달하는 데 본 교재가 보탬이 되기를 기원한다.

저자 조 상 익

이 책의 특징 및 학습법

★ 주제별 필수 어휘 총정리
주제별 iBT TOEFL 필수 어휘 및 전문 용어 수록: 독해를 위한 필수 어휘, 어휘 문제에 나왔던 단어, 그리고 최신 기출 단어뿐만 아니라, 고득점을 위한 전문 용어까지 수록하여 지문 이해력 향상을 도모할 수 있도록 하였다.

★ 수준별 학습
수준별 학습 가능: Part별로 어휘의 난이도를 차별화하는 동시에 같은 난이도끼리 너무 치우치지 않도록 하여, 본인의 수준에 맞는 가장 효과적인 학습을 가능하게 하였다.

★ 실제 시험에서 볼 수 있는 예문
실제 TOEFL 시험에서 접할 수 있는 문장 활용: Check-up Quiz와 Review Test의 문항들을 실제 시험에서 접할 수 있는 문장들로 구성하여 시험에 대한 적응력 향상을 기대할 수 있다.

★ 시간차를 염두에 둔 학습
효과적인 어휘 학습이 이루어지도록 편집: 표제어에 대한 설명에서 예문을 Check-up Quiz로 분리시킴으로써 시간차를 염두한 학습이 가능하도록 하였다.

★ TOEFL READING 어휘 문제와 연계
실제 어휘 문제에 대한 대비: 각 Chapter 마다 학습한 어휘를 바탕으로 실제 Reading 영역의 어휘 문제를 풀어 볼 수 있는 기회를 제공하였다.

Check-up Quiz 부분 ●

동일 페이지에서 학습한
어휘들을 바로 확인하고
적용해 볼 수 있음

● Chapter / Unit 부분

iBT TOEFL의 지문 내용을 4개의
카테고리로 구분, 반복
적이며 단계적인 학습을
유도함

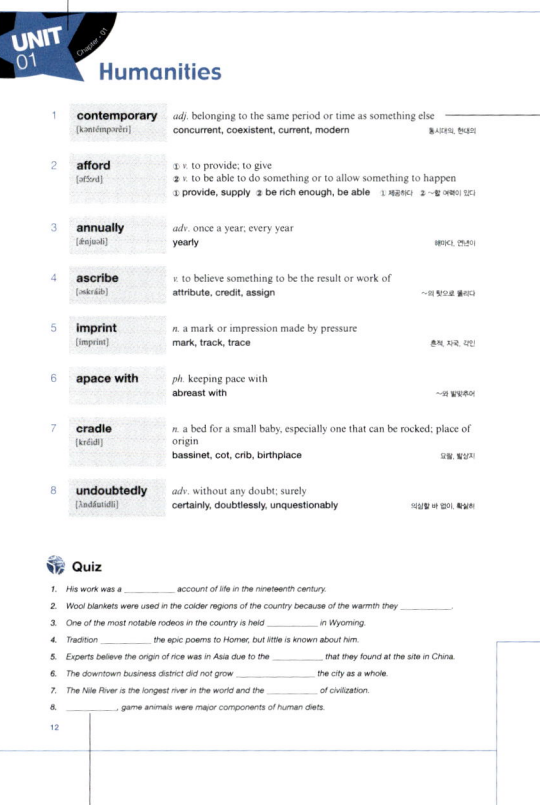

● 표제어 및 설명 부분

표제어에 대한 설명으로 영영 풀이,
한글 뜻, 동의어를 각각 제시하여
목적에 따른 학습이 가능하도록 함

Review TEST 부분 ●

iBT Reading 영역의 어휘
문제와 동일한 난이도 및 환경
으로, 학습한 어휘를 다시 한번
확인하면서 실제 시험에 대한
적응력을 증대시킬 수 있음

본 교재의 분류법

Category	HUMANITIES	SOCIAL SCIENCES	NATURAL SCIENCES	APPLIED SCIENCES
Subcategory	History	Sociology	Physics	Electronics
	Anthropology	Politics	Geology	Medicine
	Archaeology	Psychology	Meteorology	Architecture
	Literature and Authors	Economics	Astronomy	Ecology
	Linguistics	Pedagogy	Biology	Industrial Design
	Music and Music History	Business	Aquatic Organisms	City Planning
	Photography	Mass Communication	Oceanography	Extinction of Animals
	Philosophy	Child Development	Glaciers	Conservation Efforts for Plants
	Religion	Community Dynamics	Deserts	Medical Technique
	Visual and Performing Art	Education	Cosmology	Public Health
	Theater	Law	Particle Physics	Physiology
	Dance	Cultural Studies	Chemistry	
	Painting	Demography	Seismology	

목차

Part ★1

Part ★2

Part ★3

Part ★4

Part 01
VOCA

Humanities

1 contemporary
[kəntémpərèri]

adj. belonging to the same period or time as something else
concurrent, coexistent, modern

동시대의, 현대의

2 afford
[əfɔ́:rd]

① *v.* to provide; to give
② *v.* to be able to do something or to allow something to happen
① **provide, supply** ② **be able, be rich enough**   ① 제공하다 ② ~할 여력이 있다

3 annually
[ǽnjuəli]

adv. once a year; every year
yearly

해마다, 연년이

4 ascribe
[əskráib]

v. to believe something to be the result or work of
attribute, credit, assign

~의 탓으로 돌리다

5 imprint
[ímprint]

n. a mark or impression made by pressure
mark, track, trace

흔적, 자국, 각인

6 apace with

ph. keeping pace with
abreast with

~와 발맞추어

7 cradle
[kréidl]

n. a bed for a small baby, especially one that can be rocked; a place of origin
bassinet, cot, birthplace

요람, 발상지

8 undoubtedly
[ʌ̀ndáutidli]

adv. without any doubt; surely
certainly, doubtlessly, unquestionably

의심할 바 없이, 확실히

Quiz

1. His work was a _____ account of life in the nineteenth century.

2. Wool blankets were used in the colder regions of the country because of the warmth they _____.

3. One of the most notable rodeos in the country is held _____ in Wyoming.

4. Tradition _____ the epic poems to Homer, but little is known about him.

5. Experts believe the origin of rice was in Asia due to the _____ that they found at the site in China.

6. The downtown business district did not grow _____ the city as a whole.

7. The Nile River is the longest river in the world and the _____ of civilization.

8. _____, game animals were major components of human diets.

9	**cunning** [kʌ́niŋ]	*adj.* clever in deceiving **deceptive, shrewd, sly**	간사한, 약삭빠른
10	**enigmatic** [ènigmǽtik]	*adj.* mysterious and very hard to understand **obscure, ambiguous**	수수께끼 같은
11	**abundant** [əbʌ́ndənt]	*adj.* existing in large amounts **plentiful, profuse, ample**	풍부한, 많은
12	**account for**	① *ph.* to give a reason or explanation for something ② *ph.* to constitute; to form ① **explain, clarify** ② **make up**	① 설명하다 ② 차지하다
13	**cast** [kæst]	*v.* to shape by pouring something into a mold and allowing it to set **form, mold, shape**	(거푸집 등에) 뜨다, 주조하다
14	**artifact** [ɑ́ːrtəfæ̀kt]	*n.* a handcrafted object, especially one that is of archaeological interest **remain, relic, antiquity**	유물
15	**accommodate** [əkɑ́mədèit]	*v.* to provide someone with a place to stay **put up, house, lodge**	수용하다
16	**adorn** [ədɔ́ːrn]	*v.* to make more beautiful, attractive, or interesting **decorate, ornament, embellish**	장식하다, 꾸미다

UNIT 01

Quiz

9. Although they were _____ hunters, primitive humans were still threatened by certain animals.

10. The rise of Neanderthal man is somewhat _____ despite the relative abundance of fossils.

11. Some women specialized in the gathering of the _____ shellfish that lived closer to shore.

12. Various methods of spattering the glaze onto the ware _____ the extremely wide variations in color.

13. Early civilizations used bronze, an alloy that could be _____ in molds, to make tools and weapons.

14. The archaeologists examined all of evidence from sites very closely and then determined the general age of the _____.

15. The adjoining apartments could _____ dozens of families.

16. In the past, men, women, and children _____ themselves with beads.

17	**abruptly** [əbrʌ́ptli]	*adv.* in a sudden and unexpected manner; very quickly **unexpectedly, suddenly, instantly**	돌연히, 갑자기
18	**acclaim** [əkléim]	*v.* to declare something with noisy enthusiasm **hail, applaud, cheer**	환호하다
19	**bear** [bɛər]	① *v.* to have; to bring or take ② *v.* to support a weight or load; to accept something without complaining ① **carry** ② **sustain, endure**	① 지니다 ② 견디다, 참다
20	**by chance**	*ph.* without cause or reason; by accident **accidentally, incidentally**	우연히
21	**abandon** [əbǽndən]	*v.* to give something up completely **desert, cede, leave behind**	폐지하다, 버리다
22	**abstraction** [æbstrǽkʃən]	*n.* an idea of a quality considered separately from any particular object or case **conception, notion, representation**	추상, 추상 개념

* *abstract* 추상적인

23	**agile** [ǽdʒəl]	*adj.* able to move or change quickly and easily **nimble, quick, swift**	재빠른, 기민한
24	**surmount** [sərmáunt]	*v.* to be above or on top of; to overcome **ascend, mount, defeat**	오르다, 극복하다

🛡️ Quiz

17. *They didn't care for the play because it ended so _____.*

18. *The ballerina was _____ for her wonderful performance.*

19. *Alternative history _____ some relation to historical fiction as well as to science fiction.*

20. *The character gained his wealth _____, not from hard work.*

21. *Some rituals were _____, but the stories, later called myths, persisted and provided material for art and drama.*

22. *A number of sculptors have rejected the _____ of minimalist artists.*

23. *Acrobats must be extremely _____.*

24. *She managed to _____ the obstacle.*

25	**aesthetically**	*adv.* in an aesthetic manner; in a highly developed sense of beauty	
	[esθétikəli]	**artistically, beautifully, tastefully**	미적으로, 예술적으로
	* *aesthetic* 미적인		

26	**akin (to)**	*adj.* having the same appearance, character, or nature	
	[əkín]	**similar, alike, related**	같은 종류의, 혈족의

27	**diverse**	*adj.* different from each other; showing variety	
	[divə́:rs]	**different, various, assorted**	다양한

28	**acquisition**	*n.* the act of obtaining, developing, or acquiring something	
	[æ̀kwəzíʃən]	**gain, procurement, acquirement**	획득, 취득

29	**outgoing**	*adj.* eager to mix socially with others	
	[áutgòuiŋ]	**friendly, sociable**	외향적인, 사교적인

30	**nuisance**	*n.* something or someone that causes trouble	
	[njú:səns]	**annoyance, irritation, inconvenience**	성가시고 귀찮은 것, 민폐

UNIT 01

 **Quiz**

25. *Satires are read because they are _____ satisfying works of art.*

26. *Her fictitious world is strikingly _____ to the real one people live in every day.*

27. *The artwork is _____ in form and includes sculptures, paintings and photographs.*

28. *Social-interactionists believe that adults play an important part in children's language _____.*

29. *Gregarious people are friendly and _____.*

30. *After the war, the robber became a small-scale rustler – it was more a _____ than highway robbery.*

Social Sciences

| 1 | **levy**
[lévi] | *v.* to demand and collect officially
impose, charge, tax | 부과하다, 징수하다 |

| 2 | **barrier**
[bǽriər] | *n.* something that is used to keep people or things apart
bar, fence, wall | 장벽 |

| 3 | **beverage**
[bévəridʒ] | *n.* a prepared drink, especially a hot drink like coffee or tea, or an alcoholic drink like beer
drink, liquid, refreshment | 음료 |

| 4 | **brag**
[bræg] | *v.* to talk boastfully or proudly about oneself and about what one has done
boast, swagger, talk big | 자랑하다, 허풍을 떨다 |

| 5 | **breed**
[bri:d] | *v.* to reproduce sexually; to raise something, often an animal
generate, bring forth, rear | (새끼를) 낳다, 양육하다 |

| 6 | **speculator**
[spékjəlèitər] | *n.* someone who speculates, especially financially
investor, gambler | 투자가, 투기꾼 |

| 7 | **culminate**
[kʌ́lmənèit] | *v.* to reach the highest point or climax
climax, consummate | 정점에 이르다 |

| 8 | **propel**
[prəpél] | *v.* to drive or push something forward
drive, thrust, impel | 추진하다, 나아가게 하다 |

Quiz

1. A new tax was _____ on consumers of luxury goods.

2. During pioneer times, the Allegheny Mountains were major _____ to transportation.

3. The availability of synthetic fragrances has made possible a large variety of products, from _____ to used cars with applied "new car odor."

4. The owners often _____ about the quality of the facilities at their resort.

5. Nothing _____ success like success, so he kept signing deals after he got his first one.

6. Excessive investment by _____ may lead to uncontrolled economic growth.

7. The crisis _____ in the Panic of 1873, when the leading investment banking firm declared bankruptcy.

8. By the 1600s, colonial shipbuilders were strong competitors in the shipbuilding industry and helped to _____ heavy transatlantic commerce.

| 9 | **auction**
[ɔ́:kʃən] | *n.* a public sale in which each item is sold to the person who offers the most money
public sale, open sale | 경매, 장 |

| 10 | **urbanization**
[ə̀:rbənizéiʃən]

* *urban* 도시의 | *n.* the process by which cities grow or by which societies become more urban
citification | 도시화 |

| 11 | **calamity**
[kəlǽməti] | *n.* a catastrophe, or serious misfortune that causes great loss or damage
disaster, catastrophe, misfortune | 재난, 참사 |

| 12 | **infamous**
[ínfəməs] | *adj.* well known for being bad or morally wicked
notorious, disreputable, ill-famed | 악명 높은 |

| 13 | **notify**
[nóutəfài] | *v.* to tell someone, especially formally
announce, inform, alert | 통지하다, 알리다 |

| 14 | **misery**
[mízəri] | *n.* great unhappiness or suffering
affliction, distress, hardship | 불행, 비참한 신세 |

| 15 | **acute**
[əkjú:t] | *adj.* able to notice small differences; showing an ability to understand things clearly and deeply
keen, sharp, penetrating | 날카로운, 예리한 |

| 16 | **assert**
[əsə́:rt] | *v.* to state firmly; to insist on or to defend one's rights, opinions, or something else
affirm, state, insist | 단언하다, 주장하다 |

UNIT 02

 Quiz

9. _____ were another popular form of occasional trade.

10. Technological developments further stimulated the process of _____.

11. The Red Cross provides relief in case of _____ like floods, earthquakes, and hurricanes.

12. Jesse James was an _____ outlaw who was well-known as a bank robber and gunfighter.

13. Who should be _____ in case you are involved in an accident?

14. Jacob Riis, a newspaper reporter and photographer, revealed the _____ of the slums of New York City.

15. The _____ public awareness of social changes was tied to the tremendous growth in popular journalism in the late nineteenth century.

16. Slave owners _____ that their crops were a great benefit to the economy and that the slaves were needed to work the land.

17	**adversity** [ædvə́:rsəti]	*n.* circumstances that cause trouble or sorrow **hardship, misfortune, suffering**	역경, 불운
18	**retrieval** [ritrí:vəl]	*n.* the act or process of retrieving **recovery, restoration**	복구, 회복
19	**assembly** [əsémbli]	*n.* a group of people gathered together, especially for a meeting **gathering, congregation, congress**	모임, 의회
20	**bill** [bil]	*n.* a written plan or draft for a proposed law **act, measure**	법안
21	**craft** [kræft]	① *n.* a skill, or occupation, especially one requiring the use of the hands ② *v.* to make something skillfully ① **expertise, adeptness** ② **make, fabricate**	① 기술, (기술을 요하는) 일 ② 정교하게 만들다
22	**adept** [ədépt]	*adj.* skillful at doing something **proficient, versed, dexterous**	숙련된, 능숙한
23	**enact** [inǽkt]	*v.* to establish by law **pass, decree, legislate**	제정하다, 법으로 만들다
24	**eligible** [élidʒəbəl]	*adj.* suitable or deserving to be chosen for a job or something else **suitable, qualified, fit**	(뽑힐) 자격이 있는

🔵 Quiz

17. *The natives were very tough people who were able to handle _____.*

18. *Memory formation involves three main processes; encoding, storage, and _____.*

19. *All the representatives came to the capital for legislative sessions of the _____ and council.*

20. *Even if a _____ passes in Congress, it still does not become a law until the president signs it.*

21. *Much of the political activity on television news has been _____ by politicians and their public relations advisers.*

22. *He must be _____ at dealing with politicians, public interest groups, and government agencies.*

23. *Market regulations are often _____ by corrupt governments for the purpose of benefiting well-connected companies or politicians.*

24. *In the United States, citizens are _____ to vote at the age of eighteen.*

25	**conclusive**	*adj.* leaving no room for doubt or uncertainty	
	[kənklúːsiv]	**decisive, convincing, definite**	결정적인, 확실한

26	**verbal**	*adj.* relating to or consisting of words	
	[vɚːrbəl]	**oral, spoken, vocal**	말의, 구두의

27	**able**	*adj.* having the necessary knowledge, power, time, and opportunity to do something	
	[éibəl]	**capable, competent, talented**	능력 있는, 유능한

28	**adhere (to)**	*v.* to stick or remain fixed to something	
	[ædhíər]	**attach, cleave, stick**	달라붙다, 고수하다

29	**ban**	*v.* to forbid something	
	[bæn]	**prohibit, bar, outlaw**	금하다

30	**blunt**	*adj.* having no point or sharp edge; imperceptive	
	[blʌnt]	**dull, worn, abrupt**	무딘, 무뚝뚝한

UNIT 02

 **Quiz**

25. *Each circumstance may mean little, but a whole chain of circumstances can be as _____ as direct evidence.*

26. *Dreams are commonly made up of both visual and _____ images.*

27. *The head of an academic department at a university should be not only a distinguished scholar but also an _____ administer.*

28. *The child always _____ to the teacher's rules.*

29. *Some people feel that violent sports like boxing should be _____ because they are too dangerous.*

30. *The victim was apparently struck by a club or some other _____ object.*

Natural Sciences

1	**cognizant** [kágnəzənt]	*adj.* aware of something or having knowledge of it **aware, conscious, knowledgeable** 인식하고 있는
2	**cohesive** [kouhíːsiv]	*adj.* having the power of cohering; tending to unite into a mass **condensable, consolidative** 응집력이 있는, 결합력이 있는
3	**confirm** [kənfə́ːrm]	*v.* to provide support for the truth or validity of something **verify, prove, affirm** 확실하게 하다, 확인하다
4	**warp** [wɔːrp]	*v.* to make something become twisted out of shape through shrinking and expanding **bend, twist, distort** 휘다, 굽히다, 왜곡하다
5	**discharge** [distʃáːrdʒ]	*v.* to flow out or to be released; to lose some or all of something's electrical charge **let out, release, emit** 방출하다, 방전하다
6	**alert** [ələ́ːrt]	*v.* to warn someone of danger; to make someone aware of a fact or circumstance **caution, alarm, warn** 경보를 발하다, 경계태세를 취하게 하다
7	**chamber** [tʃéimbər]	*n.* a room, especially a bedroom; a room set aside for a special purpose **bedroom, room, compartment** 침실, 방
8	**classify** [klǽsəfài]	*v.* to put animals, plants, or something else into a particular group or category **categorize, divide, sort** 분류하다

Quiz

1. A scientist must always be _____ of and guard against bias skewing the results of his or her research.

2. The _____ strength permits columns of water to be pulled to great heights without being broken.

3. If observations _____ the scientists' predictions, then that will give support to their theory.

4. If boards become wet, they may _____.

5. Sharks can detect minute electrical signals _____ from their prey.

6. Fire ants make use of an alarm pheromone to _____ workers to an emergency.

7. Numerous networks of tunnels linked all the different _____ together.

8. Monkeys are _____ as primates.

9	**claw** [klɔ:]	*n.* a hard, curved, and pointed nail on the end of the foot of an animal **nail, talon** 발톱

9 **claw** [klɔ:]
n. a hard, curved, and pointed nail on the end of each digit of the foot of an animal
nail, talon
발톱

10 **aromatic** [æ̀rəmǽtik]
adj. having a strong but sweet or pleasant smell; sweet-smelling
fragrant, perfumed, pungent
향기로운

11 **demonstrate** [démənstrèit]
① *v.* to show or prove something by reasoning or providing evidence
② *v.* to show support or opposition by protesting or marching in public
① **illustrate, explain** ② **parade, protest**
① 논증[증명]하다 ② 시위하다

12 **landmark** [lǽndmɑːrk]
n. a mark showing the boundary of a piece of land; an occasion, event, or development of importance
milestone, watershed, turning point
경계표, 획기적인 사건

13 **bloom** [bluːm]
v. to be in or come into flower; to be growing well
blossom, flourish, prosper
개화하다, 번영하다

14 **venomous** [vénəməs]
adj. having the ability to poison
poisonous, toxic
독이 있는

15 **botanical** [bətǽnikəl]
adj. of, pertaining to, made from, or containing plants
phytological
식물의, 식물학상의

16 **ambidextrous** [æ̀mbidékstrəs]
adj. able to use both hands equally well; unusually skillful
talented, gifted, adept
양손잡이의, 재주가 좋은

UNIT 03

🎯 Quiz

9. Unlike other cats, the cheetah cannot fully extract its _____.

10. At least 50 different _____ compounds have been analyzed in the orchid family.

11. Many experiments _____ how some plants can survive with very little amounts of water.

12. Some experts have suggested that migrating birds find their way by following _____ like rivers and mountain ranges.

13. Most flowers _____ in the spring.

14. The rattlesnake is the most common _____ snake in the United States.

15. One of the most beautiful _____ gardens in the United States is the wild and lovely Magnolia Gardens in South Carolina.

16. Right-handers are said to make up 80% to 90% of all people and left-handers 5% to 15% while the remaining tiny percentage is _____.

17	**advent** [ǽdvent]	*n.* a coming or arrival; a first appearance	
		arrival, appearance	도래, 출현

18	**alien** [éiljən]	*adj.* from another country or society; connected with creatures from another world	
		exotic, foreign, outlandish	외래의, 외국의, 외계의

19	**boulder** [bóuldər]	*n.* a large piece of rock that has been rounded and worn smooth by weathering and abrasion	
		rock	(둥근) 바위

20	**stable** [steibl]	*adj.* firmly balanced or fixed; not likely to wobble or fall over	
		steady, secure, firm	안정적인

21	**permeable** [pɔ́:rmiəbəl]	*adj.* allowing certain liquids or gases to pass through something	
		penetrable, pervious	투과할 수 있는, 침투성이 있는

* *permeate* 스며들다

22	**eject** [idʒékt]	*v.* to throw out someone or something with force	
		banish, boot, expel	내뿜다, 분출하다

23	**hem** [hem]	*v.* to surround something closely and prevent its movement	
		enclose, encase, hedge	에워싸다, 둘러싸다

24	**core** [kɔːr]	*n.* the innermost, central, essential, or unchanging part	
		center, heart, nucleus	중심부, 핵, 핵심

Quiz

17. With the _____ of the Vietnam War, the Air Force wanted a system to help it navigate over the jungles of Southeast Asia.

18. The _____ in the Earth's core make it a far more alien world than space.

19. The mineral particles found in soil range in size from microscopic clay particles to large _____.

20. A roadbed supplies a _____ base for a highway.

21. In some cases, wells can draw water from a _____ rock layer.

22. Geysers periodically _____ streams of hot water into the air.

23. The Great Basin is _____ in by the Sierra Nevada Mountains to the west and by the Rocky Mountains to the east, giving it no outlet to the sea.

24. The asteroids' compositions are believed to be similar to that of Earth's iron _____.

25	**hamper** [hǽmpər]	*v.* to hinder the progress or movement of someone or something **impede, obstruct, block**	방해하다
26	**synthesize** [sínθəsàiz]	*v.* to combine simple parts to form a complex whole; to make or produce **combine, mix, compose**	합성하다
27	**delicate** [délikət]	*adj.* easily damaged or broken; made or formed in a very careful and detailed way **fragile, breakable, exquisite**	연약한, 섬세한
28	**fuel** [fjú:əl]	① *n.* any material that releases energy when burned ② *v.* to fill or feed with fuel ① **energy, power** ② **feed, nourish**	① 연료 ② (연료 등을) 공급하다
29	**shrink** [ʃriŋk]	*v.* to make or become smaller in size or extent **wither, shrivel, contract**	수축하다, 움츠리다
30	**efficiency** [ifíʃənsi]	*n.* the quality of doing something well with no waste of time or money **effectiveness, productivity**	효율성

UNIT 03

🌀 Quiz

25. Bad weather _____ the rescue crews trying to locate the life rafts.

26. It is important to note that animal cells cannot _____ some complex molecules from simple compounds.

27. Earth is not too close or too far away from the sun to upset the _____ temperature requirements of life.

28. The sun is _____ by thermonuclear reactions near its center that convert hydrogen to helium.

29. About 5 billion years from now, the sun's core will _____ and become hotter.

30. Even some supporters of alternative energy realize that the easiest way to cut carbon emissions is to focus more on _____.

Applied Sciences

1 **appeal**
[əpíːl]
n. an urgent or formal request for help; the quality of being attractive or interesting
solicitation, attraction, charm
호소, 매력

2 **bind**
[baind]
v. to tie or fasten tightly; to force someone to do something by making him or her promise to do it
tie, constrain, obligate
묶다, 속박하다

3 **sway**
[swei]
v. to swing or to make something swing; to incline toward a particular opinion
wave, swing, tilt
흔들리다, 기울다

4 **beneficial**
[bènəfíʃəl]
adj. having good results or benefits
helpful, useful, advantageous
유익한, 이익을 가져오는

5 **allude**
[əlúːd]
v. to mention something indirectly; to speak about something in passing
hint, mention, refer
암시하다, 언급하다

6 **alter**
[ɔ́ːltər]
v. to become different or to make something or someone become different
change, convert, transform
바꾸다, 변경하다

7 **appreciation**
[əprìːʃiéiʃən]
n. sensitive understanding of the value or quality of something
recognition, understanding, admiration
평가, 감상

8 **barren**
[bǽrən]
adj. not able to produce crops or fruit; not able to bear offspring
infertile, sterile, unproductive
황폐한, 생식 능력이 없는

Quiz

1. The _____ of iron comes from its low cost, strength, and resistance to fire.

2. Hotels were some of the earliest places that helped _____ the United States together.

3. In high winds, skyscrapers will _____ slightly.

4. Some bacteria are _____ since they stimulate plant life through food decomposition.

5. The word "zigzag" _____ to the geometric ornamentation.

6. As Earth developed, the concentrations of the pollutants were _____ by various chemical reactions.

7. With concerns about the loss of species, there is a growing _____ for the importance of biological diversity.

8. We can see large, pristine forests on one side and an almost _____ land devoid of trees on the other side.

9	**comparatively** [kəmpǽrətivli]	*adv.* according to an estimate made in comparison; not absolutely **relatively, nearly, approximately**	비교적
10	**clue** [kluː]	*n.* a fact or circumstance which helps toward the solution of a crime or a mystery **hint, evidence, indication**	실마리, 단서
11	**voluminous** [vəlúːmənəs]	*adj.* producing great quantities of writing; enough to fill many volumes **copious, bulky, huge**	저서가 많은, 부피가 큰
12	**thrive** [θraiv]	*v.* to grow strong and healthy **prosper, flourish**	번창하다, 잘 자라다
13	**facilitate** [fəsílətèit]	*v.* to make something easy or easier to do or to achieve **expedite, ease, promote**	용이하게 하다, 촉진하다
14	**boundary** [báundəri]	*n.* a line or border marking the farthest limit of an area **border, bounds, limit**	경계
15	**advocate** [ǽdvəkit]	*n.* someone who supports or recommends an idea or proposal **proponent, supporter, patron**	옹호자, 지지자
16	**cope with**	*ph.* to manage successfully; to deal with **handle, dispose of**	대처하다

UNIT 04

Quiz

9. *The first attempt to dig the canal was made by private companies, and only a _____ small portion was built.*

10. *There were no _____ as to how the animal died.*

11. *The ecologist had _____ correspondence and frequent discussions with other experts in the field.*

12. *Barley, unlike most other grains, _____ at high altitudes, so it can be grown in many places.*

13. *Research into hydrogen technology was _____ by money from Congress.*

14. *Lake Superior forms a natural _____ between the United States and Canada.*

15. *_____ of organic foods frequently proclaim that such products are safer and more nutritious than others.*

16. *The human body is usually unable to _____ extremely hot or cold temperatures.*

17	**crucial** [krúːʃəl]	*adj.* extremely important because the thing will affect others **decisive, critical, vital**	중대한, 결정적인
18	**inhibit** [inhíbit]	*v.* to hold back or prevent an action, desire, or progress; to prohibit someone from doing something **check, restrain, bar**	억제하다, 금지하다
19	**illusion** [ilúːʒən]	*n.* a deceptive or misleading appearance **fantasy, delusion, hallucination**	환상, 환각
20	**specimen** [spésəmən]	*n.* a small amount of something that shows what the rest of it is like; a sample or example of something, especially something that will be studied **example, sample, case**	표본, 견본, 연구 재료
21	**breakthrough** [bréikθrùː]	*n.* a sudden achievement; a decisive advance or discovery, especially in scientific research **advancement, improvement**	(커다란) 발전
22	**codify** [kádəfài]	*v.* to arrange something into a systematic code or laws **systematize, formulate**	(법전 등으로) 편찬하다, 체계화하다
23	**anatomy** [ənǽtəmi]	*n.* the art of dissection; the scientific study of the structure of living organisms, including humans **dissection**	해부, 해부학
24	**acrid** [ǽkrid]	*adj.* having a very bitter and pungent smell or taste **pungent, tart, bitter**	매운, 쓴, 역한 냄새나 맛이 나는

🛡️ Quiz

17. *Obviously, muscles are _____ to the human body.*

18. *Antibiotics _____ the growth of bacteria.*

19. *Optical _____ deceive the eye with tricks of perception.*

20. *Many medical tests require a blood _____.*

21. *The new vaccine represented a significant _____ in the battle against the virus.*

22. *By the 1500s in Europe, the collected knowledge of the human body was _____.*

23. *Thomas Eakins studied not only painting but also _____ when he was training to become an artist.*

24. *Burning rubber produces an _____ smoke.*

25	**corpse** [kɔːrps]	*n.* the dead body of a human being or an animal **cadaver, carcass, remains**	시체
26	**finite** [fáinait]	*adj.* having an end or limit **limited, restricted, bounded**	한정된, 유한한
27	**ignite** [ignáit]	*v.* to set fire to something **burn, inflame, kindle**	불이 붙다, 불을 붙이다
28	**manipulate** [mənípjəlèit]	*v.* to handle something or to work something with the hands, especially in a skillful way **control, operate, direct**	조종하다, 조작하다
29	**drainage** [dréinidʒ]	*n.* a process or system by which waste liquid flows away **draining, sewage**	배수, 하수 (시설)
30	**ventilate** [véntəlèit]	*v.* to allow fresh air to circulate throughout a room or a building **air**	환기시키다

UNIT 04

Quiz

25. The decomposing _____ of a dead ant is generally removed from the colony by worker ants.

26. Many people fear that Earth's supply of oil is _____ and that we will run out of energy someday.

27. When exposed to air, phosphorous _____ spontaneously and forms white fumes when it burns.

28. The pilot must _____ the controls to take off, to change directions and speed, and to land.

29. That province has a history of underground faults that has created an efficient water _____ system.

30. Most modern barns are insulated, _____, and equipped with electricity.

REVIEW TEST

Choose the closest meaning to the highlighted word or phrase.

1   Combining the grotesque and the gothic, Flannery O'Connor's fiction treats contemporary Southern life in terms of stark, brutal comedy and violent tragedy.

Ⓐ described in detail

Ⓑ written at that time

Ⓒ portayed with reality

Ⓓ got into trouble

2   But these factors do not account for the interesting question of how there came to be such a concentration of pregnant ichthyosaurs in a particular place very close to their time of giving birth.

Ⓐ record

Ⓑ repute

Ⓒ exaggerate

Ⓓ explain

3   Abruptly, the scene shifted to one where the factory workers were jostling each other on their way to work.

Ⓐ Suddenly

Ⓑ Mysteriously

Ⓒ Finally

Ⓓ Predictably

4   One researcher observed babies and their mothers in six diverse cultures and found that all the mothers used simplified syntax, short utterances, and nonsense sounds and also transformed certain sounds into baby talk.

Ⓐ intriguing

Ⓑ odd

Ⓒ different

Ⓓ similar

5   One of the less infamous ones is the colorful starfish, which feeds on plant life, coral, and other shellfish.

Ⓐ flamboyant

Ⓑ harmless

Ⓒ notable

Ⓓ notorious

6   Members of the academy and institute are not eligible for any cash prizes.

Ⓐ applied

Ⓑ responsible

Ⓒ qualified

Ⓓ known

7   The process can be very rapid, quickly creating sizable ice crystals, some of which adhere to each other to create a cluster of ice crystals or a snowflake.

Ⓐ depart from

Ⓑ thrust in

Ⓒ stick to

Ⓓ hit on

8   They were not trained in the least in the handling or proper containment of nuclear wastes, nor were they cognizant or even told by the government of the lethal levels of radioactivity they were exposing their bodies to.

Ⓐ aware

Ⓑ sure

Ⓒ igorant

Ⓓ cautious

9 Indeed, had it not been for the superb preservation of these fossils, the strange creatures might well have been classified as dinosaurs.

Ⓐ perfected

Ⓑ replaced

Ⓒ categorized

Ⓓ protected

10 Often seen close to the entrances of their burrows, fiddler crabs possess four-inch claws used for both courtship rituals and defense.

Ⓐ legs

Ⓑ bills

Ⓒ tentacles

Ⓓ nails

11 Much like the fangs of venomous snakes, the duck-billed platypus protects its young with a pair of poisonous fangs.

Ⓐ subtle

Ⓑ poisonous

Ⓒ enormous

Ⓓ graceful

12 Many large cities have taken measures to decrease the level of urban noise; the problem has received much attention with the advent of supersonic jet airplanes.

Ⓐ advance

Ⓑ appearance

Ⓒ address

Ⓓ ardent

13 At the core of Taylor's beliefs about efficiency was the idea that the "only best way" to do any kind of work could be discovered through careful scientific analysis.

Ⓐ development

Ⓑ growth

Ⓒ distribution

Ⓓ effectiveness

14 The most crucial factor behind this phenomenal upsurge in productivity was the widespread adoption of labor-saving machinery by northern farmers.

Ⓐ obvious

Ⓑ blurred

Ⓒ important

Ⓓ desirable

15 Generally, botanists compare a plant to published accounts of similar plants or to samples kept as specimens.

Ⓐ samples

Ⓑ properties

Ⓒ booties

Ⓓ commodities

16 Steamboats became the first vehicles to take advantage of this new form of power, and they were fundamental in igniting growth and industry in the United States along its major rivers and waterways.

Ⓐ deteriorating

Ⓑ curbing

Ⓒ expanding

Ⓓ inflaming

Humanities

1	**daring** [dέəriŋ]	*adj.* brave enough to do risky things; new or unusual in a way that may shock people **courageous, adventurous, bold**	용감한, 대담한

| 2 | **depress**
[diprés] | ① *v.* to weaken something; to make something lower
② *v.* to make someone sad and gloomy
① **weaken, lower** ② **dishearten, sadden** | ① 약화시키다 ② 우울하게 하다 |

| 3 | **disaster**
[dizǽstər] | *n.* an event causing great damage, injury, or loss of life
calamity, catastrophe, cataclysm | 재난, 재앙 |

| 4 | **domain**
[douméin] | *n.* the scope of any subject or area of interest
field, realm, sphere | 영역 |

| 5 | **decipher**
[disáifər] | *v.* to translate a text in an unfamiliar or strange form of writing into ordinary language
decode, unravel, interpret | 해독하다, 판독하다 |

| 6 | **ascend**
[əsénd] | *v.* to climb something or to move to a higher position
arise, climb, mount | 오르다, 올라가다 |

| 7 | **avid**
[ǽvid] | *adj.* very enthusiastic about something
ardent, eager, passionate | 열심인, 열성적인 |

| 8 | **restrict**
[ristríkt] | *v.* to keep someone or something within certain limits
confine, limit, restrain | 제한하다, 한정하다 |

Quiz

1. *Richard Bird and his pilot Floyd Bennett undertook a _____ flight to the North Pole in May 1926.*

2. *Rent controls have artificially _____ the most important long-term determinant of profitability: rents.*

3. *When their crops failed, it was a _____ that caused many people to lose their lives.*

4. *The empire was silently, but quickly, extending its _____.*

5. *They could _____ the tablets because the language was a Semitic one that scholars had first translated a decade ago.*

6. *The pueblo architects laid out a system of public roads with stone staircases for _____ cliff faces.*

7. *President Theodore Roosevelt was an _____ conservationist who believed in preserving nature.*

8. *The study of fossilized footprints is not _____ to examples from millions of years ago.*

9	**roughly** [rʌ́fli]	*adv.* not exactly approximately, around, about	대략
10	**settled** [sétld]	*adj.* established in some routine arranged, fixed, inhabited	일정한, 정착된
11	**attire** [ətáiər]	*n.* clothes, especially formal or elegant ones clothes, apparel	의류, 옷
12	**component** [kəmpóunənt]	*n.* any of the parts or elements that make up a machine, engine, or instrument constituent, element, factor	성분, 구성 요소
13	**considerable** [kənsídərəbəl]	*adj.* fairly large, especially large enough to have an effect or be important notable, sizable, substantial	고려할 만한, 상당한
14	**thanks to**	*ph.* because of owing to, as a result of	~ 때문에
15	**adversary** [ǽdvərsèri] * *adverse* 반대의	*n.* an opponent in a competition enemy, foe, opponent	적, 상대, 반대자
16	**afterlife** [ǽftərlàif]	*n.* the life that some people believe people have after death hereafter	사후세계, 내세

UNIT 05

🔵 Quiz

9. *The population _____ doubled every generation during the rest of the nineteenth centuries.*

10. *With the _____ routine of Neolithic farmers came the evolution of towns and, eventually, cities.*

11. *He indicated several weeks ago that he would wear formal _____ at his inauguration.*

12. *The time scale is divided into three time _____; eons, eras, and periods.*

13. *The book was a _____ improvement over the only other instruction manual existing at the time.*

14. *_____ the unending pressures of the work, he decided to quit his business.*

15. *By adulthood, Genghis had been through a series of rough-and-tumble encounters with various _____, who tried to enslave or kill him and his family.*

16. *It is said that death is a new beginning when the deceased passes from the restrictions of this life into the _____.*

17	**compose** [kəmpóuz]	*v.* to create music, poetry, or something else; to make up or constitute something **set to music, constitute, form**	작곡하다, 만들다, 구성하다
18	**costume** [kástjuːm]	*n.* a set of clothing of a special kind, especially of a particular historical period **apparel, attire, dress**	의상, 복장
19	**overall** [óuvərɔ̀ːl]	*adj.* including everything **total, whole, entire**	전체적인
20	**assimilate** [əsíməlèit]	*v.* to become a part of a country or community; to completely understand and begin to use new ideas, information, or something else **make similar, absorb**	동화하다, 흡수하다
21	**assumption** [əsʌ́mpʃən]	*n.* something that is accepted as true without proof **presumption, supposition**	가정, 추측
22	**attachment** [ətǽtʃmənt] * *attach* 붙이다	*n.* an act or means of fastening; liking or affection **fastening, bond, affection**	부착, 집착
23	**carry out**	*ph.* to do the work of; to bring, take, or convey something **perform, convey, transport**	실행하다, 실어 나르다
24	**coin** [kɔin]	① *v.* to invent a new word or phrase ② *v.* to manufacture coins from metal ① **originate, create** ② **mint, stamp**	① 새로운 말을 만들다 ② 주조하다

Quiz

17. Certain films had music specifically _____ for them.

18. Wearing masks and _____, they often impersonated other people, animals, or supernatural beings.

19. A book's table of contents provides readers with an _____ idea of what it is about.

20. The immigrants quickly _____ to life in their new country and learned both its language and customs.

21. The _____ of many experts is that drama evolved from various rituals.

22. Emotional _____ play a significant role in the decisions that people make.

23. African-American graphic artists _____ efforts to increase and promote the visual arts.

24. The term "beat" was _____ by Herbert Huncke, who meant it to be a synonym for tired or down and out.

25	**aristocracy** [æ̀rəstάkrəsi]	*n.* the highest social class, usually owning land and having titles
		gentry, upper class 귀족

26	**bland** [blænd]	*adj.* without any excitement, strong opinion, or special character; having very little taste
		boring, insipid, tasteless 지루한, 김빠진

27	**emphasize** [émfəsàiz]	*v.* to put an emphasis or stress on something
		stress, highlight, underscore 강조하다

28	**dialect** [dáiəlèkt]	*n.* a form of a language spoken in a particular region or by a certain social group
		vernacular, tongue 방언, 사투리

29	**come up with**	*ph.* to produce something or to have an idea
		conceive, hit upon (생각 등을) 떠올리다

30	**current** [kə́:rənt]	① *adj.* belonging to the present ② *n.* the continuous steady flow of a body of water, air, or heat in a particular direction
		① **present, contemporary** ② **flow, stream** ① 현재의 ② 흐름

UNIT 05

🏅 Quiz

25. He is a member of the _____ but has little in terms of monetary wealth.

26. The main issue was that such a rigid structure made the opera _____ and at times predictable.

27. Mothers exaggerate their facial expressions, hold vowels longer, and _____ certain words when they communicate with their children.

28. They studied the local _____ and wrote stories which focused on life in specific regions of the country.

29. Companies are being required to _____ innovative ways of cutting costs because of the economic circumstances.

30. The term "folk song" has been _____ for over a hundred years.

Social Sciences

1	**spark** [spɑːrk]	*v.* to emit sparks of fire or electricity; to stimulate, provoke, or start **ignite, stimulate, initiate**	불꽃이 튀다, 발화시키다, 자극하다
2	**devastate** [dévəstèit]	*v.* to cause great destruction in or to something **ruin, destroy, ravage**	황폐화시키다, 유린하다
3	**encourage** [enkə́ːridʒ]	*v.* to give support, confidence, or hope to someone **cheer, hearten, inspire**	고무시키다, 격려하다
4	**effect** [ifékt]	*n.* a result or condition produced by a cause; the way in which an event, action, or person changes someone or something **result, consequence, impact**	결과, 영향
5	**end** [end]	*n.* an object or purpose **aim, goal**	목적
6	**toll** [toul]	*n.* a fee or tax paid for the use of a bridge or road **charge, duty, impost**	통행료, 요금
7	**warrant** [wɔ́(ː)rənt]	*v.* to justify something; to guarantee something as being of a specified quality or quantity **justify, promise, assure**	정당화하다, 보증하다
8	**phase** [feiz]	*n.* a stage or period in growth or development **state, period, stage**	국면, 시기

Quiz

1. The booming economy _____ an explosion in real estate development.

2. After the war _____ the country, it took many years for everything to be rebuilt.

3. The state government _____ the internal improvements of the corporations in two distinct ways.

4. In the United States in the early 1800s, state governments had more _____ on the economy than the federal government.

5. Toward the _____ – to restore stability to the economy – the government pursued several courses of action.

6. The canal lived up to the investors' expectations, quickly paying for itself through _____.

7. Further explanations were not _____ since everyone understood what was happening.

8. A full-scale Keynesian policy should grant the government a role in all _____ of economic life.

9	**fragrance** [fréigrəns] * *fragrant* 향기로운	*n.* sweetness of smell **odor, scent, balm**	향기, 방향(성)
10	**sheer** [ʃiər]	*adj.* complete and not mixed with anything else **absolute, downright, plain**	순전한
11	**significant** [signífikənt]	*adj.* important; worth noting or considering **critical, weighty, meaningful**	중요한, 의미 있는
12	**concern** [kənsə́:rn]	① *n.* a feeling of worry about something important ② *n.* a company or business ① **anxiety, apprehension** ② **enterprise, firm**	① 걱정 ② 회사
13	**sparse** [spa:rs]	*adj.* thinly scattered or dotted about **meager, scant, few**	드문드문한, 희박한
14	**undertake** [ʌ̀ndərtéik]	*v.* to accept a duty, responsibility, or task **take on, assume, accept**	떠맡다
15	**catastrophic** [kæ̀təstrɑ́fik]	*adj.* relating a terrible event in which there is a lot of destruction **calamitous, disastrous**	대재앙의
16	**coincide with**	*ph.* to happen at the same time as **concur with, clash with**	동시에 일어나다

UNIT 06

Quiz

9. Natural flavorings and _____ are often costly and limited in supply.

10. The decade of the 1870s was a period in which the _____ number of newspapers doubled.

11. The Civil Rights Act of 1964 was a particularly _____ piece of legislation to African-Americans.

12. A business _____ with two or more owners is referred to as a partnership.

13. If the population in an area was _____, the Black Death usually ran out of steam within a year.

14. The Eric Canal was one of the greatest construction jobs that anyone had ever _____ up to that point.

15. A tsunami can be a _____ event that kills thousands of people and destroys their homes and buildings.

16. The rapid growth of Boston _____ the immigration of huge numbers of people there.

17	**alleviate** [əlíːvièit]	*v.* to make pain, a problem, suffering, or something else less severe **ease, relieve, mitigate**	경감하다, 누그러뜨리다
18	**antagonistic** [æntǽgənístik]	*adj.* unfriendly; opposed to an idea or group **hostile, opposing, conflicting**	적대적인, 반목의
19	**declare** [diklέər]	*v.* to announce something publicly or formally **announce, proclaim, pronounce**	선언하다, 발표하다
20	**deem** [diːm]	*v.* to think of something in a particular way or as having a particular quality **consider, judge, think**	간주하다, 생각하다
21	**equality** [i(ː)kwɑ́ləti]	*n.* the state or quality of being equal **impartiality, fairness, equivalence**	평등, 동등
22	**collapse** [kəlǽps]	*n.* a sudden failure of something, such as an institution or a business, or a course of action **break-down, downfall, disintegration**	붕괴, 와해
23	**bar** [bɑːr]	*v.* to officially prevent someone from doing something **forbid, prohibit, ban**	금지하다
24	**succinct** [səksíŋkt]	*adj.* clearly expressed in a few words; to the point **brief, concise, precise**	간결한, 간명한

🛡 Quiz

17. A support network of relatives and friends can _____ much of the burden of raising a child.

18. Most plantation owners were _____ to the development of the towns.

19. The United States _____ war and quickly sent men to the European front during World War II.

20. The president can make such regulations covering the prohibition of alcoholic liquors as may be _____ necessary.

21. In 1957, Ralph Abernathy founded an organization devoted to achieving racial _____ for black Americans.

22. The enormous size of the Roman Empire made it increasingly difficult to defend, setting the stage for its eventual _____ in 476.

23. The political party urged that immigrants be _____ from running for public office.

24. He wrote a _____ and graphic account concerning the slum and housing problem in New York City.

25	**constrict** [kənstríkt]	*v.* to make something narrower or tighter **compress, contract, squeeze**	압축하다, 수축시키다
26	**allegiance** [əlí:dʒəns]	*n.* a commitment and duty to obey and be loyal to a government or sovereign **faithfulness, fidelity, loyalty**	충성, 충실
27	**appealing** [əpí:liŋ]	*adj.* evoking or attracting interest, desire, curiosity, or sympathy **attractive, inviting, fascinating**	매력적인, 호소력 있는
28	**suit** [suːt]	*v.* to be appropriate to; in harmony with **fit, adapt, adjust**	적합하게 하다
29	**cite** [sait]	*v.* to mention something as an example, especially one that supports, proves, or explains an idea or situation **quote, mention, refer to**	인용하다, 언급하다
30	**flaw** [flɔː]	*n.* a mistake, mark, or weakness that makes something imperfect **fault, defect, blemish**	흠, 결점

UNIT 06

 **Quiz**

25. *The experts predicted that growth could not continue and that the tight labor market would _____ the economy.*

26. *While some of the Indians had formed _____ with French Jesuit priests, they were far more suspicious of the British soldiers.*

27. *The most _____ publishing investments were small books that were steady sellers.*

28. *Reformers suggested that the education programs should _____ the needs of the population.*

29. *When writing research papers, writers must _____ the sources they use.*

30. *A _____ in a jewel makes it less valuable.*

Natural Sciences

1	**disperse** [dispə́:rs]	*v.* to spread out over a wide area **diffuse, scatter, dissipate**	흩어지게 하다, 분산시키다
2	**emerge** [imə́:rdʒ]	*v.* to come out from somewhere **appear, arise, turn out**	나타나다, 등장하다
3	**emit** [imít]	*v.* to give out light, heat, a sound, or a smell **send out, discharge, eject**	방출하다, 내뿜다
4	**vertical** [və́:rtikəl]	*adj.* pointing up in a line that forms an angle of 90° with a flat surface **upright, erect, perpendicular**	수직의
5	**exhilarating** [igzílərèitiŋ]	*adj.* filling someone with a lively cheerfulness **invigorating, refreshing, cheering**	유쾌하게 하는, 상쾌한
6	**dense** [dens]	*adj.* closely packed or crowded together **compact, solid, thick**	밀집한, 밀도가 높은
7	**determine** [ditə́:rmin]	*v.* to fix or settle the exact limits or nature of something; to form a firm intention **conclude, decide, resolve**	결정하다, 결심하다
8	**dissenting** [diséntiŋ]	*adj.* disagreeing, especially openly or hostilely **discording, disagreeing, conflicting**	의견이 다른

🛡 Quiz

1. The fact that white light is composed of various wavelengths may be demonstrated by _____ a beam of light through a prism.

2. The species _____ from the water and moved onto the land.

3. Certain gases such as neon _____ light when exposed to an electrical current.

4. Although there are both horizontal and _____ movements of air, the term "wind" applies only to horizontal movement.

5. Riding a space shuttle can be an _____ experience.

6. The jungle is incredibly _____ because of the huge amount of vegetation growing in it.

7. Canadian researchers have discovered a set of genes that _____ the lifespan of the common nematode, a type of worm.

8. Our understanding of these ancient beasts has grown slowly, with many _____ opinions among the experts.

9	**edible** [édəbəl]	*adj.* fit to be eaten; suitable to eat **eatable**	먹을 수 있는
10	**entire** [entáiər]	*adj.* with nothing left out **complete, whole, total**	전적인, 전체의
11	**fatal** [féitl]	*adj.* causing or resulting in death **mortal, lethal, deadly**	치명적인
12	**succumb** [səkʌ́m]	*v.* to give in to pressure, temptation, or desire **surrender, yield, give up**	굴복하다
13	**crave** [kreiv]	*v.* to have a very strong, almost uncontrollable, desire for **desire, yearn, long for**	추구하다, 갈망하다
14	**upright** [ʌ́pràit]	*adj.* standing straight up **erect, vertical, perpendicular**	직립의, 똑바로 선
15	**venture** [véntʃər]	*v.* to be so bold as to; to attempt something dangerous **risk, gamble, dare**	감행하다, 위험을 무릅쓰고 가다
16	**brood** [bru:d]	*n.* a number of young animals, especially birds, that are produced or hatched at the same time **offspring, progeny, young**	(한배에서 난) 새끼

UNIT 07

🏆 Quiz

9. Celery, an _____ plant with long stalks topped with feathery leaves, grows best in cool weather.

10. _____ crops can be wiped out by fungal attacks both before and after harvesting.

11. Honeysuckle is a shrub that has _____ white or yellowish blossoms.

12. Most birds would _____ to the harsh weather and die if they did not migrate south for the winter.

13. Some insects may help ants by cleaning them or by giving them chemicals they _____.

14. Kangaroos use their long and powerful tails to balance themselves when sitting _____ or jumping.

15. Must crustaceans live in the sea, but some live in fresh water, and a few have _____ onto land.

16. The mother duck led her _____ into the pond.

17	**bring about**	*ph.* to cause to happen, occur, or exist	
		cause, produce, effect	야기하다, 일으키다

18	**carry** [kǽri]	① *v.* to hold something in one's hands or back while moving ② *v.* to support something's weight on one's body	
		① **convey, transport** ② **support, maintain**	① 운반하다 ② 받치다

19	**comprise** [kəmpráiz]	*v.* to contain, include, or consist of something specified	
		compose, form	구성하다, 이루다

20	**uncharted** [ʌntʃáːrtid]	*adj.* not fully explored or mapped in detail; not yet examined or fully investigated	
		unmapped, unexplored, unknown	지도에 없는, 미지의

21	**dot** [dɑt]	① *v.* to scatter; to cover with a scattering ② *n.* a small and round mark	
		① **spot, fleck** ② **speck, point**	① 산재하다 ② 점

22	**imaginary** [imǽdʒənèri]	*adj.* existing only in the mind or imagination; not real	
		imagined, fictitious, fictional	상상의, 가상의

23	**receptacle** [riséptəkəl]	*n.* a container or device that receives or holds something	
		container, holder, repository	그릇, 저장소

24	**diminish** [dimíniʃ]	*v.* to become or make something less or smaller	
		decrease, reduce, dwindle	감소하다

Quiz

17. Earthworms _____ changes in the soil by enriching it and making it more fertile.

18. Some parts of the lithosphere _____ the ocean floor, and others carry land masses or a combination of the two types.

19. The core, mantle, and crust _____ the three layers of the Earth.

20. The ocean bottom is a vast frontier that even today is largely unexplored and _____.

21. Steep, round hills called knobs _____ southern Indiana.

22. The equator is an _____ line running around the center of the Earth.

23. The broken valleys of the Great Basin provided ready _____ for the moisture.

24. The power of a hurricane becomes immediately _____ once over land because it is disconnected from its warm-water energy source.

25	**balmy** [bá:mi]	*adj.* warm and soft **gentle, mild**	온화한
26	**desperately** [déspəritli]	*adv.* recklessly or dangerously because of despair or urgency **impetuously, urgently, hopelessly**	필사적으로, 절박하게
27	**flame** [fleim]	*v.* to burn with flames **blaze, flare, glow**	타오르다, 불꽃을 내다
28	**sustainable** [səstéinəbl]	*adj.* capable of being sustained or maintained **supportable, endurable, bearable**	지속 가능한
29	**terrain** [təréin]	*n.* a stretch of land, especially with regard to its physical features **topography, territory, landscape**	지역, 지형, 지세
30	**extinguish** [ikstíŋgwiʃ]	*v.* to put out a fire **put out, quench**	불을 끄다

UNIT 07

 **Quiz**

25. The Virgin Islands, located in the Caribbean Sea, have a _____ climate.

26. The moon and Mars could be a future source of natural resources _____ needed on Earth.

27. Jupiter would have _____ as a star in its own light.

28. Something absolutely necessary for a _____ human settlement is water.

29. The moon may be divided into two major _____; the maria and the terrace.

30. After two full weeks of trying to fight it, the fire from the explosion was finally _____.

UNIT 08

Chapter • 02

Applied Sciences

1	**confine** [kənfáin]	*v.* to keep within limits; to keep in a small or enclosed space **restrict, limit, restrain**	제한하다, 한정하다
2	**dwelling** [dwéliŋ]	*n.* a house, flat, or something else where people live **habitation, house, residence**	주거, 집
3	**fasten** [fǽsn]	*v.* to make something firmly closed or fixed **tie, attach, lock**	묶다, 잠그다
4	**raze** [reiz]	*v.* to destroy something like a building or a town completely **demolish, tear down, knock down**	파괴하다
5	**annihilate** [ənáiəlèit]	*v.* to destroy something completely **exterminate, eliminate**	전멸시키다
6	**clumsy** [klʌ́mzi]	*adj.* unskillful with the hands or awkward and ungainly in movement **unhandy, ungraceful, awkward**	서투른, 우둔한
7	**conceal** [kənsíːl]	*v.* to hide; to place out of sight **hide, cover, secrete**	숨기다, 감추다
8	**critical** [krítikəl]	*adj.* of or being a moment of great danger, difficulty, or uncertainty **crucial, vital, momentous**	결정적인, 중대한

Quiz

1. *Workers in clay could generally afford to _____ themselves to either decorated wares or housewares.*

2. *A few houses in New England were built of stone, but only in Pennsylvania and adjacent areas was stone widely used in _____.*

3. *Before the plane takes off, passengers must _____ their seatbelts.*

4. *Wrecking balls are used to _____ buildings.*

5. *Human beings have the power to _____ many species as well as damage the balance of their own balance with nature.*

6. *Seals appear _____ on land, but they are able to move short distances faster than most people can run.*

7. *The researchers argued that the city was threatened by faults which lay _____ underground inside it.*

8. *Biological diversity has become widely recognized as a _____ conservation issue.*

9	**demise** [dimáiz]	*n.* the termination of existence or operation **death, loss**	사망, 소멸
10	**deplete** [diplí:t]	*v.* to reduce greatly in number or quantity; to use up supplies, money, energy, or resources **consume, expend, exhaust**	소모시키다, 고갈시키다
11	**sequence** [sí:kwəns]	*n.* a series or succession of things in a specific order; the order two or more things follow **series, succession, order**	연속, 순서
12	**turbulent** [tə́:rbjələnt]	*adj.* having a restless or uncontrolled quality; violently disturbed **wild, unruly, stormy**	몹시 거친, 격렬한
13	**typify** [típəfài]	*v.* to be an excellent or characteristic example of something **exemplify, represent, symbolize**	대표하다, 전형이 되다
14	**unprecedented** [ʌnprésədèntid]	*adj.* without precedent; not known ever to have happened before **unheard-of, unusual**	전례가 없는, 새로운
15	**feverish** [fí:vəriʃ]	*adj.* having a tendency to produce a fever; excited, restless, or uncontrolled **inflamed, fervent, passionate**	뜨거운, 열광적인
16	**permanent** [pə́:rmənənt]	*adj.* lasting or intended to last for a long time **eternal, perpetual, everlasting**	영구적이, 영속적인

UNIT 08

 ## Quiz

9. *A shortage of funds led to the _____ of the program.*

10. *The remains of organisms are recycled in the earth, which is fortunate because, otherwise, soil and water would soon become _____ of essential nutrients.*

11. *Equally interesting is the fact that the ants' execution of multiple-step tasks is accomplished in a series-parallel _____ .*

12. *Small mammals suffer hardship in the exposed and _____ environment of the uppermost trees.*

13. *High mountains _____ the terrain of Tibet and Nepal.*

14. *The developed countries of the world are using valuable resources at an _____ rate.*

15. *The Civil War created _____ manufacturing activity to supply critical materials, especially in the North.*

16. *Heavy drinking can cause _____ damage to the brain.*

| 17 | **maintain**
[meintéin] | ① *v.* to keep something in existence
② *v.* to continue to argue something
① preserve, keep ② contend, claim | ① 유지하다 ② 주장하다 |

| 18 | **screen**
[skri:n] | ① *v.* to shelter or conceal
② *v.* to test someone in order to check for the presence of a disease
① shield, cover ② examine, scan | ① 가리다 ② 조사하다 |

| 19 | **stride**
[straid] | *n.* a single long step in walking; an advance or development
pace, step, development | 활보, 진보 |

| 20 | **surpass**
[sərpǽs] | *v.* to go or be beyond in degree or extent
better, exceed, outdo | 능가하다, 뛰어넘다 |

| 21 | **unsubstantiated**
[ʌnsəbstǽnʃièitid] | *adj.* not substantiated; unable to prove the truth of something
unverified, unproved | 증거가 없는, 근거 없는 |

| 22 | **ward (off)**
[wɔːrd] | *v.* to fend off, turn aside, or parry a blow; to keep trouble, hunger, or disease away
block, avoid, avert | 막다, 피하다 |

| 23 | **articulate**
[aːrtíkjəlèit] | *v.* to pronounce words or to speak clearly and distinctly
enunciate | 또박또박 말하다, 분명하게 발음하다 |

| 24 | **element**
[éləmənt] | *n.* a part of something; a component or feature
constituent, ingredient, factor | 원소, 요소, 요인 |

Quiz

17. Consumers are misled if they believe organic foods can _____ health and provide better nutritional quality than conventionally grown foods.

18. Now, all blood is rigorously _____ for HIV and other viruses.

19. From these studies, great _____ have been made in treating patients.

20. It was reported that internal medicine would _____ surgery in value to the human race within the next twenty-five years.

21. There are numerous _____ reports that natural vitamins are superior to synthetic ones.

22. Some plants are able to _____ off animals by emitting noxious fumes that drive them away.

23. Each sound is considered and analyzed before it is _____.

24. Hydrogen, although it is the most abundant _____ in the universe, is not freely found on Earth.

25	**fabric** [fǽbrik]	*n.* woven, knitted, or felted cloth **textile, cloth**	직물, 천
26	**serve as**	*ph.* to be in the service of; to work for **function as, act as**	~로서 기능하다
27	**brittle** [brítl]	*adj.* hard but easily broken or likely to break **fragile, breakable, weak**	깨지기 쉬운, 약한
28	**vibration** [vaibréiʃən]	*n.* a vibrating motion; a single movement back and forth in vibrating **oscillation, shaking, shivering**	진동, 떨림
29	**dazzling** [dǽzliŋ]	*adj.* temporarily blinding; fascinating **brilliant, bright, dizzying**	눈부신, 현혹적인
30	**device** [diváis]	*n.* a tool or instrument made for a special purpose **instrument, apparatus, contrivance**	기구, 고안물

UNIT 08

🦭 Quiz

25. Natural silk is highly prized in spite of the availability of similar artificial _____.

26. Pheromones are substances that _____ chemical signals between members of the same species.

27. Steel is not as _____ as cast iron, so it does not break as easily.

28. The sensation of sound is produced when _____ transmitted through the air strike the eardrum.

29. The snow on the mountaintop was _____ in the bright morning sun.

30. An odometer is a _____ used to measure distance.

1   The establishment of these posts opened new roads and provided for the protection of **daring** adventures and expeditions as well as established settlers.

Ⓐ private
Ⓑ bold
Ⓒ promising
Ⓓ careful

2   Both the number and the percentage of people in the United States involved in nonagricultural pursuits expanded rapidly during the half century following the Civil War, with some of the most dramatic increases occurring in the **domains** of transportation, manufacturing, and trade.

Ⓐ fields
Ⓑ locations
Ⓒ organizations
Ⓓ occupations

3   Besides their wearability, either as jewelry or incorporated into articles of **attire**, beads possess the desirable characteristics of collectables, they are durable, portable, and available in infinite varieties, and they are often valuable in their original cultural context as well as in today's market.

Ⓐ ritual
Ⓑ furniture
Ⓒ clothing
Ⓓ utensil

4   The birds had to exercise **considerable** skill to produce the desired results, for their northern location meant fleeting growing seasons.

Ⓐ planning
Ⓑ reckless
Ⓒ physical
Ⓓ painful

5   The Mimbres would combine human and animal figures into one in order to describe their myths, legends, and history, which often resulted in humorous scenes that scholars still cannot **decipher**.

Ⓐ decode
Ⓑ agonize
Ⓒ announce
Ⓓ publish

6   The conservatism of the early English colonists in North American and their strong **attachment to** the English way of doing things would play a major part in the furniture that was made in New England.

Ⓐ indifference to
Ⓑ distaste for
Ⓒ curiosity about
Ⓓ preference for

7   Rain is **sparse** in the Atacama because of a phenomenon called rain shadow.

Ⓐ frequent
Ⓑ scanty
Ⓒ dense
Ⓓ sufficient

8   The arrival of a great wave of southern and eastern European immigrants coincided with and contributed to an enormous expansion of formal schooling.

Ⓐ was influenced by

Ⓑ happened at the same time as

Ⓒ began to grow rapidly

Ⓓ ensured the success of

9   The most significant program adopted by President Franklin D. Roosevelt was the New Deal, which helped alleviate the effects of the Great Depression.

Ⓐ stimulate

Ⓑ prevent

Ⓒ ease

Ⓓ cease

10 The water becomes part of a geyser if the rising water is constricted into a narrow passageway that connects the underground water to the surface.

Ⓐ heated

Ⓑ lowered

Ⓒ compressed

Ⓓ accelerated

11 There arc morc than 60 types of grains, and although they are all edible, only a few types are digestible by humans.

Ⓐ affordable

Ⓑ consumable

Ⓒ arable

Ⓓ feasible

12 Similarly, these boxes should be protected from direct sunlight to avoid high temperatures that are also fatal to the growing embryo.

Ⓐ beneficial

Ⓑ deadly

Ⓒ neutral

Ⓓ essential

13 The fundamental problem with the Stuyvesant and the other early apartment buildings that quickly followed, in the late 1870s and early 1880s, was that they were confined to the typical New York building lot.

Ⓐ adapted

Ⓑ transported

Ⓒ restricted

Ⓓ organized

14 Those animals that do not have highly developed modes of quick locomotion are concealed from predators by camouflage or become nocturnal feeders.

Ⓐ hidden

Ⓑ revealed

Ⓒ improved

Ⓓ escaped

15 One of the best-known examples of mass extinction occurred 65 million years ago with the demise of the dinosaurs and many other forms of life.

Ⓐ change

Ⓑ recovery

Ⓒ revival

Ⓓ death

16 Designers of the railroad stations of the new age explored the potential of iron by covering huge areas with spans that surpassed the great vaults of medieval churches and cathedrals.

Ⓐ imitated

Ⓑ exceeded

Ⓒ approached

Ⓓ included

Humanities

1 outlaw
[áutlɔ̀ː]
n. someone who has committed a crime
gangster, desperado, criminal
무법자

2 enable
[enéibəl]
v. to make someone able to do something
entitle, empower, capacitate
가능하게 하다, 힘을 주다

3 fundamental
[fʌ̀ndəméntl]
adj. serving as or being an essential part of a foundation or basis
essential, rudimentary, basic
근본적인, 기본의

4 ignorant
[íɡnərənt]
adj. lacking knowledge or information about something
unknowing, unaware, unlearned
잘 알지 못하는, 무지한

5 transportation
[trænspərtéiʃən]
n. the act of transporting or the process of being transported
conveyance, moving, carriage
운송, 교통

6 behold
[bihóuld]
v. to look at something or someone
notice, see, look at
주시하다, 지켜보다

7 mobility
[moubíləti]
n. the ability to be moved easily
movability, portability, transportability
이동성, 기동성
* *mobile* 이동성의

8 moreover
[mɔːróuvər]
adv. beside what has been said; and what is more important
in addition, besides, furthermore
게다가, 더욱이

Quiz

1. *Jesse was an _____, a bandit, and a criminal.*

2. *The economic aid would only last long enough to _____ the people to help themselves.*

3. *The _____ ideals embodied in the Constitution should not be lightly considered.*

4. *Critics _____ of the conditions attacked the proposed method to fix the problem as wasteful and dangerous.*

5. *Steam travel finally became a viable means of _____ in the late eighteenth centuries.*

6. *The steamboats must have been something to _____ on the rivers due to their size and elaborate, even luxurious, construction and appearance.*

7. *The troops' _____ was their greatest asset in warfare.*

8. *_____, even when people in different places use the material in a similar manner, the style of their work still varies.*

9	**chore**	*n.* a domestic task; a boring or unenjoyable task	
	[tʃɔːr]	**drudgery**	잡일, 허드렛일

10	**partition**	*v.* to divide into parts, pieces, or sections	
	[pɑːrtíʃən]	**separate, divide, split**	나누다, 분할하다

11	**paramount**	*adj.* greater than all others in importance or influence; of supreme importance	
	[pǽrəmàunt]	**primary, supreme, predominant**	최고의, 탁월한

12	**durability**	*n.* the ability to be strong and to last for a long time without breaking or becoming weaker	
	[djùərəbíləti]	**endurance, stability, firmness**	내구성, 내구력

13	**establish**	*v.* to set up	
	[istǽbliʃ]	**create, found, organize**	설립하다, 세우다

14	**ethnic**	*adj.* relating to or having a common race or cultural tradition	
	[éθnik]	**racial, native**	인종의, 민족의

15	**assortment**	*n.* a mixed collection	
	[əsɔ́ːrtmənt]	**group, collection, array**	분류, 유별

* *an assortment of* 다양한

16	**clarity**	*n.* the quality of being clear and pure	
	[klǽrəti]	**clearness, distinctness, definition**	명료성

Quiz

9. The earliest pottery was used for _____, with no attempt to make them works of art.

10. _____ rooms in log houses became the new style as they replaced the simple cabins people used to live in.

11. Tradition is _____, and most tribes are hesitant to make any changes.

12. The _____ of the pottery was crucial to the tribes since making ceramics was not easy for them to do.

13. The Rodeo Cowboy Association was founded in 1936 to _____ standards and regulations for the sport.

14. The Harlem Renaissance combined realism, _____ consciousness, and Americanism.

15. An _____ of bones was found at the site, which helped improved scientists' understanding of the ancient culture.

16. _____ and structure became the foundation of the opera seria.

17	**witness** [wítnis]	*v.* to see or notice something by being present when it happens observe, behold, watch	목격하다
18	**devote** [divóut]	*v.* to use or give up a resource such as time or money wholly to some purpose dedicate, pledge, consecrate	바치다, 헌신하다
19	**enforce** [infɔ́ːrs]	*v.* to cause a law or decision to be carried out effectively; to make something happen administer, implement, carry out	집행하다, 시행하다
20	**essence** [ésəns]	*n.* the basic distinctive part or quality of something, which determines its nature or character; a basic nature nature, principle, core	본질, 핵심
21	**climax** [kláimæks]	*n.* the high point or culmination of a series of events or of an experience peak, apex, culmination	절정, 정점
22	**composite** [kampázit]	*n.* a combination of two or more materials aggregate, combination, compound	합성, 혼합물
23	**encompass** [inkʌ́mpəs]	*v.* to surround completely; to include or be concerned with encircle, enclose, include	에워싸다, 포함하다
24	**deliberate** [dilíbərət]	*adj.* done on purpose or as a result of careful planning intentional, planned, careful	심사숙고한, 신중한

Quiz

17. *In 1905, he went to Paris to work with an art dealer, and it was there that he later _____ the formative years of Cubism.*

18. *Ordinary citizens sometimes _____ their entire lives to serving humanity unselfishly.*

19. *These images are meant to _____ how foolish and pitiful the character really is.*

20. *The _____ of folk music is how it reflects the humanity of the people who created it.*

21. *Arias usually followed as a _____ and revealed the emotion or internal conflict of the actors.*

22. *Some say that neither the Iliad nor Odyssey was written by a single poet but rather that each poem is a _____ of the writings of several people.*

23. *The term "art deco" has come to _____ three distinct but related design trends of the 1920s and 1930s.*

24. *The artist began the _____ process of painting the individual flowers in his landscape.*

| 25 | **husbandry** | *n.* the farming business | |
| | [hʌ́zbəndri] | farming, agriculture | (낙농, 양계를 포함한) 농업 |

| 26 | **hallmark** | *n.* a typical or distinctive feature, especially of quality | |
| | [hɔ́:lmɑ̀:rk] | characteristic, identification | (현저한) 특징, 특질 |

| 27 | **gesture** | *n.* the movement of the body as an expression of meaning | |
| | [dʒéstʃər] | motion, indication, signal | 제스쳐, 손짓, 몸짓 |

28	**discipline**	① *n.* strict training or the enforcing of rules	
	[dísəplin]	② *n.* an area of learning	
		① drilling, regulation ② field, area	① 규율 ① (학문) 분야

| 29 | **gala** | *n.* an occasion of special entertainment or a public festivity | |
| | [géilə] | celebration, festival, feast | 축제 |

| 30 | **immerse** | *v.* to put completely under water | |
| | [imə́:rs] | sink, dip, submerge | 담그다 |

 **Quiz**

25. The advent of animal _____ led to advancements in every aspect of human development from science to psychology.

26. One _____ of jazz music is the way that the best musicians can improvise so easily during their performances.

27. In all cultures, _____ are used as a form of communication.

28. Every scientific _____ tends to develop its own special language because it finds ordinary words inadequate, and psychology is no different.

29. Many people celebrate the new year with _____ parties.

30. Daguerre discovered that an image could be made permanent by _____ it in salt.

Social Sciences

1	**engage in**	*ph.* to take part in; to be involved in	
		participate in, partake in, enter into	참여하다, 종사하다
2	**exclusive** [iksklúsiv]	*adj.* involving the rejection or denial of everything else	
		sole, only, unique	배타적인, 독점적인
3	**halt** [hɔːlt]	*n.* an interruption or stop in movement, progression, or growth	
		stop, cessation, standstill	중단
4	**precious** [préʃəs]	*adj.* of great value, especially because something is very expensive or much loved	
		valuable, dear, beloved	귀중한, 소중한
5	**prosper** [práspər]	*v.* to do well, especially financially	
		flourish, thrive, succeed	번영하다
6	**sluggish** [slʌgiʃ]	*adj.* unenergetic; habitually lazy or inactive	
		stagnant, lethargic, lazy	부진한, 게으른
7	**sound** [saund]	*adj.* not damaged or injured; in good condition	
		undamaged, unimpaired, firm	온전한, 견실한
8	**ware** [wɛər]	*n.* manufactured goods of a specified material or for a specified range of use	
		merchandise, commodity, supply	제품, 상품

Quiz

1. In the early 1800s, over 80 percent of the United States' labor force was _____ agriculture.

2. A copyright is an _____ right to copy, sell, or perform a creative work such as a book or play.

3. World War II began, which brought an immediate _____ to all commercial airline service to Europe as well as Asia.

4. Salt was once so _____ that some cultures used it as a form of money.

5. Trade with Britain and the West Indies allowed Colonial seaports such as Boston to _____.

6. Some economists believe that the best way to get a _____ economy moving again is to cut taxes.

7. Government bonds and blue-chip stocks are _____ investments.

8. In the past, many salesmen tried to sell their _____ door-to-door.

9	**pervasive** [pərvéisiv]	*adj.* tending to or having the power to spread everywhere **prevalent, widespread, permeative**	널리 퍼지는, 스며드는
10	**nurse** [nəːrs]	*v.* to hold something with care; to look after sick or injured people **care for, look after, attend**	돌보다, 간호하다
11	**proceed** [prousíːd]	*v.* to make one's way; to go on **advance, progress, continue**	진출하다, 나아가다
12	**donate** [dóuneit]	*v.* to give, especially to charity **contribute, bestow, grant**	기부하다, 기증하다
13	**remarkably** [rimáːrkəbli]	*adv.* considerably; significantly **noticeably, unusually, extraordinarily**	현저하게, 두드러지게
14	**gregarious** [grigɛ́əriəs]	*adj.* seeking and enjoying the company of others **companionable, sociable**	군집의, 사회성의
15	**confer** [kənfə́ːr]	*v.* to grant someone an honor or distinction **give, award, present**	수여하다
16	**constitute** [kɑ́nstətjùːt]	*v.* to be an element or part of; to establish laws or an institution **form, compose, establish**	이루다, 구성하다

UNIT 10

Quiz

9. The influence of the thoughts has been so _____ that its theoretical approaches have come to be known in academic circles as the Chicago School.

10. Female lions cannot go into estrus and get pregnant while they are _____ lion infants.

11. Real estate subdivision in the cities _____ much faster than population growth.

12. In 1899, Mary Elizabeth Brown _____ a couple of hundred musical instruments to the museum.

13. The urban population grew _____ quickly during this time, mostly because people were moving to the cities to look for work.

14. A _____ person avoids solitude.

15. In the family, traditional cultural patterns _____ leadership on one or both of the parents.

16. A soldier's refusal to commit an illegal act does not _____ rebellion.

17	**linear** [líniər]	*adj.* of, consisting of, or using lines; extended or arranged in a line **straight, straightway**	(직)선의, 단선적인
18	**bias** [báiəs]	*n.* an inclination to favor or disfavor one side against **inclination, prejudice, leaning**	편견, 선입관
19	**exempt** [igzémpt]	*adj.* free from some obligation; not liable **excused, free, immune**	면제된
20	**negligible** [néglidʒəbəl]	*adj.* small or unimportant enough to ignore **trivial, insignificant, trifling**	보잘 것 없는, 사소한
21	**impose** [impóuz]	*v.* to make a payment of a tax or fine; to make the performance of a duty compulsory **levy, place, force**	부과하다, (의무 등을) 지우다
22	**reckless** [réklis]	*adj.* heedless of the consequences of one's actions or behavior **rash, careless, imprudent**	무모한, 부주의한
23	**bound** [baund]	*n.* a limit or boundary; a limitation **border, confines, extent**	경계, 한계
24	**atheist** [éiθiist]	*n.* a person who denies or disbelieves the existence of a supreme being or beings **nonbeliever, infidel**	무신론자

Quiz

17. *The usually uncritical acceptance of this thesis led in turn to the assumption that the application of science to industrial purposes was a _____ process.*

18. *Throughout the 19th century and into the 20th century, farmers in the U.S. maintained a _____ against big cities.*

19. *Some parents were motivated to send their children to private schools, which were _____ from governmental restrictions.*

20. *Although the accident appeared serious, only a _____ amount of damage was done.*

21. *The government _____ strict regulations on the people for the duration of the war.*

22. *Motorists can be fined for _____ driving.*

23. *Education knows no _____.*

24. *Allen was an outspoken _____ who was an advocate of deistic thought.*

25	**detect** [ditékt]	*v.* to see or to notice; to discover the presence of **uncover, discover, notice**	감지하다, 탐지하다
26	**milestone** [máilstòun]	*n.* a very important event; a significant point or stage **landmark**	획기적인 사건
27	**overthrow** [òuvərθróu]	*v.* to defeat completely an established order or a government **overpower, dethrone, defeat**	전복시키다, 뒤엎다
28	**overtax** [òuvərtǽks]	*v.* to demand too much tax from someone; to burden heavily **overload, overdo**	세금을 무겁게 걷다, 과중한 부담을 지우다
29	**headquarter** [hédkwɔ̀:rtər]	*v.* to locate the center of an organization or group from which activities are controlled **base**	본부를 설치하다, 본사를 두다
30	**zealous** [zéləs]	*adj.* enthusiastic; keen **eager, ardent, fervent**	열광적인, 열성적인

UNIT 10

 **Quiz**

25. The objective of the experiment was to _____ consciousness in animals to see if they are self-aware or not.

26. Gallup's report of the experiment was _____ in our understanding of animal minds.

27. In 509 B.C., the Roman Republic was established after the citizens of Rome _____ the ruling Etruscans.

28. The public school system suddenly found itself _____.

29. The International Herald Tribune, which is co-owned by the Washington Post and The New York Times, is _____ in Paris.

30. Although he was a sickly child, Theodore Roosevelt eventually became a _____ outdoorsman who extolled the virtues of vigorous exertion.

Natural Sciences

1	**formulate** [fɔ́ːrmjəlèit]	*v.* to express something in terms of a formula; to express something precisely and clearly **systematize, devise, articulate**	공식화하다, 명확하게 나타내다
2	**incorporate** [inkɔ́ːrpərèit]	*v.* to contain something as part of a whole; to combine something **consolidate, merge, unite**	결합하다, 통합하다
3	**strand** [strænd]	*n.* a single thin piece of thread, wire, or hair **string, fiber, thread**	(밧줄의) 가닥, 실
4	**cell** [sel]	*n.* a piece of equipment for producing electricity from chemicals, heat, or light	전지
5	**flourish** [flɔ́ːriʃ]	*v.* to be strong and healthy; to grow well **prosper, thrive, flower**	번창하다, 번영하다
6	**frigid** [frídʒid]	*adj.* cold and unfriendly **cold, frosty, chilly**	몹시 추운
7	**instance** [ínstəns]	*n.* an example, especially one of a particular condition or circumstance **case, illustration, occurrence**	경우, 사실
8	**gap** [gæp]	*n.* a space between two things or in the middle of something **rift, crevice, hole, cavity**	갈라진 틈, 구멍

Quiz

1. Some possible solutions to the problem are being _____.

2. When hypotheses are confirmed, they are _____ into theories.

3. Ropes are cords at least 0.15 inches in diameter and are made of three or more _____ which are themselves formed of twisted yarns.

4. His subsequent hydrogen fuel _____ never produced enough electricity to justify the expense of creating them.

5. Tulips also _____ in Pennsylvania.

6. During the _____ winters, food sources become scarce, and migration to more fertile feeding grounds becomes mandatory for their survival.

7. In many _____, the specimens are less than one-tenth of a millimeter in diameter.

8. The crossbill winds its long tongue into the _____ of the nut and draws out the seed.

9	**fuse** [fjuːz]	*v.* to melt as a result of the application of heat; to join by, or as if by, melting together **melt, blend, combine**	융합하다, 합치다

9 **fuse**
[fjuːz]

v. to melt as a result of the application of heat; to join by, or as if by, melting together
melt, blend, combine
융합하다, 합치다

10 **lump**
[lʌmp]

n. an irregularly shaped mass or piece
chunk, clot, bump
덩어리

11 **shed light on**

ph. to clear up; to provide information about
throw light on, clarify, elucidate
밝히다, 설명을 돕다

12 **heart**
[hɑːrt]

n. the most central part; the most important part
center, core, essence
중심, 핵심

13 **startling**
[stɑ́ːrtliŋ]

adj. causing someone to be slightly shocked or surprised
amazing, surprising, astonishing
놀라운

14 **sterile**
[stéril]

adj. incapable of producing offspring, fruit, or seeds
unproductive, infertile, barren
생식력이 없는, 불임의, 불모의

15 **canopy**
[kǽnəpi]

n. a covering over something for decoration or protection; the upper level of the trees in a rainforest
ceiling, roof, tent
덮개, 나무의 맨 위 층

16 **convert**
[kənvə́ːrt]

v. to change the form or function of one thing into another
alter, change, transform
전환하다, 변환하다

🔵 Quiz

9. *The male and female reproductive organs of orchids are _____ together into a single structure.*

10. *As centuries passed, _____ of the resin were covered by layers of soil.*

11. *This finding _____ new light on the inexorable process of aging and death.*

12. *The _____ of a comet is typically quite solid and can be more than ten kilometers in diameter.*

13. *The difference between a hummingbird and a penguin is immense, but it is hardly as _____ as the between a bat and a whale.*

14. *Typically, a colony consists of the queen, _____ female workers, and males.*

15. *The _____ holds plenty of climbing mammals that are moderately large.*

16. *The term "latent heat" refers to the energy that has to be used to _____ liquid water to water vapor.*

| 17 | **demolish**
[dimáliʃ] | *v.* to destroy or ruin a building or other structure on purpose; to tear down |
| | | **raze, smash, break down** 부수다, 폭파하다 |

| 18 | **overcome**
[òuvərkÁm] | *v.* to fight successfully in a struggle or conflict |
| | | **get over, conquer, defeat** 극복하다 |

| 19 | **texture**
[tékstʃər] | *n.* the structure formed by smaller particles; the way the surface of a substance feels |
| | | **fabric, feel** 직물, (암석 등의) 결 |

| 20 | **initiate**
[iníʃièit] | *v.* to make something begin; to be responsible for starting |
| | | **commence, launch, start** 시작하다, 착수하다 |

| 21 | **drench**
[drentʃ] | *v.* to flow or make something flow in a thin stream or drops |
| | | **drown, immerse, soak** 흠뻑 적시다, 담그다 |

| 22 | **adjunct**
[ǽdʒʌŋkt] | *n.* something attached or added to something else but which is not an essential part of it |
| | | **appendage, attachment, accessory** 부가물, 부속물 |

| 23 | **uneven**
[ʌníːvən] | *adj.* not smooth or flat; bumpy |
| | | **irregular, rough, rugged** 고르지 못한, 평탄치 않은 |

| 24 | **tepid**
[tépid] | *adj.* slightly or only just warm |
| | | **lukewarm, warmish** 미지근한 |

Quiz

17. *When Mount St. Helens erupted in 1980, it _____ a large amount of the ice field that surrounded it.*

18. *Nesting on a narrow ledge has its own peculiar problems, and the bird's behavior has become adapted to _____ them.*

19. *The _____ of the soil can be determined by physically changing the shape of the soil with one's hands.*

20. *In addition, snowfall may be _____ when mountainous regions cause moist air to elevate.*

21. *Despite the long-term lack of rain, deserts occasionally are _____ by violent storms.*

22. *In North America, potash making quickly became an _____ to the cleaning of land for agriculture.*

23. *Essentially, winds are nature's way of balancing the _____ distribution of air pressure over the Earth.*

24. *Hurricanes pose the greatest threat to human populations when they track eastward to the _____ waters of the Gulf of Mexico.*

25	**sporadically**	*adv.* at irregular intervals; not continuously	
	[spərǽdikəli]	**occasionally, intermittently**	산발적으로, 드문드문

26	**obvious**	*adj.* easily seen, recognized, or understood	
	[ábviəs]	**clear, apparent, evident**	명백한, 명확한

27	**plunge**	*v.* to dive, throw oneself, fall, or rush headlong into something; to thrust or push something	
	[plʌndʒ]	**fall, drop, pitch**	뛰어들다, 던져 넣다

28	**suitable**	*adj.* having the right qualities for a particular person, purpose, or situation	
	[súːtəbəl]	**appropriate, fitting, proper**	적당한, 알맞은

29	**trek**	*n.* a long and hard journey	
	[trek]	**trip, journey, hike**	(길고 고된) 여행

30	**peril**	*n.* grave danger, especially of being harmed or killed	
	[pérəl]	**threat, risk, jeopardy**	위험

 **Quiz**

25. Lichens and moss grow on the rocks while small tufts of grass spring up _____ in between the boulders and stones.

26. No two comets ever look identical, but they have basic features in common, one of the most _____ of which is a coma.

27. When the comet _____ into Jupiter's atmosphere and struck the planet, astronomers were watching as closely as they could.

28. If a _____ amount of water is found on the planet, it could enable colonies to be established there much more easily.

29. GPS receiving devices are becoming standard in most new car designs and are a favorite of hunters and fishermen making long _____ in the wilderness.

30. While high winds are commonly associated with the _____ of hurricanes, the most destructive factor is the accompanying storm surge as it strikes land.

Applied Sciences

1 **elaborate**
[ilǽbərət]
adj. complicated in design; carefully planned or worked out
intricate, painstaking, meticulous
정교한, 공들인

2 **erect**
[irékt]
v. to put up or build something; to set up or establish something
construct, create, found
짓다, 세우다

3 **rectangular**
[rektǽŋgjələr]
adj. relating to a four-sided figure with opposite sides of equal length
square, four-sided, right-angled
직사각형의, 직각의

4 **unify**
[júːnəfài]
v. to bring two or more things together to form a single unit
combine, integrate, unite
통합하다, 통일하다

5 **aptly**
[ǽptli]
adv. in an apt or suitable manner
fitly, appropriately, properly
적절히

6 **eliminate**
[ilímənèit]
v. to completely get rid of something that is unnecessary or unwanted
remove, exterminate, obliterate
제거하다, 없애다

7 **aquatic**
[əkwǽtik]
adj. involving or happening in water
marine, oceanic
물의, 수중의

8 **efficient**
[ifíʃənt]
adj. producing satisfactory results with an economy of effort
effective, proficient, economic
효율적인

Quiz

1. *Arriving in the New World during the 1600s, early American settlers had little resources for or interest in _____ furniture.*

2. *Many buildings in that style were _____ nationwide thanks to government programs.*

3. *Within its _____ walls, permanent houses were built, replacing the thatched dwellings of the original Manhattanites.*

4. *All of the parks and squares were meant to supplement the major road, which was to remain the _____ factor for the entire system.*

5. *The road has been _____ called "the metropolitan corridor" of the American landscape.*

6. *Certain species may be _____ while others may survive for no particular reason.*

7. *Rodents dwell in various habitats, with some species being _____ and others terrestrial.*

8. *Believe it or not, diesel is both rich in energy and highly _____.*

9	**habitat**	*n.* the natural home of an animal or plant	
	[hǽbətæ̀t]	home, niche, territory	서식지

10	**ensure**	*v.* to make something certain; to assure or guarantee something	
	[enʃúər]	assure, confirm, guarantee	확실하게 하다, 보장하다

11	**stress**	*v.* to emphasize or attach importance to something	
	[stres]	accent, underscore, spotlight	강조하다

12	**striking**	*adj.* unusual or interesting enough to be easily noticed	
	[stráikiŋ]	extraordinary, remarkable, impressive	현저한, 두드러진

13	**pliable**	*adj.* able to bend without breaking or cracking	
	[pláiəbəl]	flexible, elastic, malleable	유연한, 휘기 쉬운

14	**teem with**	*ph.* to be very full of people or animals, which are all moving about	
		proliferate with, swarm with, overflow with	~로 풍부하다, 가득 차다

15	**obtain**	*v.* to get something that is necessary	
	[əbtéin]	acquire, gain, procure	얻다, 획득하다

16	**nutritional**	*adj.* relating to the substances in food that make or stay healthy	
	[nju:tríʃənl]	nourishing, nutritive, alimentary	영양의, 영양학상의

UNIT 12

Quiz

9. Watching the behavior of diverse animal species in their natural _____, Lopez and Tinbergen observed behavior patterns that promote survival.

10. The behavioral _____ that the young will stay close to their mother and be protected from danger.

11. The woods' importance in the communities of colonial North America need hardly be _____.

12. Perhaps the most unique aspect of butterfly diversity is the _____ difference in species richness between tropical and temperate regions.

13. Platinum is harder than copper and is almost as _____ as gold.

14. The waters off the east coast of the United States once _____ immense schools of fish, some as many as a mile across.

15. Vitamin C is _____ from citrus fruits.

16. If one's basic _____ needs are being met, he or she should not need to take vitamin supplements.

17	**deter** [ditə́:r]	*v.* to discourage or restrain from acting **inhibit, prevent, check**	제지하다, 억제하다
18	**portable** [pɔ́:rtəbl]	*adj.* easily carried or moved and usually designed to be so **transportable, carryable, handy**	휴대할 수 있는, 휴대용의
19	**populate** [pápjulèit]	*v.* to inhabit or live in a certain area **settle, occupy**	~에 거주하다, (장소 등을) 차지하다
20	**precede** [pri:sí:d]	*v.* to go or be before someone or something **predate, lead, herald**	앞서다, 선행하다
21	**prescribe** [priskráib]	*v.* to advise a medicine as a remedy, especially by completing a prescription **direct, specify, order**	처방하다
22	**reaction** [ri:ǽkʃən]	*n.* a response to a stimulus **reply, feedback, repulsion**	반응
23	**respiratory** [réspərətɔ̀:ri]	*adj.* relating to breathing or the lungs **breathing, respiring**	호흡의
24	**at odds**	*ph.* at variance; in disagreement **disagreeing, conflicting, on bad terms**	다른, 불화의

Quiz

17. Another form of biological pest control is to include various plants in a garden or field that are known naturally to _____ parasitic pests.

18. Some stutterers carry a _____ device that allows them to hear their own words with a time delay.

19. Skeletal muscles _____ the human body more than any other kind of muscles.

20. Occasionally, the episode may be _____ by some visible drowsiness, but it usually just hits out of nowhere.

21. In herbal therapy, special herbs are _____ by a doctor to be taken in a hot liquid form.

22. A chemical _____ that absorbs heat is called endothermic.

23. Examples of smooth muscle can be found in the _____ tissues.

24. Scientists, physicians, and psychologists have often been _____ about how the brain functions.

25	**ingredient** [ingrí:diənt]	*n.* one of the parts that make up a whole **constituent, element, factor**	성분, 요소
26	**noxious** [nákʃəs]	*adj.* causing or capable of causing harm; poisonous **harmful, nocuous, toxic**	유해한, 유독한
27	**subject (to)** [sʌ́bdʒikt]	*adj.* likely to be affected by something, especially something bad; being under domination, control, or influence **vulnerable, prone, submissive**	걸리기 쉬운, 종속하는
28	**protein** [próuti:n]	*n.* a substance that exists in foods such as meat, eggs, and beans and which a body needs in order to grow and to remain strong and healthy	단백질
29	**artificial** [à:rtəfíʃəl]	*adj.* made by human effort; not occurring naturally **man-made, unnatural**	인공의, 인공적인
30	**harness** [há:rnis]	*v.* to control and use the natural force or power of something **utilize, apply, exploit**	(동력 등을) 이용하다

 **Quiz**

25. When the two _____ are mixed together, under certain conditions, the results can be deadly.

26. One result of the industrial complex construction was an increased concentration of _____ chemicals in the air.

27. Plants are _____ to attack and infection by a remarkable variety of symbiotic species and have evolved a diverse array of mechanisms designed to frustrate potential colonists.

28. A fever is caused when blood cells release _____ called pyrogens, which raise the body's temperature.

29. In a domed stadium, natural grass cannot be grown, so _____ turf is used on the playing field.

30. Dams can _____ the power of rivers, but they may also destroy their beauty.

REVIEW TEST

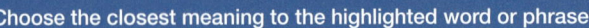

Choose the closest meaning to the highlighted word or phrase.

1   The development of the railroad led to significant improvements in the speed, volume, and regularity of shipments making possible a **fundamental** transformation in the production and distribution of goods.

Ⓐ possible

Ⓑ basic

Ⓒ gradual

Ⓓ unique

2   The trademark of Flank Lloyd Wright's style was his ability to blend the **essence** of modernity with that of nature in his architecture.

Ⓐ basic nature

Ⓑ growing importance

Ⓒ full extent

Ⓓ first phase

3   While governments abolished or abandoned slavery through much of the world, humans, **exclusively** Africans, were kept in bondage in one of the world's great democracies.

Ⓐ finally

Ⓑ relatively

Ⓒ entirely

Ⓓ solely

4   The chemical industry has introduced several herbicides that are more ecologically **sound**.

Ⓐ harsh

Ⓑ lethargic

Ⓒ magnificent

Ⓓ safe

5   The supply of wood **conferred** advantages but had some negative aspects as well.

Ⓐ eliminated

Ⓑ counteracted

Ⓒ provided

Ⓓ restricted

6   Some species seem to be very articulate creatures, but their medium of communication is difficult for humans to study and appreciate because of the technological difficulties in **detecting** and analyzing these pheromones.

Ⓐ controlling

Ⓑ storing

Ⓒ questioning

Ⓓ finding

7   **Reckless** claim that went far beyond what could actually be achieved from their use were made concerning the effects of vitamins.

Ⓐ Pertinent

Ⓑ Irresponsible

Ⓒ Urgent

Ⓓ Pungent

8   The Anasazi **flourished** over the centuries, developing a pottery tradition and carving intricate, multi-room dwellings into the sheer sides of cliffs.

Ⓐ prospered

Ⓑ vanished

Ⓒ emerged

Ⓓ transformed

9   These forms of plant life are capable
    of surviving the long winter months of
    frigid temperatures and can grow quickly
    during the short summer growing season.

    Ⓐ moderate

    Ⓑ arid

    Ⓒ freezing

    Ⓓ humid

10 With the continued rise in sea level, more
    ice would **plunge** into the ocean, causing
    sea levels to rise even higher.

    Ⓐ drop

    Ⓑ extend

    Ⓒ melt

    Ⓓ drift

11 The child is biologically prepared
    to acquire certain adaptive behavior
    but needs the support of a **suitably**
    stimulating environment.

    Ⓐ moderately

    Ⓑ inappropriately

    Ⓒ commonly

    Ⓓ approximately

12 The technology of the North American
    colonies did not differ **strikingly** from
    that of Europe, but, in one respect, the
    colonists enjoyed a greater economic
    advantage.

    Ⓐ remarkably

    Ⓑ uniquely

    Ⓒ similarly

    Ⓓ equivalently

13 Evidence **obtained** from a site known as
    the Hole in the Rock, in Papago Park
    in Phoenix, Arizona, indicates that it
    might have been used as an observatory
    by a prehistoric people known as the
    Hohokam.

    Ⓐ acquired

    Ⓑ transported

    Ⓒ disappeared

    Ⓓ removed

14 Planning, ecologists argue, must **precede**
    development, and regional planning is
    required if the use of major areas of land
    and its resources is to be brought into
    accord with environmental necessities
    and with the long-term needs of society.

    Ⓐ perceive

    Ⓑ consider

    Ⓒ lead

    Ⓓ follow

15 Obviously, none of these methods is
    entirely satisfactory although using
    landfills to create **artificial** landscapes,
    which are then covered with soil and
    planted with various kinds of vegetation,
    is a possibility that remains to be fully
    developed.

    Ⓐ native

    Ⓑ manmade

    Ⓒ luxurious

    Ⓓ superficial

16 The captains were the ones in control,
    the ones who **harnessed** and manipulated
    the massive boats and powerful steam
    engines.

    Ⓐ utilized

    Ⓑ recognized

    Ⓒ fabricated

    Ⓓ designed

Humanities

1	**implication** [ìmpləkéiʃən]	*n.* a possible effect or result of an action or a decision; something that is suggested or indirectly stated hint, insinuation, connotation	내포, 함축, 의미

2	**accompany** [əkʌ́mpəni]	*v.* to go along or in company with; to join in action attend, go with, escort	수반하다, 동반하다

3	**dexterous** [dékstərəs]	*adj.* skillful in physical movements, especially of the hands deft, artful, shrewd	솜씨 좋은, 능란한

4	**prevent** [privént]	*v.* to stop someone from doing something or from happening prohibit, inhibit, forestall	금하다, 예방하다

5	**unrestricted** [ʌ̀nristríktid] * *restrict* 제한하다	*adj.* not limited by anyone or anything unlimited, unimpeded, free	제한이 없는, 자유로운

6	**administer** [ædmínəstər]	*v.* to manage, govern, or direct one's affairs or an organization direct, manage	관리하다, 운영하다

7	**migrate** [máigreit]	*v.* to travel from one region to another; to leave one place to settle in another move, resettle, relocate	이동하다, 이주하다

8	**funeral** [fjú:nərəl]	*n.* the ceremonial burial or cremation of a dead person burial, interment	장례(식)

Quiz

1. Pennsylvania's colonial ironmasters forged iron and a revolution that had both industrial and political _____.

2. Forms of music often _____ the stories to instill emotion and climax in the history.

3. _____ with axes, snares, and fishing lines, these men blazed the trails, built the first log cabins, and confronted Native American tribes.

4. The availability of fresh meat was very limited; there was no way to _____ spoilage.

5. The herds of cattle no longer had _____ use of the plains for grazing, and the fencing led to conflict between the farmers and the cattle ranchers.

6. The National Marine Sanctuaries Program is _____ by the National Oceanic Administration.

7. At this point, early groups of humans began to _____ both east and west.

8. _____ rites have always played important roles in human history.

9	**innovative** [ínouvèitiv]	*adj.* introducing or using new ideas or ways of doing something creative, imaginative, ingenious	혁신적인, 새로운
10	**frame** [freim]	① *v.* to compose or design something ② *n.* a hard main structure or basis to something ① construct, devise ② structure, framework	① 구성하다, 입안하다 ② 틀, 뼈대
11	**recall** [rikɔ́:l]	*v.* to bring back from memory recollect, remember, reminisce	회상하다, 떠올리다
12	**excavate** [ékskəvèit]	*v.* to dig up or uncover something, especially historical remains unearth, uncover, expose	발굴하다
13	**isolated** [áisəlèitid]	*adj.* placed or standing alone or apart separated, secluded, unconnected	고립된

* *isolate* 고립시키다

14	**fashion** [fǽʃən]	① *v.* to make something into a particular shape ② *n.* a way of making or doing something ① make, manufacture ② manner, way	① 만들다, 제작하다 ② 방법, 방식
15	**coffin** [kɔ́:fin]	*n.* a box into which a corpse is put for cremation or burial casket, pall	관
16	**conduct** [kəndʌ́kt]	*v.* to carry out a particular activity or process; to lead or guide run, direct, manage	집행하다, 지도하다

Quiz

9. One _____ approach on the functions of the stone tools involves studying damage and wear on them.

10. The questions behaviorists _____ and the techniques they used were designed to help them understand how people behaved.

11. Some archeologists _____ complicated emotions when they had finally found the artifacts.

12. It was not until the 1890s that archaeologists _____ in city-states to the south of Nineveh found many thousands of tablets inscribed only in Sumerian.

13. The ideal situation for the creation of folk music is an _____ rural community.

14. The Native Americans in northern California were highly skilled at basketry, using reeds, grasses, and roots to _____ articles of all sorts and sizes.

15. The climax occurs at the end of the feast, when the body is placed in a _____ and carried to its final resting place.

16. Recently, some anthropologists _____ an interesting case study in ethnology.

UNIT 13

17	**evoke** [ivóuk]	*v.* to cause or to produce a response or reaction **invoke, raise, make**	일깨우다, 일으키다
18	**genius** [dʒíːnjəs]	*n.* someone who has an outstanding creative or intellectual ability **brain, intellect, mastermind**	천재
19	**imitate** [ímitèit]	*v.* to copy the behavior, manners, or appearance of someone; to use something as a model **mimic, copy**	흉내 내다, 모방하다
20	**exert** [igzə́ːrt]	*v.* to use power or influence in order to make something happen **exercise, expend, use**	(노력, 힘 등을) 쓰다
21	**deserving** [dizə́ːrviŋ]	*adj.* worthy of being given support or a reward **creditable, estimable, praiseworthy**	자격이 있는, 그럴 만한
22	**note** [nout]	*v.* to notice or pay careful attention to something **observe, perceive, notice**	주목하다
23	**infinite** [ínfənit]	*adj.* having no boundaries or limits in size, extent, time, or space **boundless, endless, limitless**	무한한, 막대한
24	**culmination** [kʌ̀lmənéiʃən]	*n.* the top or highest point; the attainment or arrival at the highest point of glory, power, or something else **peak, zenith, climax**	정점, 절정

Quiz

17. *The purpose of a poem need not be to inform the reader of anything but rather to _____ a feeling to create a sensual, aesthetically pleasing experience.*

18. *Today, his work tends to be poorly known among historians though some call him an intuitive _____ far ahead of his peers.*

19. *Numerous assistants, who had been trained to _____ the artist's style, applied the paint.*

20. *The pressures _____ along the foot, together with the length of the stride, which averaged 87 centimeters, indicated that the hominids had been walking slowly.*

21. *Annual cash awards are given to _____ artists in various categories.*

22. *Other investigators have _____ that when mothers talk to babies who are only a few months old, they exaggerate the pitch, loudness, and intensity of their words.*

23. *In The Library of Babel, Borges describes an _____ library that contains all possible texts.*

24. *His death was simply a _____ of years and years of trouble, pain, and suffering.*

25	**consciously** [kánʃəsli]	*adv.* with full awareness of what one is doing **intentionally, deliberately, knowingly**	의식적으로
26	**idiosyncratic** [ìdiəsiŋkrǽtik]	*adj.* peculiar to a specific individual; rather unusual **eccentric, odd, strange**	특이한
27	**elastic** [ilǽstik]	*adj.* able to return to its original shape or size after being pulled or pressed out of shape **flexible, stretchable, pliable**	탄력 있는, 탄성이 있는
28	**discrimination** [diskrìmənéiʃən]	*n.* the ability to draw fine distinctions; biased judgment **discernment, prejudice**	구별, 차별
29	**flamboyant** [flæmbɔ́iənt]	*adj.* brightly colored and easily noticed; excessively showy **flashy, garish, eye-catching**	현란한, 화려한
30	**embrace** [embréis]	① *v.* to hold someone closely in the arms affectionately or as a greeting ② *v.* to include something as a part ① **hug, clasp** ② **include, encompass**	① 껴안다 ② 포함하다

UNIT 13

Quiz

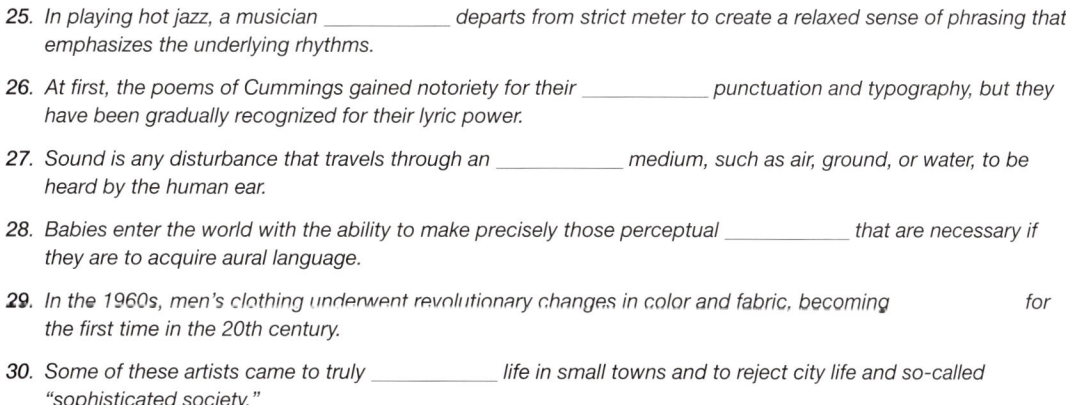

25. In playing hot jazz, a musician _____ departs from strict meter to create a relaxed sense of phrasing that emphasizes the underlying rhythms.

26. At first, the poems of Cummings gained notoriety for their _____ punctuation and typography, but they have been gradually recognized for their lyric power.

27. Sound is any disturbance that travels through an _____ medium, such as air, ground, or water, to be heard by the human ear.

28. Babies enter the world with the ability to make precisely those perceptual _____ that are necessary if they are to acquire aural language.

29. In the 1960s, men's clothing underwent revolutionary changes in color and fabric, becoming _____ for the first time in the 20th century.

30. Some of these artists came to truly _____ life in small towns and to reject city life and so-called "sophisticated society."

Social Sciences

1	**precipitous** [prisípətəs]	*adj.* very sudden; dangerously high or steep **abrupt, steep, sheer**	급격한, 가파른
2	**confront** [kənfrʌ́nt]	*v.* to face someone; to prepare to deal firmly with something **encounter, face, defy**	직면하다, 맞서다
3	**tedious** [tíːdiəs]	*adj.* tiresomely long-winded or dull **boring, overlong, monotonous**	지루한
4	**transition** [trænzíʃən]	*n.* a change or passage from one condition or place to another **alteration, change, conversion**	변화, 변이
5	**virtually** [vɚ́ːrtʃuəli]	*adv.* in practice, though not strictly speaking **substantially, practically, nearly**	실질적으로, 사실상
6	**courteously** [kɚ́ːrtiəsli]	*adv.* in a polite manner **politely, considerately, respectfully**	예의 바르게, 공손히
7	**seasoned** [síːzənd]	*adj.* rendered competent through trial and experience **trained, experienced, veteran**	익숙한, 숙련된
8	**soar** [sɔːr]	*v.* to rise or fly high into the air **rise, increase, skyrocket**	솟아오르다, 치솟다

Quiz

1. Besides ruining many thousands of individual investors, the _____ decline in the value of assets greatly strained banks and other financial institutions.

2. Staggering tasks _____ the people of the United States, both the North and the South, when the Civil War ended.

3. The use of robots and automated machinery has eliminated certain _____ factory jobs.

4. The United States economy underwent a massive _____, and the nature of work was permanently altered.

5. The land surrounding Boston had always been poor farm country, and, by the mid-eighteenth century, it was _____ stripped of its timber.

6. Workers in the service sector should be trained to act as _____ as possible.

7. _____ workers are more valuable to employers than beginners.

8. Cotton production _____ as southern farmers turned their land into cotton plantations.

9	**extraordinary** [ikstrɔ́:rdənèri]	*adj.* very unusual or surprising; much greater or more impressive than usual **strange, abnormal, outstanding**	이상한, 비범한
10	**magnify** [mǽgnəfài]	*v.* to make something seem bigger or louder, especially using special equipment **amplify, enlarge, augment**	확대하다
11	**makeup** [méikʌp]	*n.* the combination of characteristics or ingredients that form something **composition, constitution, arrangement**	구성
12	**merchandise** [mə́:rtʃəndàiz]	*n.* goods that are being sold **commodities, products, staples**	상품, 제품
13	**metropolis** [mitrápəlis]	*n.* a very large city that is the most important city in a country or area **megalopolis, municipality**	대도시, 주요 도시
14	**corruption** [kərʌ́pʃən] * *corrupt* 부패한	*n.* a sinking to a state of low moral standards **depravity, perversion**	타락
15	**descent** [disént]	*n.* family origins or ancestry **lineage, bloodline, ancestry**	혈통
16	**circulation** [sə̀:rkjuléiʃən]	① *n.* the passing of something from one person or place to another ② *n.* the distribution of a newspaper or magazine ① **distribution, diffusion** ② **issuance**	① 유통 ② 발행 (부수)

 **Quiz**

9. *The combination of new immigrants and old American "settlers" on America's "urban frontier" in the late 19th century proved _____.*

10. *Rapid industrialization and increased geographic mobility in the nineteenth century has special implications for women because these changes tended to _____ social distinctions.*

11. *As the population grew, its _____ also changed.*

12. *The men bought or traded farm animals and acquired needed _____ in the market.*

13. *By 1930, the United States had ten giant _____.*

14. *Most lived in small towns and believed cities to be centers of _____, crime, and moral degradation.*

15. *Some cultures trace a person's ancestry back through the mother's line, which is known as the matrilineal system of _____.*

16. *In fact, the _____ of weekly magazines exceeded that of newspapers in the period.*

17	**competitiveness** [kəmpétətivnis]	*n.* the ability of a company, country, or a product to compete with others **rivalry**	경쟁(력)
18	**disdain** [disdéin]	*n.* a lack of respect accompanied by a feeling of intense dislike **contempt, scorn**	경멸
19	**constraint** [kənstréint]	*n.* something that limits one's freedom of action or choice **restraint, limitation, curb**	억제, 압박
20	**budget** [bʌ́dʒit]	*n.* an estimate of expected income and expenses for a given period **fund, pool**	예산
21	**particulars** [pərtíkjulərz]	*n.* the facts and details about a job, property, or legal case **details, specifics, minutiae**	상세, 명세
22	**step in**	*ph.* to become involved in an activity, discussion, or disagreement **intervene, intercede**	개입하다
23	**plead** [pli:d]	*v.* to ask someone for something in a very strong and serious way; to state in a court of law that one is guilty or not guilty **petition, argue, assert**	탄원하다, 변론하다
24	**attune** [ətʃúːn]	*v.* to adjust or to prepare for a situation or something **adjust, accord, harmonize**	조율하다, 맞추다

Quiz

17. In the context of extreme _____ and dizzying social change, the household lost many of its earlier functions.

18. Their disputes with Hamilton over his pro-business economic program and _____ for the common man contributed to the formation of the first U.S. party system.

19. The time _____ prevented the subjects from finishing the test on time.

20. The military was restricted by its minuscule _____.

21. The study revealed _____ that seem to hold true for the general population.

22. The town board was forced to _____ and put a stop to the development in the area.

23. In 1977, Richard Helms _____ guilty to charges of inaccurately testifying about CIA activities in Chile.

24. A new type of newspaper, one that was more _____ to the spirit and needs of the new America, appeared around this time.

25	**disgust** [disgʌ́st]	*n.* a strong feeling of dislike, annoyance, or disapproval **loathing, hatred, nausea**	혐오, 구역질

26	**assessment** [əsésmənt]	*n.* the act of calculating or deciding the value or amount of something **estimation, evaluation, judgment**	평가, 판단

27	**chance** [tʃæns]	① *n.* likelihood that something will happen, especially something desirable ② *adj.* not planned or expected ① **probability, prospect** ② **accidental, causal**	① 기회, 가능성 ② 우연한

28	**integral** [íntigrəl]	*adj.* being a necessary part of a whole **essential, fundamental, elemental**	없어서는 안 될, 필수적인

29	**palatial** [pəléiʃəl] ＊ *palace* 궁전	*adj.* like a palace in magnificence or spaciousness **luxurious, grand, splendid**	궁전의, 호화로운

30	**adoption** [ədápʃən]	*n.* the act of taking and using as one's own **acceptance**	채택

UNIT 14

 **Quiz**

25. *Eight pigeons were shown photographs of people displaying emotions of happiness, anger, surprise, and _____.*

26. *One is a conscious, rational _____ of the danger, and the other is an unconscious, innate reaction.*

27. *A _____ conversation with a stranger may lead a person to discover how little is known of other religions.*

28. *Education is a lifelong process that starts long before the start of school and is one that should be an _____ part of one's entire life.*

29. *Miami Beach is a popular year-round resort, famous for its gold coast hotel strip, _____ estates, and recreational facilities.*

30. *In 1923, he began a campaign to promote the _____ of an amendment to the United States Constitution mandating equal rights for women.*

Chapter • 04

Natural Sciences

1	**minute** [mainjúːt]	*adj.* very small **tiny, minuscule, little**	미세한, 작은
2	**cross-sectional** [krɔːssékʃənəl]	*adj.* made in horizontal sections **cross-sectioned**	(횡)단면의
3	**spike** [spaik]	① *n.* a large metal nail ② *v.* to rise dramatically ① **peg, pin** ② **skyrocket**	① 큰 못 ② 치솟다
4	**literally** [lítərəli]	*adv.* according to the words and not the intention **strictly, exactly, word for word**	문자 그대로
5	**merely** [míərli]	*adv.* only as specified and nothing more **only, simply, purely**	단지
6	**random** [rǽndəm]	*adj.* having no specific pattern **accidental, haphazard, unsystematic**	임의의, 무작위의
7	**rear** [riər]	*v.* to feed and educate children; to bring up **nurture, raise, care for**	기르다, 돌보다
8	**recruit** [rikrúːt]	*v.* to enroll or obtain new members **mobilize, draft, enlist**	(신병 등을) 모집하다, 고용하다

Quiz

1. Quarks are _____ particles that are believed to be the fundamental unit of matter.

2. The strength of a rope is directly proportional to its _____ area.

3. The result was the most catastrophic nuclear disaster ever as radioactive levels _____ in the surrounding areas.

4. These animals were the pterosaurs, _____, the "winged lizards."

5. The plovers' nests are _____ scrapes in the sand or earth.

6. Far from being _____, molting is controlled by strong evolutionary forces that have established an optimal time and duration.

7. Among the species of seabirds that use the cliffs on the Atlantic coast in Canada to mate, lay eggs, and _____ their young are common murres.

8. When they fight with insects from outside their colony, Argentine ants can quickly _____ a huge army from their network of nests.

9	**refuge** [réfju:dʒ] * *refugee* 피난민	*n.* a shelter or protection from danger or trouble haven, asylum, sanctuary	피난처, 은신처
10	**respiration** [rèspəréiʃən]	*n.* the act of respiring or breathing exhalation	호흡
11	**robust** [roubÁst]	*adj.* strong and healthy; with a strong constitution vigorous, hardy, sturdy	튼튼한, 강건한
12	**rotting** [rátiŋ] * *rotten* 썩은	*adj.* decaying or causing to decay by a gradual natural process decomposing, decaying, spoiling	썩고 있는, 부패하고 있는
13	**scramble** [skrǽmbəl]	*v.* to crawl or to climb, especially hurriedly or frantically clamber, scrabble, crawl	기어오르다, 기어가다
14	**conspicuous** [kənspíkjuəs]	*adj.* visibly noticeable or obvious prominent, outstanding, vivid	눈에 띄는, 현저한
15	**seep** [si:p]	*v.* to pass slowly through small openings or pores leak, drain, ooze	스며 나오다
16	**dubious** [djú:biəs]	*adj.* feeling doubt; unsure doubtful, suspicious, ambiguous	의심스럽게 생각하는, 모호한

UNIT 15

Quiz

9. Wetlands provide _____ for many species of birds, reptiles, mammals, and amphibians.

10. The process of _____ in plants involves a complex series of chemical reactions.

11. This bird has a large, _____ bill, yet it is not the most prominent feature on the animal.

12. Both animals lived and foraged primarily in the soil and in _____ vegetation on the ground.

13. The animal's small size makes it easy for it to _____ for insects, flowers, or fruit among the twigs and branches in the canopy.

14. Many mountaineers wear orange and other bright colors in order to be as _____ as possible.

15. Millions of years ago in the Oligocene Epoch of Earth's history, clear resin _____ from pine trees growing in the Baltic Sea basin.

16. They objected to the plan because the replenishment programs are costly and of _____ value.

17	**edge** [edʒ]	*n.* the part farthest from the middle of something border, boundary, rim	테두리, 날
18	**seismic** [sáizmik]	*adj.* relating to or characteristic of earthquakes	지진의
19	**sort out**	*ph.* to separate from a mass or group classify, group, divide	분류하다, 분리하다
20	**squeeze** [skwiːz]	*v.* to grasp or embrace tightly; to get or force out by squeezing compress, press, extract	죄다, 짜내다
21	**tangled** [tǽŋgəld]	*adj.* untidy, knotted, and confused; involved especially in conflict entangled, twisted, intertwined	엉킨, 뒤얽힌
22	**consistency** [kənsístənsi]	*n.* the state of always keeping to the same principles or course of action; the degree of firmness or thickness agreement, coherence, solidity	일관성, 단단함, 경도
23	**hazardous** [hǽzərdəs]	*adj.* very risky; dangerous perilous, unsafe, precarious	위험한
24	**major** [méidʒər]	*adj.* great or greater in number, size, extent, value, or importance primary, principal, critical	주요한

🛡 Quiz

17. Prehistoric people used flint to make tools and weapons because it could be chipped into shapes with sharp _____.

18. The way that _____ waves travel shows that the Earth's interior is far from uniform.

19. To measure soil texture, the sand, silt, and clay particles are _____ by size and weight.

20. The ability of oil companies to _____ out more production by using new technology has added to the surplus.

21. Since then, over 100 tons of fossils, including 1.5 million tons from vertebrates and 2.5 million tons from invertebrates, have been recovered, often in densely concentrated _____ masses.

22. The _____ of the ocean floor determines what type of blast the trencher uses.

23. Working with toxic materials is a _____ occupation.

24. Galaxies are the _____ building blocks of the universe.

25	**subtle**	*adj.* not straightforwardly or obviously stated or displayed	
	[sʌtl]	delicate, vague, abstruse	미묘한, 난해한

26	**primeval**	*adj.* of the earliest period in the existence of something	
	[praimíːvəl]	early, prehistoric, primitive	초기의, 원시의

27	**graphic**	*adj.* described or shown vividly and in detail	
	[grǽfik]	descriptive, explicit, lifelike	생생한, 사실적인

28	**solitary**	*adj.* habitually alone, especially by choice	
	[sálitèri]	sole, single, lone	고독한, 혼자의

29	**molecule**	*n.* the smallest particle of an element or compound that can exist independently	
	[máləkjùːl]		분자

30	**realm**	*n.* a domain, province, or region; a field of interest, study, or activity	
	[relm]	territory, area, sphere	영역

UNIT 15

Quiz

25. The available weather data are generally not detailed enough to allow computers to discern the _____ atmospheric changes that precede these storms.

26. For more than 15 years, astronomers have searched for such _____ galaxies, and many gave up the task after several surveys of the sky failed to find any.

27. Dr. Dennis McCarthy, the chief of the branch that measures the Earth's rotation, expressed the meaning of a second in another, perhaps more _____, way.

28. The _____ scientist making important discoveries by himself has been replaced by a cooperative scientific team.

29. The molecular theory of matter, which considered all matter to be composed of tiny, indivisible entities called _____, was developed.

30. The invention of the visible-light microscope late in the sixteenth century introduced a previously unknown _____ of single-celled plants and animals.

Applied Sciences

1 install
[instɔ́ːl]

v. to put equipment or machinery in place and to make it ready for use
position, place, settle

설치하다, 장치하다

2 spawn
[spɔːn]

① *v.* to lay eggs; to give rise to something
② *n.* an offspring of someone or something
① generate, create   ② progeny

① 알을 낳다, 생산하다   ② 알, 새끼

3 subsequent
[sʌ́bsikwənt]

adj. happening after or following
ensuing, following, succeeding

차후의, 다음의

4 stiffen
[stífən]

v. to make or become firm
harden, solidify, thicken

굳어지게 하다, 경직시키다

* *stiff* 뻣뻣한

5 borough
[bə́ːrou]

n. a division of a large town
town, city, municipality

구역, 도시

6 obligate
[ábləgèit]

v. to force or compel somebody to do something
oblige, bind, compel

의무를 부과하다, 의무를 지우다

7 extinction
[ikstíŋkʃən]

n. the dying out of many animal species at more or less the same time
death, loss, destruction

멸종, 소멸

8 menace
[ménəs]

v. to show an intention to damage or harm someone
threaten, intimidate, frighten

위협하다

Quiz

1. The Baltimore and Ohio Railroad _____ the first air conditioning system for trains in 1931.

2. One invention often _____ many others.

3. Modern architects have ignored the _____ impact of industrialization on modern life.

4. Until the George Washington Bridge was built, modern suspension bridges were _____ with steel trusses and beams to limit their motion in traffic and wind.

5. The commercial center of New York City, the island of Manhattan is joined to the other _____ by bridges and tunnels.

6. The Endangered Species Act of 1973 _____ the government to protect all animal and plant life threatened with extinction.

7. Perhaps the human species was driving others to _____ long before the dawn of history.

8. Bald eagles were hunted both for sport and because they were thought to _____ livestock.

9	**innate** [inéit]	*adj.* belonging to or existing from birth inborn, inherent, intrinsic	타고난, 고유한, 선천적인
10	**key** [ki:]	*adj.* centrally important essential, crucial, main	주요한
11	**preponderance** [pripándərəns]	*n.* the state of being greater in amount, number, or something else supremacy, superiority, predominance	우위, 우세
12	**profound** [prəfáund]	*adj.* far below the surface; very strongly felt deep, intense, great	깊은, 심대한
13	**reveal** [riví:l]	*v.* to make a secret known; to disclose something expose, display, let out	드러내다, 누설하다
14	**evade** [ivéid]	*v.* to escape or avoid something or someone by trickery or skill avoid, elude, escape	피하다
15	**bloodcurdling** [blʌ́dkə̀:rdliŋ]	*adj.* causing a strong chilling fear or horror horrible, scary, gory	등골이 오싹해지는
16	**puzzle over**	*ph.* to make a great effort of the mind in order to find the answer to a question ponder, contemplate, consider	머리를 짜내다, 이리저리 생각하다

UNIT 16

🔵 Quiz

9. *Scientists are exploring the _____ weed-killing powers of living organisms, primarily insects and microorganisms.*

10. *Sociality has several _____ advantages over solitary behavior.*

11. *New World butterflies make up the _____ of examples because they are the most familiar species.*

12. *The wrong policy has had a _____ impact on Haiti's development and has resulted in Haiti being the poorest nation in the Western Hemisphere.*

13. *The fossil record _____ that extinctions have occurred throughout the history of Earth.*

14. *Many types of fish are continually stalking and _____ one another.*

15. *A more _____ example, especially to human beings and most other species of fish, is the shark.*

16. *Doctors and psychologists in the past _____ the cause of the disease.*

17	**skyrocketing** [skáirakitiŋ]	*adj.* increasing rapidly **soaring, rising**	급상승하는, 폭등하는
18	**solely** [sóulli]	*adv.* only and not involving anyone or anything else **alone, solitarily, exclusively**	혼자서, 오로지
19	**nervous** [nə́:rvəs]	*adj.* relating to the nerves; easily agitated **agitated, anxious, on edge**	신경(성)의, 신경질적인
20	**onslaught** [ánslɔ̀:t]	*n.* a fierce attack; an onset **assault, attack, raid**	돌격, 습격
21	**ratio** [réiʃou]	*n.* the number or degree of one class of things in relation to another **proportion**	비율, 비
22	**cautious** [kɔ́:ʃəs]	*adj.* careful to avoid risks **wary, watchful, alert**	주의 깊은, 조심성 있는
23	**physiological** [fìziəládʒikəl]	*adj.* of or pertaining to physiology	생리적인, 생리학의
24	**aversion** [əvə́:rʒən]	*n.* a strong dislike **hatred, animosity, hostility**	혐오, 반감

🛡 Quiz

17. *It was just a decade before this that many drug companies found their vitamin sales _____.*

18. *Ear acupuncture is involved _____ with the ear and its numerous activation points.*

19. *The _____ system of vertebrates is characterized by a hollow, dorsal nerve cord that ends in the head region.*

20. *In the face of this _____, living things have evolved a variety of defense mechanisms to protect their bodies from invasion by other organisms.*

21. *In the experiment, the _____ of helium to hydrogen nuclei remained about the same.*

22. *Workers must be very _____ when dealing with toxic substances.*

23. *Alternative therapies can work wonders as preventative methods for _____ as well as psychological problems.*

24. *A person suffering from claustrophobia has an _____ to confined spaces.*

25	**outrage** [áutrèidʒ]	*v.* to insult, shock, or anger someone greatly **enrage, infuriate, offend**	난폭한 짓을 하다, 격분시키다
26	**overlap** [òuvərlǽp]	*v.* to partly cover another object **overlie, overlay**	겹치다, 중첩되다
27	**odor** [óudər]	*n.* a distinctive smell, especially an unpleasant one **smell, scent, stink**	냄새
28	**petroleum** [pətróuliəm]	*n.* a naturally occurring oil consisting of a dark and thick liquid mixture of hydrocarbons	석유
29	**wholesome** [hóulsəm]	*adj.* good for the body or likely to produce good health **healthy, nutritious, beneficial**	건강에 좋은, 위생적인
30	**murky** [mə́ːrki]	*adj.* dark and unpleasant **gloomy, dim, overcast**	어두운, 음산한

UNIT 16

 **Quiz**

25. *The patient survived, but the incident _____ the religious sensitivities of the times, and no further experiments were tried.*

26. *One reason that there is much less emphasis on whether a person is considered to be "right-" or "left-brained" is that there is such an _____ in these areas.*

27. *Each ant nest has its own _____ as a result of its location, history, and local food supply.*

28. *Pipelines transport huge quantities of natural gas and liquid _____ products.*

29. *Whole grains and fresh fruits and vegetables are _____ foods.*

30. *It's difficult for scuba divers to see when the water is _____.*

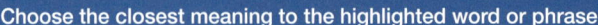

Choose the closest meaning to the highlighted word or phrase.

1   Many researchers have **conducted** studies to find out whether complex behavior must be learned during restricted time periods.

Ⓐ influenced
Ⓑ directed
Ⓒ subsidized
Ⓓ launched

2   These potters also discovered new forms of glazing as they attempted to **imitate** the Chinese white ceramics that were popular at that time.

Ⓐ remodel
Ⓑ expel
Ⓒ copy
Ⓓ promote

3   The cliff dwellings, prehistoric houses of the Pueblo Indians of the southwestern United States, are the **culmination** of this architectural development; the use of hand-hewn stone building blocks (the principal construction material) and adobe mortar was unexcelled even in later buildings.

Ⓐ accumulation
Ⓑ bottom
Ⓒ cultivation
Ⓓ summit

4   In the age of computers, it is difficult to imagine how **tedious** the work of accountants and clerks must have been in the past.

Ⓐ perplexing
Ⓑ intricate
Ⓒ boring
Ⓓ laborious

5   Tulips became an **integral** part of the gardens of the Ottoman Empire from the 16th century onward and, soon after, a part of European life as well.

Ⓐ interesting
Ⓑ fundamental
Ⓒ ornamental
Ⓓ overlooked

6   A snowfall consists of myriads of **minute** ice crystals that fall to the ground in the form of frozen precipitation.

Ⓐ tiny
Ⓑ elaborate
Ⓒ innumerable
Ⓓ ponderous

7   Some ecologists now believe that, although it was once possible to allow the development of a region to proceed more or less **at random**, such a process now holds too much risk for the well-being of society as a whole.

Ⓐ haphazardly
Ⓑ regularly
Ⓒ systematically
Ⓓ completely

8   The birds also take **refuge** in trees when they feel threatened by predators or violent storms and flooding.

Ⓐ lodge
Ⓑ nest
Ⓒ shelter
Ⓓ arena

9   Kittiwakes defecate over the edge of the nest, but this practice makes its location very **conspicuous**.

Ⓐ disordered

Ⓑ suspicious

Ⓒ noticeable

Ⓓ appealing

10   The motion of the moon around the Earth is from west to east relative to the sun so that, for an observer facing south, the shadowing of the moon begins at its left **edge**.

Ⓐ rim

Ⓑ core

Ⓒ nucleus

Ⓓ umbra

11   The most **graphic** proof that the grand spectacle of a comet develops from a relatively small and inconspicuous chunk of ice and dust was the close-up image obtained in 1986 by the European Giotto probe of the nucleus of Halley's Comet.

Ⓐ mathematical

Ⓑ popular

Ⓒ unusual

Ⓓ vivid

12   One major reason a lunar settlement is too **hazardous** is the contrast between the environments of the moon and the red planet.

Ⓐ complicated

Ⓑ plain

Ⓒ perilous

Ⓓ tangled

13   Language acquisition refers to the way in which people learn a language, whether it is their first language or a **subsequent** one.

Ⓐ previous

Ⓑ later

Ⓒ foreign

Ⓓ adjacent

14   The North American camelid, which became **extinct** in North America, evolved into the camel in Asia.

Ⓐ prosperous

Ⓑ rare

Ⓒ thrived

Ⓓ vanished

15   Linguists who support this theory argue that a child's **innate** ability to learn a language deeply and with a proficiency that is normally associated with first language acquisition will typically end at around the age of twelve.

Ⓐ inherent

Ⓑ essential

Ⓒ extraordinary

Ⓓ creative

16   The heavily populated states of Ohio, Pennsylvania, Illinois, and Michigan are **key** states for any candidate in a presidential election.

Ⓐ uncommon

Ⓑ important

Ⓒ incidental

Ⓓ temporary

Part 02
필수 VOCA

Humanities

1	**record** [rikɔ́:rd]	*v.* to set something down in some permanent form **write down, register, document**	기록하다
2	**seize** [si:z]	*v.* to take or grab suddenly, eagerly, or forcibly **grasp, grab, capture**	붙잡다
3	**concrete** [kánkri:t]	*adj.* definite or positive, as opposed to vague or general **actual, tangible, specific**	구체적인, 명확한
4	**provisional** [prəvíʒənəl]	*adj.* under terms not final or fully worked out or agreed upon **temporary, interim, conditional**	일시적인, 임시의
5	**traverse** [trǽvə:rs]	*v.* to go across or through something **cross, crisscross, intersect**	횡단하다
6	**boost** [bu:st]	*v.* to improve or encourage something or someone **lift, raise, encourage**	증대시키다, 격려하다
7	**employ** [implɔ́i]	① *v.* to use a particular object or method ② *v.* to give work, usually paid, to someone ① utilize, apply ② hire, recruit	① 사용하다 ② 고용하다
8	**expose** [ikspóuz]	*v.* to remove the cover from something or to allow this to be the case **uncover, reveal, unveil**	노출시키다, 드러내다

 Quiz

1. By 1820, it was a city of more than 10,000 people, and, by 1880, it had _____ a population of over one million.

2. Many West Africans were _____ and shipped unwillingly to the New World as slaves.

3. A good writer supports his or her generalizations with _____ examples.

4. On February 7, the seven states adopted a _____ constitution for the Confederate States of America.

5. The ships could _____ great distances and bring American and other Allied fighting forces to face the Axis powers.

6. Throughout the wilderness, bands provided entertainment and _____ morale.

7. The earliest way of keeping a count was by some simple tally method, _____ the principle of one-to-one correspondence.

8. The woolly mammoth and other mammals were periodically _____ in the tundra of Siberia.

9	**favored** [féivərd]	*adj.* enjoying favor or preferential treatment **preferred, selected, favorite**	호감을 사고 있는, 선호되는
	* *favor* 선호하다		
10	**glaze** [gleiz]	*v.* to make something shiny; to cover plates or cups with a thin liquid **polish, coat, enamel**	광택을 내다, 유약을 바르다
11	**indispensable** [ìndispénsəbəl]	*adj.* absolutely necessary; essential **requisite, vital, crucial**	없어서는 안 될, 필수 불가결한
12	**legacy** [légəsi]	*n.* an amount of property or money left in a will **heritage, bequest, inheritance**	유산
13	**inscribe** [inskráib]	*v.* to write or engrave words on something, often as a lasting record **engrave, etch**	(글을) 새기다
14	**majestic** [mədʒéstik]	*adj.* having or showing majesty; grand in manner **magnificent, imperial, grand**	위엄 있는, 장대한
15	**conjecture** [kəndʒéktʃər]	*v.* to form an opinion about something even without much information on it **guess, suppose, estimate**	추측하다, 짐작하다
16	**disguise** [disgáiz]	① *v.* to change appearance in order to escape recognition ② *n.* a disguised state ① **mask, deceive** ② **camouflage, coverup**	① 변장하다 ② 변장, 위장

UNIT 17

🔵 Quiz

9. *If such hunters first competed with the larger predators and then replaced them, they may have allowed more young to survive each year, gradually increasing the populations of _____ species.*

10. *Kilns were also used for _____ pottery when two firings were needed.*

11. *From the very beginning, music was regarded as an _____ accompaniment that people simply needed to listen to.*

12. *The empire did not last long, but its _____ was far reaching.*

13. *Many other tablets were _____ in another language that was not previously unknown and thus could not be translated.*

14. *This high land ground is _____ but not forbidding.*

15. *It is _____ that the Anasazi abandoned their settlements because of drought.*

16. *Contrary to folk songs, popular songs' origins cannot be _____, and therefore they belong primarily to the composer and not to a community.*

17	**excursion** [ikskə́:rʒən]	*n.* a short trip, usually one made for pleasure **journey, expedition, jaunt**	짧은 여행, 소풍
18	**outstanding** [àutstǽndiŋ]	*adj.* very great or clear; extremely good **distinguished, remarkable, excellent**	눈에 띄는, 뛰어난
19	**epoch** [épək]	*n.* a major division or period of history, or of a person's life **era, age, period**	시대, 시기
20	**status** [stéitəs]	*n.* a rank or position in relation to others within society or an organization **standing, position, level**	지위, 신분
21	**execute** [éksikjùːt]	*v.* to perform or carry out something **perform, fulfill, accomplish**	실행하다, 실시하다
22	**flatter** [flǽtər]	*v.* to praise someone excessively or insincerely **compliment, butter up, fawn**	아첨하다, 비위를 맞추다
23	**forefront** [fɔ́ːrfrʌ̀nt]	*n.* the very front; the most prominent or active position **vanguard, head**	최전선, 가장 중요한 위치
24	**dub** [dʌb]	*v.* to give a name, especially a nickname, to someone **call, name, entitle**	~라고 부르다, 이름을 부여하다

Quiz

17. The art society's activities also included organized sketching _____ along the Hudson River, where artists painted landscapes of the breathtaking scenery there.

18. Mark Twain became the country's most _____ realist author.

19. The year 1850 may be considered the beginning of a new _____ in American art.

20. By the outbreak of the revolution in 1778, the _____ of the artists had already undergone changes.

21. Once again, an original portrait became a luxury that was commissioned by the wealthy and _____ by the professional.

22. While the nickname was not intended to be _____, it was hardly inappropriate in his case, so he was not offended by it.

23. The Enlightenment was a period of time in Europe in which people put human reason at the _____ of thought.

24. Over time, the style of the intermezzo caught on and was put on separately, eventually being _____ the opera buffa.

25	**exponent** [ikspóunənt]	*n.* a person who supports an idea, theory, or something else and persuades others that it is good **proponent, advocate, supporter**	옹호자, 주창자
26	**extol** [ikstóul]	*v.* to praise something very much **praise, celebrate, glorify**	칭찬하다, 찬양하다
27	**mimic** [mímik]	*v.* to imitate in a way that is meant to be amusing **copy, imitate, mirror**	흉내 내다
28	**intuitive** [intʃúːitiv]	*adj.* attained by using feelings rather than by considering facts **instinctive, insightful**	직관적인
29	**caustic** [kɔ́ːstik]	*adj.* critical in a bitter or sarcastic way **biting, harsh, scathing**	신랄한, 통렬한
30	**skeptical** [sképtikəl]	*adj.* having doubts that a claim or statement is true or that something will happen **doubtful, dubious, suspicious**	회의적인, 의심이 많은

UNIT 17

🎯 Quiz

25. France produced a number of outstanding _____ of the Art Nouveau style, so many artists moved there to attempt to learn from them.

26. In the United States as well as in Great Britain, reformers _____ the virtues of handcrafted objects, thereby driving up their prices.

27. The tree seemed to _____ the Old Testament prophet Joshua waving people, with upraised arms, on toward the Promised Land.

28. The converser's tone can reflect _____ sympathy or antipathy, lack of interest, fatigue, anxiety, or even excitement.

29. _____ remarks can offend people, which is why people need to be careful of what they say in the presence of others.

30. They were _____ about the plan; a railroad built through so challenging and thinly settled a stretch of desert, mountain, and semiarid plain could not make a profit.

Social Sciences

1	**stem from**	*ph.* to arise or originate from	
		derive from, come from	~에서 나오다, 유래하다

2	**commerce** [kámə:rs]	*n.* the buying and selling of commodities and services	
		trade, business, merchandising	상업, 상거래

3	**savage** [sǽvidʒ]	*adj.* untamed or undomesticated; cruel	
		wild, barbaric, brutal	야만의, 잔인한

4	**sleek** [sli:k]	*adj.* smooth, soft, and shiny	
		glossy, satiny, slick	매끄러운

5	**recession** [riséʃən]	*n.* a period of reduced trade and business activity	
		depression, downturn, slump	불경기, 경기 후퇴

6	**tranquil** [trǽŋkwil]	*adj.* serenely quiet or peaceful; undisturbed	
		serene, calm, placid	평온한, 차분한

7	**stock** [stɑk]	*n.* the total shares issued by a particular company	
		shares, funds, assets	주식, 증권

8	**verge** [vɜ:rdʒ]	*n.* a limit, boundary, or border	
		margin, edge, brim	가장자리, 끝

＊ *on the verge of* ~직전에

🔵 Quiz

1. The impressive gain in output _____ primarily _____ the way in which workers made the goods.

2. With the growth of international _____, the economies of the world have become more interdependent.

3. The petroleum industry suffered from _____ competition, and, in the 1870s, many oil industries failed.

4. Pan Am named the airplanes after the swift, _____ clipper ships that once sailed the world's oceans during the nineteenth century.

5. During a depression, economic conditions are far worse than they are during a _____, which also lasts for a shorter period of time than a depression.

6. Manufactured in the _____ New England town of Concord, the famous Concord Coach came to symbolize the Wild West.

7. Corporations often raise funds by the sale of _____.

8. Unfortunately, by the late 1930s, the whooping crane was on the _____ of extinction and required protection in order to survive.

9	**denounce** [dináuns]	v. to inform against or to accuse someone publicly **blame, condemn, criticize**	비난하다
10	**era** [íərə]	n. a distinct period in history marked by an important event **epoch, time, age**	시대
11	**exceed** [iksíːd]	v. to be more than a particular number or amount **excel, surpass, transcend**	능가하다, 초과하다
12	**forward-looking** [fɔ́ːrwərdlùkiŋ]	adj. planning for and thinking about the future in a positive way **going ahead, progressive**	선견지명이 있는, 진보적인
13	**functional** [fʌ́ŋkʃənəl]	adj. designed for efficiency rather than decorativeness **practical, useful, effective**	기능적인
14	**burdensome** [bə́ːrdnsəm]	adj. difficult to carry, support, or tolerate **cumbersome, troublesome, bothersome**	짐이 되는, 번거로운
15	**inadequate** [inǽdikwit]	adj. not sufficient or adequate **deficient, insufficient, incomplete**	부적절한, 불충분한
16	**intensive** [inténsiv]	adj. requiring considerable amounts of effort within a relatively short period **concentrated, focused**	집중적인

UNIT 18

Quiz

9. Knight and Viner _____ economic imperialism, which viewed all social forces as having an economic explanation.

10. In every _____, the lure of the city included a major psychological element for country people as it drew them to urban centers by the thousands.

11. In 1872, only two daily newspapers could claim a circulation of over 100,000, but, by 1892, seven more newspapers _____ that figure.

12. Ice was used in hotels, taverns, hospitals, and by some _____ city dealers in fresh meat, fresh fish, and butter.

13. Only New York possesses an easy-access _____ connection to the vast Midwestern hinterland.

14. At the same time, war taxes had to be reduced to less _____ levels.

15. In the 1950s and 1960s, the baby boom hit an antiquated and _____ school system.

16. Even in this current era of large-scale, _____ research and development, the interrelationships between companies and universities are frequently misunderstood.

17	**tout** [taut]	*v.* to try to persuade people that something is important by praising it **push, promote, talk up** 권하다, 선전하다
18	**congestion** [kəndʒéstʃən]	*n.* an excessive or abnormal accumulation **overcrowding, jam** 혼잡, 밀집
19	**secession** [siséʃən] * *secede* 분리하다, 탈퇴하다	*n.* the act of an area or group becoming independent from the country or larger group that it belongs to **separation, breaking** 분리, 탈퇴
20	**position** [pəzíʃən]	*n.* a place where someone or something is **stance, posture, job** 위치, 직
21	**prevalent** [prévələnt]	*adj.* common at a particular time, in a particular place, or among a particular group **prevailing, common, widespread** 널리 퍼진
22	**supervision** [sùːpərvíʒən] * *supervise* 감독하다	*n.* the management by overseeing the performance or operation of a person or group **superintendence, oversight** 감독, 감시
23	**symbolize** [símbəlàiz]	*v.* to be a symbol of something; to stand for something **denote, exemplify, typify** 상징화하다, 상징적으로 나타내다
24	**revise** [rivàiz]	*v.* to change something because of new information or ideas **amend, modify, alter** 수정하다, 개정하다

Quiz

17. The Freudians _____ the impact of the personal subconsciousness on behavior, and the behaviorists emphasized external punishments and rewards.

18. The confusion and _____ of individual citizens looking for their letters was itself enough to discourage use of the mail.

19. The war led to the South's _____ from the Union.

20. Mary Goddard is considered to be the first woman to hold a federal _____.

21. The movie represents the idealism _____ in America in the early twentieth century.

22. The Human Genome Project, surprisingly, is under the _____ of the Department of Energy.

23. An image on a national flag can _____ political ideals that would otherwise take many words to explain.

24. Lawmakers simply _____ the vetoed bill and passed it again, daring the president to veto it despite its popular support.

25	**curb** [kə:rb]	*v.* to control or limit something in order to prevent it from having a harmful effect check, restrain, control	억제하다
26	**authorize** [ɔ́:θəràiz]	*v.* to give someone the power or right to do something empower, entitle, license	권한을 주다, 수권하다
27	**essential** [isénʃəl]	*adj.* extremely important and necessary; relating to the basic indispensable, necessary, fundamental	필수적인, 본질적인
28	**encounter** [enkáuntər]	*v.* to meet someone or something, especially unexpectedly come upon, run into	우연히 만나다
29	**illegible** [ilédʒəbəl]	*adj.* difficult or impossible to read unreadable, indecipherable	읽기 어려운
30	**expertise** [èkspərtíːz]	*n.* special skill or knowledge in a particular subject know-how, knowledge	전문 지식

UNIT 18

Quiz

25. The government hopes to _____ tax fraud, so it is simplifying the process of filing taxes to make it less confusing.

26. The National Labor Relations Board is _____ to investigate allegations of unfair labor practices on the part of either employers or employees.

27. Although there are several variations on the exact format that worksheets can take, they are all similar in their _____ aspects.

28. The memory of a past _____ with a snake would make the impression of the snake much stronger.

29. _____ handwriting does not indicate a weakness of character as even a quick glance at the penmanship of George Washington reveals.

30. A new energy policy should be developed and guided by people with apolitical science and technology _____.

Natural Sciences

1 **optical**
[áptikəl]
adj. relating to sight or to what one sees; connected with the relationship between light and sight
ocular, visual, optic
눈의, 광학의

2 **panel**
[pǽnl]
n. a rectangular board forming a section
board, pane
네모꼴의 물체, 패널판

3 **perseverance**
[pə̀:rsivíːrəns]
n. a continued effort to achieve something despite setbacks
persistence, patience, endurance
인내(력), 참을성

4 **self-consistent**
[sélfkənsístənt]
adj. not self-contradictory
self-evident, self-explaining
이치에 맞는, 자기모순이 없는

5 **scarce**
[skɛərs]
adj. less plentiful than what is normal, necessary, or desirable
scant, rare, lacking
드문, 부족한

6 **assure**
[əʃúər]
v. to state positively and confidently; to guarantee
ensure, assert
확실하게 말하다, 보증하다

7 **concede**
[kənsíːd]
v. to acknowledge as true, just, or proper
admit, accept, acknowledge
인정하다, 시인하다

8 **principal**
[prínsəpəl]
adj. first in rank or importance
chief, primary, important
주요한, 중요한

Quiz

1. The new X-ray microscopes considerably improve on the resolution provided by _____ microscopes.

2. The instrument _____ of a light airplane has at least a dozen instruments the pilot must watch.

3. The researcher's discovery was based on over thirty years of _____ and sweat.

4. Although the phlogiston theory was _____, it was awkward because it required that imaginative, even mysterious, properties be ascribed to phlogiston.

5. The _____ fossils of the Proterozoic, mostly single-celled bacteria, provide little evidence for glaciation.

6. Nesting material should be added in sufficient amounts to avoid both extreme temperature situations and to _____ that the eggs have a soft, secure place to rest.

7. Darwin himself _____ that the missing fossil record could be used as an argument against the validity of his theory.

8. Darwin was an amazing man and was the _____ founder of evolutionary biology.

9	**puncture** [pʌ́ŋktʃər]	*v.* to make a small hole in something perforate, pierce, stab	구멍을 뚫다
10	**reproductive** [rìːprədʌ́ktiv]	*adj.* producing new life or offspring generative, procreative	생식의, 번식의
11	**repertoire** [répərtwàːr]	*n.* the list of things that a performer is ready to perform repertory, stockpile, collection	연주 목록, 레퍼토리
12	**deft** [deft]	*adj.* skillful and quick dexterous, handy	능숙한, 솜씨가 좋은
13	**squirt** [skwəːrt]	*v.* to shoot a liquid or something else out in a narrow jet spout, gush, jet	분출하다, 뿜어 나오다
14	**gear** [giər]	*v.* to adjust to a particular situation in order to bring about satisfactory results adjust, fit, tailor	맞추다, 조정하다
15	**free** [friː]	*v.* to allow someone to move without restriction release, emancipate, liberate	자유롭게 하다, 해방시키다
16	**hazy** [héizi]	*adj.* not clear or exact foggy, faint, vague	흐릿한, 애매한

UNIT 19

Quiz

9. *The external surfaces of plants often carry spiky hairs known as trichomes, which either prevent feeling by insects or may even _____ and kill insect larvae.*

10. *These fish have not had a chance to mature long enough to become _____.*

11. *Plovers have an effective _____ of tricks for distracting potential nest predators from their exposed and defenseless eggs.*

12. *As a rule, large-billed crossbills are better at seeking seeds from large cones while small-billed crossbills are more _____ at removing the seeds from small, thin-scaled cones.*

13. *When the sea cucumber is attacked, it _____ all its internal organs into the water.*

14. *A consequence of right-hand dominance is that most common consumer products are _____ to right-handers only.*

15. *The increasing water pressure under the glacier might lift it off its bed, overcoming the friction between ice and rock, thus _____ the glacier.*

16. *When it comes to predicting an earthquake, it is a very _____ area.*

17	**nutrient** [njú:triənt]	*n.* a chemical or food that provides what is needed for life and growth nourishment	영양물, 영양소
18	**residue** [rézidʒù:]	*n.* what remains of something or is left over remainder, remains, rest	나머지, 찌꺼기
19	**sag** [sæg]	*v.* to bend, sink, or hang down, especially in the middle droop, dip, drop	휘다, 처지다, 떨어지다
20	**segment** [ségmənt]	*n.* a part of something that is different from the whole section, portion, fragment	부분
21	**segregate** [ségrigèit]	*v.* to set apart or to isolate divide, separate, discriminate	분리하다, 차별하다
22	**convoluted** [kánvəlù:tid]	*adj.* coiled and twisted curled, entwined, coiled	둘둘 말린, 감긴
23	**worth (of)** [wə:rθ]	*adj.* equal in value to something specified; deserving of valuable, qualified, meriting	~의 가치가 있는
24	**spot** [spɑt]	① *v.* to search for; to mark with spots ② *n.* a place; a small mark or stain ① detect, identify ② site, stain	① 위치를 찾다 ② 지점, 얼룩

Quiz

17. Since the dam was built, the sediments, rich with _____, are fewer, and the fish are also fewer.

18. The water can be drawn off and evaporated, leaving a _____ of clay, which can be weighed.

19. Each piece of clay can stand only a certain amount of heat without losing its shape through _____ or melting.

20. The cable ship will move on to repeat the process and lay another _____ of cable.

21. The one riddle was that in the Western United States, two kinds of ejecta – quartz and melted rock – are not intermingled but are _____; the quartz is layered just above the melted rock.

22. The _____ folds of the Earth's surface and its fractured geological structure tend to absorb the seismic energy of an earthquake.

23. Floods cause billions of dollars _____ of property damage annually.

24. The geographical center of the North American continent is a _____ near Balta, North Dakota.

25	**adjacent** [ədʒéisənt]	*adj.* lying beside or next to something **adjoining, bordering, touching**	인접한
26	**retain** [ritéin]	*v.* to keep or continue to have something **hold, preserve, save**	보유하다, 유지하다
27	**faint** [feint]	*adj.* difficult to see, hear, or smell **pale, dim, faded**	희미한, 어렴풋한
28	**glimpse** [ɡlimps]	*v.* to see something or someone momentarily **spot, glance, peek**	힐끗 보다, 잠깐보다
29	**mutate** [mjúːteit]	*v.* to change and develop a new form **modify, alter, transform**	변화하다, 돌연변이를 일으키다
30	**observation** [àbzərvéiʃən]	*n.* the act of noticing or watching **watching, viewing, notice**	관찰

UNIT 19

 **Quiz**

25. *Meteorology studies the currents of free air that are not _____ to the Earth's surface but which are higher up in the atmosphere.*

26. *On the moon, there is no air because the moon's gravitational field is too weak to _____ an atmosphere.*

27. *Astronomers use photography and sighting telescopes to study the motions of all of the bright stars and many of the _____ ones.*

28. *This cometary train, glistening like a string of pearls, had been first _____ only a few months before its fateful impact with Jupiter.*

29. *The radioactive rays are especially dangerous to humans because they increase the risk of cancer and can negatively alter and _____ DNA.*

30. *The scientist plans experiments, performs calculations, and makes _____ to test hypotheses.*

Applied Sciences

1	**folly** [fáli]	*n.* a foolish action, practice, or idea **idiocy, stupidity, absurdity**	어리석음, 어리석은 행동
2	**regardless of**	*ph.* in spite of; without regard for **despite, notwithstanding, heedless of**	~에 관계없이
3	**renovation** [rènəvéiʃən]	*n.* the act of improving by renewing and restoring **remodeling, reengineering, upgrade**	혁신, 개선
4	**spacious** [spéiʃəs]	*adj.* having ample room or space; extending over a large area **wide, capacious, extensive**	넓은
5	**centripetal** [sentrípətl]	*adj.* acting or moving toward the center of a circle; tending to unify **centralized, unifying**	구심력의, 중앙 집권적인
6	**compete** [kəmpíːt]	*v.* to strive to outdo another for acknowledgment, a prize, supremacy, or profit **contend, vie**	경쟁하다, 겨루다
7	**periodic** [pìəriádik]	*adj.* happening at intervals, especially regular ones **periodical, regular, cyclical**	주기적인, 정기의
8	**perch** [pəːrtʃ]	*v.* to sit or rest on an elevated place or position **roost, rest, sit**	앉다

Quiz

1. However, the artists' achievements were mocked by the artistic elite of Paris as expensive and ugly _____.

2. Potters found it convenient to locate their workshops near their source of clay, _____ their relation to the center of the settlements.

3. The _____ of the building will take longer than what had been previously estimated.

4. By the opening decades of the twentieth century, _____ buildings finally transcended the light confinement of row house building lots.

5. Social life is thus _____; that is, it is focused around the community center, the village.

6. As the populations expanded, they may have _____ with other game species for the same environmental niche.

7. This _____ extinction might be due to the intersection of the Earth's orbit with a cloud of comets.

8. In Alaska, where eagles _____ on fish traps and scared away the salmon, hunters killed more than 100,000 eagles between 1917 and 1952.

9	**conversion** [kənvə́:rʒən]	*n.* an act or process of changing something into a different state or form alteration, metamorphosis, transformation	전환, 변화
10	**jolting** [dʒóultiŋ]	*adj.* moving suddenly and roughly; giving someone a sudden shock jerking, shaking, shocking	덜컹거리는, 놀라운
11	**magnitude** [mǽgnətʃù:d]	*n.* the great size or importance of something size, enormousness, greatness	크기, 거대함
12	**perish** [périʃ]	*v.* to die; to be destroyed or ruined lose life, expire	죽다, 소멸하다
13	**poultry** [póultri]	*n.* birds such as chickens and ducks that are kept on farms in order to produce eggs and meat domestic fowl	가금(류), 가축용 날짐승
14	**choke** [tʃouk]	*v.* to prevent or be prevented from breathing by an obstruction in the throat suffocate, smother, stifle	질식시키다
15	**combustion** [kəmbʌ́stʃən]	*n.* the act or process of burning burning, flaming	연소
16	**tempting** [témptiŋ]	*adj.* attractive; inviting seductive, enticing, alluring	유혹하는, 부추기는

* *temptation* 유혹

Quiz

9. *At least 5,000 years ago, in Europe, deforestation and the _____ of wildlands to pasture began.*

10. *The high rate of species extinctions in these environments is _____.*

11. *However, nothing has ever equaled the _____ and speed with which the human species is altering the physical and chemical world and demolishing the environment.*

12. *When a species can no longer adapt to a changed environment, it may _____.*

13. *Ducks are less susceptible to infection than other types of _____.*

14. *Oil and the pollutants it causes are _____ the life from the planet.*

15. *Oil was in the depths of the planet for millions of years before man found a use for it in the Internal _____ engine.*

16. *Many people find chocolate _____, which accounts for the reason why the chocolate industry is so profitable.*

| 17 | **when it comes to** | *ph.* regarding; with regard to |
| | | **in relation to, as for, as to** ~에 대해 말하자면, ~에 관하여 |

| 18 | **impulse**
[ímpʌls] | *n.* a sudden push forward; a force producing sudden movement forward |
| | | **boots, urge, impetus, stimulus** 추진(력), 자극 |

| 19 | **in retrospect** | *ph.* in looking back on past events |
| | | **in hindsight** 되돌아보면, 회고하면 |

| 20 | **infection**
[infékʃən] | *n.* the act or process of causing or getting a disease |
| | | **contagion, communication** 감염, 전염 |

| 21 | **challenging**
[tʃǽlindʒiŋ] | *adj.* offering a challenge; testing one's ability, endurance, or something else |
| | | **defying, provoking, demanding** 도전적인, 흥미를 끄는 |

| 22 | **bolster**
[bóulstər] | *v.* to make something stronger or to hold something up |
| | | **support, reinforce, buttress** 보강하다 |

| 23 | **conjunction**
[kəndʒʌ́ŋkʃən] | *n.* a combination of different things that have come together |
| | | **combination, union** 결합, 연합 |

| 24 | **cerebral**
[séri:brəl] | *adj.* relating to or affecting the brain; involving complicated ideas |
| | | **intellectual** 뇌의, 지적인 |

Quiz

17. _____ our vision, all of the components of the eye are important.

18. The cardiac muscle will continue to pump blood without any _____ from the brain or ANS.

19. _____, vitamin and mineral therapies were much less effective when applied to health-crisis conditions.

20. His work was stimulated by the wartime need to find a cure for the fungus _____ that afflicted many military personnel.

21. Still, the brain is a great unknown in myriad ways and remains one of the most _____ and fascinating areas in the medical field.

22. Ki is fundamental in giving human strength and energy as well as _____ the immune system.

23. Sometimes, herbal medicines are used in _____ with acupuncture to magnify its effects.

24. In most cases of epilepsy, _____ electrical activity, also known as brain waves, demonstrates a characteristically abnormal rhythm.

25	**vessel** [vésəl]	*n.* a container, especially for liquids; a ship or large boat **container, holder, ship**	용기, 그릇, 선박
26	**neutralize** [njú:trəlàiz]	*v.* to cancel out the effect of something; to make a substance chemically neutral **negate, counteract, offset**	중립화하다, 중화하다
27	**nucleus** [njú:kliəs]	*n.* the positively charged tiny central part of an atom; the central part of something **heart, core**	핵, 중심
28	**alchemist** [ǽlkəmist]	*n.* a scientist who tried to discover how to change ordinary metal into gold, especially in the Middle Ages	연금술사

* *alchemy* 연금술

| 29 | **renowned**
[rináund] | *adj.* known and admired by a lot of people, especially for a special skill, achievement, or quality
famous, celebrated, noted | 유명한, 저명한 |
| 30 | **defective**
[diféktiv] | *adj.* having a defect or defects
imperfect, flawed, faulty | 결함이 있는 |

UNIT 20

 **Quiz**

25. *An Erlenmeyer flask is a glass _____ used in chemistry labs.*

26. *The insects can _____ or alter the poisonous substances that certain plants produce.*

27. *Most of the mass of an atom is made up of the _____, which contains the neutrons and protons.*

28. *Through the centuries, the dream of medieval _____ was to discover how to turn lead and other base metals into gold.*

29. *His discovery of the electric light is what he is most _____ for.*

30. *A _____ battery can cause an electrical device to malfunction.*

REVIEW TEST

Choose the closest meaning to the highlighted word or phrase.

1 30 meters deep in seawater, a diver is exposed to a pressure of about 4 atmospheres.

Ⓐ left behind
Ⓑ prepared for
Ⓒ propelled by
Ⓓ subjected to

2 The study of the embryological development of the nervous system is indispensable for an understanding of adult morphology.

Ⓐ requisite
Ⓑ usable
Ⓒ practical
Ⓓ injurious

3 The manner of the development of the counting process is largely conjectural.

Ⓐ complex
Ⓑ based on guessing
Ⓒ unbelievable
Ⓓ supported by careful research

4 Pulitzer Prizes are awarded to outstanding journalists, novelists, poets, and other writers.

Ⓐ expressive
Ⓑ serious
Ⓒ excellent
Ⓓ flashy

5 Many drug companies were quick to supply practicing physicians with generous samples of vitamins and literature extolling the virtue of supplementation for a variety of health-related conditions.

Ⓐ analyzing
Ⓑ questioning
Ⓒ praising
Ⓓ reproaching

6 A new era of aviation began in 1947 when Chuck Yaeger became the first pilot to fly faster than the speed of sound.

Ⓐ period of time
Ⓑ financial support
Ⓒ technological development
Ⓓ unique situation

7 The total number of the birds found on the British islands did not exceed 66, and the whole of Europe supported only 321.

Ⓐ exclaim
Ⓑ imprint
Ⓒ expose
Ⓓ outnumber

8 Lincoln's election made South Carolina's secession from the Union a foregone conclusion.

Ⓐ victory
Ⓑ separation
Ⓒ prosperity
Ⓓ defeat

9. Hats may symbolize social status or occupation as well as be fashion items.

Ⓐ represent

Ⓑ release

Ⓒ strengthen

Ⓓ drain

10. Mass transportation revised the social and economic fabric of the American city in three fundamental ways.

Ⓐ strengthened

Ⓑ hindered

Ⓒ changed

Ⓓ predicted

11. Industrialization and the bureaucratization of economic life combine with a new emphasis on credentials and expertise to make schooling increasingly important for economic and social mobility.

Ⓐ capacity

Ⓑ sociability

Ⓒ partition

Ⓓ know-how

12. The pale, smooth desert plain provides a perfect backdrop for spotting meteorites, which are usually dark brown or black.

Ⓐ removing

Ⓑ identifying

Ⓒ cooling

Ⓓ falling

13. For example, areas adjacent to the Great Lakes experience their own unique lake-effect storms, employing a variation of the process on a local scale.

Ⓐ isolated from

Ⓑ belonging to

Ⓒ separated from

Ⓓ adjoining to

14. If Earth had an orbit permanently outside the habitable zone, either too close or too far from the sun, most life would surely perish.

Ⓐ survive

Ⓑ die out

Ⓒ thrive

Ⓓ revitalize

15. That the ancestor of all modern domestic poultry is the red jungle fowl is widely believed.

Ⓐ cattle

Ⓑ crops

Ⓒ pets

Ⓓ fowls

16. As vitamins became recognized as essential food constituents necessary for health, it became tempting to suggest that every disease and condition for which there had been no previous effective treatment might be responsive to vitamin therapy.

Ⓐ necessary

Ⓑ attractive

Ⓒ realistic

Ⓓ additional

Humanities

1	**settle** [setl]	① *v.* to make or become quiet, calm, or still ② *v.* to come to an agreement about something ① **relax, tranquilize** ② **decide, fix**	① 안정시키다 ② 정하다
2	**oral** [ɔ́ːrəl]	*adj.* spoken; not written **verbal, vocal, voiced**	입의, 구전의
3	**peak** [piːk]	*n.* a sharply pointed mountain top; the highest point **summit, pinnacle, apex**	꼭대기, 정점
4	**initially** [iníʃəli]	*adv.* at the beginning **originally, incipiently**	초기에, 처음에는
5	**scope** [skoup]	*n.* the size or range of a subject or topic **extent, range, reach**	범위
6	**tenuous** [ténjuəs]	*adj.* slight; with little strength or substance **thin, vague, meager**	가느다란, 희박한
7	**staunch** [stɑːntʃ]	*adj.* dependably loyal **trusty, steadfast, reliable**	충실한
8	**oversee** [òuvərsíː]	*v.* to watch to see that work is being properly done **supervise, superintend, direct**	감독하다, 감시하다

🌀 Quiz

1. The place functioned as a sanctuary where the elders met to plan festivals, perform ritual dances, _____ pueblo affairs, and impart tribal lore to the younger generation.

2. Most African cultures were based on what is called an _____ tradition.

3. After the _____ year of 1957, the birth rate in Canada began to decline.

4. The characteristic of jazz is a rhythmic drive that was _____ called "hot" and later "swing."

5. How long the recession is expected to last will affect the _____ of measures the bank might adopt.

6. Oil prices were little changed last year although analysts said the stability was _____.

7. The _____ members of the ladies' group would not give up their fight for the right to vote.

8. Before the deceased _____ and conduct the lives of the people they have left behind, an elaborate funeral celebration must take place.

9	**mercy** [má:rsi]	*n.* a willingness to forgive, not to punish **pity, compassion, kindness**	자비
10	**mandate** [mǽndeit]	*v.* to give authority or power to someone or something; to command to act in a certain way **order, dictate, command**	위임하다, 명령하다
11	**marginal** [má:rdʒənəl]	*adj.* on or in the margin of a page; small in importance or amount **borderline, insignificant**	가장 자리의, 중요하지 않은
12	**meticulously** [mətíkjələsli]	*adv.* very carefully **painstakingly, particularly, scrupulously**	세심하게
13	**nomad** [nóumæd]	*n.* a member of a people without permanent homes and who travel from place to place **migrant, rover**	유목민
14	**ornament** [ɔ́:rnəmənt]	*n.* something that decorates or adds grace or beauty to a person or thing **accessory, adornment, decoration**	장식품, 장신구
15	**engulf** [engʌ́lf]	*v.* to swallow something completely **devour, swallow**	집어삼키다
16	**eternal** [itə́:rnəl]	*adj.* lasting forever and without a beginning or an end **timeless, everlasting, immortal**	영원의, 불멸의

 ## Quiz

9. *If the opponents killed their emissary or refused to surrender, the Mongols showed no _____ .*

10. *In 1938, the Fair Labor Standards Act _____ a weekly maximum of 40 hours to begin in 1940.*

11. *His tribe was one of the poorer ones, living north of the great Gobi Desert in areas with _____ resources.*

12. *In the past, things were not recorded as _____ as they are today.*

13. *The Aborigines are probably the descendants of these early _____, who made their way through southern Asia both by boats across narrow channels and across land bridges.*

14. *Articles for nearly every household activity and _____ could be bought in Rockingham ware.*

15. *Over the next ten years, a fierce civil war _____ the Mongol tribes until Genghis was master of them all.*

16. *The essence of the individual is _____ and will continue to exist in this world until a proper funeral ceremony has been performed to send the person off to the next stage of existence.*

17	**primary** [práiměri]	*adj.* first or most important **chief, fundamental, principal**	제 1의, 주요한

18	**prize** [praiz]	① *n.* something won in a competition or lottery ② *v.* to value or regard highly ① **award, reward** ② **treasure, cherish**	① 상, 상품 ② 존중하다, 소중히 여기다

19	**foremost** [fɔ́:rmòust]	*adj.* first in place, order, or rank; leading **primary, supreme, prominent**	최초의, 일류의

20	**stereotype** [stériǝtàip]	*n.* a fixed idea or image that many people have of a particular type of person or thing **type-cast**	고정 관념, 전형

21	**identical** [aidéntikǝl]	*adj.* exactly similar in every respect; exactly alike **same, twin, indistinguishable**	동일한, 일치하는

22	**representative** [rèprizéntǝtiv]	① *adj.* being an example of what other members of the same group are like ② *n.* a person or thing that represents another or others ① **typical, symbolic** ② **deputy, delegate**	① 대표하는 ② 대표자

23	**district** [dístrikt]	*n.* a division of territory, as of a country, state, or county **area, quarter, locality**	구역, 지역

24	**fabricate** [fǽbrikèit]	*v.* to invent or make up a story or evidence; to make something **imagine, fake, manufacture**	꾸며내다, 만들어내다

Quiz

17. In addition to revealing the _____ concerns of a society, the content of that society's art may also reflect the culture's social stratification.

18. The Art Nouveau style was widely copied in their time and is highly _____ today.

19. Theodore Dreiser, the _____ naturalist writer, grimly portrayed a dark world in which human beings were tossed about by forces beyond their understanding or control.

20. The minstrel show featured white actors dressed in blackface and playing up racial _____.

21. This type of writing describes an imaginary world that is _____ to ours up to a certain point in history.

22. Most of these leaders were involved in public life as reformers, activists working for women's right to vote, or authors, and were not _____ at all of the great mass of ordinary women.

23. The _____ in New York City known as Harlem was the capital of the Harlem Renaissance.

24. Dreiser thought that writers should tell the truth about human affairs, not _____ romance.

25	**fade** [feid]	*v.* to lose or cause to lose strength, freshness, or color; to become dim **wane, dull, cloud**	약해지다, 어렴풋해지다

26	**feuding** [fjuːdiŋ]	*adj.* quarreling between families, individuals, or clans; having persistent enmity **conflicting, quarreling, hostile**	불화의, 원한이 있는

27	**originate** [ərídʒənèit]	*v.* to bring or come into being **begin, derive, stem**	기원하다, 유래하다

28	**regarding** [rigáːrdiŋ]	*prep.* being talked or written about **with regard to, as to, as for**	~에 관하여

29	**distinct** [distíŋkt]	① *adj.* noticeably different or separate ② *adj.* easily seen, heard, or recognized ① **different, separate** ② **clear, explicit**	① 별개의, 다른 ② 명백한

30	**lament** [ləmént]	*v.* to feel or express regret or sadness **sorrow, grieve, mourn**	슬퍼하다, 한탄하다

UNIT 21

🔵 Quiz

25. These writers, who can genuinely be said to have created a genre, the "railroad novel," are now mostly forgotten, their names having _____ from memory.

26. West Side Story transformed the Montagues and Capulets of Shakespeare's play into _____ street gangs, the Jets and the Sharks.

27. The term etiquette _____ in France in the seventeenth century, but it is also a common term today in English.

28. The importance of punctuality can be seen through the myriad proverbs and expressions almost every culture has _____ time.

29. Every Pomo basket maker knew how to produce from fifteen to twenty _____ patterns that could be combined in a number of different ways.

30. Deeply philosophical historians _____ the role that the new frenzy for business was playing in eroding traditional values.

Social Sciences

1	**commodity** [kəmádəti]	*n.* something that is bought and sold, especially a manufactured product or raw material **product, merchandise**	상품, 제품
2	**convenient** [kənví:njənt]	*adj.* fitting in with one's plans; not causing trouble or difficulty **suitable, handy, nearby**	알맞은, 편리한
3	**monetary** [mánətəri]	*adj.* belonging or relating to, or consisting of, money **financial, fiscal, pecuniary**	통화의, 화폐의
4	**notion** [nóuʃən]	*n.* an impression, conception, or understanding **concept, idea, thought**	개념, 관념
5	**furnace** [fɔ́:rnis]	*n.* an enclosed chamber in which heat is produced for smelting metal	용광로
6	**prolific** [proulífik]	*adj.* producing plentiful fruit or offspring; producing many works **productive, fertile, fruitful**	다산의, 다작의
7	**routine** [ru:tí:n]	*n.* a regular or unvarying series of actions or a way of doing things **custom, habit, procedure**	판에 박힌 일, 일상의 과정
8	**monotonous** [mənátənəs]	*adj.* lacking in variety; tediously unchanging **repetitious, tedious**	단조로운, 지루한

Quiz

1. Corn, cotton, sugar, and many other goods are bought and sold in _____ markets.

2. Automatic teller machines provide a _____ means of banking 24 hours a day.

3. Canada adopted the dollar as its _____ unit in 1878.

4. The Depression years of the 1930s brought with them the _____ of job sharing to spread available work around.

5. The _____ in the factory was turned up as high as possible.

6. As early as 1782, the _____ Delaware inventor Oliver Evans had built a highly automated, labor-saving flour mill driven by water power.

7. The mass production of paper bags cost so little that a bag soon became a _____ part of almost every purchase.

8. While factory work was less creative and more _____, it was also more efficient and allowed mass production.

9	**posture** [pástʃər]	*n.* the general way of holding the body; a way of behaving on a particular occasion **position, pose, stance**	자세, 입장
10	**accommodating** [əkámədèitiŋ]	*adj.* helpful; willing to do what another person wants **cooperative, hospitable, kind**	도움이 되는, 친절한
11	**content** [kəntént]	*v.* to satisfy or to make oneself or another satisfied **please, gladden, gratify**	만족시키다
12	**distinguish** [distíŋgwiʃ]	*v.* to make out or identify something **discriminate, separate, differentiate**	구별하다, 분별하다
13	**justify** [dʒʌ́stəfài]	*v.* to prove or show something to be right, just, or reasonable **legitimate, vindicate, rationalize**	정당화하다
14	**oblige** [əbláidʒ]	*v.* to bind someone morally or legally; to compel **require, force, coerce**	의무를 지우다, 강요하다
15	**outbreak** [áutbrèik]	*n.* a sudden, usually violent, beginning or occurrence **outburst, rash**	발발, 발생
16	**overwhelming** [òuvərhwélmiŋ]	*adj.* physically or mentally crushing; intensely powerful **overpowering, formidable, uncontrollable**	압도적인, 막대한

UNIT 22

Quiz

9. The government established tariff barriers, provided loans and grants to build a transcontinental railroad, and assumed a studied _____ of nonintervention in private enterprise.

10. The government was nothing if not _____.

11. Most other cities _____ themselves with zoning plans for regulating future growth.

12. In 1870, the census officially _____ the nation's "urban" from its "rural" population for the first time.

13. The slave owners _____ slavery by saying it was the natural order of events and that the Africans' place in the world was as slaves.

14. Slave owners were _____ to care for the nonproductive Africans, which included the young, aged, and infirm.

15. In the fifteen years prior to the _____ of the War of Independence in 1775, more than 200,000 immigrants arrived on North American shores.

16. The new play was so successful that the demand for tickets was _____.

| 17 | **pack**
[pæk] | *v.* to stow goods compactly in cases; to put goods into a container
cram, fill, package | 꽉 채우다, 포장하다 |

| 18 | **sprawling**
[sprɔ́ːliŋ] | *adj.* spreading or extending in an irregular, straggling, or untidy way
spreading, extending, stretching | 뻗어 있는, 퍼지는 |

| 19 | **counter**
[káuntər] | *v.* to oppose, act against, or hit back
contradict, retaliate, frustrate | 반대하다, 반격하다, 상쇄하다 |

| 20 | **senator**
[sénətər] | *n.* a member of a senate
politician | (미) 상원 의원, 정치가 |

| 21 | **temporary**
[témpərèri] | *adj.* lasting, acting, or used for a limited period of time only
momentary, transient, provisional | 일시적인, 임시적인 |

| 22 | **property**
[prápərti] | ① *n.* something which is owned
② *n.* a quality, power, or effect that belongs naturally to something
① **possessions, belongings** ② **characteristic, trait** | ① 재산 ② 특성 |

| 23 | **campaign**
[kæmpéin] | ① *n.* an organized series of actions intended to gain support for or build up opposition to a particular practice or group
② *v.* to organize or take part in a campaign
① **operation, drive** ② **run, electioneer** | ① (정치적·사회적) 운동, 선거운동 ② 출마하다 |

| 24 | **urge**
[əːrdʒ] | *v.* to try very hard to persuade; to suggest strongly
press, push, request | 재촉하다, 촉구하다 |

🛡 Quiz

17. Major cities were _____ with people basically living on top of each other.

18. Los Angeles was a decentralized metropolis, _____ across the desert landscape over an area of 400 square miles.

19. One method to _____ desertification that is being used is the planting of leguminous plants.

20. A person must be at least thirty years old in order to serve as a U.S. _____.

21. The city of Memphis was an important Confederate military center during the Civil War and served as the _____ state capital in 1862.

22. Fewer than 25 percent of the 245,000 who took up land under the act obtained final title to the _____.

23. _____ on television means that, increasingly, our political world contains memorable pictures rather than memorable words.

24. The League of Women Voters _____ all citizens to vote.

25	**deploy** [diplɔ́i]	*v.* to spread out and position troops to get ready for battle <div align="right">(부대를) 전개하다, 배치하다</div>
26	**backlash** [bǽklæ̀ʃ]	*n.* a sudden violent reaction to an action or situation **backfire, counteraction, repercussion** <div align="right">격렬한 반발, 반동</div>
27	**evidence** [évidəns]	① *n.* information or something else that gives grounds for belief ② *v.* to be evidence of something; to prove ① **proof, ground** ② **demonstrate, reveal** <div align="right">① 증거 ② 입증하다</div>
28	**concentrate** [kánsəntrèit]	*v.* to give full attention and energy to something or someone **focus, center, intensify** <div align="right">집중하다</div>
29	**means** [miːnz]	*n.* the instrument or method used to achieve some object **process, manner, way** <div align="right">수단, 방법</div>
30	**compulsory** [kəmpʌ́lsəri]	*adj.* required by the rules or law **obligatory, mandatory** <div align="right">강제적인, 의무의</div>

UNIT 22

 **Quiz**

25. *The general was reluctant to _____ his troops into the enemy-controlled town.*

26. *Then came the _____ in the 1920s. America was tricked into the war by the British and French, said many.*

27. *Emotional health is _____ in the voice by free and melodic sounds of the happy, by the constricted and harsh sounds of the angry, and by the dull and lethargic qualities of the depressed.*

28. *Adults sometimes mistake children's curiosity about everything as a lack of ability to _____.*

29. *Increasingly, schools were viewed as the most important _____ of integrating immigrants into American society.*

30. *The use of seatbelts is _____ in many states; failure to wear them may result in fines.*

Natural Sciences

1	**outline** [áutlàin]	① *n.* a line that marks the outer edge of an object ② *v.* to give a brief description of something ① contour, silhouette ② delineate, draft　　① 윤곽, 외형　② 약술하다, 개설하다
2	**interchangeable** [ìntərtʃéindʒəbəl]	*adj.* capable of being put or used in place of something else equivalent, identical　　　　　　　　　　　서로 바꿀 수 있는, 교환할 수 있는
3	**mutual** [mjúːtʃuəl]	*adj.* having or based on the same relationship of one towards the other reciprocal, interactive　　　　　　　　　　　　　　　상호적인
4	**latent** [léitənt]	*adj.* present or existing in an undeveloped or hidden form dormant, potential, undeveloped　　　　　　　　　　숨은, 잠재된
5	**ooze** [uːz]	*v.* to flow or leak out gently or slowly leak, exude, secrete　　　　　　　　　　스며 나오다, 누출되다
6	**herbivore** [hə́ːrbəvɔ̀ər]	*n.* a plant-eating animal 　　　　　　　　　　　　　　　　　　　　　　초식동물
7	**hostile** [hástɪl]	*adj.* expressing enmity, aggression, or angry opposition antagonistic, inhospitable, unfriendly　　　　　　적대적인
8	**crawl** [krɔːl]	*v.* to move along the ground slowly; to move along on one's hands and knees creep, worm, squirm　　　　　　　　　　기어가다, 포복하다

Quiz

1. Charles Townes and Arthur Schawlow wrote a long paper _____ the conditions needed to amplify stimulated emission of visible light waves.

2. Potash and soda are not _____ for all purposes, but for glass- or soap-making, either will do.

3. It seems that all allosaurs worked together for _____ protection and nourishment.

4. The primary source of energy for tropical cyclones is the _____ heat released when water vapor condenses.

5. Precipitation such as rain and water can enter directly into the pool of nuclear waste, mix with it, and _____ out into the environment.

6. Any plant species often has many ways to defend itself from _____.

7. The deep-ocean bottom is a _____ environment to humans.

8. A three-foot-long octopus can _____ through a hole less than one inch in diameter.

9	**intervention** [ìntərvénʃən]	*n.* an act of intervening, especially in the affairs of other people or countries interference, interruption	간섭, 중재
10	**nocturnal** [nɑktə́:rnl]	*adj.* happening or active at night nightly	밤의, 야행성의
11	**abyss** [əbís]	*n.* a deep and bottomless hole abysm, bottomless gulf	심연, 심해
12	**palatable** [pǽlətəbəl]	*adj.* having a pleasant taste appetizing, tasty, savory	입에 맞는, 맛이 좋은
13	**fine-tuning** [faintjú:niŋ]	*n.* slight adjustments to something to obtain optimum performance	미세 조정
14	**grumble** [grʌ́mbəl]	*v.* to complain in a bad-tempered way complain, gripe, mutter	불평하다, 투덜거리다
15	**sole** [soul]	*adj.* being the only one singular, unique, lone	유일한, 오직 하나의
16	**span** [spæn]	*v.* to form an arch or bridge over; to go from one end to the other end of bridge, cross, stretch over	걸치다, 미치다

UNIT 23

🌀 Quiz

9. Ordinary light is emitted spontaneously when atoms or molecules get rid of excess energy by themselves without any outside _____.

10. Most mice are _____, but the African grass mouse is active during daylight hours.

11. In the dark _____ of the deep sea, the only light is produced by luminescent fish.

12. Menhaden are a small fish belonging to the haddock family, but they are not very _____ to humans.

13. In the world of birds, bill design is a prime example of evolutionary _____.

14. His letter the following year _____ that his livestock was all dead.

15. Pheromones are the predominant medium of communication among insects but are rarely the _____ method.

16. The plover's most famous stratagem is the broken-wing display, which is actually a continuum of injury-mimicking behavior _____ the range from slight disability to near-complete helplessness.

17 invade
[invéid]

v. to attack or overrun; to enter a country by force with an army

encroach, overrun, raid

침입하다, 침략하다

18 interval
[íntərvəl]

n. a period of time between two events

interim, intermission, pause

사이, 간격

19 intricate
[íntrəkit]

adj. full of complicated, interrelating, or tangled details or parts

complex, tangled, involved

복잡한

20 intrusion
[intrú:ʒən]

n. an act or process of intruding, especially on someone else's property

encroachment, interruption

침입, 방해

21 margin
[máːrdʒin]

n. the blank space around a page of writing or print

boundary, edge, rim

가장자리

22 modify
[mádəfài]

v. to change the form or quality of something, usually only slightly

revise, amend, adjust

수정하다, 변경하다

23 deduction
[didʌ́kʃən]

n. a process of reasoning using general rules or principles to form a judgment

conclusion, reasoning

추론, 연역

24 damp
[dæmp]

adj. slightly wet

moist, humid, dank

축축한, 습기가 있는

🛡 Quiz

17. Molten material wells out of the Earth's interior to _____ the surface layers or to flow onto the surface itself.

18. However, at _____ of 10 to 100 years, these glaciers move forward up to 100 times faster than usual.

19. The geyser is linked by an _____ plumbing network to some extremely hot rocks.

20. Man's _____ into the deltas sometimes upsets the balance of nature.

21. New oceanic crust is formed along one or more _____ of each plate by material issuing from deeper layers of the Earth's crust.

22. Rain dissolves, transports, and precipitates many chemical compounds and is constantly _____ the face of the Earth.

23. Strictly speaking, the "true" natural science is in the set of facts, not the _____.

24. Florida has a humid climate. Summers there are particularly hot and _____.

25	**recede**	*v.* to go or move back or backward	
	[ri:sí:d]	retreat, withdraw, go back	물러나다, 퇴각하다

26	**rudimentary**	*adj.* of or relating to basic facts or principles	
	[rù:dəméntəri]	basic, fundamental, elementary	기초의, 기본적인

27	**altitude**	*n.* the height, especially above sea level, of a mountain, aircraft, or something else	
	[ǽltətjù:d]	elevation, height, level	고도

28	**revolve**	*v.* to move or turn, or to make something move or turn, in a circle	
	[rivάlv]	turn, rotate, spin	돌다, 회전시키다

29	**devour**	*v.* to eat up something greedily	
	[diváuər]	gulp, swallow, gorge	집어삼키다

30	**dominate**	*v.* to have command or influence over someone or something	
	[dάmənèit]	control, govern, reign	지배하다

UNIT 23

Quiz

25. At the end of the Ice Age, the glaciers began to _____.

26. In the early nineteenth century, the knowledge of the physics of heat, which was essential to the science of refrigeration, was _____.

27. At higher _____, the particle cools, and the moisture it carries is precipitated as rain or snow.

28. All the planets in the solar system except Mercury and Venus have natural satellites, which are objects that _____ around planets.

29. Black holes are areas of massive gravitational energy that _____ all things they pass, including stars.

30. The light from the nearby Virgo Galaxy set out when reptiles still _____ the animal world.

Applied Sciences

1 presumably
[prizú:məbli]

adv. supposedly; probably
supposedly, likely, seemingly

추측상, 아마

2 picturesque
[pìktʃərésk]

adj. charming to look at, especially if it is rather quaint
scenic, pictorial, attractive

그림과 같은, 아름다운

3 predecessor
[prédisèsər]

n. the person who formerly held a job or position now held by someone else; something formerly used
forerunner, antecedent, forebear

전임자, 앞서 있었던 것

4 recommendation
[rèkəmendéiʃən]

n. an official suggestion about the best thing to do
advice, counsel, guidance

추천, 권고

5 convivial
[kənvíviəl]

adj. pleasantly merry and friendly
gala, jolly, sociable

연회의, 쾌활한

6 pursue
[pərsú:]

v. to follow someone or something in order to overtake
chase, follow, trace

추구하다, 쫓다

7 raid
[reid]

v. to attack on a person, place, or something else to do damage
attack, invade

급습하다

8 wary
[wέəri]

adj. looking out for danger; careful
circumspect, vigilant, cautious

경계하는, 주의 깊은

Quiz

1. The rural pottery establishment on the island of Thasos produced many types of pottery and roof tiles, too, _____ to meet local demand.

2. With its charming shops and restaurants, Old Town is the most _____ section of Albuquerque.

3. Eighteenth-century houses showed great interior improvements over their _____.

4. The plan impressed the university officials, and, in time, many of its _____ were implemented.

5. American hotels made other national conventions not only possible but also pleasant and _____.

6. Few predators fail to _____ such obviously vulnerable prey.

7. Even the few protected parts in Haiti are _____ for their prized trees.

8. You must be _____ when buying a used car; be sure the engine is in good condition.

9	**exposure** [ikspóuʒər]	*n.* the act of exposing or the state of being exposed disclosure, uncovering, baring	노출

* expose 노출시키다

10	**generate** [dʒénərèit]	*v.* to produce or create something create, manufacture, breed	발생시키다, 낳다
11	**pungent** [pʌ́ndʒənt]	*adj.* sharp and strong; cleverly caustic or biting bitter, biting, tart	(맛이) 얼얼한, 신랄한
12	**render** [réndər]	*v.* to cause to be or become make, become	~로 만들다, ~가 되다
13	**inhabit** [inhǽbit]	*v.* to live in or occupy a place dwell in, reside in, live in	거주하다, 서식하다
14	**genesis** [dʒénəsis]	*n.* an origin or generation origin, beginning, generation	기원, 발생
15	**crunch** [krʌntʃ]	*n.* the moment of decision or crisis crisis, critical point, decision time	위기
16	**impair** [impέər]	*v.* to damage or weaken something, especially in terms of its quality or strength damage, injure, harm	손상시키다, 저하시키다

UNIT 24

🔵 Quiz

9. *Human populations near the equator all have dark skin over many generations because of _____ to the fierce rays of the sun.*

10. *It is hoped that the errors _____ by imperfect and incomplete taxonomy will be minimized.*

11. *Certain spices give foods a _____ taste.*

12. *Rapid ecological change may _____ an environment hostile to a species.*

13. *The fact that half of the known species are thought to _____ the world's rainforests does not seem surprising.*

14. *Life's transition from the sea to the land was perhaps as much of an evolutionary challenge as was the _____ of life.*

15. *Hybrid cars have been around in one form or another since the early seventies during the oil _____ in the U.S.*

16. *Alcohol can _____ one's ability to drive.*

17	**potent**	*adj.* having a very powerful effect or influence	
	[póutənt]	**powerful, mighty, effective**	유력한, 힘센, 효능 있는

18	**curative**	*adj.* able to or tending to cure	
	[kjúərətiv]	**remedial, restorative, therapeutic**	치료용의, 치유력이 있는

19	**density**	*n.* the degree to which an area is filled with people or things	
	[dénsəti]	**solidness, thickness**	빽빽함, 밀도
	* *dense* 밀집한		

20	**elongate**	*v.* to lengthen or stretch something out	
	[ilɔ́:ŋgeit]	**extend, prolong, lengthen**	늘이다, 연장하다

21	**enthusiastic**	*adj.* showing lively interest; extremely keen	
	[enθú:ziǽstik]	**passionate, eager, fervent**	열광적인, 열성적인

22	**circulatory**	*adj.* relating to the circulation of the blood or something else	
	[sə́:rkjələtɔ̀:ri]		(혈액) 순환의, 순환성의
	* *circulate* 순환하다		

23	**concomitant (with)**	*adj.* accompanying because of or as a result of something else	
	[kɑnkɑ́mətənt]	**concurrent, coincidental, accompanying**	동시에 생기는, 동반하는

24	**crux**	*n.* the most important part of a problem, question, argument, or something else	
	[krʌks]	**core, gist, pivot**	가장 중요한 점, 핵심

Quiz

17. *Morphine, a form of synthetic heroin, is a _____ painkiller.*

18. *Some people believe that the crystals of certain minerals have _____ powers.*

19. *Our bone and muscle structures as well as their _____ are predetermined by our genes.*

20. *The actual eyeball is oblong and _____ length-wise from the front to the rear.*

21. *Some experts were _____ about the medicine while others said it was only effective for a few months.*

22. *Herbs have a more direct influence than acupuncture on the body's physical systems, such as the _____ system.*

23. *_____ with the increasing use of donor eggs, the proportion of women with multiple births over age 40 has increased as well.*

24. *The herbalists attempt to treat the source of the health problem rather than simply get rid of the symptoms, which is something that many argue is the flawed _____ of Western medicinal techniques.*

25	**resistant** [rizístənt]	*adj.* able to resist something; not affected by something defiant, unsubmissive, impervious	저항하는, 견디는
26	**impurity** [impjúərəti]	*n.* something that renders something else impure contaminant, pollutant	불순물
27	**modulate** [mádʒəlèit]	*v.* to vary the strength or nature of something; to change or alter tune, adjust, regulate	조정하다, 조절하다
28	**alloy** [ǽlɔi]	*n.* a material consisting of a mixture of two or more metals composite, compound, mixture	합금
29	**tolerate** [tálərèit]	*v.* to bear or endure someone or something bear, endure, stand	인내하다, 견디다, 참다
30	**expel** [ikspél]	*v.* to drive or force out or away eject, dislodge, remove	분출하다, 내쫓다

UNIT 24

🔵 Quiz

25. Ceramics can be harder, lighter, and more _____ to heat than metals.

26. Emeralds get their beautiful green color from titanium and chromium _____ in the stone.

27. The organism's ability to _____ a chemical signal is limited when compared with communication by visual or acoustic means.

28. Despite their light weight, aluminum _____ can be very strong.

29. Another strategy of large desert animals is to _____ the loss of body water to a point that would be fatal for non-adapted animals.

30. A sponge feeds itself by drawing water through tiny pores on its surface, filtering out food particles, and then _____ the water through larger vents.

REVIEW TEST

Choose the closest meaning to the highlighted word or phrase.

1   Since the 1790s, North American entrepreneurs had broadened the **scope** of the outwork system that made manufacturing more efficient by distributing materials to a succession of workers, who each performed a single step of the production process.

Ⓐ value
Ⓑ popularity
Ⓒ extent
Ⓓ diversity

2   The consistency of the clay was crucial; it was pounded **meticulously** and mixed with water to make it entirely even in texture.

Ⓐ heavily
Ⓑ eventually
Ⓒ carefully
Ⓓ completely

3   During the **initial** development of the human body, cholesterol guides proteins, which form bones, the spinal cord, large internal organs, and skin.

Ⓐ early
Ⓑ crucial
Ⓒ complex
Ⓓ tardy

4   The United States and the Netherlands, both **staunch** supporters of Israel, were especially targeted by the embargo and experienced immediate economic effects.

Ⓐ solitary
Ⓑ new
Ⓒ committed
Ⓓ neglect

5   Today, most astronomers accept the **notion** that the groups of stars that make up the universe are all moving farther and farther away from each other.

Ⓐ stature
Ⓑ predicament
Ⓒ idea
Ⓓ situation

6   The country had been **overwhelmingly** rural at the beginning of the century, with less than 5 percent of Americans living in large towns or cities.

Ⓐ realistically
Ⓑ hardly
Ⓒ surprisingly
Ⓓ immediately

7   Before the 1960s, geologists could not explain why active volcanoes and strong earthquakes were **concentrated** in that region.

Ⓐ scattered
Ⓑ clustered
Ⓒ exploded
Ⓓ strengthened

8   By 1920, schooling to age fourteen or beyond was **compulsory** in most states.

Ⓐ selective
Ⓑ arbitrary
Ⓒ functional
Ⓓ obligatory

9   Aside from perpetuating itself, the sole purpose of the American Academy and Institute of Arts and Letters is to "foster, assist, and sustain an interest" in literature, music, and art.

Ⓐ only

Ⓑ honorable

Ⓒ common

Ⓓ official

10   Before the arrival of the Europeans in North America, Native American Indians spoke over a thousand languages. Most of them were mutually unintelligible.

Ⓐ frequently

Ⓑ practically

Ⓒ preferably

Ⓓ reciprocally

11   Notwithstanding preening and constant care, the marvelously intricate structure of a bird's feather inevitably wears out.

Ⓐ grandiose

Ⓑ complex

Ⓒ interesting

Ⓓ historical

12   Scientists had to modify Newton's law of gravity, so they theorized that for distances as large as those between stars, the gravitational force repels rather than attracts.

Ⓐ change

Ⓑ accept

Ⓒ promote

Ⓓ deny

13   During the dry season, the waters receded, and the allosaurs had to follow their food sources.

Ⓐ intruded

Ⓑ withdrew

Ⓒ dominated

Ⓓ revolved

14   They would devour all the food available in a short time and would probably starve themselves out of existence.

Ⓐ assimilate

Ⓑ reproduce

Ⓒ reserve

Ⓓ destroy

15   At about the same time, epidemiologists noted that people who had serious bacterial infections in early childhood were less likely to develop allergies and asthma. Moreover, children born into large families were also less impaired.

Ⓐ suffered

Ⓑ prejudiced

Ⓒ damaged

Ⓓ exposed

16   A modem attached to a computer converts the digital date to an analog signal that it uses to modulate a carrier frequency.

Ⓐ regulate

Ⓑ affect

Ⓒ graft

Ⓓ interrupt

Humanities

| 1 | **vanish**
[vǽniʃ] | *v.* to become invisible or unnoticeable
disappear, dissipate, evaporate | 사라지다 |

| 2 | **longing**
[lɔ́:ŋiŋ]
＊ *long for* ~을 갈망하다 | *n.* an intense desire or yearning
craving, desire, wish | 열망, 갈망 |

| 3 | **meteoric**
[mì:tiɔ́(:)rik]
＊ *meteor* 유성 | *adj.* belonging or relating to meteors; very rapid
fleeting, swift | 유성의, 빠른 |

| 4 | **novel**
[nάvəl] | *adj.* not like anything known before
new, unusual, creative | 새로운, 참신한 |

| 5 | **obsolete**
[ὰbsəlí:t] | *adj.* no longer in use or in practice
out of date, outmoded, old-fashioned | 쓸모없는, 폐기된 |

| 6 | **coerce**
[kouə́:rs] | *v.* to force or compel someone to do something by using threats
force, fore, oblige, make | 강요하다 |

| 7 | **conquer**
[kάŋkər] | *v.* to gain possession or dominion over a territory by force
defeat, subdue, vanquish | 정복하다 |

| 8 | **consume**
[kənsú:m] | *v.* to use up time, money, goods or something else
exhaust, deplete, expend | 소비하다, 소모하다 |

🔷 Quiz

1. As the frontier _____, great factories and vast agricultural holdings marked the land.

2. Tulip bulbs were sent from Europe to the United States to satisfy the nostalgic _____ of homesick English and Dutch settlers.

3. A number of circumstances contributed to the _____ rise of Los Angeles.

4. The engine that became standard on western steamboats was a different and _____ design.

5. Until refrigerators made it _____, the ice industry supplied city dwellers with blocks of ice.

6. As for Italians, the Russians only met the reluctant few whom Hitler managed to _____ for his Russian campaign.

7. With his horse-riding, arrow-shooting hordes, he _____ a territory greater than any other leader either before or after him.

8. It is clear that humans began to carry their food to central places, called home bases, where it was shared and _____.

9	**dispute** [dispjú:t]	*n.* an argument or a disagreement between two people or groups **debate, discussion, controversy**	토론, 논쟁
10	**plateau** [plætóu]	*n.* an extensive area of relatively flat high land that is usually bounded by steep sides **mesa, tableland, highland**	고원
11	**pore** [pɔːr]	*n.* one of the similar small holes in the surface of a plant or a rock **opening, orifice, hole**	구멍
12	**sacred** [séikrid]	*adj.* religious in nature or use **holy, divine, sainted**	신성한
13	**staple** [stéipəl]	① *n.* an economically important product ② *n.* a major constituent of a particular community's diet ① **merchandise, provision** ② **necessity, basic**	① 주요 산물 ② 주성분
14	**story** [stɔ́ːri]	*n.* any of the levels on which a building is built **floor, level, tier**	층
15	**exalted** [igzɔ́ːltid]	*adj.* raised or elevated, as in rank or character; noble or elevated **lofty, noble, honored**	고귀한, 고상한
16	**foe** [fou]	*n.* a person who feels enmity or hatred toward another **enemy, adversary, opponent**	적, 적군

UNIT 25

🏆 Quiz

9. *The village chief dealt with land _____ and religious affairs.*

10. *Mesa Verde is located in the high _____ lands near Four Corners, where Colorado, Utah, New Mexico, and Arizona come together.*

11. *Fossils are frequently very dense because the _____ and other spaces in the bones have become filed with minerals taken up from the surrounding sediments.*

12. *The _____ objects of the family were under the control of the oldest female.*

13. *Though others were sometimes used, these four materials were the _____ of their finest basketry.*

14. *The largest Pueblo buildings had five _____ and more than 800 rooms.*

15. *The artisans' products, primarily silver plates and bowls, reflected their _____ status and testified to their customers' prominence.*

16. *Humans organize their societies in such a way to obtain a measure of security from a harsh and hazardous environment made up of human _____, famine, and plagues.*

17 realization
[rìːələzéiʃən]

① *n.* an awareness of something
② *n.* making something real
① recognization, comprehension ② actualization   ① 깨달음, 실감 ② 현실화

18 secure
[sikjúər]

v. to make free from danger or risk
protect, guard, defend   안전하게 하다

19 ensconce
[inskáns]

v. to hide safely
hide, conceal, cache   숨기다

20 marked
[maːrkt]

adj. obvious or noticeable
conspicuous, pronounced, evident   명료한, 두드러진

21 medium
[míːdiəm]

* *pl. media*

n. something by or through which an effect is produced
means, method, mode   매개물, 수단, 방편

22 monopolize
[mənápəlàiz]

v. to have a monopoly or exclusive control of trade in a commodity
or service
control, dominate   독점하다, 전매하다

23 optimistic
[àptəmístik]

adj. disposed to take a favorable view of events or conditions
positive, hopeful, idealistic   낙관적인

24 tantrum
[tǽntrəm]

n. an outburst of childish or petulant bad temper
blowup, rage, fury   발끈 화내기, 울화

Quiz

17. *Satire jars us out of complacence into a pleasantly shocked _____ that many of the values we unquestioningly accept are false.*

18. *In addition to _____ an exhibition space in the Library Society Building in lower Manhattan, the society founded a small school for the instruction of watercolor painting.*

19. *The key was _____ under the welcome mat.*

20. *Citizens of prosperous, essentially middle-class, republics have always shown a _____ taste for portraiture.*

21. *Implicit in it is an aesthetic principle as well that the _____ has certain qualities of beauty and expressiveness.*

22. *The older painters practiced in a mode that was often self-taught and _____ by the subject matter of the landscape.*

23. *The ending of the poem is _____, making it very different from the dark, pessimistic outcome of Smith's.*

24. *Spoiled children are apt to have _____ when they do not get their way.*

| 25 | **flush**
[flʌʃ] | *v.* to blush or to make someone blush or go red; to animate
redden, excite, encourage | 붉어지다, 활기를 띄게 하다 |

| 26 | **improvisation**
[imprὰvəzéiʃən] | *n.* the creative activity of immediate musical composition
extemporization, ad-libbing | 즉흥 연주, 즉석에서 짓기 |

| 27 | **strict**
[strikt] | *adj.* demanding obedience or the close observance of rules
austere, rigid, rigorous | 엄격한 |

| 28 | **utterance**
[ʌ́tərəns] | *n.* the act of speaking
statement, expression | 언급 |

| 29 | **fidelity**
[fidéləti] | *n.* faithfulness; devotion
loyalty, dedication | 충실(도), 성실성 |

| 30 | **irrelevant**
[iréləvənt] | *adj.* not connected with the subject at hand; beside the point
unrelated, impertinent, inappropriate | 관련 없는, 부적절한 |

* *relevant* 관련있는

UNIT 25

 **Quiz**

25. The art movement known as Regionalism began in the United States when the Depression occurred, but it really _____ before the 1930s.

26. Opera seria eschewed imagination and _____ in favor of familiar storylines, most often Greek.

27. Many parents place _____ limits on the kinds of shows their children may see and the number of hours allowed for television viewing.

28. The sounds that an infant notices might be the words that often occur at the ends of _____.

29. Most important was that the artists had all maintained, with a certain _____, a manner of technique and composition consistent with those of America's first popular landscape artist.

30. Especially because of writers who place so much importance on sound itself, the meanings of the words become all but _____.

Social Sciences

1	**durable** [djúərəbəl]	*adj.* lasting a long time without breaking **lasting, persistent, enduring**	지속하는, 내구성이 있는

| 2 | **indifferent**
[indífərənt] | *adj.* a lack of interest, feeling, or reaction toward something or someone
unconcerned, detached, uncaring | 무관심한 |

| 3 | **expendable**
[ikspéndəbəl]

* *expend* 쓰다, 소비하다 | *adj.* not valuable enough to be worth preserving
dispensable, nonessential, unnecessary | 소모할 수 있는, 필요 없는 |

| 4 | **insurance**
[inʃúərəns] | *n.* an agreement in which one party promises to pay another money in the event of a loss
assurance | 보험 |

| 5 | **kinfolk**
[kínfòuk] | *n.* one's relations; the members of one's family
kin, kindred, family | 친척, 친족 |

| 6 | **lucrative**
[lú:krətiv] | *adj.* affording financial gain
gainful, profitable | 수지맞는 |

| 7 | **appraise**
[əpréiz] | *v.* to judge the worth, quality, or condition of someone or something; to find out the value
estimate, evaluate | 평가하다, 감정하다 |

| 8 | **out-of-date**
[àutəvdéit] | *adj.* out of style or fashion; outmoded
old-fashioned, outdated, obsolete | 유행에 뒤떨어진, 구식의 |

Quiz

1. Economists define _____ goods as ones intended to last more than four months.

2. Stockholders may be too _____ to vote in corporate elections, so they let management vote for them by proxy.

3. Some workers lost their jobs when new technologies made their labor cheap or _____.

4. A number of _____ companies have their headquarters in Hartford, Connecticut.

5. In towns and cities, the nuclear family was more dependent on its immediate neighbors than on _____.

6. Even today, North Atlantic commercial flights remain the most _____ market in the world.

7. Jewelers are sometimes asked to _____ jewelry for insurance purposes.

8. Subsequent reforms have made the prior notions seem quite _____.

| 9 | **barn** [ba:rn] | *n.* a building in which grain or hay is stored or a building for housing animals |
| | | **stall** 헛간, 외양간 |

| 10 | **collective** [kəléktiv] | *adj.* belonging to or involving all the members of a group |
| | | **combined, communal** 집단적인, 집합적인 |

11	**compact** [kəmpǽkt]	① *adj.* firm and dense in form or texture
		② *adj.* neatly concise
		① **dense, condensed** ② **succinct, brief** ① 밀집한 ② 간결한

| 12 | **affluent** [ǽflu(:)ənt] | *adj.* having more than enough money |
| | | **rich, wealthy, well-off** 유복한 |

| 13 | **ponderous** [pándərəs] | *adj.* slow and awkward because of great size and weight |
| | | **heavy, massive** 무거운, 육중한 |

| 14 | **proponent** [prəpóunənt] | *n.* a supporter or advocate of something; someone who argues in favor of a cause |
| | | **advocate, backer** 지지자, 옹호자 |

| 15 | **deformity** [difɔ́:rməti] | *n.* an imperfection of the body, especially one that can be seen |
| | | **abnormality** 기형 |

| 16 | **reap** [ri:p] | *v.* to cut and gather grain or something else |
| | | **harvest, acquire, gain** 수확하다, 얻다 |

UNIT 26

Quiz

9. Other artisans worked in their homes or _____, relying on the help of family members or apprentices.

10. Expressive leadership is that which emphasizes the _____ well-being of a social group's members.

11. City dwellers also developed other pleasures, which only _____ communities made possible.

12. Scholarships allow students from less _____ families to attend college.

13. These _____ machines reaped the grain, threshed it, and bagged it, all in one simultaneous operation.

14. _____ of these reforms argued that public ownership would ensure widespread access to these utilities.

15. The offspring of animals may sometimes be born with an injury or physical _____.

16. The urban poor _____ few benefits from household improvements.

17	**brunt** [brʌnt]	*n.* the main force or shock of a blow or attack onslaught, violence, impact, shock	날카로운 공격, 맹공
18	**censorship** [sénsərʃìp]	*n.* the practice of censoring something suppression	검열
19	**pledge** [pledʒ]	*v.* to promise money or something else to someone; to offer something as a guarantee promise, oath, vow	서약하다, 약속하다, 증표를 주다
20	**cozy** [kóuzi]	① *adj.* snugly warm and comfortable ② *adj.* marked by friendly intimacy ① snug, comfortable ② intimate	① 아늑한, 편안한 ② 친밀한
21	**outspoken** [àutspóukən]	*adj.* saying exactly what one thinks; frank candid, direct, forthright	거리낌 없이 말하는, 솔직한
22	**penalize** [píːnəlàiz] * *penalty* 처벌	*v.* to impose a penalty on someone for wrongdoing punish, handicap, sentence	벌하다, 형에 처하다
23	**poll** [poul]	① *n.* a political election; a survey of public opinion ② *v.* to conduct an opinion poll among people ① vote, survey ② sample, interview	① 선거, 여론 조사 ② 여론 조사를 하다
24	**promote** [prəmóut]	*v.* to help something to develop or increase advance, boost, advertise	증진시키다, 홍보하다

Quiz

17. *The Americans bore the _____ of the Pacific fighting during the war.*

18. *Rarely could they see such a movie in the country due to _____ by the government.*

19. *The Republican Party _____ the enactment of a law granting free homesteads to settlers who would help in the opening of the West.*

20. *Before 1754, Britain and the North American colonies had a _____ relationship, but, after that, their relationship became strained.*

21. *Roger Williams was the founder of the colony of Rhode Island and an _____ advocate of religious and political freedom.*

22. *Recycling is mandatory in most major cities today, and violators may be _____ up to five hundred dollars.*

23. *A 1990 survey found that over 80 percent of those _____ claimed to believe in God.*

24. *There is an act that presidents have relied on in the past to _____ both the interests of the United States as well as their own.*

25	**prospect** [práspekt]	*n.* an expectation of something due or likely to happen **expectation, outlook, anticipation**	전망, 예상
26	**spatial** [spéiʃəl]	*adj.* belonging, referring to, or relating to space	공간의, 공간적인
27	**observe** [əbzə́:rv]	① *v.* to notice or become conscious of something ② *v.* to obey, follow, or keep a law, custom, or religious rite ① **examine, monitor** ② **obey, follow**	① 관찰하다 ② 준수하다, 지키다
28	**circumstantial** [sə̀:rkəmstǽnʃəl]	*adj.* based on something that appears to be true but is not proven **presumptive, deduced, inferred**	상황에 의한, 정황의
29	**backbone** [bǽkbòun]	*n.* the spinal column; a main support or major sustaining factor **spine, buttress, pillar**	등뼈, 중추
30	**plague** [pleig]	*n.* any of several epidemic diseases with a high mortality rate **scourge, epidemic, pestilence**	역병, 전염병

 **Quiz**

25. People in the United States in the nineteenth century were haunted by the _____ that unprecedented change in the nation's economy would bring social chaos.

26. Los Angeles was a product of the auto age; its distinctive _____ organization depended on widespread private ownership of automobiles.

27. For a long time, we've been able to _____ the effects of fear on the human body but not in the brain.

28. _____ evidence is that which is not drawn from the direct observation of a fact.

29. By 1771, when entrepreneur Mark Bird established the blast furnace in Pennsylvania, iron making had become the _____ of American industry.

30. The _____ then spread by sea trade on ships into the Mediterranean and to the island Sicily, where it got its first foothold on Europe.

Natural Sciences

1	**ample** [ǽmpl]	*adj.* more than enough **abundant, plentiful, sufficient**	풍부한
2	**penetrate** [pénətrèit]	*v.* to find a way into something; to enter something, especially with difficulty **pierce, puncture, go through**	꿰뚫다, 통과하다
3	**preliminary** [prilímənèri]	*adj.* occurring at the beginning; preparatory **prior, initial, introductory**	시초의, 예비의
4	**gravitation** [grævətéiʃən]	*n.* the force of attraction between any two masses **gravity, attraction**	중력, 인력
5	**horizontal** [hɔ̀:rəzántl]	*adj.* at right angles to vertical **level, flat, plane**	수평의, 가로의
6	**induce** [indjú:s]	*v.* to persuade, influence, or cause someone to do something; to cause **lead, urge, influence**	권유하다, 유발하다
7	**injection** [indʒékʃən]	*n.* an act of forcing liquid into something **instillation, inoculation, shot**	주입, 투입
8	**trait** [treit]	*n.* a particular quality in someone's character **characteristic, feature, property**	특성

🔷 Quiz

1. There is _____ evidence that water once existed on the surface of Mars and might return in the future if the planet warms.

2. Cleaner water allows sunlight to _____ to greater depths.

3. It takes about four years for a new aircraft model to move from the _____ design stage to the full-production stage.

4. _____ keeps the moon in orbit around Earth.

5. More air is involved in those _____ movements than in vertical movements.

6. Scientists hope to attach different chemicals to the tip of the scanning microscope to _____ chemical reactions at precise spots.

7. Fuel _____ engines employ injectors instead of a carburetor to spray fuel into the cylinders.

8. _____ such as hair color and eye color are inherited genetically from one's parents.

9	**courtship**	*n.* the courting or wooing of an intended spouse	
	[kɔ́:rtʃìp]	**courting, wooing**	구애, 구혼

10	**jeopardy**	*n.* the danger of harm, loss, or destruction	
	[dʒépərdi]	**hazard, peril, risk**	위험

11	**lair**	*n.* a wild animal's den	
	[lɛər]	**hole, burrow, cave**	굴

12	**from afar**	*ph.* far off; a long way off	
		from a distance	멀리서

13	**depart from**	*ph.* to start doing something different or not planned	
		diverge, deviate, differ from	빗나가다, 다르다

14	**mature**	*adj.* fully grown or developed	
	[mətʃúər]	**adult, ripened, aged**	성숙한

15	**heretofore**	*adv.* before or up to this time; formerly	
	[hìərtəfɔ́:r]	**hitherto, theretofore, thus far**	이제까지, 이전에는

16	**pounce**	*v.* to leap or swoop on a victim or prey, especially when trying to capture it	
	[pauns]	**jump, spring, leap**	(갑자기) 달려들다, 덤벼들다

Quiz

9. Bill clapping is a common part of _____ by storks, and bill snapping is a common threat by owls.

10. When groups of chimpanzees become fragmented and isolated from each other, their own genetic makeup is placed in _____.

11. Dinosaurs had nests or _____ where they laid the eggs.

12. To lure their pollinators _____, orchids use appropriately intriguing shapes, colors, and scents.

13. Desert mammals _____ the normal mammalian practice of maintaining a constant body temperature.

14. Its features are striking, as a _____ whooping crane is all white and stands five feet tall with a wingspan of about eight feet.

15. Researchers are confident that the discoveries will provide invaluable clues about this _____ mysterious process.

16. When a tiger spots its prey, it crouches and then _____.

17	**immunity** [imjú:nəti]	*n.* the state of being immune to a disease; the state of being protected from unpleasant things **exemption, invulnerability, nonliability**	면역, 면제
18	**rapidity** [rəpídəti]	*n.* a rapid state or quality; quickness **swiftness, speediness, promptness**	신속함, 민첩함
19	**rigid** [rídʒid]	*adj.* completely stiff and inflexible; unwilling to change **firm, hard, stubborn**	단단한, 완고한
20	**tap** [tæp]	*v.* to start using a source, supply, or something else **use, utilize**	개발하다, 이용하다
21	**grind** [graind]	*v.* to crush something into small particles or powder between two hard surfaces **pound, pulverize, mill**	갈다, 빻다, 연마하다
22	**groundwater** [gráundwɔ̀:tər]	*n.* water which occurs in the rocks beneath the surface of the Earth **underground water, subsurface water**	지하수
23	**inaccessible** [ìnəksésəbəl]	*adj.* difficult or impossible to approach, reach, or obtain **unapproachable, unobtainable, unreachable**	접근할 수 없는
24	**infringe (on)** [infríndʒ]	*v.* to break or to violate a law or oath **intrude, impinge, trespass**	침해하다

🌀 Quiz

17. The human immune system reacts defensively, and _____ is stimulated without illness.

18. The last figure shows the importance of the ocean as the principal reservoir of the hydrosphere and also the _____ of water transport on the continents.

19. The hard, _____ plates that form the outermost portion of the Earth are about 100 kilometers thick.

20. Geothermal energy is a potentially inexhaustible energy source that has been _____ by humans for centuries but, until recent years, only on a small scale.

21. Because of their hardness, industrial diamonds can be used for cutting, _____, and drilling.

22. Many communities are dependent on _____ obtained from wells for their water supply.

23. Until about a century ago, the deep-ocean floor was completely _____.

24. While many anxious parents may welcome this, others are already beginning to wonder if the GPS revolution is just another way for the government to _____ on its citizens' privacy.

| 25 | **delta** | *n.* a more-or-less triangular area of sediments deposited at the mouth of a river | |
| | [déltə] | | 삼각주 |

| 26 | **sturdy** | *adj.* thick and strong-looking | |
| | [stə́ːrdi] | **strong, solid, well-built** | 견고한, 튼튼한 |

| 27 | **instantaneously** | *adv.* in an instant; at a particular instant | |
| | [ìnstəntéiniəsli] | **immediately, directly, promptly** | 순간적으로, 즉각적으로 |

28	**phenomenon**	*n.* something that happens or exists in society, science, or nature	
	[finámənàn]	**event, happening, occurrence**	현상
	* *pl.* phenomena		

| 29 | **compile** | *v.* to collect and organize information | |
| | [kəmpáil] | **put together, collect, gather** | 자료를 모으다 |

| 30 | **vast** | *adj.* extremely great in size, extent, or amount | |
| | [væst] | **great, enormous, huge** | 거대한 |

UNIT 27

 **Quiz**

25. The Amazon River has the largest _____ in the world, and the Yellow River in China has the greatest sediment flow, which is very important in delta formation.

26. Because they must be able to break a path through icebound waters, icebreakers have to be very _____ boats.

27. Communications satellites can transmit data around the world cheaply and _____.

20. The spectacular aurora light displays that appear in Earth's atmosphere around the north and south magnetic poles were once mysterious _____.

29. Modern computers can quickly _____ and analyze a large volume of weather information.

30. It is now known that the _____ majority of the moon's craters were formed by the impact of solid bodies with the lunar surface.

Applied Sciences

1	**combine** [kəmbáin]	*v.* to join together connect, link, unite	결합하다
2	**projection** [prədʒékʃən]	① *n.* the process of being projected ② *n.* something that protrudes from a surface ① presentation ② bulge, protrusion	① 투사, 투영 ② 돌출(부)
3	**meager** [míːgər]	*adj.* lacking in quality or quantity scant, sparse, thin	빈약한
4	**mural** [mjúərəl]	*n.* a painting that is painted directly onto a wall wall painting, fresco	벽화
5	**deck** [dek]	*n.* a platform extending from one side of a ship to the other and forming a floor or covering floor	갑판, 바닥
6	**unique** [juːníːk]	*adj.* being the only one of its kind; unusually good and special single, only, unequaled	유일한, 독특한
7	**ultimately** [ʌ́ltəmitli]	*adv.* at last; in the end finally, eventually, in the long run	궁극적으로, 마침내
8	**rare** [rɛər]	*adj.* not done, found, or occurring very often scarce, unusual, uncommon	드문, 진기한

🎯 Quiz

1. Because of the urban heat island effect, several characteristics of urban areas _____ to elevate artificially the ambient temperature.

2. The hatch dome is a smooth design with no _____ to easily attach to.

3. Seattle's park development was very limited, and its funding was _____.

4. _____ tell narrative stories through visual images.

5. The observation _____ at the Empire State Building has been featured prominently in several movies.

6. What unusual or _____ biological trait led to the remarkable diversification and unchallenged success of ants for over 50 million years?

7. Other species may become better adapted to an environment, resulting in competition, and, _____, the death of a species.

8. On the _____ occasion when a fine piece of sculpture was desired, Americans turned to foreign sculptors.

9	**ecosystem**	*n.* a community of living things and their relationships to their surroundings
	[ékousìstəm]	생태계

10	**measure**	*n.* a system of measurement; the process of ascertaining the quantity of something
	[méʒər]	gauge, scale, estimation
		측량, 측정

11	**equivalent**	*adj.* equal in value, power, or meaning
	[ikwívələnt]	comparable, corresponding, equal
		동등한, 같은

12	**eschew**	*v.* to avoid, keep away from, or abstain from something
	[istʃú:]	evade, escape, avoid
		피하다, 삼가다

13	**eternity**	*n.* time regarded as having no end
	[itə́:rnəti]	perpetuity, infinity, timelessness
		영원

14	**custodian**	*n.* someone who cares for something, like a public building or ancient monument
	[kʌstóudiən]	caretaker, guardian, watchman
		관리인

15	**debilitate**	*v.* to make someone weak or weaker
	[dibílətèit]	weaken, enervate
		쇠약하게 하다

16	**flora**	*n.* the wild plants of a particular region, country, or time period
	[fló:rə]	vegetation, greenery, herbage
		시물군

Quiz

9. *Humans have become experts at destroying the world and the _____ in which they live.*

10. *Absent an objective _____, therefore, the range of estimates is wide.*

11. *Studies have shown that it costs the _____ of about a dollar a gallon to recharge a plug-in hybrid's energy tank.*

12. *We should accept the responsibility of saving the environment by _____ non-hybrid cars for more environmentally friendly plug-in hybrids.*

13. *The animal may soon be another one lost for _____ to human greed.*

14. *Therefore, both the ocean and the human body have a kind of _____ that maintains their bacteria levels.*

15. *If bacteria levels increase and get out of control, they can take hold of a system, overrun it, and become _____.*

16. *These plans have been designed to protect the endangered _____ and fauna as well.*

17	**aggravate** [ǽgrəvèit]	*v.* to make something worse; to exasperate or irritate **exacerbate, worsen, bother**	악화시키다, 괴롭히다
18	**circulate** [sə́:rkjəlèit]	*v.* to move or to cause to move around freely, especially in a fixed route **circle, flow, move around**	순환하다
19	**blockage** [blákidʒ]	*n.* the state of being blocked or prevented; something that is stopping movement in a narrow place **obstruction, impasse**	봉쇄, 방해(물)
20	**clot** [klɑt]	*n.* a thick, almost solid, mass formed when blood or milk dries **coagulation, lump**	(엉긴) 덩어리
21	**compatible** [kəmpǽtəbəl]	*adj.* able to associate or coexist agreeably **agreeable, consistent, harmonious**	양립하는, 모순되지 않는
22	**besiege** [bisí:dʒ]	*v.* to surround a town or stronghold with an army **lay siege to, blockade, surround**	포위하다, 공격하다
23	**intoxication** [intɑ̀ksikéiʃən]	*n.* a condition in which certain centers in the brain are affected by toxic substances **poisoning**	중독
24	**chronic** [kránik]	*adj.* long-lasting, usually of gradual onset, and often difficult to treat **long-lasting, lingering, continuing**	만성적인, 고질적인

Quiz

17. *The treatment only _____ the condition.*

18. *The heart must beat more forcefully if it is to _____ the same amount of blood.*

19. *These pathways might suffer _____ or be disrupted for various reasons.*

20. *This can cause serious problems. A _____, or a lump of blood, can form.*

21. *In a transfusion, a patient must receive a blood type that is _____ with his blood.*

22. *Almost daily, the public is _____ by claims for "no-aging" diets, new vitamins, and other wonder foods.*

23. *A sudden increase in caffeine consumption can easily produce caffeine _____.*

24. *More often than not, _____ pain is untreated or undertreated, but it does not have to be this way.*

25	**filter** [fíltər]	*v.* to pass something through a filter, often to remove impurities sieve, purify, refine	거르다, 여과하다

26	**detonate** [détənèit]	*v.* to explode or to make something explode explode, burst, blow up	폭파하다, 폭발시키다

27	**duplicate** [djú:pləkeit]	*v.* to make or be an exact copy or copies of something; to repeat something copy, reproduce, repeat	복사하다, 되풀이하다

28	**amenable** [əmí:nəbəl]	*adj.* ready to accept someone else's idea, proposal, advice, or guidance agreeable, receptive, obedient	(의견 등에) 따르는, 쾌히 받아들이는

29	**pupa** [pjú:pə]	*n.* the inactive stage during which a larva is transformed into a sexually mature adult while enclosed in a protective case chrysalis	번데기

30	**brilliant** [bríljənt]	*adj.* very bright and sparkling; showing outstanding intelligence or talent shining, radiant, intelligent	밝은, 찬란한, (두뇌가) 명석한

UNIT 28

 **Quiz**

25. Commercial honey is heated and _____ in order to stabilize and clarify it.

26. Dynamite is ordinarily _____ with a device called a blasting cap.

27. In science, the results of an experiment are not generally accepted until they have been _____ in other laboratories.

28. Glass is _____ to a greater number of heat-forming techniques than most other materials.

29. Eight to eleven days later, an adult moth emerges from the _____.

30. Robert Goddard was a _____ pioneer in the field of rocketry.

1. The very few who knew about it viewed it as a **novelty**, so there was no great rush to produce more hydrogen vehicles.

   Ⓐ usefulness

   Ⓑ commonness

   Ⓒ newness

   Ⓓ fearfulness

2. The Bessemer process was once the most common method of making steel, but today this process is considered **obsolete**.

   Ⓐ outmoded

   Ⓑ latest

   Ⓒ controversial

   Ⓓ methodical

3. This green corn was boiled, dried, and shelled, with some of the maize slated for immediate **consumption** and the rest stored in animal-skin bags.

   Ⓐ transporting

   Ⓑ planting

   Ⓒ eating

   Ⓓ distributing

4. The **dispute**, of course, has been that older fossils could be out there, somewhere, so the Africa source cannot be completely proven.

   Ⓐ discussion

   Ⓑ argument

   Ⓒ convention

   Ⓓ occurrence

5. The techniques of pottery manufacture had evolved well before the Greek period, but **marked** stylistic developments occurred in shape and in decoration.

   Ⓐ obvious

   Ⓑ obscure

   Ⓒ opponent

   Ⓓ oval

6. Like all artists, jazz musicians strive for an individual style, and **improvisation** or paraphrasing is a jazz musician's main opportunity to display his or her individuality.

   Ⓐ producing

   Ⓑ altering

   Ⓒ ad-libbing

   Ⓓ adorning

7. Glass is lightweight, impermeable to liquids, readily cleaned and reused, **durable** yet fragile, and often very beautiful.

   Ⓐ lasting

   Ⓑ delicate

   Ⓒ feeble

   Ⓓ flat

8. Secondary groups are large groups whose relationships are formal or based upon certain social **circumstances**, such as those between schoolmates or work colleagues.

   Ⓐ levels

   Ⓑ classes

   Ⓒ infrastructures

   Ⓓ surroundings

9 With no mass and no electric charge, neutrons can penetrate a solid object such as the Earth.

Ⓐ cut down

Ⓑ go through

Ⓒ fill up

Ⓓ take over

10 Such a dangerous event could happen if a passing massive gravitation field influenced Earth's orbit.

Ⓐ pressure

Ⓑ magnetism

Ⓒ tension

Ⓓ attraction

11 While a tendency towards anxiety and fear may well be an inherited trait, the specific form that fear takes has more to do with the individual's environment.

Ⓐ significance

Ⓑ method

Ⓒ characteristic

Ⓓ reliability

12 This immunity has been followed by a relaxation of the defenses, and kittiwakes do not react to predators nearly as fiercely as do ground-nesting gulls.

Ⓐ exposure

Ⓑ avoidance

Ⓒ approach

Ⓓ measure

13 Flight requires certain rigid aeronautical principles of design, yet birds, bats, and insects have all conquered the air.

Ⓐ inflexible

Ⓑ ideal

Ⓒ unnatural

Ⓓ steep

14 It was 1969, when Boeing came out with the 747, that the Clipper was ultimately eclipsed in size by a new design.

Ⓐ exceptionally

Ⓑ dramatically

Ⓒ eventually

Ⓓ unfortunately

15 Unlike Keynesianism, monetarism eschews direct government control by means of taxation and spending in favor of imposing limits on the nation's money supply.

Ⓐ avoids

Ⓑ favors

Ⓒ reinforces

Ⓓ involves

16 For decades, people suffering from chronic fatigue syndrome have struggled to convince doctors, employers, friends, and even family members that they were not imagining their debilitating symptoms.

Ⓐ painful

Ⓑ trifling

Ⓒ tolerable

Ⓓ lasting

Humanities

1 **fragile**
[frǽdʒəl]

adj. easily broken, shattered, or damaged
brittle, feeble, frail

깨지기 쉬운, 무른

2 **grueling**
[grúːəliŋ]

adj. very difficult and tiring
exhausting, laborious, arduous

기진맥진하게 만드는

3 **fixture**
[fíkstʃər]

n. a permanently fixed piece of furniture or equipment
appliance, fitting, equipment

고정물, 설비, 붙박이

* *fix* 고정시키다

4 **hollow**
[hálou]

adj. containing an empty space within or below; not solid
empty, vacant, void

속이 빈

5 **intent**
[intént]

n. something which is aimed at or intended; a purpose
intention, goal, object

의도, 목적

6 **subterranean**
[sʌ̀btəréiniən]

adj. beneath the surface of the Earth
underground

지하의

7 **be derived from**

ph. to have arisen from something; to be traced back to something
stem from, be originated from

~로부터 기원하다, 유래하다

8 **besides**
[bisáidz]

prep. in addition to; apart from something or someone
as well as, additionally, aside from

~ 이외에도, 그 밖에도

🔷 Quiz

1. The fibers were short and _____, but he predicted that spun glass fibers as thin as spider silk would be flexible and could be woven into fabric.

2. The 26-mile-long Boston Marathon is a _____ foot race.

3. The icebox became a _____ in most homes and remained so until the mechanized refrigerator replaced it in the 1920s and 1930s.

4. As they continued this oral tradition, they were able to fill up what was _____ and what was missing inside of them.

5. Despite the _____ of the law, speculators often managed to obtain large tracts of land.

6. Separate _____ rooms in three pueblos were set aside for religious ceremonies.

7. The name of the ware was probably _____ its resemblance to English earthenware made in South Yorkshire.

8. _____ overhunting, at least three other reasons for the extinction have been suggested.

9	**blend** [blend]	*v.* to mix different sorts or varieties into one **mix, mingle, combine**	섞다, 혼합하다

10	**casual** [kǽʒuəl]	① *adj.* intended for informal situations ② *adj.* happening by chance ① **informal** ② **accidental, fortuitous**	① 형식적이지 않은 ② 우연한

11	**butt** [bʌt]	*n.* a person who is often the target of jokes, ridicule, or criticism **object, target, victim**	(조소 등의) 대상, 표적

12	**supernatural** [sùːpərnǽtʃərəl]	*adj.* relating to phenomena that cannot be explained by the laws of nature **paranormal, unnatural, mysterious**	초자연적인

13	**supposedly** [səpóuzidli]	*adv.* seemingly; probably **presumably, allegedly, reputedly**	짐작컨데, 아마도

14	**supreme** [səpríːm]	*adj.* highest in rank, power, or importance; most outstanding **uppermost, prime, excellent**	최고의, 최상의

15	**forge** [fɔːrdʒ]	*v.* to shape metal by heating and hammering; to develop something new **mold, invent, form**	(쇠를) 벼리다, (노력하여) 만들어내다

16	**hearth** [hɑːrθ]	*n.* the floor of a fireplace or the area surrounding it **firoplace, fireside**	난로, 노변

UNIT 29

🔷 Quiz

9. *The funeral tradition of the Toraja people _____ ancient animist beliefs with the Western influences of Christianity.*

10. *Spoken language is generally more _____ than written language.*

11. *These so-called couch potatoes are often the _____ of jokes or regarded as being unintelligent.*

12. *The belief in the _____ powers of a stone or tree may cause a sculptor to be sensitive to that material.*

13. *English goods were _____ being smuggled into that city at a time when the Dutch controlled trading in the area.*

14. *The anthropologist suggested that all human belrigs have tho capacity to understand that there is a _____ god.*

15. *Genghis was able to _____ his people into the greatest class of warriors the world has ever known.*

16. *Most early pottery was fired over open _____.*

17	**shield** [ʃiːld]	① *n.* a piece of armor consisting of a broad plate ② *v.* to protect from danger or harm ① buckler ② guard, defend	① 방패 ② 가리다, 보호하다
18	**sketch** [sketʃ]	*v.* to do a rough drawing or drawings of something outline, delineate	사생하다, 스케치하다
19	**outnumber** [àutnʌ́mbər]	*v.* to exceed in number; to be more than	~보다 수가 많다
20	**overtake** [òuvərtéik]	*v.* to go past a moving vehicle or person in the same direction overhaul, catch, reach	추월하다, 따라잡다
21	**pessimistic** [pèsəmístik]	*adj.* emphasizing or expecting the worst negative, cynical, hopeless	염세적인, 비관적인
22	**prevail** [privéil]	*v.* to be victorious; to be the common, usual, or generally accepted thing predominate, preponderate, spread	우세하다, 널리 퍼지다
23	**prominent** [prámənənt]	*adj.* important or well-known; easily seen eminent, celebrated, conspicuous	저명한, 두드러진
24	**inception** [insépʃən]	*n.* the start of an organization, institution, or something else beginning, outset, dawn	시작, 개시

Quiz

17. *Locks and escutcheon plates - the latter to _____ the wood from the metal key - would often be imported.*

18. *Sometimes a talented man or woman who began by _____ family members gained a local reputation.*

19. *The greatest musical expansions and experimentations have involved percussion instruments, which _____ strings and winds.*

20. *Art Nouveau was eventually _____ by a new school of thought known as Functionalism, which had been practiced since the turn of the century.*

21. *Most people mix a _____ and an optimistic outlook to some degree.*

22. *After the 1870s, a number of important authors began to reject the romanticism that had _____ immediately following the Civil War.*

23. *Forty-two _____ artists living in New York City founded the American Society of Painters in Water Colors.*

24. *Since its _____ in Italy around the year 1600, opera has experienced a number of shifts and trends.*

| 25 | **insanity** | *n.* the state of being insane | |
| | [insǽnəti] | lunacy, madness | 광기, 발광 |

＊ insane 미친

| 26 | **acculturation** | *n.* the adoption of the behavior patterns of a surrounding culture | |
| | [əkʌltʃəréiʃən] | socialization | 문화 변용, 사회화 |

| 27 | **self-sacrificing** | *adj.* forgoing one's own needs or interests for the sake of others | |
| | [sélfsǽkrəfàisiŋ] | selfless, self-immolating | 자기 희생의, 헌신하는 |

| 28 | **snap** | *v.* to break suddenly and cleanly with a sharp cracking noise | |
| | [snæp] | crack, break, fracture | 부러지다, 꺾이다 |

| 29 | **feed** | *v.* to supply food to animals or something else; to supply a machine with fuel | |
| | [fiːd] | nurture, nourish, supply | 먹이다, (연료 따위를) 공급하다 |

| 30 | **hull** | *n.* the frame or body of a ship or airship | |
| | [hʌl] | framework, structure, body | 선체, 동체 |

UNIT 29

 **Quiz**

25. *Hers is a world of violence, _____, fractured love, and hopeless loneliness.*

26. *One crucial outcome of these musical _____ was the development by blacks of the so-called blues scale, with its "blue notes."*

27. *The Hopi people of Arizona stress the institutions of family and religion in a harmonious existence which makes the _____ individual the ideal.*

28. *Before barbed wire came into general use, fencing was often made from serrated wire, which could _____ in cold weather due to contractions.*

29. *The wire to make the barbs is _____ into the machine from the sides and cut to length by knives that cut diagonally through the wire to produce a sharp point.*

30. *The clipper has a knifelike bow to slice easily through the water and a narrow _____ so that the ship can move smoothly.*

Social Sciences

1 prudent
[prú:dənt]
adj. sensible and careful, especially by trying to avoid unnecessary risks
wary, cautious, discreet
신중한, 사려 깊은

2 raw
[rɔː]
adj. not cooked; not processed, purified, or refined
unprepared, untreated, crude
날 것의, 가공하지 않은

3 cling (to)
[kliŋ]
v. to hold firmly or tightly; to stick
adhere, attach, stick
고수하다, 달라붙다

4 domesticate
[douméstəkèit]
v. to train an animal for life in the company of people
tame
길들이다, 가축으로 기르다

5 eager
[íːgər]
adj. feeling great desire or enthusiasm; keen to do something
avid, enthusiastic, longing
열망하는, 간절히 바라는

6 reconstruction
[rìːkənstrʌ́kʃən]
n. constructing or forming again
restoration
재건

7 entrepreneur
[àːntrəprəná:r]
n. someone who engages in business enterprises
industrialist
기업가

8 bust
[bʌst]
n. a failure; a sudden decline in the economic conditions of a country
failure, recession
실패, 불황

Quiz

1. A _____ investor never takes unnecessary financial risks.

2. _____ materials have less economic value than processed ones.

3. In the nineteenth century, the former colonies lagged behind Britain in industrial development because their supply of wood led them to _____ to charcoal iron.

4. Huge numbers of people began to rely on the grain they grew and the animals they _____.

5. This new technology enabled them to build factories in the largest cities, taking advantage of urban concentrations of inexpensive labor and _____ customers.

6. The desperate plight of the South eclipsed the fact that _____ had to be undertaken in the North as well.

7. North American _____ increased productivity by reorganizing work and building factories.

8. The more-or-less rhythmic succession of economic booms and _____ is referred to as the business cycle.

9	**buttress** [bʌ́tris]	*v.* to support a system, idea, argument, or something else **brace, sustain, reinforce**	지지하다, 보강하다
10	**clamp** [klæmp]	*v.* to put or hold something in a position so that it cannot move **clasp, clip, fasten**	고정시키다, 죄다
11	**avail** [əvéil]	*v.* to provide with something useful or desirable **benefit, pay, profit**	쓸모가 있다, 이익이 되다
12	**rational** [rǽʃənl]	*adj.* related to or based on reason or logic **logical, reasonable, sensible**	이성적인, 합리적인
13	**resolve** [rizálv]	① *v.* to determine to do something ② *v.* to find a solution for something ① **decide, determine** ② **solve, answer**	① 결심하다 ② 해결하다
14	**afterthought** [ǽftərθɔ̀ːt]	① *n.* a thought after a main plan has been formed ② *n.* something added later ① **reconsideration** ② **addition**	① 고쳐 생각함, 재고 ② 추가 부분, 보충
15	**stimulate** [stímjəlèit]	*v.* to cause physical activity or increased activity; to initiate or to get going **rouse, spur, provoke**	자극하다
16	**superb** [supə́ːrb]	*adj.* extremely good **perfect, marvelous, exccllent**	최고의, 웅대한, 훌륭한

UNIT 30

Quiz

9. *The population flow from farms to cities increased, and the labor force it provided was _____ by millions of newly arrived immigrants.*

10. *In 1789, he invented a machine in which the cutter was _____ into a moveable slide that could be advanced precisely by a hand crank.*

11. *With much of the labor force inducted into the army and with grain prices on the rise, northern farmers rushed to _____ themselves of the new labor-saving equipment.*

12. *Your _____ mind tells you it's just a stick, but your innate mind tells you it could be a snake.*

13. *They were quick to lighten serious moments with humor and tried to _____ issues that threatened to divide the group.*

14. *In most of the earliest books for children, illustrations were an _____.*

15. *The agricultural revolution _____ many in the countryside to seek new lives in the cities.*

16. *The city had a _____ natural harbor as well as excellent rail connections.*

17	**tenement** [ténəmənt]	*n.* a large building divided into several self-contained flats or apartments **apartment, flat**	주택, 가옥
18	**determinant** [ditə́:rmənənt]	*n.* a thing that decides whether or how something happens	결정 요소
19	**dilute** [dailú:t]	*v.* to make a liquid weaker; to make a quality or belief weaker or less effective **water down, weaken, lessen**	묽게 하다, 희석하다
20	**uniformly** [jú:nəfɔ́:rmli]	*adv.* without variation or diversity **consistently, evenly, equally**	일률적으로, 균등하게
21	**inspection** [inspékʃən]	*n.* a close look at or over someone or something in order to judge its condition **scrutiny, examination, audit**	조사, 감시
22	**jury** [dʒúəri] ＊*juror* 배심원	*n.* a body of people sworn to give an honest verdict	배심(원단)
23	**legislative** [lédʒislèitiv]	*adj.* concerned with making laws **lawmaking**	입법의
24	**mock** [mɑk]	① *v.* to make someone or something the object of unkind laughter ② *adj.* not real, but intended to be similar to a real situation or substance ① **deride, ridicule** ② **fake, sham**	① 조롱하다, 비웃다 ② 가짜의, 거짓의

🔵 Quiz

17. *Urban slum wards often had no sewers, garbage collection, or gas or electric lines, and _____ lacked both running water and central heating.*

18. *Economics was probably the most important _____ for the baby boom.*

19. *As a result, it changes far more slowly than regular DNA, which is _____ by fifty percent each generation.*

20. *To be fair, laws must be _____ applied to all people.*

21. *The perishable commodities of trade generally came under state _____.*

22. *Many Americans still feel that the _____ system is at the core of their democracy.*

23. *Members of congress have to spend most of their time in Washington taking care of their _____ duties.*

24. *He was asked to be a juror in the _____ trial which will take place at the law school next week.*

25	**conspiracy** [kənspírəsi]	*n.* a secret plan made by two or more people to do something that is harmful or illegal collusion, plot, intrigue	음모, 공모
26	**demographic** [dì:məgrǽfik]	*adj.* pertaining to demography; relating to the dynamic balance of a population	인구(학)의, 인구 통계(학)의
27	**characteristic** [kæ̀riktərístik]	*n.* a quality or feature of something or someone that is typical of that thing or person and is easy to recognize mark, trait, property	특성, 특질
28	**assign** [əsáin]	*v.* to give a task or something else to someone allocate, allot, apportion	할당하다, 배정하다
29	**sponsor** [spánsər]	*v.* to act as a sponsor for someone or something patronize, support, back	후원하다, 지지하다
30	**dismay** [disméi]	*v.* to break down the courage of completely, as by sudden danger or trouble discourage, dishearten	낙담시키다

UNIT 30

 **Quiz**

25. *The details of John Kennedy's death continue to elude the most relentless of _____ theorists.*

26. *Today, the elderly comprise the fastest growing _____ group in many developed countries.*

27. *These factors ensured that Chicago would become a great city regardless of the disadvantageous _____ of the available site.*

28. *In the research, each consideration is _____ a numerical value to reflect its relative importance.*

29. *Classes for adult immigrants were _____ by public schools, corporations, unions, churches, settlement houses, and other agencies.*

30. *Some visitors were _____ by the endless urban sprawl and dismissed Los Angeles as a mere collection of suburbs in search of a city.*

Natural Sciences

1	**candidate** [kǽndədèit]	n. someone who is competing with others for a parliamentary seat or some other position **runner, nominee, applicant**	후보, 후보자
2	**cushion** [kúʃən]	v. to make the effect of a fall or hit less painful **soften, mitigate, absorb**	완화시키다, (충격 등을) 흡수하다
3	**bewildering** [biwíldəriŋ]	adj. thoroughly confusing, disorientating, or puzzling **baffling, perplexing, confusing**	당황스럽게 만드는, 당혹케 하는
4	**quantify** [kwántəfài]	v. to determine the quantity of something **measure**	양을 재다, 양을 표시하다
5	**refrigerate** [rifrídʒərèit]	v. to freeze something or to make it cold **chill, cool, ice**	냉장하다, 냉각하다
6	**condense** [kəndéns]	v. to decrease the volume, size, or density of a substance **compress, compact, concentrate**	압축하다, 농축하다
7	**constituent** [kənstítʃuənt]	n. a forming part of a whole **component, element, ingredient**	구성 요소, 성분
8	**diffuse** [difjúːz]	v. to spread or to send out in all directions **disperse, distribute, scatter**	발산하다, 방산하다

Quiz

1. Mars would be a more successful _____ for exploration and settlement.

2. The big surprise, though, is the role of air resistance in _____ the shock of collisions.

3. Telescopic images of the planet permitted the cataloging of a _____ array of land forms.

4. Scientists have tried to _____ the proportion of the sun's energy.

5. Florists often _____ cut flowers to protect their fresh appearance.

6. The water stored as vapor in the atmosphere will _____ to a liquid again, and the energy will be released to the atmosphere.

7. Helium nuclei have also been found to be _____ of cosmic rays that fall on the Earth.

8. The nitrogen _____ from the tissues into the blood and from the blood into the lungs.

| 9 | **friction**
[fríkʃən] | *n.* the rubbing of one thing against another; disagreement or unfriendliness between people
abrasion, scrape, conflict | 마찰 |

| 10 | **wander**
[wándər] | *v.* to walk, move, or travel about with no particular destination
ramble, roam, range | 방랑하다, 돌아다니다 |

| 11 | **ferocious**
[fəróuʃəs] | *adj.* violently unfriendly or aggressive
fierce, savage, cruel | 사나운, 잔인한 |

| 12 | **humidity**
[hjuːmídəti] | *n.* the amount of water vapor in the atmosphere
dampness, moisture | 습도, 습기 |

| 13 | **instill**
[instíl] | *v.* to impress ideas, feelings, or something else slowly or gradually
implant, imbue, infuse | (사상이나 감정 등을) 주입하다 |

| 14 | **intact**
[intǽkt] | *adj.* not broken or damaged; untouched
undamaged, unimpaired, unblemished | 손상되지 않은, 손대지 않은 |

| 15 | **intake**
[íntèik] | *n.* a thing or quantity taken in or accepted; the act of taking in
consumption, ingestion | 섭취량, 섭취 |

| 16 | **expenditure**
[ikspénditʃər] | *n.* a payment made in the course of achieving a result
outlay, expense, cost | 지출, 소비 |

UNIT 31

 ## Quiz

9. *The air of the upper atmosphere is dense enough to ignite meteors by _____.*

10. *Some of the mice _____ around the box and did not appear to be bothered by being so exposed.*

11. *Barracudas are _____ predators and are sometimes called the "tigers" of tropical waters.*

12. *When parrots incubate their eggs in the wild, the temperature and _____ of their nests are controlled naturally.*

13. *Through this process, the conservationists _____ in the whooping cranes a natural sense of migration.*

14. *The finding of a perfectly _____ massive dinosaur fossil may seem exciting, but to paleontologists, it is just evidence that one beast died for some reason.*

15. *An important consideration of fat _____ is the ratio of saturated fats to unsaturated fats.*

16. *Each of the functions of the body, even thinking, requires the _____ of energy.*

17	**incubator** [ínkjəbèitər]	*n.* a transparent container in which a prematurely born baby can be nurtured
		인공부화기, 인큐베이터

18	**ingest** [indʒést]	*v.* to take food or liquid into the body **consume, eat**
		섭취하다

19	**insulation** [ìnsəléiʃən]	*n.* the state of being alone or kept apart from others **isolation, secludedness, separateness**
		차단, 절연

20	**jostle** [dʒásl]	*v.* to push something in an annoying way **hustle, jolt, push**
		(난폭하게) 떠밀다, 밀치다

21	**submerge** [səbmə́:rdʒ]	*v.* to plunge, sink, or cause to plunge or sink under the surface of some liquid **immerse, drench, dive**
		물에 잠그다, 잠수하다

22	**decompose** [dì:kəmpóuz]	*v.* to rot, usually as a result of the activity of fungi and bacteria **decay, break down, disintegrate**
		부패시키다, 분해하다

23	**deposit** [dipázit]	*v.* to put something down; to leave a layer of a substance on the surface of something **place, store, bank**
		쌓이게 하다, 퇴적시키다

24	**fine** [fain]	*adj.* consisting of tiny particles **dusty, floury, powdery**
		미세한, 고운

🛡 Quiz

17. The eggs were placed in _____, hatched, and continually monitored and eventually raised by specialists.

18. The nectar of flowers is _____ by worker bees and converted to honey in a special sac in their digestive systems.

19. Fat acts as _____ against the cold and as cushioning for the internal organs.

20. Eventually, large rocks may be _____ around enough to be broken into sand-sized grains.

21. As the Bering land bridge had been _____ before the Eskimos came from Asia, they must have arrived by boat.

22. It is the rock that gradually _____ into clay.

23. When a river overflows, the coarser sand sediment is sometimes _____ on the river banks, which forms natural levees.

24. Table salt is _____ than rock salt.

25	**erode** [iróud]	*v.* to wear away, destroy, or be gradually destroyed **wear down, grind down, corrode**	침식하다, 부식시키다

26	**give way to**	*ph.* to give priority to; to collapse under pressure **concede, succumb, yield**	~에게 자리를 내어 주다, 굴복하다

27	**labyrinth** [lǽbərìnθ]	*n.* a highly complex network of interconnected passages **maze**	미궁, 미로

28	**glowing** [glóuiŋ]	*adj.* giving out a steady heat or light without flames **burning, luminous, incandescent**	빛나는, 작열하는

29	**inflow** [ínflòu]	*n.* a flowing or coming in **influx, inrush**	유입

30	**evaporate** [ivǽpərèit]	*v.* to change or cause something to change from a liquid into a vapor **vaporize, boil off, dehydrate**	증발하다

UNIT 31

 **Quiz**

25. *Rock is _____ by wind and water, and many of the eroded parts end up in the water system at some point and, eventually, in the great rivers of the world.*

26. *Beyond a depth of around 2,900 kilometers, a great change takes place, and the mantle _____ the core.*

27. *Located inside Rainer's two ice-filled summit craters, these caves form a _____ of tunnels and vaulted chambers about one and one-half miles in total length.*

28. *Viewed from outer space, auroras can be seen as dimly _____ belts wrapped around each of the Earth's magnetic poles.*

29. *For a snowfall to continue once it starts, there must be a constant _____ of moisture to supply the nuclei.*

30. *Rain and melting snow quickly _____ in the dry desert climate.*

Applied Sciences

1	**outlook** [áutlùk]	*n.* a view from a particular place **viewpoint, perspective, prospect**	견해, 전망
2	**inviting** [inváitiŋ]	*adj.* attractive or tempting **alluring, captivating, enticing**	유혹하는, 마음을 끄는
3	**loop** [luːp]	*n.* a rounded or oval-shaped single coil in a piece of thread, string, or rope **circle, hoop, ring**	고리
4	**magnificent** [mægnífəsənt]	*adj.* splendidly impressive in size, extent, or appearance **great, grand, impressive**	장엄한, 굉장한
5	**draw on**	*ph.* to utilize or make use of something as a source **employ, exploit, use**	이용하다, 활용하다
6	**toxic** [táksik]	*adj.* relating to the characteristics of poison or toxin **poisonous, venomous**	유독한, 독성의
7	**cosmic** [kázmik]	*adj.* relating to the universe **universal**	우주의, 천체의
8	**drastically** [drǽstikəli]	*adv.* with force or violence; severely or extensively **severely, violently, forcefully**	격렬하게, 강렬하게

Quiz

1. *The town planning commission said that its financial _____ for the next fiscal year was optimistic; it expects an increase in its tax revenues.*

2. *In spite of Hunt's _____ façade, the living space was awkwardly arranged.*

3. *The Loop, which is the commercial heart of Chicago, is enclosed within a rectangular _____ of elevated train tracks.*

4. *Even though many are taller, the building's history and the _____ view from the top have helped its popularity endure throughout the decades.*

5. *A public library is a resource the entire community can _____.*

6. *In her book Silent Spring, Rachel Carson wrote about insecticides and their _____ effects on animal life.*

7. *The extinction of the dinosaurs was caused by some physical event, either climatic or _____.*

8. *The weather can change _____ in the desert over the course of a mere day.*

9	**bleak** [bliːk]	*adj.* cold and cheerless **dreary, dismal, desolate**	황량한
10	**comparably** [kámpərəbli]	*adv.* in a similar way or to a similar degree **similarly, equivalently, likely**	비교될 정도로, 동등하게
11	**conserve** [kənsə́ːrv]	*v.* to keep safe from damage, deterioration, loss, or undesirable change **keep, preserve, save**	보존하다, 보호하다
12	**decline** [dikláin]	*n.* a lessening of strength, health, or something else **weakening, decrease, downturn**	쇠퇴, 하락
13	**deficient** [difíʃənt]	*adj.* not good enough; not having all that is needed **lacking, wanting, insufficient**	모자라는, 불충분한
14	**mitigate** [mítəgèit]	*v.* to make pain, anger, or something else less severe **moderate, relieve, lessen**	완화시키다
15	**discrepancy** [diskrépənsi]	*n.* a failure of sets of information or something else to correspond to something **disparity, disagreement, inconsistency**	불일치
16	**exhale** [ekshéil]	*v.* to breathe out **blow, puff**	숨을 내쉬다, 내뿜다

UNIT 32

🛡 Quiz

9. With its massive population and _____ future, many Haitians are sneaking across the border and hoping for a better one in the Dominican Republic.

10. Crows are less well known than many _____ common species.

11. In winter especially, it is important for birds to _____ their precious food reserves.

12. There are two major factors which contributed to the _____ of the bird in the early twentieth century.

13. If one of them is missing or _____, an entire system can be placed in jeopardy.

14. One strategy for _____ the impact of the heat island effect is to use construction materials in houses, pavements, and highways that reflect, not absorb, the sunlight.

15. The two nations have followed different paths of forest management, which has resulted in the current _____.

16. When the pressure inside the lungs increases, the air is _____.

17	**abuse** [əbjúːs]	*n.* the wrong use of one's power; the excessive use of harmful substances **perversion, misuse, ill-use**	오용, 남용
18	**come about**	*ph.* to happen **occur, take place, come up**	발생하다, 일어나다
19	**methodically** [məθádikəli]	*adv.* in a systematic way; systematically **neatly, tidily, regularly**	방법론적으로, 질서 있게
20	**ironic** [airánik]	*adj.* containing, characterized by, or expressing irony **sarcastic, satirical, sardonic**	반어의, 풍자적인
21	**holistic** [houlístik]	*adj.* considering a person or thing as a whole rather than as separate parts	전인적인, 전체론적인
22	**imbibe** [imbáib]	*v.* to drink, especially alcoholic drinks **drink, take**	마시다, 섭취하다
23	**tissue** [tíʃuː]	*n.* a group of cells with a similar structure and particular function	조직 (세포)
24	**alternative** [ɔːltáːrnətiv]	*adj.* secondary or different, especially in terms of being less favorable as a choice **substitute, surrogate**	대안의, 대신의

🔵 Quiz

17. The therapy is excellent for treating individuals with eating disorders and drug _____.

18. The train wreck _____ as a result of the engineer's negligence.

19. Hazen _____ screened and cultured scores of soil samples, which she then sent to her partner.

20. It is somewhat _____ that without cholesterol, a person's body would not be able to function correctly.

21. Many individuals are taking a more _____ approach to their bodies and health rather than simply looking for a quick cure.

22. Traditionally, herbal teas are _____ to boost the immune system.

23. Free radicals of oxygen, common byproducts of the metabolic processes in the body, are capable of causing _____ damage.

24. Natural gas really is an excellent _____ fuel to gasoline.

25	**cease** [siːs]	*v.* to bring or to come to an end **end, halt, stop**	그치다, 그만두다
26	**concise** [kənsáis]	*adj.* brief but comprehensive **compact, succinct, abridged**	간결한
27	**tarnish** [tɑ́ːrniʃ]	*v.* to make or become dull and discolored **sully, stain, spoil**	더럽히다, 변색되다
28	**homology** [həmɑ́lədʒi]	*n.* the same relation; the quality of being similar or corresponding in position, value structure, or function	상동 관계, 상동
29	**pectoral** [péktərəl]	*adj.* referring to or relating to the breast or chest **thoracic**	가슴의, 흉근의
30	**affliction** [əflíkʃən]	*n.* distress or suffering **hardship, pain, disease**	고통, 병

UNIT 32

 **Quiz**

25. *By the time the universe was a few minutes old, helium production had effectively _____.*

26. *The system of chemical symbols, first devised around 1800, gives a _____ and instantly recognizable description of an element or compound.*

27. *In the metal industry, hydrogen is used to prevent metals from _____ while undergoing heat treatments.*

28. *The concepts of analogy and _____ are probably easier to exemplify than to define.*

29. *The _____ fins of a fish, the wings of a bird, and the forelimbs of a mammal are all homologous structures.*

30. *Future studies of the brain may make it possible to create microchips that can be implanted, thus curing stutterers of their _____ for good.*

REVIEW TEST

Choose the closest meaning to the highlighted word or phrase.

1   The intent of this legislation was to provide protection to selected coastal habitats similar to that existing for land areas designated as national parks.

Ⓐ repetition
Ⓑ approval
Ⓒ goal
Ⓓ revision

2   Composed of a series of subterranean chambers and narrow passages formed by the dissolution of limestone, Mammoth Cave has five separate levels.

Ⓐ exposed
Ⓑ protruded
Ⓒ marvelous
Ⓓ underground

3   The organ, the clavichord, and the harpsichord became the chief instruments of the keyboard group, a supremacy they maintained until the piano supplanted them at the end of the eighteenth century.

Ⓐ a suggestion
Ⓑ an improvement
Ⓒ a dominance
Ⓓ a development

4   The social-Darwinism of British philosopher Herbert Spencer and American economist William Graham Summer prevailed at the time.

Ⓐ predominated
Ⓑ veiled
Ⓒ premiered
Ⓓ evolved

5   Wealthy and socially prominent settlers made quilts of the English type that were cut from large lengths of cloth of the same color and texture.

Ⓐ isolated
Ⓑ stingy
Ⓒ generous
Ⓓ distinguished

6   Meteorologists and computer scientists now work together to design computer programs capable of transforming raw weather data into words, symbols, and vivid graphic displays.

Ⓐ massive
Ⓑ inaccurate
Ⓒ synthesized
Ⓓ unprocessed

7   Most national parks have a built-in paradox: Although their existence often depends on tourism stimulated by public interest in nature, the preservation of their wildlife depends on the parks not being molested.

Ⓐ activated
Ⓑ impeded
Ⓒ discouraged
Ⓓ inhibited

8   Jurors are not government officials. Being a juror is more akin to voting, a civic duty that occurs in private.

Ⓐ judge
Ⓑ lawyer
Ⓒ hearer
Ⓓ prosecutor

9 In the eighteenth century, Antoine Lavoisier was led to propose a different theory of burning, one that required a constituent of air – later shown to be oxygen – for combustion.

Ⓐ component

Ⓑ layer

Ⓒ principle

Ⓓ sphere

10 A tall tree attracts lightning and is a poor conductor of electricity. However, steel buildings and vehicles provide good paths to the ground for electricity and are well insulated.

Ⓐ insulted

Ⓑ isolated

Ⓒ included

Ⓓ attached

11 It is relict seashore, tossed up millions of years ago when ocean levels were higher and the rest of the peninsula was submerged.

Ⓐ created

Ⓑ underwater

Ⓒ destroyed

Ⓓ modified

12 In soils with a high proportion of clay, the fine particles are measured on the basis of their settling velocity when suspended in water.

Ⓐ tiny

Ⓑ light

Ⓒ excellent

Ⓓ various

13 The stump speech, a political speech given by traveling politicians and lasting one and a half to two hours, has given way to the 30-second advertisement and the 10-second "sound bite" in broadcast news.

Ⓐ added interest to

Ⓑ given rise to

Ⓒ been superior to

Ⓓ been replaced by

14 How a speaker perceives the listener's receptiveness, interest, or sympathy in any given conversation can drastically alter the tone of the presentation by encouraging or discouraging the speaker.

Ⓐ frequently

Ⓑ exactly

Ⓒ severely

Ⓓ equally

15 Cells and tissues are said to be cancerous when, for reasons not clearly understood, they grow more rapidly than normal, assume abnormal shapes and sizes, and cease functioning in a normal manner.

Ⓐ verify

Ⓑ sign

Ⓒ feature

Ⓓ end

16 An abstract is a concise form of an academic article. Many journals publish abstracts, so readers can decide if it is worthwhile to read the full version of the article.

Ⓐ changeable

Ⓑ brief

Ⓒ elongated

Ⓓ uniform

Part 03
쓰다 VOCA

	Chapter 9	Chapter 10	Chapter 11	Chapter 12
Humanities	Unit 33	Unit 37	Unit 41	Unit 45
Social Sciences	Unit 34	Unit 38	Unit 42	Unit 46
Natural Sciences	Unit 35	Unit 39	Unit 43	Unit 47
Applied Sciences	Unit 36	Unit 40	Unit 44	Unit 48

Chapter 09

Humanities

1	**enthusiasm** [enθúːziæzəm]	*n.* lively or passionate interest or eagerness **fervor, passion, ardor**	열광, 열정
2	**eradicate** [irǽdəkèit]	*v.* to get rid of something completely **eliminate, obliterate, remove**	근절하다, 없애다
3	**trend** [trend]	*n.* a general direction or tendency **inclination, leaning, direction**	경향, 추세
4	**progressive** [prəgrésiv]	*adj.* favoring or advocating progress, change, improvement, or reform **advancing, liberal, radical**	진보적인
5	**crisscross** [krískrɔ̀ːs]	*v.* to cross one another in different directions **weave, traverse**	종횡으로 움직이다
6	**designate** [dézignèit]	*v.* to name, choose, or specify someone or something for a particular purpose **nominate, appoint, select**	지정하다
7	**attain** [ətéin]	*v.* to complete successfully **accomplish, achieve, reach**	달성하다
8	**attribute** [ətríbjuːt]	*n.* a trait or characteristic of something **trait, quality, feature**	특성, 속성

Quiz

1. There seemed to be nothing that men are so afraid of as religious _____.

2. Governmental attempts to _____ the black market were less than successful.

3. A generation in pop-culture terms measures about two years, and a _____ can come and go in weeks.

4. The _____ movement is an umbrella term referring to some reform efforts that emerged in the early 1900s.

5. Wagons and coaches continued to _____ the West wherever the rails had not yet been laid.

6. The Antiquities Act gives the president the unobstructed power to _____ land as national monuments.

7. The natives _____ one of the most complex social organizations of any nonagricultural people in the world.

8. The physical _____ of the Hole in the Rock in Arizona allow its use as a natural calendar.

9	**surmise** [sərmáiz]	*v.* to conclude something from the information available suppose, assume, guess	추측하다
10	**synonymous (with)** [sinánəməs]	*adj.* having the character of synonyms or a synonym; equivalent in meaning equal, tantamount, identical	동의어의, 같은 뜻의
11	**henceforth** [hènsfɔ́:rθ]	*adv.* from now on; from this point forward hereafter, henceforward	지금부터는, 이제부터는
12	**immutable** [immjú:təbəl]	*adj.* unable to be changed changeless, invariable, constant	변하지 않는, 불변의
13	**imperative** [impérətiv]	*adj.* absolutely essential; urgent necessary, requisite, pressing	필수적인, 긴급한
14	**incise** [insáiz]	*v.* to cut into, especially precisely and with a specialized sharp tool cut, gash, slash	절개하다, 새기다
15	**incur** [inkɔ́:r]	*v.* to bring something unpleasant upon oneself; to become liable for debts draw, arouse, provoke	(위험을) 초래하다, (손해를) 입다
16	**iridescent** [irədésənt]	*adj.* having many bright rainbow-like colors which seem to change constantly opalescent	빛에 따라 색이 변하는, 무지개 빛깔의

UNIT 33

Quiz

9. One might _____ that these dwellings were built for protection, but the Anasazi had no known enemies.

10. They thought of the Industrial Revolution as _____ with mechanization, with human labor replaced by machines.

11. In 1926, he announced that, _____, his factories would close for the entire day on Saturday.

12. Adjustments in various places show that the standard is not _____.

13. With the gradual evolution of society, more complex counting became _____.

14. Some pots were adorned with _____ or stamped decorations.

15. The reason is due to the cost since the family will _____ heavy expenses because of the funeral.

16. A favored device of the style was to imitate the _____ surface seen on ancient glass.

17	**fate** [feit]	*n.* the apparent power that determines the course of events over which humans have no control **fortune, destiny, doom**	운명, 숙명
18	**proclivity** [prouklívəti]	*n.* a natural liking or tendency, especially towards something bad **inclination, preference, tendency**	경향, 기질
19	**undergo** [ʌndərgóu]	*v.* to experience something especially unpleasant or difficult **suffer, bear, endure**	겪다, 경험하다
20	**revere** [rivíər]	*v.* to feel or show great respect or reverence for someone or something **respect, admire, worship**	존경하다, 숭배하다
21	**rotate** [róuteit]	*v.* to turn or make something turn about an axis like a wheel **revolve, spin, whirl**	돌다, 회전하다
22	**myriad** [míriəd]	*adj.* an exceedingly great number **countless, limitless**	무수한, 수많은
23	**norm** [nɔːrm]	*n.* a typical pattern or situation; a standard, especially for achievement in industry **criterion, standard, model**	표준, 기준
24	**preoccupation** [priːὰkjəpéiʃən]	*n.* the state or condition of being preoccupied **obsession, absorption**	몰두, 열중

🔵 Quiz

17. *Some writers wrote of a world in which a cruel and merciless environment determined human _____.*

18. *The _____ to play hot distinguished jazz musicians from other instrumentalists.*

19. *The surrounding area was _____ tremendous economic and demographic growth.*

20. *Founded by John Ruskin and William Morris, the movement _____ craft as a form of art.*

21. *Committee membership _____ every year so that new voices and opinions are constantly heard.*

22. *A series of mechanical improvements finally produced an instrument capable of _____ tonal effects.*

23. *The organization of the opera never deviates from the usual _____.*

24. *An examination of the art of the Middle Ages tells us something about the medieval _____ with theological doctrine.*

25	**rage** [reidʒ]	*n.* a widespread, usually temporary, fashion **fashion, vogue, craze**	대유행
26	**refreshing** [rifréʃiŋ]	*adj.* producing a feeling of comfort and new strength **invigorating, rejuvenating, exhilarating**	상쾌한, 기운을 돋우는
27	**exuberant** [igzú:bərənt]	*adj.* overflowing with life and cheerful excitement **joyful, lively, vigorous**	생기가 넘치는
28	**delivery** [dilívəri]	*n.* the carrying of goods, letters, or something else to a person or place **distribution, conveyance, transportation**	배달, 전달
29	**insulting** [insʌ́ltiŋ] ＊ *insult* 모욕하다	*adj.* rude or offensive with lack of respect **contemptuous, rude, offensive**	모욕적인
30	**formidable** [fɔ́:rmidəbəl]	*adj.* causing fear, doubt, or anxiety; very impressive **appalling, awesome, overwhelming**	가공할 만한, 엄청난

 **Quiz**

25. In the late eighteenth century, portraiture was the _____, so Raphaelle Peale found few buyers for his still lives.

26. Satire exists because readers appreciate a _____ stimulus, an irreverent reminder they live in a world of platitudinous thinking.

27. Self-image can be indicated by a tone of voice that is confident, shy, aggressive, or _____.

28. The free _____ service was at first confined to cities, and soon home delivery became a mark of urbanism.

29. After the Civil War, Jefferson Davis, president of the Southern Confederacy, was the subject of an _____ popular Northern song.

30. The northwest coast of the United States is uniquely characterized by the _____ Cascade Mountain Range.

Social Sciences

1	**prior** [práiər]	*adj.* existing or arranged before something else or before the present situation **earlier, former, previous**	앞선, 이전의
2	**output** [áutpùt]	*n.* the quantity or amount of something produced **production, yield**	산출(량)
3	**capacity** [kəpǽsəti]	① *n.* someone's ability to do something ② *n.* the amount of space a container or room has to hold things or people ① **ability, faculty** ② **space, volume**	① 능력 ② 용량
4	**cohesion** [kouhí:ʒən]	*n.* the process or state of sticking together; the tendency to unite **cohesiveness, connection, bond**	결합, 유대, 응집(력)
5	**colossal** [kəlásəl]	*adj.* extraordinarily great in size, extent, or degree **vast, gigantic, enormous**	거대한, 굉장한
6	**cramped** [krǽmpt]	*adj.* uncomfortably restricted in size **tight, crowded, close**	비좁은, 답답한
7	**defunct** [difʌ́ŋkt]	*adj.* no longer living, existing, active, usable, or in use **extinct, outmoded, expired**	현존하지 않는
8	**dictate** [díkteit]	*v.* to say words for someone to write down; to tell someone what to do **command, order, demand**	구술하다, 지시하다

Quiz

1. Employers often require job applicants to have _____ experience in the field.

2. The innovations in manufacturing boosted _____ and living standards to an unprecedented extent.

3. The economic heart of Canada, Ontario accounts for more than 40 percent of the nation's productive _____.

4. The airplanes contributed to a kind of international _____, which was beginning to emerge due to air travel across the oceans.

5. The Lincoln Memorial features a _____ statue of the sixteenth president.

6. Having a lower income generally forces people to live in more _____ quarters than those typically occupied by wealthier people.

7. The city cannot legally sign a contract with a _____ corporation.

8. The quality of the hinterland _____ the pace of growth of the cities.

| 9 | **astounding** | *adj.* so surprising that it is almost impossible to believe | |
| | [əstáundiŋ] | astonishing, shocking, stunning | 놀라운 |

| 10 | **turmoil** | *n.* a state of confusion, excitement, or anxiety | |
| | [tə́:rmɔil] | disorder, confusion, unrest | 소동, 소란, 혼란 |

11	**valid**	① *adj.* based on truth or sound reasoning	
	[vǽlid]	② *adj.* drawn up according to proper legal procedure	
		① concrete, sound ② lawful, legitimate	① 타당한 ② (법적으로) 유효한

| 12 | **vigilance** | *n.* the state of being watchful or observant | |
| | [vídʒələns] | alertness, watchfulness, caution | 경계, 조심 |

| 13 | **exorbitant** | *adj.* going beyond a normal or acceptable limit in degree or amount | |
| | [igzɔ́:rbətənt] | excessive, outrageous, disproportionate | (가격 등이) 터무니없는, 엄청난 |

| 14 | **exponential** | *adj.* becoming faster and faster | |
| | [èkspounénʃəl] | | 기하급수적인 |

| 15 | **filthy** | *adj.* extremely dirty | |
| | [fílθi] | foul, tainted, unclean | 불결한, 더러운 |

| 16 | **foothold** | *n.* a place to put one's foot when climbing; a firm or secure position | |
| | [fúthòuld] | footing, bridgehead, base | 발판, 거점 |

UNIT 34

Quiz

9. The circulation of Ladies' Home Journal reached an _____ 700,000 copies.

10. There were a number of major causes for the social and religious _____ experienced in Europe during the fourteenth century.

11. In some societies, both male and female lines are considered equally _____.

12. From this point until the first green corn could be harvested, the crop required labor and _____.

13. Reformers argued that the privately owned utility companies would charge _____ rates for these essential services.

14. Except for Boston, cities grew by _____ leaps through the eighteenth century.

15. The _____ living conditions were definitely a major reason why the Black Death was so devastating to Europe.

16. The five-day working week gained a firm _____ in England during the past year.

17	**foreshadow** [fɔ:rʃǽdou]	*v.* to give or have some indication of something in advance **augur, indicate, presage**	미리 암시하다, 전조가 되다
18	**ghastly** [gǽstli]	*adj.* making someone very frightened, upset, or shocked **awful, terrible, appalling**	무시무시한
19	**go along with**	*ph.* to comply with something, even if reluctantly **agree to, assent to, concur with**	찬성하다, 동의하다
20	**grant** [grænt]	*n.* something granted, especially an amount of money from a public fund for a specific purpose **subsidy, subvention**	보조금
21	**herald** [hérəld]	*v.* to proclaim or usher in something **announce, proclaim, declare**	알리다, 포고하다
22	**discourse** [dískɔ:rs]	*n.* an exchange of views for the purpose of exploring a subject or deciding an issue **discussion, colloquy**	담론, (사회적) 논의
23	**emissary** [émərsèri]	*n.* a person sent on a mission, especially on behalf of a government **messenger, envoy, legate**	밀사, 사자
24	**entanglement** [entǽŋglmənt]	*n.* a difficult situation or relationship that is hard to escape from **involvement, complication**	얽힘, 분규, 연루

Quiz

17. *The beginning of a major change was _____ in the later 1860s.*

18. *The date of the pandemic's _____, horrific assault on Europe was probably around the mid-fourteenth century.*

19. *The president would _____ the decision to hire more people if the department could bring in more revenue.*

20. *Many universities receive _____ to do research for the federal government.*

21. *The Declaration of Independence included the names of its signers and therefore _____ the support of all thirteen colonies.*

22. *Much of what constituted the traditional political _____ of earlier ages has been lost.*

23. *When the British sent _____ demanding the surrender of the colony, the leader wanted to fight.*

24. *The first president advised the nation to avoid foreign _____, and, for the first century, the country was quite adept at doing so.*

25	**facilitation**	*n.* the act of making something easy or easier	
	[fəsìlətéiʃən]	**aid, assist, promotion**	촉진, 조장

* *facilitate* 용이하게 하다

26	**fatigue**	① *v.* to exhaust or to become exhausted	
	[fətí:g]	② *n.* tiredness after work or effort	
		① **tire, exhaust** ② **weariness, tiredness**	① 피곤하게 만들다 ② 피로

27	**insatiable**	*adj.* not able to be satisfied; extremely greedy	
	[inséiʃəbəl]	**greedy, ravenous, unquenchable**	만족할 줄 모르는

28	**antecedent**	*n.* an event or circumstance which precedes another	
	[æ̀ntəsí:dənt]	**forerunner, precursor, predecessor**	앞선 것, 전례, 조상

29	**blunder**	*n.* a foolish or thoughtless, and usually serious, mistake	
	[blʌ́ndər]	**error, mistake, howler**	실수

30	**ideal**	① *n.* the best or most suitable that something could be	
	[aidí:əl]	② *adj.* perfect in every way	
		① **perfection, nonpareil** ② **supreme, complete**	① 이상적인 것 ② 이상적인

UNIT 34

 **Quiz**

25. *The goals of the federal government were the _____ of western settlements and the development of native industries.*

26. *People make more mistakes when they are _____ than when they are fresh.*

27. *One characteristic that many psychologists have agreed is common to creative types is an _____ curiosity.*

28. *A book was generally bound simply, in boards or merely stitched in paper wrappers, which was an _____ of modern-day paperbacks.*

29. *The airline _____. It sent him to Atlanta but his luggage to Montreal.*

30. *Many people feel that Hawaii has an almost _____ climate.*

Natural Sciences

1	**postpone** [poustpóun]	*v.* to delay or put off something till later **defer, adjourn, suspend**	연기하다
2	**atmosphere** [ǽtməsfìər]	*n.* the layer of gas surrounding a planet; the general or prevailing climate or mood **aerosphere, air, mood**	대기, 분위기
3	**axis** [ǽksis]	*n.* an imaginary straight line around which an object, like a planet, rotates	축
4	**bypass** [báipæs]	*v.* to avoid a congested or blocked place by taking a route which goes round it **evade, circumvent, sidestep**	피해가다, 우회하다
5	**related** [riléitid]	*adj.* connected with something or someone in some way **associated, linked, allied**	관련된, 연관된
6	**capsize** [kǽpsaiz]	*v.* to turn over completely **invert, overturn, upset**	뒤집다, 전복되다
7	**abrasion** [əbréiʒən]	*n.* the process of rubbing a surface very hard so that it becomes damaged or disappears **erosion, friction, wear**	마모, 마멸
8	**atom** [ǽtəm]	*n.* the smallest unit of a chemical element that can display the properties of that element	원자

Quiz

1. NASA sometimes _____ the launch of space vehicles on account of bad weather or technical problems.

2. _____ is crucial because it protects humans and all other life from the continuous bombardment of cosmic radiation.

3. The _____ is tilted so that Earth has various seasons at the northern and southern regions.

4. The moon's relatively harsh environment is the major reason why it should be _____.

5. In science, a theory is a reasonable explanation of observed events that are _____.

6. Small sailboats can easily _____ if they are not handled carefully.

7. _____ due to daily wear alters the surface features of beads.

8. Physicists have known since the early nineteenth century that all matter is made up of extremely tiny particles called _____.

9	**aurora** [ɔːrɔ́ːrə]	*n.* an atmospheric phenomenon consisting of bands of light caused by charged solar particles following the Earth's magnetic lines of force
		오로라, 극광

10	**keen** [kiːn]	① *adj.* having a sharp edge or point ② *adj.* enthusiastic about something or someone
		① sharp, pointed ② eager, enthusiastic ① 날카로운, 예리한 ② 열광하는

11	**gigantic** [dʒaigǽntik]	*adj.* extremely large in size, amount, or degree
		enormous, huge, massive 거대한

12	**grasp** [græsp]	① *v.* to take a firm hold of something or someone ② *v.* to completely understand
		① grip, seize ② understand, comprehend ① 붙잡다 ② 파악하다

13	**groundbreaking** [ɡráundbrèikiŋ]	*adj.* making new discoveries; using new methods
		innovative 획기적인

14	**hibernation** [hàibəːrnéiʃən]	*n.* passing the winter in a sleeping or inactive condition
		동면, 겨울잠

15	**hue** [hjuː]	*n.* a color or type of color
		tint, shade, tone 색조

16	**fertilize** [fə́ːrtəlàiz]	*v.* to make new animal or plant develop; to supply soil or land with extra nutrients
		impregnate, pollinate, enrich 수정시키다, 기름지게 하다

UNIT 35

Quiz

9. The colors of an _____ depend on the atoms emitting them.

10. The rhinoceros has a poor sense of sight but a _____ sense of smell.

11. Like the dinosaurs, some of the pterosaurs became _____.

12. A couple of major contrasts between ant and human societies are perhaps easier to _____.

13. The _____ work of primatologists Louis Leakey and Jane Goodall has shown that the chimpanzee is not just another monkey.

14. Some animal activities, such as mating, migration, and _____, have a yearly cycle.

15. The bird's head is colored red and black, and its eyes are a deep, golden _____.

16. The male ants serve one purpose only; to _____ the eggs of the queen.

| 17 | **lacerate**
[lǽsərèit] | *v.* to cut skin deeply with something sharp; to wound or hurt someone's feelings
gash, rip, wound, hurt | 갈기갈기 찢다, 상처를 주다 |

| 18 | **litter**
[lítər] | ① *n.* discarded rubbish lying in a public place
② *v.* to make something untidy
① **rubbish, debris** ② **clutter, scatter** | ① 쓰레기, 잡동사니 ② 어지르다, 흐트러뜨리다 |

| 19 | **huddle**
[hʌ́dl] | *v.* to gather or crowd together in a close mass
cluster, crowd, pack | 붐비다, 떼지어 몰리다 |

| 20 | **nostril**
[nástril] | *n.* either of the two external openings in the nose
nare | 콧구멍 |

| 21 | **summit**
[sʌ́mit] | *n.* the highest point of a mountain or hill
pinnacle, zenith, peak | 정상, 꼭대기 |

| 22 | **igneous**
[ígniəs] | *adj.* of rocks formed when magma becomes solid, especially after it has poured out of a volcano | 화성(암)의 |

| 23 | **crack**
[kræk] | *n.* a partial fracture in a material produced by an external force or internal stress
split, crevice, rift | 틈, 균열 |

| 24 | **facet**
[fǽsit] | *n.* any of the flat sides of something; an aspect of a problem
side, aspect, phase | 면, 측면 |

⭐ Quiz

17. *The weed has sharp, spiny leaves that can _____ the flesh of ranchers and horses alike.*

18. *The ground under towering oaks is often _____ with thousands of half-eaten acorns, each one only bitten from the top.*

19. *The effect of sheltering is magnified by several birds, including wrens, swifts, and brown creepers, _____ together in the roosts.*

20. *The sea otter is well adapted to its marine existence, with ears and _____ that can be closed under water.*

21. *The snow-covered _____ of Mount Hood is the highest point in the state of Oregon.*

22. *Even today, approximately 95 percent of the entire crust is _____.*

23. *If there is a _____ in the rock, a crack that runs from the aquifer to the surface pushes the water up through it.*

24. *The more _____ a diamond has, the more it glitters.*

| 25 | **expedition** | *n.* an organized journey with a specific purpose | |
| | [èkspədíʃən] | excursion, exploration | 원정(대), 탐험 |

| 26 | **entomb** | *v.* to put a body in a tomb; to bury someone or something | |
| | [intú:m] | bury, inter | 매장하다, 매몰시키다 |

| 27 | **fleck** | *n.* a spot or marking | |
| | [flek] | speck, dot, mark | 반점, 점 |

| 28 | **oscillation** | *n.* a movement of swinging or making something swing backward and forward | |
| | [àsəléiʃən] | fluctuation, vibration, swing | 진동, 진폭 |

| 29 | **consecutive** | *adj.* following one after the other; in sequence | |
| | [kənsékjətiv] | successive, succeeding, sequential | 연속적인, 계속되는 |

| 30 | **embed** | *v.* to set or fix something firmly and deeply | |
| | [imbéd] | root, entrench, implant | 꽂아 넣다, 끼워 넣다 |

UNIT 35

🌀 Quiz

25. The Lewis and Clark _____, sponsored by President Jefferson, was the most important examination of the high plains and the northwest before the War of 1812.

26. Although they were _____ in rock for millions of years, many fossils have organic remains in them.

27. The Glass Mountains of northwestern Oklahoma are covered with _____ of gypsum, which shine in the sunlight.

28. In the diurnal type of tidal _____, the alternate rise and fall of sea level, a single high water and a single low water occur each tidal day.

29. The driest deserts are called hyper-arid, and rain is absent for at least twelve _____ months.

30. When meteorites fell on the continent, they were _____ in the moving ice sheets.

Applied Sciences

1	**harmonize** [háːrmənàiz]	v. to form or be made to form a pleasing whole **coordinate, conform**	조화시키다
2	**intimacy** [íntəməsi]	n. a state of having a close personal relationship with someone **familiarity, closeness, nearness**	친밀함, 절친함
3	**impetus** [ímpətəs]	n. the force with which something moves; a driving force **thrust, impulse, stimulus**	추진력, 자극
4	**edifice** [édəfis]	n. a building, especially a large and impressive one **building, hall, palace**	건축물, 전당
5	**foliage** [fóuliidʒ]	n. the green leaves on a tree or plant; the sprays of leaves used for decoration **leafage, greenery**	잎, 무성함
6	**archaic** [ɑːrkéiik]	adj. from or relating to ancient times; old and no longer used **antiquated, outmoded, out-of-date**	고풍의, 낡은
7	**bark** [baːrk]	n. the tough and protective outer layer which covers the stems and roots of woody plants	나무껍질
8	**emission** [imíʃən]	n. the act of sending out light, heat, or gas **discharge, ejection, radiation**	방사, 방출

* *emit* 방출하다

🔵 Quiz

1. Frank Lloyd Wright is known for his highly original methods of _____ buildings with their surroundings.

2. The American farmer is as free of the _____ of the village as the urbanite.

3. Brick houses became common in Boston, where the danger of fire gave an _____ to using more durable materials.

4. The Executive Mansion, constructed in the 1790s and now called the White House, is the oldest _____ in Washington, D.C.

5. Art deco regularized the forms into abstracted repetitive patterns rather than presenting them as flowing, asymmetrical _____.

6. In fact, hybrid technology was _____ as was battery technology.

7. The _____ of a tree thickens with age.

8. _____ from the new diesel release up to 30% less carbon dioxide into the air than gas burners.

9	**encroach (on)** [enkróutʃ]	*v.* to advance beyond proper, established, or usual limits intrude, trespass, infringe	침입하다, 침해하다

10	**entrench** [entréntʃ]	*v.* to fortify something with trenches dug around it; to establish something firmly establish, embed, fix	참호로 에워싸다, 확립하다

11	**environs** [inváiərənz]	*n.* surrounding areas, especially the outskirts of a town or city environment, neighborhood	주위 환경, 주변 지역

12	**impede** [impíːd]	*v.* to prevent or delay the start or progress of an activity or something else obstruct, hamper, hinder	방해하다

13	**epic** [épik]	*adj.* having the features of an epic; very great and impressive heroic, imposing, impressive	서사(시)의, 웅장한

14	**forage** [fɔ́ːridʒ]	*v.* to gather food or provisions from an area graze, pasture	(먹이를 찾아) 돌아다니다

15	**fraction** [frǽkʃən]	*n.* a small part of something segment, portion, bit	파편, 단편, 소량

16	**layman** [léimən]	*n.* someone who is not a member of the clergy; someone who does not have specialized knowledge worldling, nonprofessional	평신도, 일반인

UNIT 36

Quiz

9. As populations in Africa explode and _____ on chimpanzee societies, they begin to become infected with disease, suffer, and die.

10. This combination of resources and technology is _____ in man's way of life.

11. The numbers of bacteria are vast, which allows them both to dominate and maintain a healthy balance within their _____.

12. Weeds clog waterways, destroy wildlife habitats, and _____ farming.

13. This is unfortunate since the loss of the menhaden spells an eco-disaster of _____ proportions.

14. During the day, parties of birds will have spread out to _____ over a very large area.

15. Only a small _____ of all the organisms that have ever lived are preserved as fossils.

16. Both doctors and _____ talk about both hemispheres of the brain as if each has specially assigned functions.

17	**ailment**	*n.* an illness, especially a minor one	
	[éilmənt]	sickness, affliction, disease	우환, 병

18	**nausea**	*n.* a sensation that one is about to vomit	
	[nɔ́ːziə]	queasiness, squeamishness	메스꺼움, 구역질

19	**perspiration**	*n.* the secretion of fluid by the sweat glands of the skin	
	[pə̀ːrspəréiʃən]	sweating	발한 (작용), 땀

20	**pharmaceutical**	*n.* the preparation of drugs and medicines; medicine	
	[fɑ̀ːrməsúːtikəl]	medication, drug	조제(약)

21	**pulsate**	*v.* to make sounds or movements that are strong and regular like a heart beating	
	[pʌ́lseit]	beat, throb, pulse	고동치다, (맥박이) 뛰다

22	**rectify**	*v.* to correct a mistake; to adjust something	
	[réktəfài]	correct, revise, fix	교정하다, 고치다

23	**spinal**	*adj.* belonging, relating, or referring to the spine	
	[spáinl]		척추의, 등뼈의
	* *spine* 척추		

24	**stamina**	*n.* energy and staying power	
	[stǽmənə]	vigor, robustness, indefatigability	정력, 체력

🔵 Quiz

17. Anthrax is generally an _____ of sheep and cattle but may also be transmitted to humans.

18. Early signs characteristic of the acute phase of viral hepatitis are abdominal pain, _____, and fever often accompanied by chills.

19. Anyone working under conditions that cause a heavy amount of _____ can suffer heat exhaustion.

20. Thousands today claim that _____ have done wonders, helping them manage stress better on a day-to-day basis.

21. Ki is a kind of life force that _____ through every human's body.

22. Research has demonstrated that rapid weight loss can be _____ by providing adequate protein associated with certain foods.

23. The _____ column is like the brain in that its main functions can be classified as either sensory or motor functions.

24. Some teas build _____ and are good for digestive purposes.

25	**correlate** [kɔ́ːrəlèit]	*v.* to have a connection or correspondence; to relate one thing to another **link, associate, connect**	연관되다, 서로 관련시키다
26	**corrosive** [kəróusiv]	*adj.* capable of eating away; tending to cause corrosion **caustic**	부식하는, 부식성의
27	**detergent** [ditə́ːrdʒənt]	*n.* a liquid or powder used for washing clothes, dishes, or something else **cleanser**	세제
28	**tart** [tɑːrt]	*adj.* sharp or sour in taste **acidic, sour, tangy**	시큼한
29	**haphazard** [hǽphǽzərd]	*adj.* happening or done in a way that is not planned or organized **casual, random, arbitrary**	되는 대로의
30	**tamper (with)** [tǽmpər]	① *v.* to interfere or to meddle ② *v.* to handle thoughtlessly, ignorantly, or mischievously ① **intervene** ② **fiddle, mess**	① 간섭하다 ② (변경, 손상 등을 위해) 주무르다

UNIT 36

Quiz

25. One function of a virus that does not _____ with its size is its ability to cause a serious disease.

26. The chemical element chlorine is a _____, greenish-yellow gas that has a sharp odor and is 2 1/2 times heavier than air.

27. _____ clean clothes by first removing particles of dirt from the fabric and then suspending the particles until they can be washed away.

28. Citric acid gives citrus fruit their _____ taste.

29. At first, the results of the experiment seemed _____, but a pattern finally emerged.

30. One should never buy food or medicine if the package has obviously been _____ with.

Choose the closest meaning to the highlighted word or phrase.

1   The good economic conditions of the 1950s supported a growth in the population, but the expansion also derived from a **trend** toward earlier marriages and an increase in the average size of families.

Ⓐ tendency
Ⓑ situation
Ⓒ growth
Ⓓ direction

2   Jupiter might have **attained** internal temperatures as high as the ignition point for nuclear reactions.

Ⓐ attempted
Ⓑ changed
Ⓒ surpassed
Ⓓ reached

3   Beginning with the Industrial Revolution, 10- to 12-hour workdays with six workdays a week were the **norm**.

Ⓐ minimum
Ⓑ example
Ⓒ possibility
Ⓓ standard

4   The woods in late summer often seem so quiet when compared with the **exuberant** choruses of birds in spring.

Ⓐ reversed
Ⓑ abundant
Ⓒ scarce
Ⓓ excellent

5   The cost of tools, draft animals, a wagon, a well, fencing, and the building of the simplest house might come to $1,000, which is a **formidable** barrier.

Ⓐ obvious
Ⓑ predictable
Ⓒ difficult
Ⓓ manageable

6   Another population wave would be composed of the children who were born during the period of high birth rates **prior to** 1957.

Ⓐ behind
Ⓑ following
Ⓒ during
Ⓓ preceding

7   The first passengers paid almost ten thousand dollars in today's monetary equivalent, fairly equal to the cost of a flight on the now **defunct** Concorde.

Ⓐ perished
Ⓑ existent
Ⓒ improved
Ⓓ available

8   A pioneering study by Donald Appleyard made the **astounding** discovery that a sudden increase in the volume of traffic through an area affects people in a way that a sudden increase in crime does.

Ⓐ startling
Ⓑ disappointing
Ⓒ dubious
Ⓓ alternative

9　The suburbs were perceived by some whites as a peaceful haven, free from the urban **turmoil** caused by poor blacks and the decline of city schools.

Ⓐ pollution

Ⓑ poverty

Ⓒ agitation

Ⓓ crowdedness

10　Certain feminists showed a **keen** sense of history by keeping records of activities in which women were engaged.

Ⓐ sarcastic

Ⓑ extensive

Ⓒ sharp

Ⓓ proximate

11　The column is designed so that a single pollination will **fertilize** hundreds of thousands of seeds.

Ⓐ disperse

Ⓑ pollinate

Ⓒ decrease

Ⓓ exterminate

12　In order to use this system to calculate Mount Everest's elevation, scientists needed to put a special receiver on its **summit** to receive signals on the satellite.

Ⓐ estuary

Ⓑ pinnacle

Ⓒ ridge

Ⓓ hillside

13　Reinforced concrete is concrete that is strengthened by metal bars that have been **embedded** in it.

Ⓐ enabled

Ⓑ encased

Ⓒ enhanced

Ⓓ enlarged

14　**Edifices** were built with succeeding stories set back, creating a row of terraces on each level that gives the structure the appearance of a ziggurat.

Ⓐ Buildings

Ⓑ Editions

Ⓒ Volumes

Ⓓ Tenements

15　Although the round dance does not have any information about direction, by tasting the nectar, the foragers can identify a scent which helps the bees **forage** nearby.

Ⓐ fly

Ⓑ assemble

Ⓒ feed

Ⓓ rest

16　Such caves testify to the enormous pressures exerted by waves and to the **corrosive** power of wave-carried sand and gravel.

Ⓐ permeating

Ⓑ dissolvable

Ⓒ intensive

Ⓓ erosive

Humanities

1	**fort** [fɔːrt]	*n.* a fortified military building, enclosure, or position fortress, base, stronghold	요새, 주둔지
2	**imposing** [impóuziŋ]	*adj.* impressive, especially in size, dignity, or appearance majestic, magnificent, grand	인상적인, 당당한
3	**retract** [ritrǽkt]	*v.* to refuse to keep an agreement, a promise, or something else withdraw, revoke, cancel	철회하다, 취소하다
4	**apparent** [əpǽrənt]	*adj.* easy to see or to understand obvious, evident, clear	명백한, 뚜렷한
5	**unearth** [ʌnə́ːrθ]	*v.* to dig something up out of the ground excavate, disclose, uncover	파내다, 발굴하다
6	**utmost** [ʌ́tmoust]	*adj.* the greatest possible in degree, number, or amount paramount, ultimate, supreme	최대의, 극도의
7	**luster** [lʌ́stər]	*n.* the shiny appearance of something in reflected light radiance, luminosity, sheen	광택
8	**mundane** [mʌndéin]	*adj.* connected with ordinary daily life rather than religious matters everyday, prosaic	속세의, 일상적인

🎯 Quiz

1. In addition to their military role, the _____ of the nineteenth century provided numerous other benefits for the American West.

2. The First Bank of the United States still stands in the _____ building constructed in the 1790s.

3. Once determined, little can be done to _____ or stop the establishment of monuments.

4. The way in which a society views its environment is sometimes _____ in its choice and use of artistic materials.

5. Vast quantities of tablets in Sumerian have been _____ during the intervening years from numerous sites.

6. The clay used in prehistoric pot making was invariably selected with the _____ care.

7. The distinctive color and _____ of pottery were the results of skillful adjustments of the kiln's temperature.

8. A man remains a creation eternally torn between the divine and the _____.

9	**ornate** [ɔ:rnéit]	*adj.* covered with a lot of decoration **elaborate, flamboyant**	화려하게 장식된
10	**procure** [proukjúər]	*v.* to manage to obtain something or to bring something about **acquire, gain, come by**	획득하다, 조달하다
11	**ramble** [ræmbəl]	*v.* to go where one pleases; to wander **stroll, amble, meander**	거닐다, 돌아다니다
12	**rebuke** [ribjú:k]	① *n.* a stern reprimand or reproach ② *v.* to speak severely to someone ① **criticism** ② **reprove, scold**	① 비난 ② 비난하다, 꾸짖다
13	**sufficient** [səfíʃənt]	*adj.* as much as is needed for a particular purpose **enough, adequate**	충분한
14	**setting** [sétiŋ]	*n.* a set of surroundings; a background within or against which action takes place **environment, background, scene**	환경, (무대 등의) 배경
15	**solemn** [sáləm]	*adj.* very serious and not happy; performed in a very serious way **grave, serious, sober**	진지한, 엄숙한
16	**contrasting** [kəntræstiŋ]	*adj.* different or dissimilar between things or people that are being compared **different, dissimilar, distinct**	대조적인, 뚜렷이 구별되는

UNIT 37

Quiz

9. *These tools were highly _____, with elaborate barbs and points on them.*

10. *Hunting is a precarious way of _____ food even when the person's diet is supplemented with seeds and fruits.*

11. *The Anasazi began to build their homes above ground and joined them together into _____ multistoried complexes.*

12. *Fighting, bullying, or attempting to surpass others brings automatic _____ from the community.*

13. *They enjoyed _____ patronage to allow them to maintain an image of themselves as professional artists.*

14. *The museum featured paintings by Peale and his family and displays of animals in their natural _____.*

15. *Within a very short time, the incongruity of playing lively music for a _____ film became apparent.*

16. *The new taste demanded dramatic effects of _____ stark outline and complex textural surfaces.*

| 17 | **struggle** [strʌ́gəl] | *n.* a long and hard fight to get freedom, political rights, or something else; a task requiring strenuous effort |
| | | **fight, strife, effort** 투쟁, 노력 |

| 18 | **prodigious** [prədídʒəs] | *adj.* very large or great in a surprising or impressive way |
| | | **huge, enormous, immense** 거대한, 막대한 |

| 19 | **protrude** [proutrúːd] | *v.* to stick out from somewhere |
| | | **project, extend** 튀어나오다 |

| 20 | **score** [skɔːr] | *n.* a written or printed copy of music for several parts and which is set out vertically down the page |
| | | **music** 스코어, 악보 |

| 21 | **spontaneous** [spɑntéiniəs] | *adj.* unplanned and voluntary or instinctive; not provoked or invited by others |
| | | **natural, instinctive, involuntary** 자연적인, 자발적인 |

22	**criterion** [kraitíəriən]	*n.* a standard or principle on which to base a judgment
		standard, benchmark, touchstone 기준, 표준
	* *pl. criteria*	

| 23 | **in vain** | *ph.* without success; to no purpose |
| | | **unsuccessfully, vainly, fruitlessly** 헛되이, 쓸데없이 |

| 24 | **rugged** [rʌ́gid] | *adj.* not having a level or smooth surface |
| | | **jagged, rough, bumpy** 우둘투둘한, 울퉁불퉁한 |

Quiz

17. The Hudson River School seems to have emerged in the 1870s as a direct result of the _____ between the old and new generations of artists.

18. Her productivity has been _____, as she has, in less than two decades, written nearly thirty works.

19. The painter stands out with his life-sized painting of a woman's bent back from which _____ real thorns.

20. The most famous _____ was composed and arranged for D. W. Griffith's film Birth of a Nation.

21. Music began playing a greater role in opera, was _____, and often mirrored the characters' emotions.

22. Some groups judged potential members through a complex set of _____ that often included class, education and skin tone.

23. Supply ships were essential during the war because, without the supply ships, all would be _____.

24. The glass fibers were brittle, _____, and no longer than ten feet.

| 25 | **in proportion to** | *ph.* having due proportion |
| | | corresponding | ~에 비례하여 |

| 26 | **obsessed** | *adj.* completely or constantly occupied by thoughts or the mind |
| | [əbsést] | haunted, preoccupied, possessed | (생각 등에) 사로잡힌, 몰두한 |

| 27 | **option** | *n.* the power, right, or opportunity to choose |
| | [ápʃən] | choice, selection | 선택 |

* *opt* 선택하다

| 28 | **ridge** | *n.* a long and narrow strip of relatively high ground with steep slopes on either side |
| | [ridʒ] | crest, strip, top edge | 산마루, 산등성이 |

| 29 | **resort (to)** | *v.* to turn to something as a means of solving a problem |
| | [ri:sɔ́:rt] | turn, fall back | 호소하다, 의존하다 |

| 30 | **aid** | *v.* to help or support in the form of money, supplies, or services |
| | [eid] | assist, help, back | 돕다, 원조하다 |

UNIT 37

 **Quiz**

25. The high-pressure engine was far lighter _____ its horsepower and was much easier and cheaper to repair than the previous one.

26. Evans quickly became _____ by the possibilities of mechanized production and steam power.

27. Their speed of travel made steamboats the most attractive and practical _____ for shipping as well as for human travel.

28. The distance was more than 350 miles, and there were _____ to cross and a wilderness of woods and swamps to penetrate.

29. It is pleasant to imagine a woodworker carefully matching lumber and joining a chest together without _____ nails or glue.

30. The swamp's environment kept bacterial decay down, which _____ in the preservation of plants and animals.

Social Sciences

1 **wage**
[weidʒ]
n. a regular payment from an employer to an employee
salary, pay, earnings
임금

2 **communal**
[kəmjúːnl]
adj. for or by a group rather than individuals
collective, shared, common
공동의, 공용의

3 **boom**
[buːm]
v. to become rapidly prosperous; to increase sharply in value
prosper, flourish, roar
번창하다, 급증하다

4 **ploy**
[plɔi]
n. a stratagem or maneuver to gain an advantage
artifice, trick, wile
책략, 계략

5 **follow suit**
ph. to do the same thing; to follow the example of another
follow in one's tracks, conform to
남이 하는 대로 하다, 선례를 따르다

6 **foment**
[foumént]
v. to encourage or foster ill-feeling or something else
agitate, inflame, provoke
선동하다, 조장하다

7 **implement**
[ímpləmənt]
① *v.* to take action or make changes that have been decided
② *n.* a tool, especially one used for outdoor physical work
① **execute, carry out** ② **instrument, utensil**
① 실행하다 ② 도구

8 **jolt**
[dʒoult]
n. a jarring shake; an emotional shock
bounce, blow, shock
급격한 충격, 동요

Quiz

1. Congress sets the minimum _____, which is the lowest amount of money workers may be paid per hour.

2. _____ violence broke out in different parts of the country.

3. The glass factories of Toledo, Ohio, _____ after Michael Owens invented a process that turned out bottles by the thousands.

4. At this point, she may use one of several _____ to deceive her enemy.

5. When Britain developed coke smelting, the colonies did not _____ because they had plenty of wood.

6. The event was a major issue that _____ the break between England and the British colonies.

7. A plow is a farm _____ used to break up soil and to prepare the land for planting.

8. The coach's rugged body and suspension system of leather straps could handle the hard _____ from rough roads.

9	**altogether** [ɔ̀ːltəgéðər]	*adv.* wholly; with all or everything included **entirely, totally, utterly**	완전히, 전적으로
10	**assassinate** [əsǽsənèit] ＊ *assassin* 암살자	*v.* to kill suddenly or secretively **kill, murder**	암살하다
11	**optimal** [áptəməl]	*adj.* most favorable; most suitable **optimum**	최적의, 최선의
12	**hygiene** [háidʒiːn]	*n.* a condition of cleanliness that helps maintain health **cleanliness, sanitation**	위생
13	**influx** [ínflʌks]	*n.* a continual stream or arrival of large numbers of people or things **inflow, inrush**	유입
14	**ingenuity** [ìndʒənjúːəti]	*n.* inventive cleverness, skill, or originality; inventiveness **handiness, brilliance, creativity**	재간, 창의(력)
15	**instability** [ìnstəbíləti] ＊ *stability* 안정성	*n.* a lack of physical or mental steadiness or stability **insecurity, precariousness, shakiness**	불안정성
16	**gulf** [gʌlf]	*n.* a portion of an ocean or sea partly enclosed by land; a large difference between two people or groups **bay, cove, gap**	만, 큰 간격

UNIT 38

Quiz

9. *The interrelationship of science, technology, and industry is summed up, not _____ accurately, as "research and development."*

10. *A group who favored the restoration of the Roman Republic _____ Caesar in 44 B.C.*

11. *Proponents of the worksheet procedure believe that it will yield _____, that is, the best decisions.*

12. *City streets were crowded with citizens, and _____ was not at the top of a fourteenth-century European's list of priorities.*

13. *This black _____ to cities increased during World War II as blacks came seeking jobs in the war industries.*

14. *Some functions of the park are direct results of the _____ of the citizenry.*

15. *The rezoning plan would catalyze physical expansion and accelerate the inherent _____ of urban life.*

16. *A _____ that at times seemed unbridgeable was created between husbands and wives.*

17	**intriguing** [intrí:giŋ]	*adj.* arousing curiosity or interest **interesting, fascinating, immersing**	호기심을 자극하는, 매혹적인
18	**cooperation** [kouὰpəréiʃən]	*n.* an act or instance of working or acting together for a common purpose **collaboration, teamwork, interaction**	협동, 협조
19	**accuse** [əkú:z]	*v.* to make a claim of wrongdoing against **blame, denounce, indict**	비난하다, 고소하다
20	**eloquently** [éləkwəntli]	*adv.* in an eloquent manner; by powerful discourse **fluently, persuasively, effectively**	웅변조로, 설득력 있게
21	**feeble** [fí:bəl]	*adj.* lacking strength **fragile, weak, infirm**	연약한, 미약한
22	**intertwine** [ìntərtwáin]	*v.* to twist or be twisted together **interweave, interlace, entangle**	얽히게 하다, 짜 넣다
23	**nominate** [námənèit]	*v.* to suggest someone formally for a position, office, or something else **appoint, designate, name**	지명하다, 지정하다
24	**decree** [dekrí:]	*v.* to order or decide something formally or officially **ordain, proclaim, pronounce**	포고하다, 명하다

🛡️ Quiz

17. The bustle and social interaction of urban life seemed particularly _____ to those raised in rural isolation.

18. The original motivation for the space station was to foster _____ between the United States and the Soviet Union.

19. In the United States, every person _____ of a crime has the right to a trial by a jury of his or her peers.

20. Few American politicians have spoken more _____ than William Jennings Bryan.

21. The national government made a _____ attempt to reduce taxes.

22. The American Constitution clearly states that religious worship and governmental activities shall not be _____.

23. In 1884, Belva Lockwood, a lawyer who had appeared before the Supreme Court, became the first woman _____ for president of the United States.

24. The president _____ that no more money would be spent on missile defense.

25	**fair** [fɛər]	*n.* an event at which people or businesses show and sell their products; a market
		exhibition, exposition, bazaar	박람회, 장

26	**bond** [bɑnd]	① *n.* something used for tying, binding, or holding ② *n.* a written agreement to pay money
		① tie ② contract, covenant	① 묶는 것, 유대 ② 채권, (차용) 증서

27	**condemn** [kəndém]	① *v.* to declare something to be wrong or evil ② *v.* to give someone a punishment after deciding the person is guilty of a crime
		① criticize ② convict, sentence	① 비난하다 ② 유죄를 선고하다

28	**nurture** [nə́:rtʃər]	① *n.* care or nourishment given to a growing child ② *v.* to nourish and tend to a growing child
		① raising ② foster, nourish	① 양육, 후천(성) ② 양육하다

29	**statutorily** [stǽtʃutɔ:rili]	*adv.* in terms of rules or laws which have been formally written down
		legally, legitimately	법적으로

30	**intrude** [intrú:d]	*v.* to force or impose oneself without welcome or invitation
		encroach, interfere, break in	억지로 밀고 들어가다, 끼어들다

UNIT 38

Quiz

25. The _____ provided a means of bringing handmade goods from outlying places to would-be buyers in the city.

26. Investment banking deals with corporate stocks and bonds as well as the government _____.

27. When Martin Luther was _____ as a religious outlaw, he experienced profound spiritual and physical torment.

28. The other theory maintains that a child is defined by environment – _____ – not nature.

29. The name "charter" refers to the _____ defined performance contract that the schools are expected to meet.

30. The printed word, unquestionably, was _____ on the insulation that had characterized the United States society in an earlier period.

Natural Sciences

1	**fickle** [fíkəl]	*adj.* likely to change suddenly and without reason **capricious, inconstant**	변덕스러운

2	**celestial** [siléstʃəl]	*adj.* belonging or relating to the sky **astronomical, heavenly**	천체의

3	**staggering** [stǽgəriŋ]	*adj.* almost unbelievable **amazing, surprising, unpredictable**	놀라운, 예측할 수 없는

4	**contradict** [kàntrədíkt]	*v.* to assert the opposite of a statement or something else made by a person; to disagree with **controvert, counter**	반박하다, 모순되다

5	**crater** [kréitər]	*n.* the bowl-shaped mouth of a volcano or geyser **hole, cavity, pit**	(분)화구

6	**retreat** [ri:trí:t]	*v.* to move back or away from the enemy or to retire after defeat **withdraw, recede, evacuate**	퇴각하다, 물러나다

7	**interstitial** [ìntərstíʃəl]	*adj.* pertaining to, situated in, or forming a space or crack	틈의, 빈틈을 이루는

8	**misconception** [mìskənsépʃən]	*n.* a wrong or misguided attitude, opinion, or view **misapprehension, misjudgment, misunderstanding**	오인, 오해

Quiz

1. *This, along with the _____ nature of hurricanes, adds to the turmoil that hurricanes inflict on the populations of the areas they hit.*

2. *The orbit of a _____ body is usually in the shape of an ellipse.*

3. *The process could take hundreds or even thousands of years to complete, and the cost would be _____.*

4. *Newton's idea of gravity as a force of attraction, which _____ the idea of a universe that is static, was unchanging.*

5. *The roughness of the moon's surface is mostly caused by the abundance of _____.*

6. *Some 800 years ago, Alaska's Hubbard Glacier advanced toward the sea, _____, and advanced again 500 years later.*

7. *Some fossil bones have all of their _____ spaces filled with foreign minerals.*

8. *That all deserts are hot is a common _____.*

9	**granular**	*adj.* made of or containing tiny particles or granules	
	[grǽnjələr]	**grainy, gritty, particulate**	알갱이로 된, 과립의

10	**hemisphere**	*n.* one half of a sphere	
	[hémisfiər]		반구, 반구체

11	**ornamental**	*adj.* serving as an ornament	
	[ɔ́ːrnəméntl]	**decorative, adorning, beautifying**	장식의, 장식적인

12	**estimate**	*v.* to judge or calculate size, amount, or value roughly or without measuring	
	[éstəmèit]	**approximate, gauge, guess**	추산하다, 어림잡아 계산하다

13	**disproportionately**	*adv.* out of proportion, as in size or number	
	[dìsprəpɔ́ːrʃənətli]	**asymmetrically, unevenly**	불균형하게

14	**stash**	*v.* to put aside or away for safekeeping or future use, usually in a secret place	
	[stæʃ]	**cache, secrete**	따로 간직해 두다, 은닉하다

15	**forerunner**	*n.* a person or thing that goes before; an earlier type or version	
	[fɔ́ːrrʌ̀nər]	**predecessor, forebear, precursor**	선임자, 선조, 전조

16	**fragrant**	*adj.* having a pleasant scent or aroma	
	[fréigrənt]	**sweet-smelling, sweet-scented, aromatic**	향기로운, 방향성의

UNIT 39

🔵 Quiz

9. *As new snow falls and buries the older snow, the layers of _____ snow further compact.*

10. *Logically, in the Northern _____ , a north wind turns to bring colder weather and the south wind warmer weather.*

11. *An _____ plant is cultivated chiefly for its beauty.*

12. *A professor _____ that each large white oak produced between two and eight thousand acorns.*

13. *Humans are _____ right-handed.*

14. *The ant colony contains all of the ants' important possessions, such as the queen and their _____ food reserves.*

15. *Experts have concentrated their studies on the species called the Allosaur, a _____ of the massive Tyrannosaurus Rex.*

16. *The daylily is an attractive, _____ flower.*

17	**dehydration** [dìːhaidreíʃən]	*n.* dryness resulting from the removal of water; an abnormal loss of water from the body evaporation	탈수, 탈수 현상
18	**obedient** [oubíːdiənt]	*adj.* doing what one is ordered to do; willing to obey observant, docile, compliant	복종하는, 고분고분한
19	**impinge** [impíndʒ]	① *v.* to interfere with or encroach on something or someone ② *v.* to make an impression ① infringe, encroach ② impact	① 침해하다 ② 영향을 주다
20	**omnivorous** [ɑmnívərəs]	*adj.* eating any type of food, especially both meat and vegetable matter polyphagous	잡식성의
21	**pandemonium** [pæ̀ndəmóuniəm]	*n.* any very disorderly or noisy place or assembly chaos, turmoil, uproar	대혼란, 아수라장
22	**transmit** [trænsmít]	*v.* to pass or hand on, especially a message, an inheritance, or disease transfer, convey, send	전달하다, 전송하다
23	**bound** [baund] * *bind-bound-bound*	*adj.* tied with or as if with a rope or other binding; stuck together fastened, tied, fixed	묶여져 있는, 굳어져 있는
24	**ore** [ɔːr]	*n.* rock, earth, or something else from which metal can be obtained	광물, 광석

Quiz

17. _____ occurs when more water is lost through perspiration or diarrhea than is replaced by fluid intake.

18. They are wild animals and do not make _____, domesticated pets.

19. Florida's surrounding lushness cannot _____ on its desert scrubbiness.

20. Chimpanzees are _____, which means that they rely on meat, plant life, and fruit for subsistence.

21. The chimpanzee's ability to use tools caused near _____ in the scientific world.

22. Paths, roads, and trails made journeys easier, and the creation of maps _____ this knowledge to others.

23. The process by which individual crystals become _____ together in a collection of ice crystals produces glacial ice.

24. The _____ is broken up in a series of blasting operations.

25	**bunch** [bʌntʃ]	① *n.* a number of things fastened or growing together ② *v.* to group together in or to form a bunch or bunches of something ① bundle, cluster ② collect, gather	① 다발, 무리 ② 모으다, 모이다

26	**acronym** [ǽkrənìm]	*n.* a word made from the first letters of other words and pronounced as a word in its own right abbreviation	머리글자로 된 말

27	**conflict** *n.*[kánflikt]*v.*[kənflíct]	① *n.* a disagreement; a fierce argument ② *v.* to be incompatible or in opposition; to fight ① dispute, opposition ② disagree, clash	① 갈등 ② 대립하다, 충돌하다

28	**outfit** [áutfìt]	① *n.* a set of equipment; an organization ② *v.* to provide someone with an outfit ① apparatus, group ② equip, furnish	① 장비, 조직 ② 장비를 제공하다

29	**percolate** [pə́:rkəlèit]	*v.* to pass slowly through a material that has small holes in it filter, seep, permeate	거르다, 여과하다

30	**insurmountable** [ìnsərmáuntəbəl]	*adj.* too large or difficult to be dealt with unbeatable, indomitable, invincible	극복할 수 없는, 넘을 수 없는

UNIT 39

 **Quiz**

25. In the polar regions, the magnetic lines of force of the Earth and of the solar wind _____ together.

26. The word laser was coined as an _____ for Light Amplification by the Stimulated Emission of Radiation.

27. When Jules Verne wrote Journey to the Center of the Earth in 1864, there were many _____ theories about the nature of the Earth's interior.

28. The cable ship crew will pull the trencher back up to the surface and _____ it with a burying apparatus.

29. All of the minerals deposited within the bone have been recrystallized from solution by the action of water _____ though them.

30. The difficulties involved in rapidly collecting and processing the raw weather data from such an old network were _____.

Applied Sciences

1 commission
[kəmíʃən]

v. to give a commission or authority to someone
authorize, license, charge

위임하다, 위탁하다

2 engage
[engéidʒ]

① *v.* to take someone on as a worker
② *v.* to involve or to occupy
① employ, hire ② occupy, absorb

① 고용하다 ② 몰두하다

3 frenetic
[frənétik]

adj. wildly excited or active; in an uncontrolled way
frantic, frenzied

열광적인, 발광한

4 hurl
[hə:rl]

v. to throw something with force
cast, throw, pitch

집어 던지다, 세게 던지다

5 suspension
[səspénʃən]

n. the act of suspending or the state of being suspended

매달림, 걸림

6 arbitrary
[á:rbitrèri]

adj. not based on any principle
capricious, erratic

임의적인, 독단적인

7 fringe
[frindʒ]

n. a border of loose threads on a garment or something else
border, edge, trimming

가장자리, 외변

8 germinate
[dʒə́:rmənèit]

v. to cause a seed to start growing; to show the first signs of development
sprout

싹트게 하다, 발아하다

 **Quiz**

1. The city's social leadership _____ mansions while apartments and hotels began to sprout on multiple lots.

2. In 1903, the governing board of the University of Washington _____ a firm of landscape architects.

3. Hotels were both creatures and creators of communities as well as symptoms of the _____ quest for community.

4. Passenger terminals, like the luxury express trains that _____ people over spots, spotlight the romance of railroading.

5. The George Washington Bridge is a _____ bridge between New York City and Fort Lee, New Jersey.

6. In constructing the botanical gardens, some _____, practical decisions were made.

7. In terrestrial ecosystems and in _____ marine ecosystems, the most common problem is habitat destruction.

8. These acorn halves, many of which contain seeds, may later _____.

| 9 | **hack** | *v.* to cut or chop something roughly | |
| | [hæk] | hew, slash, slice | (도끼 등으로) 마구 패서 자르다 |

| 10 | **herbicide** | *n.* a substance used to kill weeds | |
| | [hə́ːrbəsàid] | weed-killer | 제초제 |

| 11 | **scurry** | *v.* to move hurriedly or briskly | |
| | [skə́ːri] | hurry, rush, dash | 허둥지둥 달리다, 급히 가다 |

12	**inclination**	① *n.* the degree at which an object slopes away from a vertical line	
	[ìnklənéiʃən]	② *n.* a particular tendency	
		① tilt, slope ② disposition, preference	① 기울기 ② 경향, 성향

| 13 | **infrastructure** | *n.* the basic inner structure of a society, organization, or system | |
| | [ínfrəstrʌ̀ktʃər] | base | 하부 조직, 토대, 기반 시설 |

| 14 | **iron out** | *ph.* to solve or get rid of problems or difficulties, especially small ones | |
| | | resolve, clear up | 해소하다, 제거하다 |

| 15 | **lurking** | *adj.* lying in wait, especially in ambush, with some sinister purpose in mind | |
| | [lə́ːrkiŋ] | hiding, sneaking, slinking | 숨어 있는, 잠복하는 |

| 16 | **stimulant** | *n.* any substance that produces an increase in particular activity | |
| | [stímjələnt] | stimulus, spur, incentive | 흥분제, 자극(물) |

UNIT 40

 ## Quiz

9. *What is so worrisome is that acre upon acre of the animals' habitat is being _____ to the ground every day.*

10. *The _____ are effective, but some pose serious problems, particularly if misused.*

11. *The ducks respond by _____ to gather around her.*

12. *Individual birds have markedly different interests, _____, and strategies.*

13. *They have established another company to help develop the _____ of hydrogen separation and hydrogen supply points.*

14. *Until these basic problems are _____ , hydrogen will not turn into a major source of energy.*

15. *Still, there is another predator _____ invisibly in the bodies of water of the world; bacteria.*

16. *Occasionally, doctors will provide _____, but these can cause addiction and are usually avoided except in the most extreme cases.*

17	**stroke** [strouk]	*n.* a interruption to the supply of blood to the brain, thereby causing unconsciousness **cerebral apoplexy, attack, seizure**	뇌졸중
18	**stutter** [stʌ́tər]	*n.* an inability to form words at what is considered a normal speed of speech **stammer, slur**	말더듬기
19	**subconscious** [sʌbkɑ́nʃəs]	*adj.* denoting mental processes which a person is not fully aware of **subliminal**	잠재의식의
20	**transfusion** [trænsfjúːʒən]	*n.* the process of introducing blood directly into the bloodstream of a person	수혈
21	**transplanted** [trænsplǽntid]	*adj.* having taken a living organ from someone and using it as an implant; having taken a plant out of the ground and put it in a different place **relocated, uprooted, removed**	이식된
22	**equilibrium** [ìːkwəlíbriəm]	*n.* a state in which various forces balance each other **balance**	평형
23	**outage** [áutidʒ]	*n.* a period of time during which a power supply fails to operate **power failure, power cut**	정전
24	**infinitesimal** [ìnfinitésəməl]	*adj.* infinitely small; with a value too close to zero to be measured **tiny, minute, slight**	극소의, 아주 작은

🛡 Quiz

17. *If a blood clot goes to the brain, it can cause a _____ or even death.*

18. *The newest theories on _____ concentrate on how the brain functions during speech.*

19. *Specialists believe stutterers are listening to themselves as they talk but at a _____ level of understanding.*

20. *You may know that, nowadays, blood _____, or the giving of one person's blood to another, are a common practice.*

21. *The immune system takes action against foreign invaders and _____ tissues that are treated as foreign cells.*

22. *Illness can result when bodily systems are not in _____.*

23. *The 1979 power _____ in New York City caused half of the city to be without electricity for several hours.*

24. *A virus is so _____ that it can be seen only with an electron microscope.*

25	**inert** [inə́:rt]	*adj.* tending to remain in a state of rest or uniform motion inactive, inanimate, motionless	활발하지 못한, 비활성의
26	**integrity** [intégrəti]	*n.* the quality or state of being whole and unimpaired completeness, entirety, soundness	완전(성), 무결
27	**malleable** [mǽliəbəl]	*adj.* able to be beaten into a different shape or bent without breaking flexible, pliable, tractable	펴 늘릴 수 있는, 유순한
28	**fortuitously** [fɔːrtjúːətəsli]	*adv.* by chance or haphazardly incidentally, haphazardly, accidentally	우연히, 우발적으로
29	**prow** [prau]	*n.* the projecting front part of a ship bow, head	뱃머리, 기수
30	**counterpart** [káuntərpɑ̀:rt]	*n.* one of two parts which form a corresponding pair rival, equivalent, parallel	상대물, 대응물, 동자격자

UNIT 40

 **Quiz**

25. These gases include helium, neon, and argon and are called _____ because they bond with other elements only with extreme difficulty.

26. The colony odor allows ants to identify intruders and to maintain colony _____.

27. The mixture becomes soft and _____ and can be formed into many shapes and sizes.

28. On a 1948 vacation, Hazen _____ collected a clump of soil from the edge of a cow pasture in Fauquier County, Virginia.

29. To ensure proper identification, the _____ of Viking warships were either adorned with carved figures or vividly painted.

30. Digital cameras are likely to replace their traditional _____ as prices of electronic components go down.

Choose the closest meaning to the highlighted word or phrase.

1   The museum's most popular display was the skeleton of a mastodon — a huge, extinct elephant — which Peale unearthed on a New York farm in 1801.

Ⓐ carved
Ⓑ ornamented
Ⓒ uncovered
Ⓓ retracted

2   By the late 1700s, the influence of the Enlightenment was beginning to lose its luster.

Ⓐ impetus
Ⓑ brilliance
Ⓒ originality
Ⓓ fascination

3   Stoneware grew increasingly ornate throughout the nineteenth century

Ⓐ elaborate
Ⓑ puzzling
Ⓒ durable
Ⓓ simple

4   Not only did Abraham Lincoln project an image of solemnity and dignity, but he also had a sharp sense of humor.

Ⓐ honesty
Ⓑ seriousness
Ⓒ peculiarity
Ⓓ humor

5   The mortise is the hole chiseled and cut into one piece of wood while the tenon is the tongue of the protruding element shaped from another piece of wood so that it fits into the mortise.

Ⓐ parallel
Ⓑ rugged
Ⓒ projecting
Ⓓ sinking

6   Given these conditions, the common people opted to patronize the village apothecary, who was typically a local grocer that sold ineffectual herbal remedies.

Ⓐ chose
Ⓑ conceived
Ⓒ refused
Ⓓ planned

7   Pan American Airways implemented a fleet of planes, called Clippers, to become the first commercial planes to cross the vast oceans.

Ⓐ conceded
Ⓑ rebuilt
Ⓒ realized
Ⓓ abolished

8   The 1960s will always be remembered for the Vietnam War, hippies, and the assassination of John F. Kennedy.

Ⓐ dismissal
Ⓑ murder
Ⓒ retirement
Ⓓ election

9 These and many other applications of science and **ingenuity** resulted in a new level of productivity in almost every field.

Ⓐ invention

Ⓑ cleverness

Ⓒ adaptation

Ⓓ development

10 Bill the Kid was the most famous and **intriguing** outlaw-gunfighter of the frontier in the Southwest.

Ⓐ provocative

Ⓑ fascinating

Ⓒ primitive

Ⓓ unscrupulous

11 Stars may be spheres, but not every **celestial** object is spherical.

Ⓐ visible

Ⓑ heavenly

Ⓒ glowing

Ⓓ scientific

12 Another way that lakes have been formed is through volcanic action. In many parts of the world, the **craters** of extinct volcanoes hold small lakes.

Ⓐ creeps

Ⓑ holes

Ⓒ convexes

Ⓓ bows

13 A very **dehydrated** person cannot drink enough water to rehydrate in one session, partly because the human stomach is not big enough.

Ⓐ infectious

Ⓑ poisoned

Ⓒ sturdy

Ⓓ desiccated

14 Fessenden began experimenting with radio detectors in order to explore the possibility of voice **transmission**.

Ⓐ detection

Ⓑ transcription

Ⓒ conveyance

Ⓓ interpretation

15 Since even one speck of dust would easily create a groove deep enough in the **malleable** plate surfaces to render the daguerreotypes worthless, they required extensive polishing until completely smooth.

Ⓐ soft

Ⓑ angled

Ⓒ persistent

Ⓓ flat

16 Anyone who has handled a fossilized bone knows that it is usually not exactly like its modern **counterpart**, the most obvious difference being that it is often much heavier.

Ⓐ species

Ⓑ version

Ⓒ change

Ⓓ material

Humanities

1 **veil**
[veil]
① *n.* a fabric covering for a woman's head or face
② *v.* to cover something
① cloak, curtain ② conceal, hide
① 베일 ② 베일을 씌우다, 감추다

2 **worldly**
[wə́:rldli]
adj. relating to this world; material, as opposed to spiritual or eternal
earthly, secular, mundane
속세의

3 **relent**
[rilént]
v. to become less severe or unkind
relax, soften
누그러지다

* *relentlessly* 가차없이

4 **sanitation**
[sæ̀nətéiʃən]
n. the system that keeps places clean, especially by removing human waste
위생, 보건

5 **scorch**
[skɔ:rtʃ]
v. to burn or be burned slightly or superficially
char, sear, roast
태우다, (불에) 그슬리다

6 **stalk**
[stɔ:k]
① *v.* to walk in a proud proved or angry way and with long steps
② *v.* to hunt, follow, or approach stealthily
① strut, prance ② chase, hunt
① 활보하다 ② 살그머니 접근하다

7 **stringent**
[stríndʒənt]
adj. not allowing for any exceptions or loosening of standards
rigid, strict, inflexible
엄격한, 엄중한

8 **subjugate**
[sʌ́bdʒugèit]
v. to dominate someone; to bring someone under control
subdue, suppress, subject
정복하다, 복종시키다

Quiz

1. Eventually, stories arose which explained or _____ the mysteries of the rites.

2. An elaborate funeral celebration is also important to impress the gods with the individual's _____ importance and wealth.

3. He could have _____, but he decided to attack.

4. In Sacramento, an excavation at a site revealed garbage in the building basement despite _____ laws to the contrary.

5. This timber might be _____ occasionally, but it was far enough in front of the rising column of heat to be safe from catching fire.

6. Many accounts say that Genghis Khan _____ and killed his older half-brother.

7. The archaeologists stated that they have subjected their findings to _____ and numerous tests.

8. The peoples _____ by the Nazis labored, sometimes without pay and sometimes for a pittance.

9 lavish
[lǽviʃ]

adj. spending or giving generously
generous, unsparing, open-handed

후한, 성대한

10 vital
[váitl]

adj. relating to or essential for life; extremely important and necessary
essential, requisite, crucial

생명의, 중대한

11 supplant
[səplǽnt]

v. to take the place of someone or something, often by force or unfair means
replace, substitute, supersede

대신하다, 대체하다

12 frustration
[frʌstréiʃən]

n. the fact that something is preventing someone from succeeding; the feeling of being frustrated
prevention, disappointment, dissatisfaction

좌절(감)

* *frustrate* 좌절시키다

13 trace
[treis]

① *v*. to track by following clues
② *n*. a sign of presence in a particular place
① **pursue, shadow** ② **print, footmark**

① 추적하다 ② 흔적, 자취

14 vividly
[vívidli]

adv. in a very clear and detailed manner
distinctly, clearly, lively

생생하게, 활발하게

15 accomplished
[əkámpliʃt]

adj. expert or skilled
versed, adept, proficient

통달한, 뛰어난

16 subject
[səbdʒékt]

v. to cause something to undergo something unpleasant
expose, submit, lay open

당하게 하다, 받게 하다

* *be subject to* ~를 당하다

 **Quiz**

9. In most cultures, it is traditional to prepare _____ meals to celebrate holidays.

10. From colonial times, sailing ships were _____ to the economy.

11. Modern dictators are using art to help their states _____ religion with political myths.

12. Expressionist drama often shows the influence of modern psychology by reflecting the inner _____ of the dramatist.

13. Another theory _____ the theater's origin from the human interest in storytelling.

14. In his novel The Red Badge of Courage, Stephen Crane _____ describes a Civil War battle.

15. An _____ saxophonist and composer, John Coltrane began his career playing in the big bands of the early 1950s.

16. When songs have been _____ to complex processes, their origins are usually impossible to trace.

UNIT 41

17	**unadorned** [ʌnədɔ́ːrnd]	*adj.* without unnecessary or special features or decorations **undecorated, unornamented, unembellished**	꾸미지 않은, 있는 그대로의
18	**inflection** [inflékʃən]	*n.* a change in the tone or pitch of a voice **accent, intonation**	억양
19	**vary** [vɛ́əri]	*v.* to be different from each other in size, shape, or something else **differ, diverge**	다양하다
20	**apply (to)** [əplái]	*v.* to use something like a method, idea, or law in a particular situation, activity, or process **use, utilize, employ**	적용하다
21	**periphery** [pərí:fəri]	*n.* the edge or boundary of something **perimeter, circumference, rim**	주위, 주변
22	**persist** [pəːrsíst]	*v.* to continue with something in spite of resistance and difficulty **continue, preserve, insist**	지속하다, 고집하다
23	**indigenous** [indídʒənəs]	*adj.* belonging naturally to a country or area **native, local, aboriginal**	토착의
24	**submission** [səbmíʃən]	*n.* a bending to the authority or control of another **surrender, concession, obedience**	항복, 복종

Quiz

17. *Many early jazz bands played _____ published arrangements of popular songs.*

18. *Babies can detect the difference between syllables pronounced with rising and falling _____.*

19. *In the early days of the United States, postal charges were paid by the recipient, and charges _____ according to the distance carried.*

20. *This term was usually _____ to a fabric of wool and linen used in heavy clothing and quilted petticoats worn in the wintertime.*

21. *Over 100 areas designated as conservation of wildlife preserves exist around the _____ of the Caribbean Sea.*

22. *Along with market days, the institution days of twice-yearly fairs _____ in Philadelphia.*

23. *The _____ people of Australia were called Aborigines by the English settlers.*

24. *Genghis Khan often sent an emissary ahead to a city to ask for its _____.*

25	**thereby** [ðɛ̀ərbái]	*adv.* with the result that something else happens **thus, therefore, hence**	따라서, 그러므로

26	**agent** [éidʒənt]	① *n.* someone or something that affects or changes a situation ② *n.* someone who represents an organization and acts on its behalf ① **factor, means** ② **proxy, representative**	① 요인 ② 대행인, 직원

27	**trickle** [tríkəl]	*v.* to flow in a thin and slow stream or drops **drip, drop, flow**	졸졸 흐르다, 똑똑 떨어지다

28	**perishable** [périʃəbəl] * *perish* 소멸하다	*adj.* liable to rot or to go bad quickly	썩기 쉬운

29	**preside** [prizáid]	*v.* to take the lead at an event; to be in charge **chair, supervise, oversee**	의장을 맡아보다, 감독하다

30	**anonymous** [ənánəməs]	*adj.* having no name; from someone whose name is not known **nameless, incognito, unidentified**	익명의, 작가 불명의

UNIT 41

 Quiz

25. *Non-Western music typically divides an interval between two pitches more finely than Western music does, _____ producing a great number of distinct tones, or microtones, within the same interval.*

26. *Organisms must be buried rapidly to escape destruction by the elements and to be protected from _____ of weathering and erosion.*

27. *The climate is dry, but tiny streams _____ at the bottom of deeply cut canyons.*

28. *Before refrigerators came into common use, people in rural areas often had a well or a springhouse to keep _____ foods fresh.*

29. *Mr. Kennedy was scheduled to _____ at 4 p.m. over a meeting of the National Security Council.*

30. *The terminology by which artists were described at the time suggests their status: "limner" was usually applied to _____ portrait painters up to the 1760s.*

Social Sciences

1 **yield**
[jiːld]

① *v.* to give up or to give in
② *n.* the amount of profits or crops that something produces
① **surrender, hand in** ② **production, output**   ① 포기하다, 양도하다 ② 생산(량)

2 **allot**
[əlát]

v. to give a share of something to each member of a group
allocate, apportion, distribute   할당하다

3 **discriminate**
[diskrímənèit]

v. to recognize a difference between things; to treat a person or group differently from another in an unfair way
differentiate, discern, segregate   식별하다, 차별하다

4 **lull**
[lʌl]

v. to make someone relaxed and calm
soothe, calm, tranquilize   달래다, 잠잠해지다

5 **lure**
[luər]

v. to tempt or to entice, often by the offer of some reward
tempt, attract, seduce   유인하다, 꾀다

6 **mason**
[méisən]

n. someone who is skilled in shaping stones for building work
stonecutter   석공, 벽돌공

7 **merger**
[mɔ́ːrdʒər]

n. a joining together, especially of business firms
consolidation, amalgamation, combination   합병, 흡수

8 **mint**
[mint]

v. to manufacture coins
coin   (화폐를) 주조하다

Quiz

1. Fertilizers can increase farmers' _____.

2. Rationing is a system for _____ scarce resources.

3. It is illegal for universities and colleges to _____ on the basis of sex, religion, or national origin.

4. Parents often sing to children to _____ them to sleep.

5. Many adults were _____ to the cities by promises of steady employment.

6. Where stone was the local building material, a _____ was sure to appear on the list of people who paid taxes.

7. A _____ is achieved when a company purchases the property of other firms.

8. Both the United States silver dollar and half-dollar, first _____ in 1794, had the figures of Liberty on one side and an eagle on the reverse side.

9	**ratify** [rǽtəfài]	*v.* to give formal consent to a treaty or agreement approve, endorse, validate	비준하다, 승인하다
10	**reverse** [rivə́:rs]	*v.* to move backward or in an opposite direction invert, transpose, overturn	거꾸로 하다, 반대로 하다
11	**irrigation** [ìrəgéiʃən]	*n.* the artificial application of water to land watering	관개, 물 대기
12	**lineage** [líniidʒ]	*n.* the way in which members of a family are descended from other members ancestry, genealogy, bloodline	혈통, 가계
13	**divulge** [divʌ́ldʒ]	*v.* to make something known; to reveal a secret expose, unveil, disclose	누설하다, 폭로하다
14	**monarchy** [mánərki]	*n.* the system in which a country is ruled by a king or queen autocracy, absolutism, monocracy	군주제
15	**municipal** [mjuːnísəpəl]	*adj.* relating to or belonging to the local government of a town or region civic, urban	시의, 도시의
16	**potential** [pouténʃəl]	*adj.* possible or likely, though as yet not tested or actual possible, dormant, latent	잠재적인, 잠재력이 있는

🎯 Quiz

9. Congress must write and _____ the declaration much like a law.

10. Today, there is a high demand for people who might be able to control or _____ the aging process.

11. The agricultural potential of the area was enormous if water for _____ could be found.

12. It can always be proven that the members of a _____ share blood ties.

13. A person who has been accused of a crime cannot be forced to _____ any information that is self-incriminating

14. Patrilineal descent is often used in _____ to determine who has the best claim on the throne.

15. Water and sewage systems were usually operated by _____ governments.

16. Real estate developers added 800,000 _____ building sites to the Chicago region in just fifty years.

17	**precarious** [prikέəriəs]	*adj.* not in complete control of something unsafe **unreliable, perilous, risky**	불안정한, 위험한

18	**notoriety** [nòutəráiəti:] * *notorious* 악명 높은	*n.* the state of being known for something bad or unfavorable **disgrace, dishonor, disrepute**	악명

19	**prejudice** [prédʒədis]	*n.* a biased opinion based on insufficient knowledge **partiality, bias, prejudgment**	편견, 선입관

20	**split** [split]	*n.* a tear or crack in something; a separation or division through disagreement **crack, rift, division**	쪼개짐, 분열

21	**appliance** [əpláiəns]	*n.* a piece of equipment, especially something electrical **gadget, contrivance**	(가정용) 기구, 장치

22	**loom** [luːm]	① *v.* to appear in an enlarged form ② *v.* to appear important or threatening and likely to happen soon ① **appear, emerge** ② **predominate**	① 어렴풋이 나타나다 ② 중요하게 생각되다

23	**dramatically** [drəmǽtikəli]	*adv.* forcefully in appearance or effect **sensationally, strikingly, suddenly**	극적으로

24	**snippet** [snípit]	*n.* a scrap of information, news, or something else **snatch, extract**	단편적인 지식

Quiz

17. Thousands abandoned their _____ lives on the farm for more secure and better paying jobs in the city.

18. He achieved _____ as chief counsel to President Nixon during the Watergate break-in.

19. Ethnic and religious _____ often influences politics.

20. It was the _____ of eleven southern states from the Union in 1861 that led to the Civil War in the United States.

21. The electric toaster was one of the earliest _____ to be developed for the kitchen.

22. After the Civil War, financial problems _____ large in both the North and the South.

23. Critics argue that urbanization has created many problems and has _____ decreased people's quality of life in cities.

24. In _____, politicians assert but do not argue.

25	**superintendent**	*n.* someone whose job is to manage a department	
	[sùːpərinténdənt]	supervisor, overseer, foreman	감독자, 관리자

26	**pertinent**	*adj.* relating to or concerned with something	
	[pə́ːrtənənt]	appropriate, pertaining, relevant	적절한, 관련이 있는

27	**trigger**	*v.* to pull a trigger or detonating device; to start a train of events	
	[trígər]	activate, propel, spark	방아쇠를 당기다, 촉발시키다

28	**cursive**	*adj.* having letters which are joined rather than printed separately	
	[kə́ːrsiv]	flowing, running	흘림으로 쓰는

29	**rank**	① *v.* to have a particular status in relation to others	
	[ræŋk]	② *n.* a position of seniority within an organization	
		① rate, grade ② status, standing	① 위치를 차지하다 ② 계급

30	**preoccupied**	*adj.* lost in thought and unaware of one's surroundings or actions	
	[priːɑ́kjəpàid]	engrossed, absorbed, rapt	몰두한, 여념이 없는

UNIT 42

 **Quiz**

25. She served as the _____ of a group of hospital nurses for the federal government.

26. It is an ability to ask _____ questions, recognize defensible answers, and reject spurious or irrelevant ones.

27. A sense of danger nearby, whether real or imagined, _____ various reactions in the body.

28. The children moved from writing in block capital letters to _____ script.

29. Despite its greater number of dead, the Russian effort _____ second place to the American effort during World War II.

30. People were becoming more and more _____ with their own lives.

Natural Sciences

1	**descend** [disénd]	*v.* to go or move down from a higher to a lower position **get down, decline, slope**	내려가다, 하강하다
2	**inexorable** [inéksərəbəl]	*adj.* incapable of being made to change a position; unrelenting **unavoidable, inevitable, merciless**	변경할 수 없는, 멈추지 않는, 용서 없는
3	**docket** [dákit]	*n.* any label accompanying a package; a list of things to be done **tag, timetable, agenda**	꼬리표, 의제
4	**commence** [kəméns]	*v.* to begin or start something **begin, initiate, launch**	시작하다, 개시하다
5	**entity** [éntiti]	*n.* something that has a physical existence as opposed to a quality or mood **being, object, thing**	실체
6	**extract** [ikstrǽkt]	*v.* to pull or draw something out, especially by force or with effort **extricate, pull, derive**	추출하다
7	**rear** [riər]	*n.* the back of something, as distinguished from the front **back, end, hind part**	뒤, 후미
8	**intense** [inténs]	*adj.* very great or extreme, especially in quality or feeling **powerful, severe, extreme**	강렬한, 극도의

Quiz

1. Smokejumpers are firefighters who _____ into remote areas by parachute to fight forest fires.

2. A glacier's process is slow but _____.

3. The moon is already on NASA's _____ for further exploration within the next couple of decades.

4. The Space Age _____ in October 1957 when Sputnik was launched by the Soviet Union.

5. But none of the shapes on the list describes the largest single _____ in the universe.

6. Hydrogen can be _____ from water sources and used as fuel.

7. As the cat rotates the front of its body clockwise, its _____ and tail twist counterclockwise so that the total spin remains zero.

8. A laser uses a synthetic ruby to concentrate light into an extremely _____ high-energy beam.

9	**plate** [pleit]	*n.* a thin and flat piece of metal; any of the rigid sections that make up the Earth's crust
		panel, layer 판, (대륙의) 판

10	**kinetic** [kinétik]	*adj.* relating to or producing motion
		motive 운동의, 운동에 의한

11	**lubricant** [lú:brəkənt]	*n.* oil, grease, or something else used to reduce friction
		윤활유, 감마제

12	**extend** [iksténd]	*v.* to make something longer or larger
		stretch, elongate, broaden 뻗다, 확장하다

13	**cast off**	*ph.* to remove something or someone that becomes unnecessary
		throw off, shed 버리다, 제거하다

14	**colony** [káləni]	① *n.* an area under the political control of a distant country ② *n.* a group of the same kind of animals or plants
		① **settlement** ② **community** ① 식민지 ② 군락, 군체

15	**porous** [pɔ́:rəs]	*adj.* referring or relating to a material that contains pores or cavities
		spongy, permeable, pervious 구멍이 많은, 침투성의

16	**discard** [diská:rd]	*v.* to get rid of something as useless or unwanted
		dispense with, dispose of, abandon 버리다, 폐기하다

 Quiz

9. *They can measure the movement of the _____ but not when they will spawn an earthquake.*

10. *When each fragment slammed into the atmosphere, its immense _____ energy was transformed into heat.*

11. *Subglacial streams of meltwater might act as a _____, allowing the glacier to flow rapidly toward the sea.*

12. *The evaporated water is replaced by water moving from inside the plant in unbroken columns that _____ from the top of a plant to its roots.*

13. *When attacked, the sea cucumber also _____ attached structures such as tentacles.*

14. *When it comes to ant _____, certain kinds of ants are divided into highly specialized positions.*

15. *_____ rocks such as chalk and sandstone allow water to soak through them.*

16. *Using its bill and tongue, the bird cracks open and _____ the woody seed covering and swallows the nutritious inner kernel.*

17	**counteract** [kàuntərǽkt]	*v.* to reduce or prevent the effect of something **counterbalance, neutralize, nullify**	거스르다, 중화하다

18	**parasite** [pǽrəsàit]	*n.* a plant or animal that lives on or in other living things **hanger-on, freeloader**	기생 동식물, 기생충

19	**peculiar** [pikjúːljər]	*adj.* strange or unusual, especially in a way that is unpleasant or worrying **odd, weird, quaint**	기묘한, 이상한

20	**predator** [prédətər]	*n.* any animal that obtains food by eating other animals	포식자, 육식 동물

21	**dwindle** [dwíndl]	*v.* to shrink in size, number, or intensity **decrease, diminish, reduce**	줄어들다, 감소하다

22	**application** [æpləkéiʃən]	*n.* the act of using something for a particular purpose **utilization, operation, use**	적용, 사용

23	**primate** [práimeit]	*n.* a member of the group of animals that includes humans and monkeys	영장류

24	**pry** [prai]	*v.* to move, raise, or open by leverage **lever, jimmy, prize**	지레로 올리다, 비틀어 열다

🛡 Quiz

17. Increased protection by the mass roots is _____ since they attract predators and are vulnerable if they are on the ground.

18. Perhaps the most straightforward dependence of one species on another occurs with _____.

19. All birds have wings, too, but wings are not _____ to birds.

20. Fish are not the only _____ of menhaden as birds also depend on them as a source of nourishment.

21. The amount of open space has _____ as more and more land is developed.

22. The _____ of GPS are wide-ranging.

23. Their astonishing research reveals that these _____ exhibit numerous highly developed physical as well as mental characteristics.

24. Squirrels _____ off the caps of acorns and bite through the shells to get at the inner kernels.

25	**benign** [bináin]	*adj*. kind and gentle; not dangerous or likely to cause death **gentle, mild, nonfatal**	온화한, 양성의
26	**hydraulic** [haidrɔ́:lik]	*adj*. moved or operated by the pressure of water or other liquid	수력의
27	**discrete** [diskrí:t]	*adj*. separate and distinct from each other **separate, individual, disconnected**	분리된, 별개의
28	**quarry** [kwɔ́:ri]	*v*. to dig stone or sand from a quarry **mine, extract**	캐다, 채굴하다
29	**scuff** [skʌf]	*v*. to brush, graze, or scrape, especially shoes or heels while walking **scrape, abrade**	문지르다, 닳게 하다
30	**sediment** [sédəmənt]	*n*. solid particles that have settled at the bottom of a liquid **deposit, grounds, remains**	침전(물), 퇴적(물)

 **Quiz**

25. Following the early Proterozoic, the climate appears to have been fairly _____ for a very long time.

26. _____ elevators are still used in some old buildings, but almost all new buildings are equipped with electrical elevators.

27. By such ingenious adaptations to specific pollinators, orchids have avoided the hazards of rampant crossbreeding in the wild, assuring the survival of species as _____ identities.

28. One of the latest methods of _____ stone is cutting the stone with a jet torch.

29. Caves are usually created by carbonate acid trickling down, but the cave was _____ out by powerful acid that rose from below.

30. A delta can build up for many centuries, and, if there is enough _____, it can produce islands.

Applied Sciences

1 adjoin
[ədʒɔ́in]

v. to be next to; to be contiguous to

neighbor, abut, border

인접하다, 접하다

2 cluster
[klʌ́stər]

① *n.* a small group or gathering
② *v.* to form into a cluster or clusters

① **collection, bunch** ② **gather**

① 떼, 집단 ② 밀집하다, 떼를 짓다

3 lug
[lʌg]

n. a part of something that sticks out and can be used as a handle or a support

grip, handle

손잡이, 자루

4 sumptuous
[sʌ́mptʃuəs]

adj. very impressive and expensive

costly, expensive, luxurious

값비싼, 호화로운

5 motif
[moutíːf]

① *n.* an idea or subject repeated throughout a work
② *n.* a single design

① **theme, topic** ② **pattern, figure**

① 주제 ② 의장

6 aerial
[ɛ́əriəl]

adj. relating to or found in the air; from a plane

공기의, 항공(기)의

7 mar
[mɑːr]

v. to spoil something; to make something less attractive or enjoyable

damage, spoil, impair

손상시키다, 훼손하다

8 pneumatic
[njuːmǽtik]

adj. filled with air; worked by air pressure

공기가 든, 공기압으로 움직이는

Quiz

1. Their rooms on upper floors could be entered both by doorways from _____ rooms and by a hole in the ceiling.

2. The motels _____ along transcontinental highways such as U.S. Routes 40 and 66.

3. Wood from a freshly cut tree was used for the _____ pole, so it would resist heat.

4. These who could afford the buildings were quite content to live in the more _____, single-family homes.

5. Stone carvers engraved _____ of skulls and crossbones and other religious icons of death into the tombstones in old burial grounds.

6. An _____ view of the border between Haiti and the Dominican Republic shows a remarkable sight.

7. _____ our gardens is one of the milder effects of weeds.

8. Compressed air provides the power to drive _____ tools.

| 9 | **paucity**
[pɔ́:səti] | *n.* less than is needed of something
lack, shortage, scarcity | 부족, 결핍 |

| 10 | **perpetuation**
[pərpètʃuéiʃən] | *n.* an endless existence for an indefinite period of time
continuance, eternity, immortality | 영속, 불멸 |

| 11 | **pesky**
[péski] | *adj.* annoying
troublesome, bothersome, disturbing | 성가신, 귀찮은 |

| 12 | **pillage**
[pílidʒ] | *v.* to steal things from a place or region, especially in a war, by using violence
loot, plunder | 약탈하다 |

| 13 | **pollutant**
[pəlú:tənt]
* *pollute* 오염시키다 | *n.* any substance or agent that pollutes
adulterant, contaminant, impurity | 오염 물질 |

UNIT 44

| 14 | **proliferate**
[proulífərèit] | *v.* to reproduce rapidly; to increase in number
grow, increase, multiply | 증식하다, 확산하다 |

| 15 | **purification**
[pjùərəfikéiʃən]
* *purify* 정화시키다 | *n.* the act or an instance of cleansing or purifying
cleansing, sanctification | 정화 |

| 16 | **fracture**
[frǽktʃər] | *n.* a crack or broken part in a bone or other hard substance
break, breakage | 골절, 분쇄 |

Quiz

9. Because of skyrocketing populations and the _____ of housing in many regions of Africa, developers are cutting back the jungle.

10. Migration is the second major hurdle the whooping crane and conservationists alike needed to overcome in order to secure the birds' _____.

11. Are squirrels dispersers and planters of oak forests or _____ seed predators?

12. Once the eggs were _____ from nests, future generations became placed even more in jeopardy.

13. In the future, even water vapor might be considered an air _____ under certain conditions.

14. The species will continue to expand and to _____ in most regions of the world.

15. Human output may temporarily overload the natural _____ scheme of the cycle.

16. We are able to repair damage such as bone _____ and injuries to the skin and muscles.

17	**cranial** [kréiniəl]	*adj.* relating to or in the region of the skull	두개골의
18	**dissection** [disékʃən]	*n.* the separation and identification of the parts of a whole **breakdown, anatomizing**	해체, 해부
19	**vein** [vein]	*n.* one of the tubes which carries blood to the heart from other parts of a body	정맥
20	**champion** [tʃǽmpiən]	*v.* to strongly support or defend a person or cause **advocate, back, support**	옹호하다
21	**acupuncture** [ǽkjupʌ̀ŋktʃər]	*n.* a treatment for pain and disease that involves pushing special needles into parts of the body	침술
22	**appendage** [əpéndidʒ]	*n.* anything added or attached to a larger or more important part **accessory, attachment, addition**	부속물, 부속기관
23	**artery** [ɑ́ːrtəri]	*n.* one of the tubes that carries blood from the heart to the rest of the body	동맥
24	**complication** [kàmpləkéiʃən]	*n.* a second disease that arises as a result of an existing one	합병증

Quiz

17. The peripheral nervous system is responsible for controlling _____, spinal, and autonomic nerves.

18. Early studies of anatomy were hampered by the authorities' disapproval of _____, and by the lack of refrigeration.

19. Cholesterol tends to get built up as excess residue in the arteries and _____ of the body.

20. For many years, doctors have _____ the view that cholesterol is a dangerous substance.

21. Two of the most popular forms of alternative therapies in the West today are _____ and herbal medicine.

22. The muscles are responsible for the actual, physical movement of our limbs and _____.

23. The pulmonary _____ carries blood from the right side of the heart to the lungs.

24. A painful _____ of diabetes may be caused by an underproduction of a hormone that nourishes and maintains the body's nervous system.

25	**microbe** [máikròub]	*n.* an extremely small living thing that can only be seen under a microscope and that may cause diseases **microorganism, germ**	미생물, 세균
26	**resin** [rézin]	*n.* a thick and sticky liquid that comes out of some trees	(나무의) 진
27	**saturated** [sǽtʃərèitid]	*adj.* extremely wet; containing as much of a solute as can be dissolved **drenched, soaked**	흠뻑 젖은, 포화 상태가 된
28	**treble** [trébəl]	*v.* to become three times as much or as many **triple, threefold**	3배가 되다
29	**summon** [sʌ́mən]	*v.* to order someone to come to a place **call, assemble, convene**	불러 모으다, 소환하다
30	**helical** [hélikəl]	*adj.* relating to or like a helix **spiral, coiling, screwlike**	나선형의

* *helix* 나선

UNIT 44

 **Quiz**

25. When fish populations become depleted due to factors like overfishing, _____ such as algae expand and threaten the fragile ecosystems of the ocean.

26. Amber is a hard, yellow-brown substance formed from the _____ of pine trees that lived millions of years ago.

27. All fats are combinations of _____ and unsaturated fatty acids.

28. A baby usually doubles his birth weight at the end of four months and _____ it at the end of one year.

29. Ultrasonic whistles, which cannot be heard by human beings, are audible to dogs and are used to _____ them.

30. Franklin used the technique known as X-ray crystallography to show that DNA has a _____, or spiral, shape.

REVIEW TEST

Choose the closest meaning to the highlighted word or phrase.

1   The organ, the clavichord, and
the harpsichord became the chief
instruments of the keyboard group, a
supremacy they maintained until the
piano supplanted them at the end of the
eighteenth century.

Ⓐ supported

Ⓑ promoted

Ⓒ replaced

Ⓓ dominated

2   Fossils are the remains and traces of
ancient plant and animal life that are
more than 10,000 years old.

Ⓐ structures

Ⓑ descendants

Ⓒ skeletons

Ⓓ imprints

3   Although the mechanisms vary
considerably, all major groups of animals
are capable of detecting and reacting to
the presence of "foreign" cells.

Ⓐ differ

Ⓑ abound

Ⓒ balance

Ⓓ exist

4   While this sort of amateur genealogy can
be entertaining, lineages used to be far
more vital to a person's social status.

Ⓐ crucial

Ⓑ deadly

Ⓒ applicable

Ⓓ dynamic

5   Chimpanzees are indigenous to Africa,
where the tree canopy provides them
with shelter, food, and protection.

Ⓐ endangered

Ⓑ rare

Ⓒ insignificant

Ⓓ native

6   The lot could also accommodate a
rectangular tenement though it could
not yield the well-lighted and logically
arranged rooms that great apartment
buildings require.

Ⓐ harvest

Ⓑ produce

Ⓒ amount

Ⓓ provide

7   With Mars looming as the eventual long-
term goal, serious questions exist as to
whether the dangers and difficulties of
a lunar settlement are too extreme and
unnecessary.

Ⓐ expanding

Ⓑ contracting

Ⓒ disappearing

Ⓓ emerging

8   In rational decision making, the pertinent
considerations that will be affected by
each decision are listed, and the relative
importance of each consideration or
consequence is determined.

Ⓐ relevant

Ⓑ preceding

Ⓒ insightful

Ⓓ instant

9   His 1969 novel, *Portnoy's Complaint*, won critical praise while triggering a storm of controversy with its candid and raw descriptions of adolescent lust and adult sexuality.

Ⓐ eliminating

Ⓑ activating

Ⓒ capturing

Ⓓ relieving

10   This finding sheds new light on the aging process that may eventually allow them to delay the inexorable process of aging and death.

Ⓐ insignificant

Ⓑ unstoppable

Ⓒ essential

Ⓓ incomprehensible

11   The drill ship was able to maintain a steady position on the ocean's surface and to drill in very deep waters, extracting samples of sediments and rock from the ocean floor.

Ⓐ breaking

Ⓑ locating

Ⓒ removing

Ⓓ analyzing

12   The range of the New York canal system was further extended when the states of Ohio and Indiana, inspired by the success of the Erie Canal, provided water connections between Lake Erie and the Ohio River.

Ⓐ increased

Ⓑ constructed

Ⓒ deepened

Ⓓ measured

13   Parasites such as the acarids or itch mites or scabies are barely visible, and helminths, or worms, may grow to be several feet long.

Ⓐ Hosts

Ⓑ Bacteria

Ⓒ Fragments

Ⓓ Leeches

14   Each stone tool had its own peculiar characteristics that demanded a certain way of cutting or drying the meat.

Ⓐ unique

Ⓑ uniform

Ⓒ universal

Ⓓ biological

15   Benign tumors usually do not cause death although they may if they interfere with a normal body function by virtue of their location or size.

Ⓐ Extreme

Ⓑ Moderate

Ⓒ Catastrophic

Ⓓ Infectious

16   The simplest of these is the carbon dioxide from the respiration of an ant cluster, a chemical that acts as a pheromone to promote aggregation.

Ⓐ organ

Ⓑ activity

Ⓒ group

Ⓓ collision

Humanities

1. **maritime**
[mǽrətàim]
adj. connected with the sea in relation to navigation; pertaining to the sea
marine, nautical, oceanic
해상의, 해양의

2. **jolly**
[dʒáli]
adj. good-humored; pleasant and enjoyable
joyful, cheerful, merry
명랑한, 기분이 좋은

3. **shun**
[ʃʌn]
v. to intentionally avoid or keep away from someone or something
avoid, eschew, stay away from
피하다, 멀리하다

4. **envision**
[invíʒən]
v. to picture mentally some future events
envisage, imagine, visualize
상상하다, 마음 속에 그리다

5. **depict**
[dipíkt]
v. to describe something or someone in writing or to show someone or something in a painting
describe, characterize, picture
묘사하다

6. **tremendously**
[triméndəsli]
adv. greatly in size, amount, or intensity
enormously, vastly, utterly
막대하게, 엄청나게

7. **vigorous**
[vígərəs]
adj. strong and active
brisk, dynamic, energetic
활기찬, 정력적인

8. **vocalize**
[vóukəlàiz]
v. to utter or produce something with the voice
articulate, verbalize, speak
소리 내어 말하다

Quiz

1. The Native American people of the north Pacific Coast created a highly complex _____ culture.

2. The _____ character Falstaff is one of Shakespeare's finest comic creations.

3. The Shakers were a strict religious group that _____ all types of pleasure.

4. Before hunting, hunters would draw and study migrating animals and _____ having a successful hunt.

5. In their novels, Joel Chandler Harris and Ellen Glasgow _____ life in the South.

6. During the Great Depression, the economy suffered _____.

7. The Board of Health took _____ measures to bring the tenement houses of New York up to the best sanitary condition.

8. The Malcolm X march has often been used as an outlet to _____ discontent over the development of Harlem.

| 9 | **puzzling**
[pʌ́zliŋ] | *adj.* confusing and difficult to understand or explain
baffling, perplexing, bewildering | 당황스러운, 헷갈리게 하는 |

| 10 | **usher**
[ʌ́ʃər] | *v.* to escort someone into a place
guide, direct, lead | 안내하다, 인도하다 |

| 11 | **complement**
[kámpləmənt] | ① *v.* to make up a lack of something
② *n.* something that completes or perfects another
① **complete, enhance** ② **supplement** | ① 보충하다 ② 보완물 |

| 12 | **eerie**
[íəri] | *adj.* strange and disturbing or frightening
uncanny, weird, creepy | 기묘한, 섬뜩한 |

| 13 | **entice**
[intáis] | *v.* to tempt by arousing hopes or desires or by promising a reward
seduce, lure, tempt | 꾀다, 유혹하다 |

| 14 | **jargon**
[dʒá:rgən] | *n.* the specialized vocabulary of a particular profession
argot, cant, lingo | 은어, 특수 용어, 전문 용어 |

| 15 | **roll back** | *ph.* to return to a lower level of prices, wages, or something else | (물가 등을) 어느 수준까지 도로 내리다 |

| 16 | **maintenance**
[méintənəns] | *n.* the process of keeping something in good condition
continuance, persistence | 지속, 유지 |

🎯 Quiz

9. Sherlock Holmes, a fictional detective, solved many _____ crimes.

10. In 1839, the daguerreotype was introduced to America, _____ in the age of photography.

11. Movie directors use music to _____ the action on the screen.

12. The writer H.P. Lovecraft wrote many _____ stories about the supernatural.

13. Vance Packard's book, The Hidden Persuaders deals with the tactics advertisers use to _____ consumers.

14. Technical _____ greatly accelerate changes in usage, often blurring the definitions of words and fracturing the grammatical rules of purists.

15. In 1979, Santa Monica's municipal government ordered landlords to _____ their rents to the levels charged in 1978.

16. Rental prices promote the efficient _____ of existing housing and stimulate the construction of new housing.

17	**kiln** [kiln]	*n.* a heated oven or furnace used for drying or for firing something **furnace, oven**	가마, 노
18	**carve** [kɑ:rv]	*v.* to cut wood, stone, or something else into a shape **hew, sculpt, engrave**	조각하다
19	**rehearse** [rihə́:rs]	*v.* to practice something before performing it in front of an audience **exercise, practice**	예행연습을 하다, 리허설하다
20	**time-wise** [taimwaiz]	*adv.* with regard to time	시간에 대해서
21	**mythology** [miθɑ́lədʒi]	*n.* ancient myths in general **folklore, lore, stories**	신화
22	**deteriorate** [ditíəriərèit]	*v.* to grow worse **worsen, degrade**	악화시키다, (가치가) 저하되다
23	**homage** [hɑ́midʒ]	*n.* a display of great respect toward someone **respect, admiration, esteem**	존경, 경의
24	**carcass** [kɑ́:rkəs]	*n.* the dead body of an animal **corpse, remains**	(동물의) 시체

 **Quiz**

17. More and more large _____ were built to create the high-fired stoneware.

18. Sculptors use hammers and chisels to _____ statues out of stone.

19. Musicians have to _____ before performing.

20. Because the railroad was more efficient and reliable _____, it quickly became the dominant mode of transportation.

21. In the seventh and sixth centuries, potters depicted episodes from _____ and ancient Greek heroic narratives.

22. Fired clay does not _____ over time.

23. The priests transcribed their _____ in Egyptian and Greek using the three prevailing scripts of the day.

24. An important function of early stone tools was to extract highly nutritious food from large animal _____.

25	**tactics** [tǽktiks]	*n.* the art or science of disposing military forces for battle maneuvers, strategy, plans	전술
26	**cathartic** [kəθάːrtik]	*adj.* helping someone to remove strong or violent emotions purgative, cleansing	카타르시스의, 정화의
27	**logistical** [loudʒístikəl]	*adj.* relating to supplies carried by an army	병참의
28	**spectacular** [spektǽkjələr]	*adj.* impressively striking to see or watch dramatic, splendid, sensational	장관인, 멋진
29	**unravel** [ʌnrǽvəl]	*v.* to separate the strands of a knitted fabric; to explain something that is mysterious or complicated untwine, untangle, solve	풀다, 해명하다
30	**obscure** [əbskjúər]	*adj.* not clearly understood or expressed uncertain, confusing, ambiguous	불명료한, 애매한

UNIT 45

 **Quiz**

25. *It is a reflection of the American and Russian commanders' battle _____, with the former being more concerned with saving lives.*

26. *Through songs and the oral tradition, slaves were able to be free in a sense, which became _____ for them.*

27. *A great _____ effort was required to support both its own forces and those of many other nations.*

28. *D.W. Griffith was the first director of _____ films. There were movies made on a colossal scale.*

29. *The pot's history, manufacture, cultural context, economic role, and ornamental use are all points of information one hopes to _____.*

30. *The poetry of Ezra Pound is sometimes difficult to understand because it contains so many _____ references.*

Social Sciences

1	**preach** [priːtʃ]	*v.* to deliver a sermon as part of a religious service; to talk about something in order to persuade people to accept it evangelize, sermonize, urge	설교하다, 전도하다
2	**abound** [əbáund]	*v.* to present in large numbers teem, overflow	풍부하다
3	**accelerate** [æksélərèit]	*v.* to increase the speed of something hasten, quicken, speed	가속하다
4	**pastoral** [pǽstərəl]	*adj.* relating to the countryside or country life rustic, rural, provincial	전원의, 목가적인
5	**plush** [plʌʃ]	*adj.* expensively or showily luxurious luxurious, opulent, lavish	사치스러운, 호화로운
6	**shrewd** [ʃruːd]	*adj.* possessing or showing keen judgment gained from practical experience astute, clever, sharp	기민한
7	**stabilize** [stéibəlàiz]	*v.* to make or become firm or steady balance, steady, fix	안정(화)시키다
8	**rejuvenate** [ridʒúːvənèit]	*v.* to make someone feel young again reinvigorate, renew, revitalize	활기차게 하다, 원기를 회복하다

Quiz

1. Before the Great Depression, classical economics _____ the theory of laissez-faire.

2. All sorts of fine trees were _____, and those who pushed westward encountered new forests as well.

3. The opening of the Erie Canal in 1825 _____ the development of commerce on the Great Lakes.

4. Some hunters and gatherers continued the old _____ and nomadic ways.

5. The accommodations were by no means _____.

6. A _____ businesswoman, Oprah has inspired trends in the marketplace simply by mentioning a product on the air.

7. The International Monetary Fund was created to _____ exchange rates without interfering with the growth of trade.

8. Music can help to _____ or soothe the patient.

9	**vying** [vaiiŋ] * *vie* 경쟁하다	*adj.* competing with someone for some gain or advantage competing, contending, struggling	경쟁하는, 겨루는
10	**abolish** [əbáliʃ]	*v.* to put an end to customs, laws, or something else eliminate, terminate, obliterate	폐지하다
11	**precursor** [priːkə́ːrsər]	*n.* something that comes before another and leads to it forerunner, harbinger, herald	선임자, 전조
12	**uncanny** [ʌnkǽni]	*adj.* having a supernatural or inexplicable basis; beyond the ordinary supernatural, unnatural, unaccountable	초인적인
13	**reciprocal** [risíprəkəl]	*adj.* giving and receiving or given and received mutual, complementary, shared	상호적인, 호혜의
14	**replicate** [répləkèit]	*v.* to reproduce or copy something exactly copy, duplicate, transcribe	복제하다, 복사하다
15	**revolt** [rivóult]	① *v.* to rise up against a government ② *v.* to provoke a feeling of disgust ① rebel, mutiny ② disgust, offend	① 반란을 일으키다 ② 불쾌하게 하다
16	**gratify** [grǽtəfài]	*v.* to give pleasure to a person by satisfying desires please, satisfy, delight	만족시키다, (욕구 등을) 채우다

UNIT 46

🛡 Quiz

9. In the 1880s, five railroads were _____ for traffic between New York and Chicago.

10. In 1864, the House resumed the consideration of the constitutional amendment to _____ slavery.

11. The icebox was a _____ of the modern refrigerator.

12. Abraham Maslow possessed an _____ intelligence that put him in the company of the greatest social thinkers of the day.

13. The _____ relationship ensured that all would have a means of survival.

14. Researchers make tools that _____ excavated specimens as closely as possible.

15. While infanticide may _____ the vast majority of people, it has its purpose within the animal kingdom.

16. He observed that individuals whose basic needs had been _____ performed differently from dissatisfied people.

17	**sire** [saiər]	*v.* to be a father of young **father, generate, create**	~의 아버지가 되다, ~을 낳게 하다
18	**upheaval** [ʌphíːvəl]	*n.* a strong or violent change or disturbance, as in a society **upset, disruption, disturbance**	대이변, 격동
19	**aspiration** [æspəréiʃən]	*n.* a strong desire for high achievement **ambition, dream, yearning**	포부, 열망
20	**coordinate** [kouɔ́ːrdəneit]	*v.* to integrate and adjust a number of different parts or processes **systematize, organize, harmonize**	종합하다, 조정하다
21	**union** [júːnjən]	*n.* an association, confederation, or group of people united for a common goal; a trade union **alliance, coalition, league**	연합, 노동조합
22	**autocratic** [ɔ́ːtəkrǽtik]	*adj.* pertaining to autocracy or exercising power or authority without interference by others **tyrannical, despotic, dictatorial**	독재의, 전제의
23	**lucid** [lúːsid]	*adj.* bright or shining; clearly presented and easily understood **luminous, distinct, clear**	빛나는, 명료한
24	**morale** [mouræl]	*n.* the level of confidence or optimism in a person or group **spirit, confidence, self-esteem**	사기

Quiz

17. *Among some species, males that take over a group of females kill every child _____ by the other males.*

18. *Political discontent arises when existing political parties fail to give voice to those frustrated by social _____ .*

19. *In addition to his political _____, he served as the leader of the Green Mountain Boys.*

20. *Political parties help to _____ the campaigns of their members.*

21. *In 1886, many national _____ formed the American Federation of Labor under the leadership of Samuel Gompers.*

22. *An _____ ruler who serves his people well is sometimes called a benevolent dictator.*

23. *Julius Caesar is known for his political skills and for his _____, informative writing.*

24. *The USO is a service organization that entertains U.S. troops and improves their _____ .*

| 25 | **substantially** | *adv.* in real worth, value, or effect | |
| | [səbstǽnʃəli] | **actually, practically, virtually** | 실질적으로, 실제적으로 |

| 26 | **dogma** | *n.* a belief or principle laid down by an authority as unquestionably true | |
| | [dɔ́(:)gmə] | **creed, doctrine, tenet** | 교의, 교리 |

| 27 | **endow** | *v.* to provide a source of income for an organization | |
| | [endáu] | **donate, grant, contribute** | 기부하다, 기여하다 |

| 28 | **inevitably** | *adv.* without possibility of escape | |
| | [inévitəbli] | **inescapably, unavoidably, certainly** | 불가피하게, 어쩔 수 없이 |

| 29 | **wharf** | *n.* a landing-stage built along a waterfront for loading and unloading vessels | |
| | [hwɔːrf] | **pier, dock** | 부두 |

| 30 | **arable** | *adj.* suitable or used for plowing and growing crops | |
| | [ǽrəbəl] | | 경작할 수 있는 |

UNIT 46

 **Quiz**

25. *The effect of advertising increased _____ as ads for products like coffee, tea, and chocolate appeared in newspapers.*

26. *The experiments with the animals eroded the behaviorist _____ that only humans have minds.*

27. *Massachusetts used much of its funds to _____ the Massachusetts Institute of Technology.*

28. *The focus of educators _____ turned toward the lower grades and back to basic academic skills and discipline.*

29. *The largest companies have fired many employees, and many of their vessels sit idle at the _____.*

30. *Land refers to all natural resources usable in the production process: _____ land, forests, and so on.*

Natural Sciences

| 1 | **arid**
[ǽrid] | *adj.* having so little rain as to be very dry and unproductive
desert, dry, torrid | 메마른 |

| 2 | **precipitation**
[prisìpətéiʃən] | *n.* water that falls from clouds in the atmosphere to the Earth's surface
rainfall, shower, downpour | 강수(량) |

| 3 | **rim**
[rim] | *n.* the outside edge or border of, especially a round object
edge, brim, border | 가장자리 |

| 4 | **incinerate**
[insínərèit] | *v.* to burn or reduce to ashes
burn | 태우다, 재로 만들다 |

| 5 | **inhospitable**
[inháspitəbəl] | *adj.* not friendly or welcoming to others
unwelcoming, unfriendly, unfavorable | 대접이 나쁜, 불친절한 |

| 6 | **intensity**
[inténsəti] | *n.* the quality or state of being intense
power, strength, forcefulness | 강도, 세기 |

| 7 | **lethal**
[líːθəl] | *adj.* causing or enough to cause death
fatal, mortal, deadly | 치명적인, 치사의 |

| 8 | **ambient**
[ǽmbiənt] | *adj.* relating to the surrounding area
surrounding | 주위의, 주변의 |

Quiz

1. *Southern Arizona has an _____ climate, and there are some deserts.*

2. *Deserts are regions that receive less than 25 centimeters of annual _____.*

3. *The totally eclipsed moon will appear to have a bright _____ along its southern edge.*

4. *The asteroid impact caused an explosion that quickly expanded as each icy mass _____ itself.*

5. *According to the evidence gathered by space probes and astronomers, Mars is an _____ planet.*

6. *The habitable zone is the region 75 to 140 million miles away from a star with the _____ of our sun.*

7. *Mars has no ozone layer to screen out the sun's _____ radiation.*

8. *The report, which was prepared for the Environmental Protection Agency, stated that the level of lead in _____ air poses a significant threat to infants.*

9	**acidic** [əsídik]	*adj.* like, or containing, acid; very sour **sour, tart**	산성의, 매우 신
10	**ominous** [ámənəs]	*adj.* containing a warning of something evil or bad that will happen **foreboding, sinister**	불길한
11	**radiation** [rèidiéiʃən]	*n.* the energy in the form of heat or light that is sent out as waves **emission, emanation, diffusion**	(빛, 열 등의) 방사, 발산
12	**resonance** [rézənəns]	*n.* the sound produced in an object by sound of a similar frequency from another object **vibration, echo, reverberation**	공명, 반향
13	**aggression** [əgréʃən]	*n.* the act or tendency of attacking another person or country without being provoked **attack, belligerence, hostility**	공격(성)
14	**speculate** [spékjəlèit]	*v.* to consider the possibilities regarding something **postulate, hypothesize, conjecture**	추측하다
15	**bizarre** [bizá:r]	*adj.* weirdly odd or strange **odd, peculiar, weird**	별난, 기묘한
16	**carnivore** [ká:rnəvɔ̀:r]	*n.* an animal that feeds mainly on the flesh of other animals	육식 동물

UNIT 47

🔵 Quiz

9. *Rain is slightly _____ even in unpolluted air.*

10. *The black clouds of a gathering thunderstorm look quite _____.*

11. *The nuclear chamber continues to smolder and to emit harmful _____ into the air and water.*

12. *The musical tone of an electric guitar is created not by the _____ of the body of the guitar but by electronic amplification.*

13. *Within this colony, there is little _____ among ants from different nests.*

14. *Experts have _____ that there may have been a cycle of dry and wet seasons.*

15. *What else can be said about the _____ animal that eats mud is that it feeds almost continuously day and night.*

16. *Our image of dinosaurs is either of massive herbivores like the Brontosaurus or of _____ such as the Tyrannosaurus Rex.*

17	**torque** [tɔːrk]	*n.* the measured ability of a rotating element to overcome turning resistance	회전력, 토크
18	**scale** [skeil]	① *v.* to climb up ② *n.* an extent or level relative to others ① ascend, mount ② range, scope	① 오르다 ② 규모
19	**scavenger** [skǽvindʒər]	*n.* a person or animal that searches among waste for usable items or food prowler	청소부, 청소 동물
20	**blistering** [blístəriŋ]	*adj.* viciously angry and aggressive harsh, critical	호된, 통렬한
21	**untamed** [ʌntéimd] ＊ *tame* 길들이다	*adj.* undomesticated or uncultivated unsubdued, savage, wild	길들지 않는, 야성의
22	**accessible** [æksésəbəl]	*adj.* able to be reached easily approachable, attainable, available	접근할 수 있는
23	**apparatus** [æpəréitəs]	*n.* the equipment needed for a specified purpose device, gear, machine	장치, 기계
24	**sieve** [siv]	① *n.* a utensil with a meshed or perforated bottom ② *v.* to strain or sift with a sieve ① mesh, net ② filter, screen	① 체, 조리 ② 체로 거르다

🧭 Quiz

17. While nobody can acquire spin without _____, a flexible one, like a cat, can readily change its orientation.

18. One of the most popular peaks for mountain climbers to _____ is El Capitan in Yosemite National Park.

19. Like vultures, condors are _____, so they eat animals that are already dead.

20. Its climate, despite more than 50 inches of annual rainfall, is _____.

21. Hawaii's variety of _____ volcanic ranges and pristine beaches attracts many tourists who enjoy the diverse wilderness.

22. Rivers also reveal clay along their banks, and erosion on a hillside may make the clay easily _____.

23. Though delicate _____ are used, volcanoes have been great mysteries.

24. Clay is far too small to _____ accurately.

| 25 | **scourge** | *n.* a cause of great suffering and affliction | |
| | [skə:rdʒ] | affliction, misery, plague | 원한, 재앙 |

| 26 | **skim** | *v.* to remove floating matter from the surface of a liquid | |
| | [skim] | cream, scoop, take off | (위에 뜬 찌끼를) 걷어내다 |

| 27 | **trench** | *n.* a long and narrow ditch in the ground | |
| | [trent□] | channel, furrow, pit | 도랑, 참호, 해구 |

| 28 | **thruster** | *n.* a rocket attached to a spacecraft used to control its attitude | |
| | [θrʌ́stər] | | 추진 장치 |

| 29 | **accumulate** | *v.* to collect or gather something in an increasing quantity | |
| | [əkjú:mjəlèit] | amass, stock, pile up | 축적하다, 쌓이다 |

| 30 | **homogeneous** | *adj.* made up of elements that are all of the same kind or nature | |
| | [hòumədʒí:niəs] | uniform, consistent, identical | 동질적인 |

UNIT 47

Quiz

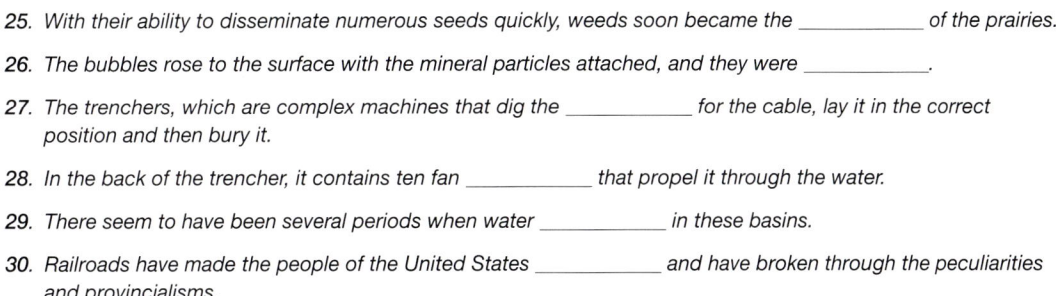

25. *With their ability to disseminate numerous seeds quickly, weeds soon became the _____ of the prairies.*

26. *The bubbles rose to the surface with the mineral particles attached, and they were _____.*

27. *The trenchers, which are complex machines that dig the _____ for the cable, lay it in the correct position and then bury it.*

28. *In the back of the trencher, it contains ten fan _____ that propel it through the water.*

29. *There seem to have been several periods when water _____ in these basins.*

30. *Railroads have made the people of the United States _____ and have broken through the peculiarities and provincialisms.*

Chapter 12

Applied Sciences

#	Word	Definition
1	**reorient** [ri:ɔ́:riènt]	*v.* to set or arrange in a new or different determinate position **modify** 재정립하다

* *orient* 방향을 정하다

2 deciduous [disídʒuːəs]
adj. involving plants which shed all their leaves at a certain time of year
낙엽성의

3 expedient [ikspí:diənt]
adj. useful or helpful for a purpose
beneficial, effective, practical
편리한

4 stake [steik]
① *n.* an interest, especially a financial one
② *n.* a sum of money risked in betting
① **interest, share** ② **bet**
① 이해관계 ② 내기에 건 돈

5 adverse [ædvə́:rs]
adj. going against; unfavorable to one's interests
contrary, negative, hostile
역의, 거스르는, 적대적인

6 replenish [ripléniʃ]
v. to fill up or make complete again
refill, restock, restore
보충하다, 다시 채우다

7 resilient [rizíljənt]
adj. able to recover quickly
elastic, flexible, springy
복원력이 있는

8 sanctuary [sǽŋktʃuèri]
① *n.* a holy or sacred place, like a church or temple
② *n.* an area for birds or animals where they cannot be hunted
① **sanctum, shrine** ② **reservation**
① 성역 ② 보호 구역

 **Quiz**

1. Railroads reshaped the North American environment and _____ North American behavior.

2. This pest defoliates ornamental trees such as _____ oaks.

3. He felt that there must be a more _____ way to send messages.

4. Holding a large _____ in the community, nineteenth-century American hotelkeepers exercised power to make it prosper.

5. Penicillin can have an _____ effect on a person who is allergic to it.

6. There is no easy source of hydrogen to _____ the supply.

7. By ridding the ocean of weaker fish, predators allow the stronger ones to multiply, making their species more _____.

8. The designation of a marine _____ indicates that it is a protected area, just as a national park is.

9	**sedentary** [sédəntèri]	*adj.* involving much sitting; not moving from one place to another **seated, stationary, unmoving**	앉아 있는, 정착의
10	**stagnant** [stǽgnənt]	*adj.* not flowing; not developing or growing **motionless, standing, stale**	괴어 있는, 정체된
11	**suffocate** [sʌ́fəkèit]	*v.* to kill or be killed by a lack of air **choke, stifle**	~의 숨을 막다, 질식하다
12	**nemesis** [néməsis]	*n.* a person or thing that causes serious harm as punishment **enemy, foe, rival**	적, 천벌
13	**hatch** [hætʃ]	*v.* to break out of an egg; to produce young animals from eggs **breed, incubate, brood**	부화하다, 알을 품다
14	**surrender** [səréndər]	*v.* to admit defeat by giving oneself up to an enemy **give up, concede, yield**	항복하다, 굴복하다
15	**symbiotic** [sìmbaiátik]	*adj.* relating to a relationship in which organisms, people, or living things involved depend on each other	공생의, 공생관계의
16	**glucose** [glúːkous]	*n.* a natural form of sugar found in fruit and used in the body	포도당

UNIT 48

 ## Quiz

9. *Aphids are particularly vulnerable to predators because of their gregarious habits and _____ nature.*

10. *A cupful of _____ water may contain millions of microorganisms.*

11. *If the bacteria are not kept in check, they could _____ the oceans.*

12. *He believed AIDS is our collective _____.*

13. *Female sea turtles swim as much as 2,000 kilometers to return to the beaches where they were _____.*

14. *The military was charged with defending the nation's forests and had orders to kill illegal loggers who did not _____.*

15. *A _____ relationship is when two organisms of different species "work together" and each benefit from the relationship.*

16. *_____ does not have to be digested, so it can be put directly into the bloodstream.*

| 17 | **prosthetic**
[prɑsθétik] | *adj.* relating to a device that substitutes for or supplements a missing or defective part of the body |
| | | 보철의, 의치의 |

| 18 | **amnesia**
[æmníːʒə] | *n.* a loss of memory, either in part or completely
forgetfulness |
| | | 기억 상실(증), 건망증 |

| 19 | **analgesic**
[æ̀nəldʒíːziks] | *n.* a remedy that relieves or allays pain
painkiller |
| | | 진통제 |

| 20 | **antibiotic**
[æ̀ntibaiátik] | *n.* a substance like penicillin which is used in the treatment of bacterial infections |
| | | 항생제 |

| 21 | **hypnosis**
[hipnóusis] | *n.* an induced sleeplike state in which a person is deeply relaxed
hypnotism, mesmerism |
| | | 최면 (상태) |

| 22 | **insomnia**
[insámniə] | *n.* a condition where the individual has trouble falling asleep or wakes up repeatedly during the night
sleeplessness, wakefulness |
| | | 불면증 |

| 23 | **terminology**
[tə̀ːrmənálədʒi] | *n.* the words and phrases used in a particular subject or field
jargon, lingo, argot |
| | | 전문 용어, 술어 |

| 24 | **ulcer**
[ʌ́lsər] | *n.* a sore place appearing on the skin inside or outside the body which may bleed or produce poisonous matter
sore, abscess, canker |
| | | 궤양, 종기 |

Quiz

17. A _____ leg enables a person to function without the assistance of a wheelchair or crutches.

18. In cases of a minor injury to the brain, _____ is likely to be a temporary condition.

19. _____ are used to relieve *pain and reduce fever.*

20. Fungi are the source of many of the most potent _____ used in clinical medicine, including penicillin.

21. _____ is sometimes employed as a means of helping people to quit smoking.

22. The causes of _____ are usually psychological in the form of stress, depression, and too much worrying.

23. In very loose _____, the right hemisphere of the brain controls the left side of the body.

24. People with _____ must eat bland foods.

25	**secrete** [sikríːt]	*v.* to form and release a substance release, ooze, exude	분비하다
26	**volatility** [vὰlətíləti]	*n.* the property of changing readily from a solid or liquid to a vapor	휘발성
27	**weld** [weld]	*v.* to join two pieces of metal; to unite something together firmly join, unite, combine	용접하다, 결합시키다
28	**streamlined** [stríːmlàind]	*adj.* designed to offer the least possible resistance; optimally shaped hydrodynamic, aerodynamic, efficient	유선형의, 효율적인
29	**revolutionize** [rèvəlúːʃənàiz]	*v.* to bring about revolution; to change dramatically	혁명을 일으키다, 대변혁을 일으키다
30	**serene** [səríːn]	*adj.* calm and composed tranquil, peaceful, pacific	고요한, 평온한

Quiz

25. Pheromones are _____ to the outside of the body and cause other individuals to have specific reactions.

26. The chemical signal can be persistent depending upon the _____ of the chemical.

27. There are two gas tanks connected to the _____ equipment; one is full of oxygen, and the other is full of acetylene.

28. The challenge is to build a wing _____ enough to fly at high speeds for long distances.

29. Iron production was _____ in the early eighteenth century when coke was first used instead of charcoal for refining iron ore.

30. The architects emphasized the need for natural, _____ settings where hurried urban dwellers could periodically escape from the city.

Choose the closest meaning to the highlighted word or phrase.

1　His characters were used to **depict** real people, and he was interested in showing the reality of human weakness as much as possible.

　Ⓐ ridicule

　Ⓑ amuse

　Ⓒ describe

　Ⓓ imitate

2　The harpsichord, with its bright, **vigorous** tone, was the favorite instrument to support the bass in the small orchestra's of the period.

　Ⓐ gloomy

　Ⓑ denouncing

　Ⓒ hesitating

　Ⓓ energetic

3　The purpose of this **special jargon** is not to mystify non-psychologists; rather, it allows psychologists to accurately describe the phenomena they are discussing and to communicate with each other effectively.

　Ⓐ lingo

　Ⓑ credit

　Ⓒ statement

　Ⓓ symbol

4　Whereas the surfaces of the Earth-like planets are visible with telescopes and space probes, the cores of the Jovian planets remain **obscured** by thick layers of gaseous atmosphere.

　Ⓐ disclosed

　Ⓑ heated

　Ⓒ hidden

　Ⓓ untouched

5　By centering politics on the person of the candidate, television **accelerated** the citizen's focus on character rather than on issues.

　Ⓐ allowed

　Ⓑ increased

　Ⓒ required

　Ⓓ started

6　By 1885, a **substantial** amount of indirect evidence indicated that chromosomes — dark-staining threads in the cell nucleus — carried information on cell heredity.

　Ⓐ consequent

　Ⓑ meager

　Ⓒ intensive

　Ⓓ noticeable

7　Accordingly, Whistler preferred to describe these paintings as an arrangement — much as music is an arrangement of pure forms — making him a **precursor** to abstract art.

　Ⓐ descendant

　Ⓑ follower

　Ⓒ patron

　Ⓓ ancestor

8　An airplane can fly because of its ability to **coordinate** four forces: lift, weight, thrust, and drag.

　Ⓐ evaluate

　Ⓑ prove

　Ⓒ display

　Ⓓ harmonize

9 The University of Texas, which has several branches, is one of the most heavily **endowed** schools in the country.

Ⓐ framed

Ⓑ donated

Ⓒ trained

Ⓓ regulated

10 The Great Lakes of North America lie in ancient river valleys or lowlands that were gouged deeper by glaciers while their **rims** were built up by glacial deposits.

Ⓐ portions

Ⓑ cores

Ⓒ edges

Ⓓ decks

11 The other effect precipitation has on nuclear waste is much more immediate and **ominous**.

Ⓐ evident

Ⓑ threatening

Ⓒ meager

Ⓓ complicate

12 Any type of electromagnetic energy, such as transformers and power lines, may produce harmful **radiation**.

Ⓐ emanations

Ⓑ evaporation

Ⓒ explosives

Ⓓ consolidation

13 The advantage of nesting on cliffs is the immunity it gives from foxes, which cannot **scale** the sheer rocks, and from ravens and other species of gulls, which have difficulty landing on narrow ledges to steal eggs.

Ⓐ climb

Ⓑ descend

Ⓒ approach

Ⓓ measure

14 Limestone is rock that is created in shallow seas from the gradual **accumulation** of dead marine animals such as coral.

Ⓐ deterioration

Ⓑ exposure

Ⓒ motion

Ⓓ collection

15 A useful definition of an air pollutant is a compound added directly or indirectly by humans to the atmosphere in such quantities as to affect humans, animals, vegetation, or materials **adversely**.

Ⓐ negatively

Ⓑ swiftly

Ⓒ admittedly

Ⓓ considerably

16 The Malthusian catastrophe has already occurred in isolated cultures that had no means of **replenishing** their resources.

Ⓐ refilling

Ⓑ protecting

Ⓒ creating

Ⓓ altering

Part 04
피수 VOCA

Humanities

1	**subsidize** [sʌ́bsidàiz]	*v.* to provide or support with a subsidy finance, fund, sponsor	보조금을 지급하다, (자금 등을) 후원하다

2 **utter**
[ʌ́tər]

① *adj.* having no exceptions or restrictions
② *v.* to express a thought or emotion in words
① complete, thorough ② state

① 전적인, 철저한 ② 말하다, 언급하다

3 **article**
[áːrtikl]

① *n.* an object
② *n.* a short written composition in a newspaper
① item ② essay, report

① 물품 ② 기사

4 **convergence**
[kənvə́ːrdʒəns]

n. the coming together of two or more things to the same point
confluence, conjunction, meeting

(한 점으로의) 집중, 수렴, 모임

5 **hilarious**
[hilέəriəs]

adj. very funny or humorous
amusing, comical, merry

아주 재미있는, 즐거운

6 **jester**
[dʒéstər]

n. a colorfully-dressed professional clown
clown, joker

어릿광대

7 **puppet**
[pʌ́pit]

n. a type of doll that can be operated by strings or sticks
marionette

꼭두각시

8 **memoir**
[mémwɑːr]

n. a record of events written by a person having knowledge of them
biography, life, reminiscence

전기, 회고록

Quiz

1. One award _____ a promising American writer's visit to Rome.

2. This movie illustrates people's _____ helplessness in the face of machines meant to serve their basic needs.

3. The Pomo people used four distinct variations on the basic twining process, often employing more than one of them in a single _____.

4. From this unity created by the _____ of artists from various social and geographical backgrounds came a new spirit.

5. Shirley Jackson's sometimes chilling, sometimes _____ stories were largely ignored by critics when they were published.

6. This funny costume reminds you of a _____ or even a woman.

7. Music based on Indonesian music was used in the shadow _____ theater of that region.

8. A _____ is restricted in scope, and it is usually shorter than an autobiography.

9	**obscenity** [əbsénəti] * *obscene* 음란한	*n.* the state or quality of being obscene **bawdiness, vulgarity, filthiness**	외설, 음란
10	**prosaic** [prouzéiik]	*adj.* not poetic; boring or ordinary **unimaginative, common, routine**	산문조의, 평범한, 단조로운
11	**auditory** [ɔ́ditɔ̀ːri]	*adj.* referring to hearing or the organs involved in hearing **acoustic, aural, auricular**	청각의
12	**utensil** [juːténsəl]	*n.* an implement or tool, especially one for everyday or domestic use **tool, implement, device**	도구, 용구
13	**cumbersome** [kʌ́mbərsəm]	*adj.* difficult to use or operate, especially because of size, weight, or design **awkward, clumsy, unhandy**	방해가 되는, 성가신
14	**strategic** [strətíːdʒik]	*adj.* done as a part of a plan, especially in a military or business **tactical**	전략적인
15	**coarse** [kɔːrs]	*adj.* of low quality; not having a level or smooth surface **crude, inferior, rough**	조잡한, (천 등이) 거친
16	**infiltrate** [infíltreit]	*v.* to filter something like a liquid; to pass into a territory **insinuate, permeate, sneak**	스며들다, 침투하다

UNIT 49

🌀 Quiz

9. *Also influential was a novel by Williams S. Burroughs, Naked Lunch, which also survived an _____ trial.*

10. *For babies, language is a sensory-motor delight rather than the route to _____ meaning that it often is for adults.*

11. *Babies' responses to the sound of the human voice are different from their responses to other sorts of _____ stimuli.*

12. *The fork has been used as an eating _____ at least since the twelfth century.*

13. *As a part of a _____ process, a pit was dug, and a platform was set up across it.*

14. *Another area to take into consideration was the _____ bombing campaign.*

15. *The Egyptians made _____ fibers by 1600 B.C., and fibers survived as decorations on Egyptian pottery dating back to 1375 B.C.*

16. *Using the cover of darkness, the soldiers _____ the enemy's defenses.*

17	**niche** [nitʃ]	*n.* a shallow recess suitable for a thing; a position in life in which one feels fulfilled
		alcove, hollow, place 벽감, 적합한 장소, 적소

18	**eccentricity** [èksentrísəti]	*n.* an odd or peculiar habit
		unusualness, strangeness, peculiarity 이상함, 엉뚱함

19	**rote** [rout]	*n.* the mechanical use of the memory to perform something without thinking
		memory 기계적 기억, 기계적인 암기

20	**shard** [ʃɑːrd]	*n.* a fragment of something brittle
		chip, fragment, piece 파편

21	**chronicle** [kránikl]	*v.* to record historical events in the order in which they occurred
		record, list, document 연대순으로 기록하다

22	**libation** [laibéiʃən]	*n.* a liquid suitable for drinking; the pouring of wine or something else in honor of a god
		drink 술, 제주

23	**figurine** [fìgjurí:n]	*n.* a small carved or molded figure
		figure, statuette 작은 입상

24	**conventional** [kənvénʃənəl]	*adj.* conforming to established practice or accepted standards
		customary, traditional, ordinary 전통적인, 관습적인

🛡 Quiz

17. *The archaeological site contained _____ for ceremonial objects and a central fire pit.*

18. *Playwright Oscar Wilde distinguished himself for his wit and _____ in dress, taste, and manners.*

19. *John Dewey strongly believed that children should not be taught by _____.*

20. *By digging up different _____ from different stratum layers, archaeologists can easily date the stages of a culture's development.*

21. *The book vividly _____ the writer's struggle to overcome alcoholism.*

22. *Large quantities of food and _____ are consumed during the festivities.*

23. *At the archaeological site, there were many poor-quality _____ and painted pots produced in quantity by easy, inexpensive means.*

24. *The European influences on jazz can be heard in its use of such _____ instruments as the trumpet, string bass, and piano.*

25	**betray** [bitréi]	*v.* to be disloyal or unfaithful to **sell out, let down, fail**	배반하다, (기대 등을) 저버리다
26	**sentiment** [séntəmənt]	*n.* a subjective response to a person, thing, or situation **feeling, emotion**	감정, 정서
27	**dilapidated** [dilǽpədèitid]	*adj.* falling to pieces because of neglect or age; in great need of repair **ruined, destroyed, broken-down**	황폐화된, 파괴된
28	**aviation** [èiviéiʃən]	*n.* the science of mechanical flight through the air; the industry that makes aircraft **aeronautics**	항공학, 항공업
29	**pluck** [plʌk]	*v.* to pull out something with one's fingers; to sound the strings of a violin or something else using the fingers **pick, extract, draw out**	잡아 뜯다, (현악기의 줄 등을) 튕기다
30	**decode** [di:kóud]	*v.* to translate a coded message into ordinary language **decipher, interpret**	해독하다, 번역하다

* *encode* 암호화하다

Quiz

25. *Arthur Miller's masterpiece, Death of Salesman, is the tragic story of a salesman _____ by his own hollow values.*

26. *Modern Times does accurately reflect the _____ of many who feel they are victims of an over-mechanized world.*

27. *These painters usually chose subjects that were interesting only because they were so ordinary; a closed-down gas station, an old man waiting for a bus, a _____ billboard.*

28. *Charles Lindbergh's first transatlantic flight opened a whole new world of possibilities for _____, especially commercial aviation.*

29. *The harp is a stringed musical instrument of ancient origin, and its strings are _____ by the fingers.*

30. *In order to _____ Egyptian numerals, long stretches of symbol groupings had to be sorted out and added together.*

Social Sciences

1 **pivotal**
[pívətl]

adj. constructed as or acting like a pivot; crucially important

central, vital, crucial

주축의, 중요한

2 **barter**
[bá:rtər]

① *n.* a trade by exchanging goods rather than by selling them for money
② *v.* to trade or exchange goods or services without using money

① **trade** ② **exchange, bargain**

① 물물 교환 ② 물물 교환을 하다

3 **lay off**

ph. to stop employing someone because there is no work for that person to do

dismiss, sack

(일시적으로) 해고하다

4 **reprieve**
[riprí:v]

n. a delay or cancellation of someone's punishment

postponement, suspension

일시적 구제, 집행 유예

5 **juggernaut**
[dʒʌ́gərnɔ̀:t]

n. a mighty force sweeping away and destroying everything in its path

불가항력

6 **per capita**

ph. by or for each individual person

per head, per each person

1인 당

7 **arduous**
[á:rdʒuəs]

adj. needing a lot of work, effort, or energy

hard, laborious, exhausting

힘든, 험한

8 **frivolous**
[frívələs]

adj. not sufficiently serious; silly or amusing

insignificant, trivial, childish

하찮은, 사소한, 경박한

🔵 Quiz

1. The development of steam engines played a _____ role in the spread of the factory system.

2. Before currency came into use, people used the _____ system to exchange goods directly for goods.

3. The Brindley Corporation had to _____ ten percent of its employees due to decreased sales.

4. To famers, factories offered a _____ from the backbreaking work and financial unpredictability associated with farming.

5. They were the _____ of the sky and by far the largest commercial planes of their day.

6. Fifteen hundred dollars a year was the _____ income in the United States in 1950.

7. Mountain climbing is an _____ sport.

8. He was frustrated because his boss assigned him some _____ work.

9　**consistent**
[kənsístənt]

adj. in agreement with something; in keeping with something
conforming, accordant, constant

일치하는, 일관된

10　**subdue**
[səbdjúː]

v. to overpower and bring under control; to reduce in intensity
conquer, suppress, quell

정복하다, 진압하다, 진정시키다

11　**patent**
[pǽtənt]

① *n.* a sole right to make and sell a particular article
② *v.* to obtain a patent for an invention

① 특허　② 특허를 얻다

12　**strain**
[strein]

n. a type of animal, plant, or disease
family, bloodline, race

종족, 종류

13　**abortion**
[əbɔ́ːrʃən]

n. the deliberate ending of a pregnancy at an early stage
termination

낙태

14　**census**
[sénsəs]

n. an official count of a population carried out at periodic intervals
poll

인구 조사

15　**locale**
[loukǽl]

n. the scene of some event or occurrence
site, location, spot

현장, 장소

16　**ovulate**
[óuvjulèit]

v. to release an ovum or egg cell from the ovary

배란하다

UNIT 50

🛡 Quiz

9. Decades of research have failed to produce _____ evidence.

10. Policemen armed with riot shields and batons were called in to _____ the angry soccer fans.

11. Barbed wire, first _____ in the United States in 1867, played an important part in the development of American farming.

12. The second _____ was the pneumonic plague, which was probably a mutation of the bubonic plague.

13. In some societies like China, with its one-child policy, the preference for sons is a driving reason for _____.

14. The United States _____ for 1970 showed that the French-speaking residents of Louisiana were one of the country's most compact regional linguistic minorities.

15. The information on the alarm pertained to the _____ in which it would be used.

16. During estrus, a female is _____ and can become pregnant.

17 put down

① *ph.* to criticize someone to make that person feel silly
② *ph.* to stop a revolution or something else by using force

① belittle, insult ② overpower, suppress   ① 모욕하다 ② 진압하다

18 falter
[fɔ́ːltər]

v. to move unsteadily; to become weaker

totter, stumble, weaken   비틀거리다, 약해지다

19 federal
[fédərəl]

adj. belonging to a country consisting of a group of states

                                                    연방의, 연합의

20 electorate
[iléktərit]

n. all the people in a city or country who have the right to vote

                                                (전체) 선거인, 유권자

21 hierarchical
[hàiərɑ́ːrkikəl]

adj. classified according to various criteria into successive levels or
layers   위계질서의

22 amendment
[əméndmənt]

n. a small change or improvement that is made to a law or a document

correction, alteration   수정(법)

23 ammunition
[æ̀mjuníʃən]

n. bullets, shells, bombs, or something else made to be fired from a
weapon   탄약, 무기

24 bladder
[blǽdər]

n. a hollow sac-shaped organ in which liquid waste is stored before it
is passed out of the body

vesica   방광

🛡 Quiz

17. The leaders _____ a rebellion in their country by appeasing the different groups.

18. After starting out in the lead, he began to _____ near the finish line.

19. The _____ system of government in Canada is similar to that of the United States.

20. The British Reform Bill of 1867 more than doubled the _____ by granting the right to vote to common working men.

21. Because of the fierceness of their army and their _____ organization, they became the largest Native American society.

22. The first ten _____ to the Constitution are known as the Bill of Rights.

23. Many of the Frenchmen had provided all sorts of things, from food to _____, for the Indians.

24. Your bowels and _____ prepare to empty their contents because, if they experience an injury, their contents could infect your body.

25	**ruthless** [rú:θlis]	*adj.* having or showing a lack of sympathy or tender feeling; hard and cruel **relentless, pitiless, merciless**	가차 없는, 무자비한

25 **ruthless**
[rú:θlis]
adj. having or showing a lack of sympathy or tender feeling; hard and cruel
relentless, pitiless, merciless
가차 없는, 무자비한

26 **incest**
[ínsest]
n. sexual intercourse between closely related people
근친상간

27 **inaugural**
[inɔ́:ɡjurəl]
adj. coming before all others in time or order; relating to a ceremony that officially marks the beginning of something
initial, introductory, maiden
개시의, 취임(식)의

28 **soothe**
[su:ð]
v. to bring relief from pain or something else
comfort, calm, mitigate
달래다, 완화시키다

29 **interdisciplinary**
[ìntərdísəplənèri]
adj. involving two or more subjects of study
둘 이상 분야에 걸치는, 학문간 연계의

30 **dignify**
[dígnəfài]
v. to make something impressive or dignified
ennoble, glorify, exalt
위엄을 갖추게 하다, 고상하게 하다

UNIT 50

Quiz

25. *The pirate Blackbeard had a reputation for being a harsh, _____ man.*

26. *While virtually all cultures have rules prohibiting _____, the definition of what constitutes incest fluctuates widely.*

27. *On the _____ flight of the Dixie Clipper across the Atlantic, twenty-two passengers enjoyed a main sitting area equipped with plush sofas.*

28. *Food, drink, and celebration after the group work provided relaxation and _____ weary muscles.*

29. *Cognitive science is an _____ field of research that employs psychology, linguistics, and biology.*

30. *Agriculture was not even considered a science until it was _____ by the work of research stations.*

Natural Sciences

1 hexagonal
[hekségənl]
adj. having a plane figure with six sides and angles
육각형의
* *hexagon* 육각형

2 torrential
[tɔːrénʃəl]
adj. caused by or like a torrent; falling in large amounts
rushing, streaming, violent
급류의

3 luminous
[lúːmənəs]
adj. full of or giving out light
bright, shining, glowing
빛을 발하는, 발광의

4 spiral
[spáiərəl]
adj. moving in a continuous curve that winds around a central point
coiled, helical, screw
나선의, 나선 모양의

5 tentacle
[téntəkəl]
n. long and thin appendages which are used as sense organs
촉수, 촉각

6 sinuous
[sínjuəs]
adj. marked by a long series of irregular curves
curving, twisting, winding
꾸불꾸불한, 굽이진

7 rupture
[rʌ́ptʃər]
v. to be broken or to burst apart; to burst or break apart something
break, split, breach
터지다, 터뜨리다

8 tension
[ténʃən]
① *n.* a feeling of anxiety and stress that makes it impossible to relax
② *n.* the state of being stretched tight
① **nervousness, distress** ② **strain, pressure**
① 긴장(감) ② 장력

Quiz

1. Simple snowflakes possess a variety of beautiful forms, most of which are _____.
2. The _____ rains and heavy winds the hurricane brought are contributing to its storm surge.
3. The most _____ objects seen by telescopes are probably ten thousand million light years away.
4. The Milky Way is a _____ galaxy, a flattish disc of stars with two spiral arms emerging from its central nucleus.
5. Giant squid have eight short arms and two long _____.
6. The large circular maria were seen as strange, and _____ features were observed in the maria.
7. This change in the volume of air may cause the lungs to distend and even to _____.
8. As water is lost from the surface of the leaves, a negative pressure or _____ is created on it.

9	**translucent** [trænsljúːsənt]	*adj.* allowing light to pass diffusely **semi-transparent, see-through**	반투명의
10	**borealis** [bɔ̀ːriǽlis]	*n.* a luminous display of colors in the night sky of the Northern Hemisphere	북극광
11	**reactor** [riːǽktər]	*n.* a large structure used for the controlled production of nuclear energy	반응로, 원자로
12	**oval** [óuvəl]	*adj.* with the outline of an egg or shaped like an egg **egg-shaped, ovoid, elliptical**	달걀 모양의, 타원형의
13	**gyration** [dʒaiəréiʃən]	*n.* a rapid turning about on an axis or central point **whirl, rotation, spin**	선회, 회전
14	**anomaly** [ənáməli]	*n.* something that is unusual or different from what is expected **abnormality, freak, exception**	변칙, 이례적인 것, 예외
15	**antler** [ǽntlər]	*n.* either of a pair of solid bony outgrowths on the head of an animal	(사슴 등의) 가지진 뿔
16	**epidermis** [èpədɔ́ːrmis]	*n.* the outer layer of skin **skin**	표피, 외피, 피부

UNIT 51

Quiz

9. One cannot see through _____ materials, but light can pass through them.

10. It is almost impossible to capture the beauty of the aurora _____ in photographs.

11. In late April 1986, the number four _____ at the Chernobyl nuclear power plant exploded.

12. The pear tree has simple, _____ leaves that are smoother and shinier than those of the apple.

13. The _____ of the cat in midair are too fast for the human eye to follow, so the process is obscured.

14. If we stand above nature and if technology is all powerful, then AIDS is a horrifying _____ that must be trying to tell us something.

15. Deer use their _____ chiefly to fight for mates or for leadership of a herd.

16. The external surfaces of plants, in addition to being covered by an _____ and a waxy cuticle, often carry spiky hairs.

17	**conifer** [kóunəfər]	*n.* a tree with narrow needle-like leaves and which produce pollen and seeds in cones	침엽수
18	**pique** [piːk]	*v.* to hurt someone's pride; to arouse curiosity or interest **annoy, offend, intrigue**	성나게 하다, 자극하다
19	**phosphorescent** [fàsfərésənt]	*adj.* producing a faint light in the dark; luminous without sensible heat **light, radiant, luminous**	인광성의
20	**vascular** [væskjələr]	*adj.* relating to the blood vessels of animals or the sap-conducting tissues of plants	혈관이 있는, 관다발의
21	**pollinate** [pálənèit]	*v.* to put pollen into a flower or plant so that it produces seeds **fertilize**	수분시키다
22	**unfurl** [ʌnfə́ːrl]	*v.* to spread out or unroll something from a rolled-up state **spread, unfold, open**	펴다, 펼치다
23	**aquifer** [ǽkwəfər]	*n.* an area of rock underneath the surface of the Earth that absorbs and holds water	대수층 (지하수를 담고 있는 지층)
24	**cartographer** [kɑːrtágrəfər]	*n.* a person who makes charts or maps **mapmaker**	지도 제작자

Quiz

17. The _____, which is among the tallest trees, has an unusually low root pressure.

18. Although this impact event was of considerable scientific important, it especially _____ the public's curiosity and interest.

19. Fish living in complete darkness at the bottom of deep-sea trenches have evolved incredibly sensitive eyes and _____ organs.

20. Club mosses, considered to be advanced because they are _____, often inhabit moist places.

21. Some honeybees are raised for their ability to _____, which ensures plant fertilization that increases fruit yields.

22. The water _____ in the sunlight with the colors of the rainbow playing across it.

23. The first condition for a geyser's eruption is that water must be contained in an _____.

24. The task of a _____ is to represent the Earth's surface at a greatly reduced scale.

25	**fault** [fɔːlt]	*n.* a break or crack in the Earth's crust resulting in the slippage of a rock mass slip	단층
26	**parole** [pəróul]	*n.* the release before the end of one's sentence on the promise of good behavior	가석방
27	**ensue** [ensúː]	*v.* to happen after or as a result of another event follow	(잇따라) 일어나다
28	**impending** [impéndiŋ]	*adj.* being soon to appear or take place imminent, approaching, nearing	임박한, 절박한
29	**overcast** [òuvərkǽst]	*adj.* covered by clouds cloudy, gloomy, dark	구름으로 덮인, 흐린
30	**gauge** [geidʒ]	*n.* a standard against which things are measured; an instrument used to measure a quantity yardstick, measure, indicator	측정 기준, 척도, 측정 기구

UNIT 51

 **Quiz**

25. The original architects of the University of California at Berkeley built the campus directly on top of a _____.

26. GPS is even used to keep track of criminals on day leave or _____.

27. In 1906, much of San Francisco was destroyed by an earthquake and the fires that _____.

28. Even with our improved ability to identify hazardous areas and to warn of _____ eruptions, increasing numbers of people face certain danger.

29. Because ultraviolet light from the sun can penetrate clouds, it is possible to get a sunburn on an _____ day.

30. The _____ known as potential evaporation totals the water lost through both normal evaporation and the evaporation that occurs from plant life.

Applied Sciences

1	**minuscule** [mínʌskjùːl]	*adj.* extremely small **minute, tiny**	아주 작은
2	**ledge** [ledʒ]	*n.* a narrow horizontal shelf or shelf-like part **shelf, projection, overhang**	선반, 쑥 내민 곳
3	**tendon** [téndən]	*n.* a cord of strong fibrous tissue that joins a muscle to a bone	힘줄
4	**electron** [iléktrɑn]	*n.* a particle which has a negative electric charge in atoms	전자
5	**scaffolding** [skǽfəldiŋ]	*n.* a temporary framework of metal poles and planks **frame, rack**	비계 (건물 등의 임시적인 골격)
6	**terrestrial** [təréstriəl]	*adj.* relating to the land or to the Earth **earthly, earthbound**	지구(상)의
7	**thwart** [θwɔːrt]	*v.* to prevent or hinder someone or something **impede, obstruct, block**	방해하다, 막다
8	**parched** [páːrtʃt]	*adj.* dried up; slightly roasted **dry, torrid, burned**	바짝 마른, 불에 탄

Quiz

1. In order to build his dream, he borrowed $50 million, which sounds _____ by today's standards.

2. Two _____ were built across from each other on the inside of the chimney.

3. Muscle fibers are attached bones by _____.

4. The proton has a positive charge, and the _____ has a negative charge.

5. Construction workers have begun dismantling the _____ that has encased the Guggenheim Museum for nearly three years.

6. Much has been written about the diversity of _____ organisms.

7. Ocean predators play a critical role by _____ bacteria growth and maintaining the oceans' equilibrium by reducing vulnerable links in the food chain.

8. According to one of the scientists, most _____ trees transmit their plight in the 50- and 500-kilohertz range.

9	**saline** [séili:n]	*adj.* containing sodium chloride or salt **briny, salty**	염분이 있는, 짠
10	**seemingly** [síːmiŋli]	*adv.* in appearance **apparently, ostensibly, superficially**	겉보기에는, 표면적으로는
11	**bog** [bɑg]	*n.* an area of low and wet muddy ground that sometimes contains bushes or grasses **marsh, swamp, fen**	습지, 소택지
12	**propagation** [prὰpəgéiʃən]	*n.* multiplication by natural reproduction; dissemination **proliferation, generation, spread**	증식, (병의) 만연
13	**groom** [gruːm]	*v.* to clean the fur or skin of another animal or itself **dress, neaten up, tidy up**	몸단장하다
14	**cetacean** [sitéiʃən]	*n.* an animal belonging to the order which includes dolphins, porpoises, and whales	고래류의 동물
15	**antigen** [æntidʒən]	*n.* a foreign substance that stimulates the body's immune system to produce antibodies	항원
16	**capillary** [kǽpəlèri]	*adj.* having a very small diameter; relating to capillarity **hair-like**	털 (모양)의, 모세 혈관의

UNIT 52

Quiz

9. When the _____ water table rises to within two meters of the surface, evaporation concentrates salt at the surface.

10. Why did the huge, _____ successful mammoths disappear?

11. Many animals became trapped in _____ overgrown by vegetation.

12. Our problems do not stem from evaporated water supplies but from a _____ of carbon dioxide and other greenhouse gases due to industrial and automobile emissions.

13. Monkeys are highly social animals. A good example of this is the fact that they _____ one another.

14. It is widely believed that _____ are highly intelligent.

15. Each blood cell has an _____, a kind of protein, on its surface.

16. Oxygen and nutrients reach the body's tissues by passing from the blood through the _____ wall.

17	**canine** [kéinain]	*n.* one of the long, sharp, and pointed teeth in front of a human's or animal's mouth **cuspid, dogtooth**	송곳니

18	**incisor** [insáizər]	*n.* one of the eight sharp teeth at the front of the mouth and which are used for biting **front tooth, fore-tooth**	앞니

19	**diaphragm** [dáiəfræm]	*n.* the layer of muscle between the lungs and the stomach and which is used especially to control breathing	횡경막

20	**iris** [áiris]	*n.* the colored part of the eye that controls the opening and closing of the pupil	홍채

21	**neurosis** [njuəróusis]	*n.* a mental disorder that causes obsessive fears and unreasonable behavior **nervous breakdown**	신경증, 노이로제

22	**pneumonia** [nju:móunjə]	*n.* an inflammation of the lungs, usually as a result of bacterial or viral infection	폐렴

23	**pupil** [pjú:pəl]	*n.* the dark and circular opening in the center of the iris	눈동자, 동공

24	**paralysis** [pərǽləsis]	*n.* a temporary or permanent loss of muscular function or sensation **numbness, palsy**	마비, 불수

Quiz

17. The front teeth are used to bite food, the _____ to tear it, and the molars to grind it.

18. A baby's first teeth to appear are generally the lower _____.

19. The power required for breathing comes from the intercostal muscles and the _____.

20. The _____ is basically the aperture of the eye, which is similar to that of a camera.

21. A psychosis is a severe mental disorder that is more serious than a _____.

22. The symptoms of _____, a lung infection, include high fever, chest pains, breathing difficulty, and coughing.

23. The _____ regulates the amount of light allowed into the eye.

24. Although complete _____ is rare with neuritis, it is common for some muscles to become weak.

25	**arthritis** [ɑːrθráitis]	*n.* a disease that causes pain and swelling in one or more joints of the body
		관절염

26	**viable** [váiəbəl]	*adj.* capable of being done or carried out **feasible, possible, practical**
		실행 가능한, 실용적인

27	**carbohydrate** [kɑ̀ːrbouháidreit]	*n.* a group of organic compounds which consist of carbon, hydrogen, and oxygen
		탄수화물

28	**viscosity** [viskásəti]	*n.* the degree to which a fluid can resist flowing **cohesion**
		점성, 점성도

29	**pavilion** [pəvíljən]	*n.* a large and elaborate tent; a large ornamental building
		대형 천막, 특설 건축물

30	**prodigy** [prádədʒi]	*n.* a child of extraordinary brilliance; something extraordinary or surprising **genius, wonder, marvel**
		신동, 놀라운 것

UNIT 52

 **Quiz**

25. Isadora Martinez invented a knee implant that lets people with _____ bend their knees easily.

26. During the nineteenth century, further advances were made, notably Bessemer's process for converting iron into steel, which made the material more commercially _____.

27. _____ such as sugar or starches are important energy sources for humans and animals.

28. _____ is a measurement describing the relative difficulty or easiness with which liquids flow.

29. The Liberty Bell, formerly housed in Independence Hall, was moved to a separate glass _____ in 1976.

30. Edison has been referred to as a child _____ since he began working on his first inventions at the age of twelve.

Choose the closest meaning to the highlighted word or phrase.

1. The chair of the congressional committee bluntly stated that without a government subsidy, no one would undertake so unpromising a venture.

   Ⓐ persuasion
   Ⓑ financing
   Ⓒ interference
   Ⓓ penalty

2. Although synthetic nylon is mainly synthesized for fabric, it is also manufactured to make ropes, insulation, fiberglass, and other common household utensils.

   Ⓐ decorations
   Ⓑ plows
   Ⓒ weapons
   Ⓓ tools

3. It is no wonder that, during the years of these cumbersome arrangements, private letter-carrying and express businesses developed.

   Ⓐ burdensome
   Ⓑ handsome
   Ⓒ loathsome
   Ⓓ quarrelsome

4. The quilts were made of a top layer of woolen or glazed worsted wool fabric, consisting of smooth, compact yarn from long, wool fibers dyed dark blue, green, or brown with a bottom layer of a coarser woolen material.

   Ⓐ older
   Ⓑ less heavy
   Ⓒ thinner
   Ⓓ rougher

5. Collecting pottery shards has proven to be one of the best ways for archaeologists to identify the developmental levels of ancient cultures.

   Ⓐ fragments
   Ⓑ carvings
   Ⓒ coverings
   Ⓓ pigments

6. In time, the increasing complexity of Neolithic societies led to the development of writing since the people were prompted by the need to keep records and later by the urge to chronicle their experiences, learning, and beliefs.

   Ⓐ repeat
   Ⓑ exchange
   Ⓒ analyze
   Ⓓ describe

7. Because female scientists in the early 1950s were often forced to work in the shadow of their male counterparts, Franklin's pivotal work has been relegated to a footnote in the history of science.

   Ⓐ delicate
   Ⓑ essential
   Ⓒ original
   Ⓓ preliminary

8. Surpluses of food could also be bartered for other commodities.

   Ⓐ examined
   Ⓑ exerted
   Ⓒ extended
   Ⓓ exchanged

9 Whether abstract, stylized, or realistically treated, the consistent theme in virtually all arts and crafts designs is nature.

Ⓐ conservative

Ⓑ considerable

Ⓒ constant

Ⓓ consecutive

10 By modern standards, these early advertisements were quite small and subdued — not the splash sheet whole page spreads of today — yet some of them appeared on the front page of newspapers.

Ⓐ calm

Ⓑ colorful

Ⓒ limited

Ⓓ sizable

11 The Roman Republic began to falter from within as the victories abroad were not matched by successes in supporting its own citizens at home.

Ⓐ come up

Ⓑ slow down

Ⓒ integrate

Ⓓ unite

12 Many of the most damaging and life-threatening types of weather — torrential rains, severe thunderstorms, and tornadoes — begin quickly, strike suddenly, and dissipate rapidly.

Ⓐ continuous

Ⓑ intermittent

Ⓒ occasional

Ⓓ heavy

13 The resin was hardened by time and pressure into a fossil called amber. It is a brittle, yellow-to-brown, translucent substance.

Ⓐ viscous

Ⓑ transparent

Ⓒ liquid

Ⓓ solid

14 In the 20th century, electron microscopes have provided direct views of viruses and minuscule surface structures.

Ⓐ circular

Ⓑ dangerous

Ⓒ complex

Ⓓ tiny

15 Another unusual feature of glass is the manner in which its viscosity changes as it turns from a cold substance into a hot, ductile liquid.

Ⓐ hardness

Ⓑ adhesiveness

Ⓒ intensity

Ⓓ density

16 Born in France, Robert Laurent was a prodigy who received his education in the United States.

Ⓐ painter

Ⓑ novice

Ⓒ genius

Ⓓ expert

Humanities

1   **caliber**
    [kǽləbər]
    n. the level of quality or ability that someone or something has achieved
    talent, capacity, merit
    능력, 재간

2   **cardinal**
    [káːrdənl]
    adj. highly important; having other things based on something
    essential, main, principal
    가장 중요한, 주요한

3   **hiss**
    [his]
    n. a sound like a long 's'; unwanted background noise in a sound system
    sibilance
    쉿 하는 소리, 히스 (고음역의 잡음)

4   **luminosity**
    [lùːmənásəti]
    n. the property of emitting light
    radiance, glow, splendor
    발광(성), 광명

5   **lurid**
    [lúːrid]
    adj. too bright in color; arousing a strong and superficial interest or emotional reaction
    flaming, sensational, startling
    번쩍번쩍하는, 선정적인

6   **choreography**
    [kɔ̀ːriágrəfi]
    n. the arrangement of the pattern of movements in dancing
    안무법

7   **punctuality**
    [pʌ̀ŋktʃuǽləti]
    n. the quality or habit of arriving on time
    promptness, timeliness
    시간 엄수

8   **babble**
    [bǽbəl]
    v. to talk or say something quickly
    prattle, chatter, jabber
    재잘거리다, 지껄이다

Quiz

1. The actors may be of the highest _____ or simply part-time novices.

2. A _____ rule for players of the lute, a stringed instrument, is that every note is sustained for as long as possible.

3. Environmental sounds and electrically generated _____ can be incorporated into a musical composition.

4. His paintings show the same _____ and attention to detail that the works of the Dutch masters show.

5. Paperback novels in the 1940s often had _____ covers to attract readers' attention.

6. It was around 1925 that an accurate, convenient system for recording the _____ of ballet was developed.

7. You will no doubt meet people with varying attitudes towards _____.

8. Between four months and eight months, infants begin to _____ meaningless syllables.

9	**cliché** [kliːʃéi]	*n.* a phrase which has become stale and hackneyed through overuse **trite saying, banality**	진부한 표현, 상투적인 말
10	**sprout** [spraut]	*v.* to develop a new growth of leaves, hair, or something else **come up, bud, germinate**	자라기 시작하다, 발아하다
11	**supplement** [sʌ́plmənt]	*n.* something that is added to make something else complete **addition, annex, accessory**	추가, 보충
12	**treacherous** [trétʃərəs]	*adj.* not to be trusted; ready or likely to betray **unreliable, faithless, disloyal**	신뢰할 수 없는, 충실하지 못한
13	**discretion** [diskréʃən]	*n.* the right to make decisions; the quality of behaving in a discreet way **volition, discernment, discrimination**	결정권, 재량, 분별(력)
14	**feudal** [fjúːdl] * *feudalism* 봉건제도	*adj.* relating to the feudal structure that was used in medieval Europe 봉건(제도)의	
15	**mutiny** [mjúːtəni]	*n.* a rebellion or an act of rebellion; open fighting against authority **rebellion, revolt, uprising**	반란, 폭동
16	**detectable** [ditéktəbl] * *detect* 탐지하다	*adj.* able to be noticed or discovered **perceptible, observable, discernible**	탐지할 수 있는, 알아낼 수 있는

UNIT 53

🛡 Quiz

9. *Some of the American expressions are so common they have become _____; "Time is money," "Time waits for no one," and so on.*

10. *Thanks to the steamboat, numerous towns and industries began to _____ up along the rivers.*

11. *Wagon freighting, stage coaching and steamboating became _____ of feeders for the first train.*

12. *The early slave songs provided them with a kind of spiritual escape from the _____ bonds of slavery.*

13. *Establishing monuments is at the president's _____.*

14. *Although based on _____ models, the colony of Pennsylvania developed a reputation for a progressive political and social outlook.*

15. *The _____ of a ship's crew signifies the breakdown of obedience and discipline.*

16. *The fact that DNA in _____ amounts has survived for 40,000 years has given scientists hope that genetic material of other long-vanished species may be found.*

17	**limbo** [límbou]	*n.* an area between heaven and hell	연옥
18	**hominid** [hámənid]	*n.* a primate belonging to the family of modern man and his ancient ancestors **human**	인간, 인류
19	**vault** [vɔːlt]	*n.* an underground burial chamber **crypt, catacomb**	납골당
20	**freakish** [fríːkiʃ]	*adj.* very unusual or unexpected **odd, weird, peculiar**	변덕스러운, 기묘한
21	**characterize** [kǽriktəràiz]	*v.* to describe something; to be a typical feature of something **depict, label, mark**	특성을 묘사하다, 특징 지우다
22	**glorify** [glɔ́ːrəfài]	*v.* to make someone or something seem more important or beautiful than he, she, or it really is **exalt, dignify, ennoble**	찬양하다, 찬미하다
23	**delineate** [dilínièit]	*v.* to describe, draw, or explain something in detail **describe, outline, portray**	서술하다, 묘사하다
24	**embark (on)** [imbáːrk]	*v.* to begin a task, especially a lengthy one **commence, launch, start**	착수하다, 시작하다

🎯 Quiz

17. *The natives believe that only through a funeral are they able to break the _____ of their dead family member.*

18. *A great deal can be learned from the actual footprints of early _____.*

19. *The body is placed in a horizontal _____ and enclosed with stone or wood.*

20. *A trumpeter of _____ gift, Louis Armstrong will be remembered as the most influential jazz musician of all time.*

21. *Her works can not be _____ in a few words.*

22. *The art did not _____ any specific rulers.*

23. *The regional novel _____ the lives of people in a particular place to demonstrate how an environment influences its inhabitants.*

24. *The Dadaists _____ on their crusade by trying to shock the public by constructing offensive or outrageous works of art and literature.*

| 25 | **rekindle**
[riːkíndl] | *v.* to relight a fire; to revive or renew something
restore, revitalize, renew | 다시 불을 붙이다, (흥미 등을) 다시 일으키다 |

| 26 | **relegate**
[réləgèit] | *v.* to move someone down to a lower grade
banish, exile, demote | 내쫓다, 좌천시키다 |

| 27 | **come of age** | *ph.* to become established and accepted | 확립하다, 자리를 잡다 |

| 28 | **in regards to** | *ph.* with regard to; regarding or about
as regards, in respect of | ~에 관하여 |

| 29 | **impostor**
[impástər] | *n.* someone who pretends to be someone else in order to deceive others
pretender, deceiver, trickster | 사기꾼 |

| 30 | **lyrics**
[líriks] | *n.* the words of a song
libretto, book, words | (노래) 가사 |

UNIT 53

Quiz

25. In 1912, O'Keeffe's creative spark was _____ when she attended an art class at the University of Virginia summer school.

26. The show was hounded off the legitimate stage and found itself _____ to saloons and barrooms.

27. Colonial coppersmithing also _____ in the early eighteenth century and prospered in northern cities.

28. Pay particular attention to details, especially _____ Poe's work, because they are there for a reason.

29. The character looks very much like a fool or even an _____; that is, he might have wealth, but, essentially, he is a clown, a fake.

30. Louis Armstrong was one of the first musicians to sing in the scat style, using rhythmic nonsense syllables instead of _____.

Social Sciences

1 spearhead
[spíərhèd]

v. to lead a movement, campaign, attack, or something else
lead, initiate, pioneer
앞장서다, 선두에 서다

2 haul
[hɔːl]

v. to pull with great effort or difficulty
drag, draw, tow
끌어당기다, 잡아끌다

3 arithmetic
[əríθmətìk]

n. the branch of mathematics that uses numbers to solve problems
calculation, computation
산수, 산술

4 encyclopedia
[insàikloupíːdiə]

n. a reference containing information on every branch of knowledge
백과사전

5 protocol
[próutəkàl]

n. the version of an agreement; correct, formal, or diplomatic etiquette or procedure
treaty, manners, convention
의정서, 의례

6 hinge on

ph. to be dependent or contingent on, or as if on a hinge
depend on, rely on, turn to
~에 의지하다, ~에 달려있다

7 lathe
[leið]

n. a machine tool used to cut, drill, or polish a piece of metal
선반, 녹로

8 subsist
[səbsíst]

v. to live or to manage to stay alive
exist, live, survive
살아가다, 생활하다

Quiz

1. Taylor was an American engineer who _____ the Efficiency Movement at the beginning of the 20th century.

2. Farm women had to _____ large quantities of water into the house from wells or pumps for every purpose.

3. Reading, writing, and _____ were the basics of an elementary school education.

4. Publishers of _____ employed hundreds of specialists and large editorial staffs.

5. This endless repetition, combined with strict schedules and office _____, has a very wearing effect on workers.

6. Industrial growth _____ several economic factors.

7. Until the late 1700s, metal could not be turned on a _____ to make it uniformly smooth and round.

8. Many prehistoric people _____ as hunters and gathers.

9	**heading** [hédiŋ]	*n.* a word or series of words, often in larger letters, placed at the beginning of a passage in order to introduce or categorize **headline, rubric, title**	범주, 항목
10	**disseminate** [disémənèit]	*v.* to make something be widely circulated or diffused **disperse, spread, dissipate**	널리 퍼뜨리다
11	**windfall** [wíndfɔ̀:l]	*n.* a fruit, especially an apple, blown down from its tree; an unexpected fortune **jackpot, bonanza, lucky strike**	뜻밖의 횡재
12	**linger** [líŋgər]	*v.* to remain for a long time **remain, stay, loiter**	질질 끌다, (떠나지 않고) 꾸물거리다
13	**ideology** [àidiálədʒi]	*n.* the body of ideas which forms the basis for a social system **beliefs, doctrine, philosophy**	이념, 사상
14	**litter** [lítər]	*n.* a number of animals born to the same mother at the same time **offspring, young, brood**	한배에서 난 새끼
15	**puberty** [pjú:bərti]	*n.* the stage of change in the human body from childhood to the adult state **adolescence, pubescence, teens**	사춘기
16	**chaos** [kéiɑs]	*n.* a state of utter confusion or disorder **disorder, pandemonium, turmoil**	혼돈, 대혼란

Quiz

9. The work of a factory worker and an office worker falls under the general _____ of labor.

10. Hollywood _____ an image of the good life in Southern California on screens all across the nation.

11. The South received great financial _____ from its agricultural produce.

12. Some people like to _____ after dinner over coffee and dessert.

13. The farmers' distrust of a city was caused, in part, by a national _____ that proclaimed farming the greatest occupation and rural living superior to urban living.

14. Many animal species produce large _____ at birth.

15. Adolescence is a transitional stage in human development from the beginning of _____ to the attainment of the emotional, social, and physical maturity of adulthood.

16. These new urbanities eagerly embraced the progressive reforms that promised to bring order out of the _____ of the city.

17	**institution** [ìnstətjúːʃən]	*n.* a public body founded for a special purpose; a custom or tradition **establishment, foundation, practice**	기관, (사회적) 제도, 관례
18	**gullible** [gʌ́ləbəl]	*adj.* easily tricked or fooled **innocent, naive, unwary**	속기 쉬운, 잘 속는
19	**pending** [péndiŋ]	*adj.* waiting to be decided or dealt with **impending, undecided**	현안의, 미결정의
20	**ravage** [rǽvidʒ]	*v.* to cause extensive damage to a place **demolish, destroy, raze**	파괴하다, 황폐화시키다
21	**epithet** [épəθèt]	*n.* a word applied to a person or thing to describe an actual quality **nickname, label, tag**	통칭, 별칭
22	**cabinet** [kǽbənit]	*n.* an executive policy-making body made up of senior ministers **council, ministry**	내각
23	**credential** [kridénʃəl]	*n.* the personal qualifications that can be quoted as evidence of one's competence **identification, reference, license**	증명서, 신임장
24	**isolationism** [àisəléiʃənìzəm]	*n.* the policy of not joining with other countries in international affairs	고립주의

Quiz

17. The _____ of slavery has been a part of human history for thousands of years.

18. Con artists are criminals who take advantage of _____ people by tricking them and taking their money.

19. The _____ plan for the improvement of New York Harbor was discussed at a conference, but, unfortunately, it was not agreed to.

20. The country currently is being _____ by ancient religious conflicts.

21. Even the name is an _____, a synonym for the stunted, the scruffy, and the insignificant.

22. In the United States, the attorney general is the _____ member in charge of the administration of the Department of Justice.

23. Whatever their opinion of Mr. Jelks was, he had very impressive _____.

24. A whole movement, known as _____, which called for America to remain out of world affairs unless threatened directly, grew.

25	**arena** [ərí:nə]	*n.* a playing field where sporting events take place; a place of great activity **stadium, theater**	경기장, 활동 무대

25 **arena**
[ərí:nə]

n. a playing field where sporting events take place; a place of great activity

stadium, theater

경기장, 활동 무대

26 **bowels**
[báuəlz]

n. an intestine, especially the large intestine in humans

intestines, guts, innards

창자

27 **variable**
[vɛ́əriəbəl]

n. a factor which may change or be changed by another

변수

* *constant* 상수

28 **exaltation**
[ègzɔ:ltéiʃən]

n. the act of exalting or raising high

elevation, glory, praise

고양, 찬양

29 **cost-effective**
[kɔ:stiféktiv]

adj. giving an acceptable financial return in relation to the initial outlay

profitable, economical, worthwhile

비용 효과적인, 가격대비 효과적인

30 **territory**
[térətɔ́:ri]

n. an area of land, especially considered with regard to the government that owns or controls it

land, area, domain

영토, 영역

UNIT 54

 # Quiz

25. *In foreign affairs, he led the United States into the _____ of international power politics, thrusting aside the American tradition of isolationism.*

26. *An estimated one in five Americans suffers from irritable _____ syndrome, a disorder that can cause disabling cramping, constipation, and diarrhea.*

27. *A worksheet can be especially useful when the decision involves a large number of _____ with complex relationships.*

28. *The Second Chicago School adhered to neoclassical economics and rejected the Keynesian _____ of government regulation.*

29. *Pamphlets and chapbooks could be printed in large, _____ editions and sold cheaply.*

30. *Canada, which has a small population, covers slightly more _____ than the United States does.*

Natural Sciences

1 **concentric**
[kənséntrik]

adj. having a common center

동일한 중심을 갖는, 동심의

2 **wisp**
[wisp]

n. a thin and fine tuft or shred; a thin or delicate untidy piece
bit, tuft, snippet

작은 다발, 작은 물건

3 **eclipse**
[iklíps]

① *v.* to cause an eclipse of a heavenly body
② *v.* to surpass or to outshine
① **veil, overshadow** ② **surpass**

① 그늘지게 하다 ② 능가하다

4 **skewed**
[skju:d]

adj. sloping or twisted
oblique, distorted

비스듬한, 뒤틀린

5 **constellation**
[kànstəléiʃən]

n. a group of stars which form a pattern and have a name

별자리, 성운

6 **tributary**
[tríbjutèri]

n. a stream or river that flows into a larger stream or river
branch, offshoot, streamlet

지류

7 **velocity**
[vəlásəti]

n. a rate of motion; a speed in a certain direction
speed, pace, rapidity

속도

8 **refraction**
[rifrǽkʃən]

n. a change in the direction of a wave of light when it passes from one medium to another

(빛의) 굴절

 ## Quiz

1. The planets in our solar system are arrayed on nearly the same flat plane, with their orbits forming roughly _____ ellipses around the sun.

2. Daytime temperatures may reach above freezing, but because the planet is blanketed by the mere _____ of an atmosphere, the heat radiates back into space.

3. The moon has been _____ by mankind, and it is only natural that Mars be the next step for space exploration.

4. Made of hard wood, the boomerang is roughly V-shaped with arms slightly _____.

5. In addition to the twelve ones of the Zodiac, thirty other _____ were familiar to people in ancient times.

6. A western _____, called Valerie Glacier, advanced up to 122 feet per day.

7. The _____ of a river is controlled by the slope, depth, and toughness of the riverbed.

8. Because of _____, the water in a tank never looks as deep as it actually is.

| 9 | **narcotic**
[nɑ:rkátik] | *adj.* taking away pain or especially causing sleep
anesthetic, hypnotic, soporific | 마취의, 최면의 |

| 10 | **petal**
[pétl] | *n.* one of the modified leaves, often scented and brightly colored | 꽃잎 |

| 11 | **hitch**
[hitʃ] | *n.* a small and temporary setback or difficulty
problem, snag, obstacle | 장애, 걸림돌 |

| 12 | **molt**
[moult] | *v.* to shed feathers, hair, or skin to make way for a new growth
shed | 허물을 벗다, 털갈이를 하다 |

| 13 | **coronary**
[kɔ́:rənèri] | *adj.* denoting vessels, nerves, or something else belonging or relating to the heart | 관상(동맥)의, 심장의 |

| 14 | **hypersensitive**
[hàipərsénsətiv] | *adj.* unusually sensitive; having feelings which are too easily hurt
temperamental, touchy | 과민한, 과민증의 |

| 15 | **embryo**
[émbriou] | *n.* a developing young organism until hatching or birth | 배아 |

| 16 | **fauna**
[fɔ́:nə] | *n.* the animals of a given region or period considered as a whole | 동물군 |

UNIT 55

 ## Quiz

9. *Some doctors have questioned whether surgical treatments, injections, and _____ pain medications are being used appropriately in many patients.*

10. *The most noticeable of the _____ is called the labellum, or lip.*

11. *There was a _____ in the program, which caused a two-hour delay.*

12. *All adult birds _____ their feathers at least once a year.*

13. *Cholesterol may lead to _____ heart disease by building up in the arteries of the heart.*

14. *In an allergy, the animal's immune system is _____ to some substances it encounters, called allergens.*

15. *Eggs should not become chilled to a point where the _____ can no longer survive.*

16. *Crows are probably the most frequently met and easily identifiable members of the native _____ of the United States.*

17	**intestine** [intéstin]	*n.* the long tube that carries waste matter from the stomach out of the body **bowls, guts**	장
18	**resilience** [riзíljəns]	*n.* the power or ability to return to an original form or position after being bent, compressed, or stretched **elasticity, springiness, flexibility**	복원력
19	**metabolism** [mətǽbəlìzəm]	*n.* the chemical reaction that occurs within the cells of a living organism	신진대사
20	**crevice** [krévis]	*n.* a narrow crack **fissure, cleft, cranny**	틈, 구멍
21	**grid** [grid]	*n.* a network of evenly spaced horizontal and vertical lines that can be superimposed on a chart	격자 눈금
22	**quicksand** [kwíksæ̀nd]	*n.* wet sand that can suck down anything that lands or falls on it	유사 (물질을 빨아들이는 모래)
23	**dune** [dʒuːn]	*n.* a ridge or hill, usually on a seashore or in a hot desert	사구, 모래 언덕
24	**geyser** [gáizər]	*n.* a type of hot spring that intermittently spouts hot water and steam into the air	간헐천

Quiz

17. *Protein digestion begins in the stomach and ends in the small _____.*

18. *The tiny ant could be one of the most successful and marvelous species ever witnessed due to its unrivaled _____.*

19. *Virtually all species have biological clocks that regulate their _____ over a 24-hour period.*

20. *Cactus range from the three-inch fishhook cactus nestled in a rock _____ to the towering Saguaro Cactus, which reaches heights of 30 to 40 feet.*

21. *On more modern GPSs used in vehicles, it even shows an animated car exactly where it is on a city _____.*

22. *Although _____ can be found all over the world, little was known about its composition until recently.*

23. *Sand _____ are made of loose sand built up by the action of the wind.*

24. *_____ have often been compared to volcanoes because they both emit hot liquids from below the Earth's surface.*

25	**incandescent** [ìnkəndésənt]	*adj.* white-hot or glowing with intense heat **glowing, flaming, flaring**	백열의, 빛나는

26	**synchronize** [síŋkrənàiz]	① *v.* to happen or make something happen in exact time with something else or each other ② *v.* to set clocks and watches so that all show the same time ① **coincide** ② **coordinate, mate**	① 동시에 일어나다 ② 같은 시각을 표시하다

27	**basalt** [bəsɔ́:lt]	*n.* a fine-grained dark volcanic rock formed by the solidification of molten lava	현무암

28	**stratum** [stréitəm] * *pl. strata*	*n.* a layer of sedimentary rock; a layer of the atmosphere or the ocean **level, layer**	층

29	**weathering** [wéðəriŋ]	*n.* the action of weather on rocks making them change shape or color **efflorescence, erosion**	풍화 (작용)

30	**symmetrical** [simétrikəl]	*adj.* characterized by or exhibiting symmetry; proportionally balanced **proportional, well-balanced**	대칭적인

UNIT 55

 **Quiz**

25. Some geologists thought that the Earth's interior contained a highly compressed ball of _____ gas.

26. The GPS receiver _____ its clock with that of the satellites' atomic clocks.

27. The black obsidian cliffs of Yellowstone National Park are the result of a lava flow of _____ running head on into a glacier.

28. The formation of snow begins with these ice crystals in the subfreezing _____ of the middle and upper atmosphere.

29. _____ involves the interaction of the lithosphere with the atmosphere and hydrosphere.

30. The elliptical galaxies have a _____ elliptical or spheroidal shape with an obvious structure.

Applied Sciences

1	**thaw** [θɔː]	*v.* to melt; to make snow or ice melt **melt, deice, unfreeze**	녹다, 녹이다

2	**crooked** [krúkid]	*adj.* bent or curved, angled, or twisted; not straight **bowed, askew, distorted**	구부러진, 뒤틀린

3	**hoist** [hɔist]	*v.* to lift or heave something up, especially something heavy **elevate, raise, uplift**	내걸다, 올리다

4	**opulent** [ápjulənt]	*adj.* having or showing great wealth **affluent, wealthy, well-to-do**	부유한, 유복한

5	**barge** [baːrdʒ]	*n.* a long and flat-bottomed boat used on rivers and canals	거룻배 (바닥이 평평한 짐배), 바지

6	**peg** [peg]	*n.* a little shaft of some wood shaped for any of various fixing **pin, rod, bolt**	못, 쐐기

7	**canal** [kənǽl]	*n.* an artificial channel or waterway	운하

8	**vindicate** [víndəkèit]	*v.* to prove that something is true or right; to clear someone of blame or criticism **justify, support, exonerate**	정당함을 입증하다, 변호하다

Quiz

1. During the summer, the permafrost _____ enough so that plants are able to grow and reproduce.

2. Lombard Street in San Francisco, which zigzags its way up a steep hill, is known as the most _____ street in the world.

3. During the construction of skyscrapers, cranes are used to _____ building materials to the upper floors.

4. Many of the world's most _____ restaurants are located in luxury hotels.

5. Coal, grain, steel, and other products are often shipped by _____ on inland waterways.

6. Early carpenters, having no nails, had to use wooden _____ to secure their constructions.

7. It is said that George Washington was one of the first to realize how important the buildings of _____ would be to the nation's development.

8. Carson's work was _____ by a 1963 report of the President's Science Advisory Committee.

9	**roam**	*v.* to ramble or wander with no fixed purpose or direction	
	[roum]	wander, range, rove	거닐다, 방랑하다

10	**pasture**	*n.* an area of grasslands suitable or used for the grazing of livestock	
	[pǽstʃər]	meadow, grassland, range	목초지, 방목장

11	**pulverization**	*n.* the action of reducing to dust or powder	
	[pʌ̀lvərizéiʃən]	grinding, shattering, crushing	분쇄
	* *pulverize* 빻다		

12	**enzyme**	*n.* a specialized protein molecule that acts as a catalyst	
	[énzaim]		효소

13	**stasis**	*n.* a situation in which there is no change or development	
	[stéisis]	counterpoise, equilibrium, equipoise	정지 상태, 안정 상태

14	**mileage**	*n.* the number of miles traveled or to be traveled	
	[máilidʒ]		마일수, 연비

15	**tusk**	*n.* one of a pair of long and projected teeth certain animals, like the elephant, have	
	[tʌsk]		(코끼리 등의) 엄니

16	**camouflage**	*n.* the way that the color or shape of something can make it difficult to see	
	[kǽməflɑ̀:ʒ]	cover, disguise, concealment	변장, 위장

 Quiz

9. *Millions of bison once _____ the plains of North America.*

10. *Overgrazing is a result of too much livestock being kept on a given area of _____.*

11. *The result of cattle grazing in an area is the reduction of the natural vegetation and the _____ of the soil.*

12. *In fact the _____ may cause a reaction to proceed billions of times faster than it would otherwise.*

13. *Basil works together in conjunction with helpful predatory insects to create a state of _____ in which the levels of harmful pest damage are minimized without the use of any chemicals.*

14. *Tests have shown that the new diesel gets between 25% and 45% better _____ than gasoline.*

15. *Mammoths were distinguished from today's elephants by their thick, shaggy coats and their huge, upward-curving _____.*

16. *These snakes have _____ patterns on them and can be very difficult to see.*

17	**splice** [splais]	*v.* to join two pieces of rope by weaving the strands of one into the other **knit, unite, bind** <div align="right">(꼬아) 잇다, 접합하다</div>
18	**arboretum** [à:rbərí:təm]	*n.* a botanical garden where trees and shrubs are grown <div align="right">수목원, 식물원</div>
19	**infrared** [ìnfrəréd]	*n.* a wavelength between the red end of the visible spectrum and microwaves and radio waves <div align="right">적외선</div>
20	**kingdom** [kíŋdəm]	*n.* a category in biological taxonomy; one of the five major groups into which all living things are organized <div align="right">계(界), 분야</div>
21	**veterinarian** [vètərənɛ́əriən]	*n.* a person trained in the medical care and treatment of sick animals <div align="right">수의사</div>
22	**slash and burn**	*ph.* characterized by a system of agriculture in which trees are cut down and burned in order to make land available for crops <div align="right">화전의, 화전 농업의</div>
23	**astigmatism** [əstígmətìzəm]	*n.* the inability of the eye to see properly because of its shape <div align="right">난시안, 난시</div>
24	**dementia** [diménʃiə]	*n.* a loss or severe lessening of normal mental ability <div align="right">치매</div>

Quiz

17. *Another possible solution to the problem of overfishing is gene _____, which can accelerate the reproduction of fish many times.*

18. *In an _____, trees are cultivated for scientific and educational purposes.*

19. *The greenhouse effect is a process by which the sun's _____ radiation is more readily absorbed by the atmosphere.*

20. *Members of the animal _____ have developed a variety of defense mechanisms for dealing with parasites.*

21. *A dog should be checked regularly by a _____ to ensure that it remains in good heath.*

22. *This terrible loss of vegetation and farmland is due to the _____ agricultural practices used by the indigenous people.*

23. *Symptoms of _____ are blurred vision and, in more extreme cases, headaches.*

24. *Alzheimer disease is the most common form of _____.*

| 25 | **hepatitis**
[hèpətáitis] | *n.* an inflammation of the liver caused by a viral infection |
| | | 간염 |

| 26 | **plasma**
[plǽzmə] | *n.* the component of blood or lymph in which the blood cells are suspended |
| | | 혈장 |

| 27 | **hypersomnia**
[hàipərsámniə] | *n.* the condition of sleeping for excessive periods |
| | | 수면과다증 |

| 28 | **ligament**
[lígəmənt] | *n.* a band of tough connective tissue that holds two bones together at a joint
sinew, string |
| | | 인대 |

| 29 | **anesthesia**
[æ̀nəsθíːʒə] | *n.* a reversible loss of sensation in all or part of the body
narcosis |
| | | 마취 |

| 30 | **pituitary gland** | *ph.* a small and oval endocrine gland attached to the base of the vertebrate brain |
| | | 뇌하수체 |

UNIT 56

 **Quiz**

25. Early signs characteristic of the acute phase of viral _____ are abdominal pain, nausea, and fever often accompanied by chills.

26. Blood is usually stored as whole blood or _____.

27. Contrary to popular belief, many studies have shown that _____ could actually be even more common than its nocturnal cousin, insomnia.

28. They are also the muscles that connect to tendons and _____, which connect them to our bones.

29. Frontier surgeon Ephraim MacDonald had to perform operations without _____.

30. Endocrine is used to refer to glands like the thyroid and _____, which secrete products directly into the bloodstream.

REVIEW TEST

Choose the closest meaning to the highlighted word or phrase.

1   For the many small mammals that **supplement** their insect diet with fruits or seeds, an inability to span open gaps between tree crowns may be problematic.

Ⓐ control
Ⓑ replace
Ⓒ look for
Ⓓ add to

2   For example, sulfur dioxide has **detectable** health effects at 0.08 parts per million.

Ⓐ noxious
Ⓑ latent
Ⓒ measurable
Ⓓ adverse

3   In a period **characterized** by the abandonment of so much of the realistic tradition by authors such as John Barth, Donald Barthelme, and Tomas Pynchon, Joyce Carol Oates has seemed at times determinedly old-fashioned in her insistence on the essentially mimetic quality of her fiction.

Ⓐ shocked
Ⓑ affected
Ⓒ distinguished
Ⓓ helped

4   The artists created scenes from everyday life in small towns or farming areas, and their styles were not at all neutral; really, they **glorified** or romanticized country life, showing it to be stable, wholesome, and embodying important American traditions.

Ⓐ extolled
Ⓑ defied
Ⓒ denounced
Ⓓ disagreed

5   Wagon trains had been used to **haul** freight and passengers between the Eastern Seaboard and the Ohio Valley since 1812.

Ⓐ tow
Ⓑ promote
Ⓒ push
Ⓓ bestow

6   Television has transformed politics in the United States by changing the way in which information is **disseminated** and by altering political campaigns.

Ⓐ collected
Ⓑ discussed
Ⓒ spread
Ⓓ stored

7   Winter often **lingered**; spring could be ushered in by a severe frost.

Ⓐ dropped
Ⓑ loitered
Ⓒ fleeted
Ⓓ changed

8 They keep their bosses informed about pending legislation, organize hearings, and also keep their local congressional representatives up to date and informed on what's going on in other parts of Congress.

Ⓐ deliberate

Ⓑ intense

Ⓒ imminent

Ⓓ infinite

9 At least 92 people died, and tens of thousands were left homeless in floods that ravaged large areas of southern India.

Ⓐ devastated

Ⓑ restored

Ⓒ refrigerated

Ⓓ generated

10 Mathematicians took centuries to develop the methods that now are used in arithmetic.

Ⓐ construction

Ⓑ calculation

Ⓒ combustion

Ⓓ connotation

11 Once the system becomes stronger and sustained wind speeds eclipse speeds of seventy-five miles per hour, the storm can be classified as a true hurricane.

Ⓐ exceed

Ⓑ decrease

Ⓒ propel

Ⓓ maintain

12 With the aid of humans, the birds have migrated the 1,250 miles from north to south with few hitches.

Ⓐ aids

Ⓑ enemies

Ⓒ dissolutions

Ⓓ difficulties

13 The tiny, delicate skeletons are usually scattered by scavengers or destroyed by weathering before they can be fossilized.

Ⓐ decomposition

Ⓑ decaying

Ⓒ efflorescence

Ⓓ corrosion

14 Replicas of Greek statues and figures that could not be restored were recast, and the opulent detailing returned to moldings, ceilings, and fixtures.

Ⓐ luxurious

Ⓑ flickering

Ⓒ profuse

Ⓓ murky

15 The Supreme Court rejected a plea from Manton to give him a last chance to vindicate himself.

Ⓐ defend

Ⓑ accuse

Ⓒ suppress

Ⓓ promote

16 Many other animals and insects have structures that produce iridescence, contrast, or strong colors used for camouflage or communication.

Ⓐ forage

Ⓑ hunting

Ⓒ protection

Ⓓ disguise

Humanities

1 **footage**
[fútidʒ]

n. a clip from a film used in a TV program or a movie

(영화, TV의) 장면

2 **chisel**
[tʃízl]

n. a hand tool which has a strong metal blade with a cutting edge at the end of the blade, used for cutting into or shaping wood, stone, or something else

끌, 정

3 **snide**
[snaid]

adj. expressing criticism or disapproval in an unpleasant manner
scornful

헐뜯는, 깔보는

4 **intonation**
[ìntənéiʃən]

n. the rise and fall of the pitch of the voice in speech
inflection, accent, tone

억양, 어조, 발성법

5 **vowel**
[váuəl]

adj. pertaining to any of the human speech sounds in which the breath is let out without any closing of the air passage in the mouth or throat

모음의

6 **stationary**
[stéiʃənèri]

adj. not moving; standing still
fixed, immovable, static

움직이지 않는, 고정된

7 **surge**
[səːrdʒ]

v. to move up and down or to swell with force
wave, bulge, rise and fall

파도가 일다, 동요하다

8 **salvage**
[sǽlvidʒ]

v. to rescue property or a ship from potential destruction or loss
save, rescue, retrieve

구조하다, 인양하다

Quiz

1. Scenes of factory interiors account for only about one third of the _____ of Modern Times.

2. Neoclassical sculptors seldom held a mallet or _____ in their own hands.

3. Although many intellectuals make _____ remarks about TV viewing, there are a number of "high-brow" shows.

4. These differences in adult stress and _____ can influence babies' emotional states and behavior.

5. Most common are those words beginning with p, b, d, or n sounds followed by a _____ sound.

6. As early as 1802, he was using a _____ steam engine of high-pressure design in his mill.

7. Most of the _____ population growth came from a natural increase.

8. Even after a ship has sunk, its cargo can often be _____.

9	**hinterland**	*n.* a region lying inland from the coast or the banks of a river
	[híntərlænd]	interior, province (항구의) 배후 지역, 지방

10	**semantics**	*n.* the branch of linguistics that deals with the meanings of words
	[simǽntiks]	의미(론)

11	**utilitarian**	*adj.* intended to be useful rather than beautiful
	[ju:tìlətɛ́əriən]	functional, practical, useful 실용의, 실리의

12	**derogatory**	*adj.* showing disapproval, dislike, scorn, or a lack of respect
	[dirágətɔ̀:ri]	depreciating, lowering, insulting (권위 등을) 떨어뜨리는, 모욕적인

13	**polygamy**	*n.* the custom of having more than one husband or wife
	[pəlígəmi]	복혼, 일부다처제

14	**hieroglyphs**	*n.* a symbol representing a word, syllable, sound, or idea
	[háiərəglìfs]	상형 문자

15	**etch**	*v.* to make designs on metal by using acid to eat out the lines
	[etʃ]	engrave 에칭하다, 식각하다

16	**humanitarian**	*adj.* concerned with improving people's lives and welfare
	[hju:mænətɛ́əriən]	인도주의의, 박애의

UNIT 57

 **Quiz**

9. *Philadelphia became an increasingly important marketing center for a vast and growing agricultural _____.*

10. *One important branch of linguistics is _____, which analyzes the meanings of words.*

11. *Pottery usually has _____ purposes, and sometimes it is designed purely for decorative reasons.*

12. *We used to call them Eskimos, but, today, that term is regarded by many Inuit as _____.*

13. *Marriages were not always monogamous. Some men practiced _____.*

14. *_____ catered to religious rules and represented important concepts with stylized pictures.*

15. *The monument at Mount Rushmore is a giant sculpture of four United States presidents that is _____ into the highest peak in the Black Hills mountain range.*

16. *She is remembered for her work in literature and also for her _____ work.*

17	**evacuate** [ivǽkjuèit]	*v.* to leave a place, especially because of danger
		leave, vacate, decamp 피난하다, 철수하다

18	**hoard** [hɔːrd]	*v.* to store or gather something especially for use in the future
		store, reserve, set aside 저장하다

19	**consort** [kánsɔːrt]	*v.* to associate or keep company with someone
		mingle, mix, pal 교제하다, 어울리다

20	**gruff** [grʌf]	*adj.* having a deep and rough voice
		hoarse, husky, rough 쉰 목소리의, 거친 목소리의

21	**faction** [fǽkʃən]	*n.* an active or trouble-making group within a larger organization
		group, cabal, bloc 당파, 파벌

22	**morph** [mɔːrf]	*v.* to form, shape, or structure
		형성되다

23	**fiddle** [fídl]	*n.* a violin, especially when used to play folk music or jazz
		바이올린

24	**prop** [prɑp]	*n.* a small article, such as a weapon or piece of furniture, that is used on stage in the acting of a play
		(연극 등의) 소품

 # Quiz

17. The Bucks returned to China in the year 1927 only to be _____ to Japan during the Chinese Civil War.

18. The famous miser Ebenezer Scrooge would _____ his money and never spend it.

19. Some colonial urban portraitists _____ with affluent patrons.

20. Louis Daniel Armstrong is known for the beautiful, clear tone of his trumpet-playing and for his _____, gravelly singing voice.

21. Those who were pro-slavery joined the Democrats, and the anti-slavery _____ switched to the Republicans, who were led by Abraham Lincoln.

22. Their distinct styles reflected the social mentality of the era and its ability to _____ and grow in a new direction.

23. After work, the people of the frontier sang and danced to _____ tunes or country dances.

24. Provincial theaters frequently lacked heat and even minimal _____ and scenery.

25	**pretend** [priténd]	① *adj.* imaginary ② *v.* to make believe; to act as if ① **imagined, fake** ② **make believe, feign**	① 가짜의, 허구의 ② ~인 체하다

26	**lexicon** [léksəkən]	*n.* a dictionary; the vocabulary of terms used in a particular branch of knowledge **dictionary**	사전, (특정 분야의) 어휘

27	**metaphysical** [mètəfízikəl]	*adj.* belonging or relating to metaphysics **abstract, psychic**	형이상학적인

28	**template** [témplit]	*n.* a piece of metal cut in a particular shape and used as a pattern when cutting out material **pattern, model**	모형, 원형

29	**catalyze** [kǽtəlàiz]	*v.* to bring about a change in the rate of a chemical reaction; to alter significantly	촉매작용을 하다, 변하다

* *catalyst* 촉매제

30	**thermal** [θə́:rməl]	*adj.* belonging or relating to, caused by, or producing heat	열의, 온도의

 **Quiz**

25. In the experiment, the child was presented with a picture of some kind of _____ creature.

26. Whether the term "couch potato" was first said in jest or not, it has stuck and is now a part of the _____ of modern-day people.

27. _____ philosophy is concerned with the principles, structures, and meanings that underlie all observable reality.

28. The Rainbow provided the _____ for a new generation of ships that amazed the world.

29. Mass transportation _____ physical expansion, it sorted out people and land uses, and it accelerated the inherent instability of urban life.

30. Glass fibers were little more than a novelty until the 1930s, when their _____ and electrical insulating properties were appreciated.

Social Sciences

1	**premise** [prémis]	*n.* a statement or idea assumed to be true as a basis for stating something further **assumption, proposition, supposition**	전제
2	**heyday** [héidèi]	*n.* the climax of the most success and prosperity **golden age, best days**	전성기, 한창 때
3	**consensus** [kənsénsəs]	*n.* a general agreement; the opinion of most of the people in a group	합의, 의견 일치
4	**sweatshop** [swétʃàp]	*n.* a workshop in which the employees work hard, often in terrible conditions	(노동자를 착취하는) 공장
5	**depression** [dipréʃən]	① *n.* a period of low business and industrial activity ② *n.* a mental state of prolonged sadness and pessimism ① **recession, slump** ② **dejection, gloom**	① 경기침체 ② 우울(증)
6	**tariff** [tǽrif]	*n.* the tax to be paid on a particular class of goods imported or exported	관세
7	**microcosm** [máikrouk̀àzəm]	*n.* any structure which contains, in miniature, all of the larger structure	소우주, 축소판
8	**surplus** [sə́ːrplʌs]	*n.* an amount that exceeds the amount required **leftover, oversupply, excess**	잉여물, 여분, 과잉

Quiz

1. *Keynes' _____ was that the rate of economic growth depends on an aggregate demand for goods.*

2. *Clipper ships saw their _____ in the early to mid-1800s.*

3. *The conference came to a _____, overcoming a variety of challenges.*

4. *There were _____ in city tenements, where groups of men and women manufactured clothing or cigars.*

5. *The Wall Street Crash of 1929 leads to years of economic _____ in the United States.*

6. *The federal government set up a system of _____ that was basically protectionist.*

7. *The settlement at Jamestown in Virginia was in many ways a _____ of the economy of colonial North America.*

8. *The administration raised the possibility that the slowing economy could drive the federal budget _____ down this year.*

9	**embargo** [embáːrgou]	*n.* an official order forbidding something, especially trade with another country **ban, prohibition, proscription**	통상 금지, 출항 금지

| 10 | **laissez-faire**
[lèseiféər] | ① *adj.* with minimally restricted freedom in commerce
② *n.* a policy of not interfering in what others are doing | ① 자유방임의   ② 자유방임정책 |

| 11 | **tenet**
[ténit] | *n.* a principle or belief held by a person, group, or something else
creed, doctrine, dogma | 교리, 신조 |

| 12 | **pluralism**
[plúərəlìzəm] | *n.* the belief or theory that reality consists of more than two kinds of substances | 다원주의 |

| 13 | **decimal**
[désəməl] | *adj.* based on the number 10 | 십진법의 |

| 14 | **pseudo**
[súːdou] | *adj.* not actual but having the appearance of; false or spurious
quasi, sham, deceptive | 사이비의 |

| 15 | **breadbasket**
[brédbæ̀skit] | *n.* an area which produces large amounts of grain for export
rich grain district, granary | 주요 농업 지대 |

| 16 | **genealogy**
[dʒìːniǽlədʒi] | *n.* the history of the members of a family from the past to the present; a person's direct line of descent from an ancestor
pedigree, lineage | 족보, 혈통 |

UNIT 58

 ## Quiz

9. The Nazi's _____ immediately affected the United States and many of its allies.

10. He reversed the traditional federal policy of _____ and sought to bring order, social justice, and fair dealings to American industry and commerce.

11. Not all of the members accepted the church's _____.

12. Locke recommended a cultural _____ through which artists could enrich the culture of America.

13. Canada adopted the _____ system of coinage in 1867.

14. According to the _____-science of racial classification, Africans were deemed inferior and unintelligent.

15. The regions around New York and Philadelphia became the _____ of North America.

16. Today, individuals, driven by an urge to learn more about their family's history, often trace their personal lineages through online _____ sites.

17	**miscarriage** [mìskǽridʒ]	*n.* a case of accidentally giving birth to a child too early for it to live <div align="right">자연유산</div>
18	**commentary** [kámantèri]	*n.* a spoken description of an event while it is happening, especially on the radio or television; a criticism or discussion of something **comment, exposition, criticism** <div align="right">논평, 비평</div>
19	**questionnaire** [kwèstʃənέər]	*n.* a set of questions formulated as a means of collecting information <div align="right">설문지, 조사표</div>
20	**treaty** [trí:ti]	*n.* a formal agreement between states or governments **agreement, compact, protocol** <div align="right">조약</div>
21	**veto** [ví:tou]	① *n.* the right to formally reject a proposal ② *v.* to formally and authoritatively reject or forbid ① **turndown, rejection** ② **deny, proscribe** <div align="right">① 거부(권) ② 거부하다</div>
22	**bracket** [brǽkit]	*n.* a group or category fixed according to certain upper and lower limits **class, group, rank** <div align="right">집단, 계층</div>
23	**egalitarian** [igæ̀lətέəriən]	*adj.* relating to the principle that all human beings are equal <div align="right">평등(주의)의</div>
24	**cognition** [kɑgníʃən]	*n.* the mental processes which enable humans to experience and process knowledge and information <div align="right">인식, 인지</div>

🛡 Quiz

17. Abortion exists in some animals as a natural phenomenon in the form of _____.

18. James Franklin was the first editor to see the newspaper as a means of expressing social and political _____.

19. One of the most important tools for research in social science is a well-written _____.

20. The defeated were forced to sign a _____ with their opponents.

21. If it's not to the president's liking, the bill can be _____ or killed in two other ways.

22. Unfortunately, such options are not available to all, especially those in a lower income _____.

23. Olmstead's concept was to make the park a symbol of democracy and _____ ideals.

24. What psychologists call _____ is a general category that includes all mental states and activities.

25	**ethology** [i(:)θάləd͡ʒi]	*n.* the study of animal behavior with an emphasis on their behavioral patterns 행동 생물학
26	**paranoia** [pæ̀rənɔ́iə]	*n.* a rare mental disorder characterized by delusions of persecution by others 편집증
27	**traumatic** [trɔːmǽtik]	*adj.* relating to, resulting from, or causing physical wounds; of an experience deeply and unforgettably shocking 외상(성)의, 정신적 쇼크의
28	**supersede** [sùːpərsíːd]	*v.* to take the place of something **displace, replace, supplant** 대신하다, 대체하다
29	**hub** [hʌb]	*n.* the center of a wheel; the center of activity or importance **center, core, pivot** (연결의) 중심
30	**anarchy** [ǽnərki]	*n.* lawlessness and social and political disorder caused by absence of government or control; any state of disorder and confusion 무정부 상태, 정치 사회적 혼란

UNIT 58

Quiz

25. _____ began to be applied to research on children in the 1960s but has become even more influential today.

26. The memories of the terrible events were so powerful that they suffered from insomnia, _____, and other dramatic side effects.

27. Anyone who has been in a car accident, been robbed, or been in any kind of _____ event can suffer from post-traumatic stress disorder.

28. Plastic and fiberglass have _____ metal in the replacement of such body parts as eyeballs, teeth, and bones.

29. Phoenix is the ninth largest city in the United States and is the _____ of the rich agricultural region of the Salt River Valley.

30. The Dadaists' answer was to embrace _____ and the irrational.

Natural Sciences

1	**tilt** [tilt]	*n.* a sloping position or angle; a slant **incline, pitch, slope**	기울기, 경사

2	**nebula** [nébjulə]	*n.* a mass of gas and dust among the stars, appearing often as a bright cloud at night	성운

3	**tug** [tʌg]	① *v.* to pull sharply or strongly ② *n.* a strong, sharp and sudden pull ① **draw, haul** ② **drag, yank**	① 세게 끌어당기다, 끌다 ② 끌기, 잡아당기기

4	**elliptical** [ilíptikəl]	*adj.* relating to, or having the shape of, an ellipse; rounded like an egg **oval**	타원(형)의

5	**plasma** [plǽzmə]	*n.* a gas that has a nearly equal number of positively and negatively charged particles	플라즈마, 전리 기체

6	**diffraction** [difrǽkʃən]	*n.* the spreading out of light waves as they emerge from a small opening or slit	회절

7	**spell** [spel]	*n.* a period or bout of illness, work, weather, or something else **interval, period**	한 차례, 짧은 기간

8	**imprinting** [impríntiŋ]	*n.* the process by which animals rapidly learn the characters of their own species	각인(현상)

Quiz

1. Earth's _____, which gives us the seasons, is probably due to the impact of a large object at its birth.

2. Jupiter is the best-preserved sample of the early solar _____.

3. Tides are caused by the _____ of the moon's gravity.

4. The satellite is following an _____ path 680 miles from the Earth at its farthest point.

5. The gas is stripped of its electrons by heat, and each atom thereby acquires a positive electric charge. In this form, the gas is called "_____."

6. Two young scientists boldly published the results of their experiments on the _____ of light.

7. High-pressure cells may bring brief warm _____ even in the middle of winter.

8. Like all migratory birds, they have a natural instinct called _____, which means they will follow and trust the first object they open their eyes to.

9	**gill** [gil]	*n.* a respiratory organ of a fish that extracts dissolved oxygen from the surrounding water **branchia**

아가미

10	**herbarium** [hə:rbɛ́əriəm] * *pl. herbaria*	*n.* a classified collection of preserved plants in a room

식물 표본실

11	**biodiversity** [bàioudivə́:rsəti]	*n.* the existence of different species of living organisms within a given area

생물 다양성

12	**pathological** [pæ̀θəláːdʒikəl]	*adj.* of or pertaining to pathology; caused by or involving disease **morbid**

병리학의, 병리상의

13	**vertebrate** [və́:rtəbrit]	*n.* any animal that has a backbone

척추동물

14	**invertebrate** [invə́:rtəbrit]	*n.* any animal that does not possess a backbone

무척추동물

15	**metamorphosis** [mètəmɔ́:rfəsis] * *metamorphose* 변형하다	*n.* a change in physical form that occurs during the development process; a complete change **transformation, change**

변태, 변형

16	**superficial** [sù:pərfíʃəl]	*adj.* apparent rather than actual or substantial **external, shallow**

표면적인, 외형적인

 ## Quiz

9. Menhaden swim with their mouths open, allowing water to flow through their _____.

10. Unfortunately, no book described the weed, and no samples existed in any _____ in the United States.

11. One definitive characteristic of tundra is a very low level of _____.

12. Some researchers have argued that some left-handedness may have a _____ origin, having been caused by brain trauma during birth.

13. The first flying _____ were true reptiles which had one of the fingers from their front limbs become very elongated.

14. Some marine _____ migrate from deep water to shallow water to spawn during spring and early summer.

15. Butterflies undergo _____ changing from caterpillar to pupa.

16. There was only a _____ resemblance between the two creatures.

17	**avalanche** [ǽvəlæ̀ntʃ]	*n.* the rapid movement of a large mass of snow down a mountain slope **snowslide**	눈사태
18	**estuary** [éstʃuèri]	*n.* the broad mouth of a river that flows into the sea	강어귀, 하구
19	**longitude** [lándʒətjùːd]	*n.* the imaginary circles that pass through both poles measured from Greenwich	경도, 경선
20	**coma** [kóumə]	*n.* the envelope of gas which forms around the nucleus of a comet	코마 (혜성의 핵 둘레의 대기)
21	**reclamation** [rèkləméiʃən]	*n.* the conversion of wasteland to commercial use **recovery**	(재)개발, 간척, 개간
22	**congregate** [káŋgrigèit]	*v.* to gather together into a crowd **assemble, collect, cluster**	모이다, 집합하다
23	**granite** [grǽnit]	*n.* a hard and coarse-grained igneous rock widely used in buildings and roads	화강암
24	**lava** [lávə]	*n.* the magma that has erupted from a volcano; a rock in a very hot liquid state flowing from a volcano	용암, 화산암

◆ Quiz

17. Occurring predominantly in mountainous areas, _____ are triggered by earthquake tremors, human disturbances, or excessive rainfall.

18. Other deltas do not appear to be deltas at all but are more like _____ because the strength of the tides and waves is so strong in those areas.

19. Lines of _____ run from the North to South poles.

20. The visible _____ is a huge cloud of gas and dust that has escaped from the nucleus.

21. _____ is the successful attempt to make unusable land suitable for farming.

22. Like stars, galaxies tend to _____ in clusters.

23. _____ is a coarse-grained igneous rock whose individual mineral crystals have formed to a size easily seen by the naked eye.

24. In its molten state, the material is called magma when it pushes into the crust and _____ when it runs out onto the surface.

25	**asteroid** [ǽstərɔ̀id]	*n.* a small rocky object or a celestial body orbiting a star 소행성
26	**bulge** [bʌldʒ]	*v.* to swell outwards **swell, protrude, stick out** 부풀다, 불룩해지다
27	**scrap** [skræp]	① *v.* to discard or cease to use ② *n.* a small piece ① **abandon, discard** ② **piece, fragment** ① 버리다, 폐기하다 ② 작은 조각
28	**tectonics** [tektániks]	*n.* the study of continental drift and how mountains and volcanoes form 구조학, 판구조론
29	**latitude** [lǽtətjùːd]	*n.* the imaginary circles drawn around the Earth parallel to the equator 위도, 위선
30	**stark** [staːrk]	*adj.* barren or severely bare; harsh or simple **vacant, severe, desolate** 삭막한, 황량한

UNIT 59

 **Quiz**

25. Our solar system has 240 moons, or natural satellites, that circumnavigate the planets and _____.

26. A planet's rotation generally causes a slight flattening at the poles and _____ at the equator.

27. Denver's plan to build a subway system was _____ in the 1970s.

28. With an understanding of plate _____, geologists have put together a new history of the Earth's surface.

29. _____ lines start at zero degrees at the equator and then run north to the North Pole.

30. Mars is an inhospitable planet, more similar to Earth's moon than to Earth itself – a dry, _____, seemingly lifeless world.

Applied Sciences

1	**vicinity** [visínəti]	*n.* an area very near to or around a stated place **neighborhood, environs, locale**	근처, 부근

2	**feasibility** [fì:zəbíləti] * *feasible* 실현 가능한	*n.* the capability of being done or achieved **practicability, workability, viability**	실행할 수 있음, 실현 가능성

3	**arch** [á:rtʃ]	*n.* a curved and both-side supported structure forming an opening of a roof, post, or pillar	아치, 호

4	**divergence** [divə́:rdʒəns]	*n.* the act of moving away in a different direction from a common point; a difference between two or more things **separation, division, difference**	분기, 발산, 상이함

5	**topography** [toupágrəfi]	*n.* the science of describing the character of an area; the natural and constructed features on the surface of land **terrain**	지형학, 지형

6	**order** [ɔ́:rdər]	*n.* the groups into which a class is divided and subdivided into more families	목 (class와 family의 중간 분류)

7	**environmentally-kind** [invàiərənméntlikáind]	*adj.* suitable to the surroundings; harmonizing with the circumstances **eco-friendly, nature friendly, green**	환경친화적인

8	**adrenal** [ədrí:nəl]	*adj.* pertaining to the adrenal glands; relating to the kidneys **suprarenal**	부신의, 신장 부근의

Quiz

1. A metropolitan area consists of a central city and any suburban areas in its _____.

2. The canal was never completed, but it showed the nation the _____ of canals.

3. The committee appointed by the mayor will undertake the erection of a memorial _____ in honor of the soldiers who died in the war.

4. Most domestic architecture during the first three-quarters of the eighteenth century displays a wide _____ of tastes.

5. He and his brothers believed that parks should be adapted to the local _____.

6. Scientists cannot agree on how fleas are related to other _____ of insects.

7. There is a number of what we call green fuels, more _____ fuels, on the market right now.

8. The _____ glands, one on top of each kidney, secrete many important hormones.

| 9 | **cardiac**
[káːrdiæk] | *adj.* relating to or affecting the heart | 심장의 |

10 inflammation
[ìnfləméiʃən]

n. the presence of redness and swelling from an infection

염증

11 hyperopia
[hàipəróupiə]

n. a condition in which distant objects are seen more distinctly than near ones

farsightedness

원시

12 narcolepsy
[náːrkəlèpsi]

n. a condition marked by sudden episodes of irresistible sleepiness

기면증

13 antidepressant
[æntidiprésənt]

n. a drug that prevents or relieves the symptoms of depression

항우울제

14 neutron
[njúːtrɑn]

n. one of the electrically uncharged particles in the nucleus of an atom

중성자

15 photosynthesis
[fòutousínθəsis]

n. the process of manufacturing carbohydrates from carbon dioxide and water by using light

광합성

16 genetics
[dʒinétiks]

n. the scientific study of heredity and of its mechanisms

유전학

UNIT 60

 **Quiz**

9. As the name implies, _____ muscle is the tissue that surrounds the heart and allows it to pump blood throughout our bodies.

10. Encephalitis is an _____ of the brain that can be caused by rabies.

11. As they grow and develop, sometimes the shape of the eye does as well, thereby alleviating the _____.

12. Scientists believe that _____ is a genetic disorder passed down through generations.

13. Seven out of ten practicing health care professionals in Alaska prescribe _____ to their patients.

14. The _____ is neutral, meaning it has no charge.

15. During the process of _____ in green plants, light energy is captured and used.

16. Our body types are usually fixed by heredity, that is, _____.

17	**antioxidant** [æ̀ntiɑ́ksədənt]	*n.* a substance that slows down the oxidation of other substances <div align="right">항산화제</div>
18	**asthma** [ǽzmə]	*n.* a long-lasting disease which causes difficulty in breathing **chronic respiratory disease** <div align="right">천식</div>
19	**chromosome** [króuməsòum]	*n.* the microscopic thread-like structures of a cell which contain all the genetic information <div align="right">염색체</div>
20	**endocrine** [éndəkrin]	*adj.* relating to internal secretions or to a pathway or structure that secretes internally <div align="right">내분비(선)의</div>
21	**cornea** [kɔ́ːrniə]	*n.* the convex transparent membrane that covers the front of the eyeball <div align="right">각막</div>
22	**lens** [lenz]	*n.* a piece of round and transparent flesh behind the pupil in the eye <div align="right">수정체</div>
23	**myopia** [maióupiə]	*n.* a condition in which distant objects appear blurry **shortsightedness** <div align="right">근시, 근시안</div>
24	**measles** [míːzəlz]	*n.* a highly infectious disease characterized by fever, a sore throat, and a blotchy red rash **rubeola** <div align="right">홍역</div>

 **Quiz**

17. *One excellent example of an herbal remedy is mushroom tea, which is an excellent _____.*

18. *Hot, humid weather can make an _____ sufferer's condition much worse.*

19. *Almost all the hereditary material of an individual organism resides in the _____.*

20. *The _____ system functions in close relationship with the nervous system.*

21. *The _____ protects the internal workings of the eye from things like foreign debris.*

22. *The _____ focuses the image before it moves inwardly onto the retina.*

23. *People with _____ have difficulty seeing objects far away but can see things up close very easily.*

24. *Among the symptoms of _____ are a high fever, the swelling glands and a cough.*

25	**polio** [póuliòu]	*n.* a viral disease of the brain and spinal cord which can result in paralysis **poliomyelitis** 소아마비
26	**receptor** [riséptər]	*n.* an element of the nervous system adapted for reception of stimuli 수용기, 감각 기관
27	**kidney** [kídni]	*n.* an organ whose function is the removal of waste products from the blood 신장
28	**pancreas** [pǽnkriəs]	*n.* an organ that is situated behind the stomach and which produces insulin 췌장
29	**isotope** [áisətòup]	*n.* one of two or more atoms with the same atomic number but with different numbers of neutrons 동위 원소
30	**proton** [próutɑn]	*n.* the positively charged particles that are found at the center of an atom 양성자

🎯 Quiz

25. The _____ vaccine was discovered by a physician named Jonas Salk.

26. These are genes that are associated with particular nerve-cell _____ in the brain.

27. The _____ play a vital role in maintaining health by removing impurities from the bloodstream.

28. The hormone secretin travels through the bloodstream and stimulates the _____ to liberate digestive fluid.

29. Carbon can have _____ like carbon-12, carbon-13, and carbon-14.

30. The number of _____ in the nucleus of an atom varies from element to element.

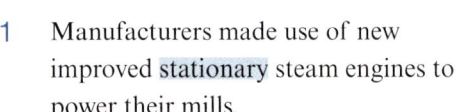

REVIEW TEST

Choose the closest meaning to the highlighted word or phrase.

1   Manufacturers made use of new improved **stationary** steam engines to power their mills.

Ⓐ potable

Ⓑ fixed

Ⓒ locomotive

Ⓓ advanced

2   One of the results of the conflict between the two **factions** was that what in previous years had been referred to as the "American," "native," or occasionally "New York" school, had by 1890 become firmly established in the minds of critics and public alike as the Hudson River School.

Ⓐ sides

Ⓑ fragments

Ⓒ cities

Ⓓ regions

3   There is strong **consensus** in society that property rights encourage property holders to develop the property and efficiently to allocate resources based on the operation of the market.

Ⓐ rift

Ⓑ division

Ⓒ dispute

Ⓓ agreement

4   Their regulations kept **tariffs** high, and that helped protect American industrialists against foreign competition.

Ⓐ safeguards

Ⓑ tolls

Ⓒ interests

Ⓓ duties

5   Neolithic farmers usually raised more food than they could consume, and their **surpluses** permitted larger, healthier populations.

Ⓐ remainders

Ⓑ inventions

Ⓒ proscriptions

Ⓓ provisions

6   The basic **tenet** of functionalism — that function should determine form — was not a new concept.

Ⓐ hymn

Ⓑ doctrine

Ⓒ sermon

Ⓓ demand

7   In 1992, 150 nations signed a **treaty** on global warming at a UN-sponsored summit on the environment in Rio de Janeiro.

Ⓐ application

Ⓑ agreement

Ⓒ adaptation

Ⓓ adherence

8   Social Security benefits are already heavily taxed. For example, a retired couple in the 28 percent **bracket** receiving $20,000 in benefits pays $2,800 in taxes.

Ⓐ state

Ⓑ class

Ⓒ revenue

Ⓓ income

9   If one of these parts becomes injured through trauma or does not develop correctly, problems with our vision will occur.

Ⓐ alias

Ⓑ awareness

Ⓒ shock

Ⓓ pandemic

10 The small tilt of the moon's orbit with respect to the plane of the ecliptic and the small eccentricity of the lunar orbit make such eclipses much less common than they would be otherwise, but partial or total eclipses are actually rather frequent.

Ⓐ portion

Ⓑ incline

Ⓒ path

Ⓓ bulge

11 In fact, give and take is an example of the way scientists tug and haul at their own and others' findings until a consensus takes shape.

Ⓐ thrust

Ⓑ pull

Ⓒ snatch

Ⓓ push

12 The dry spell parched the soil in the metropolitan region and has endangered corn, tomatoes, hay and dairy forage, and probably would reduce supplies and prompt price increases of the favorite fruits and vegetables of summer.

Ⓐ area

Ⓑ pitch

Ⓒ atmosphere

Ⓓ period

13 Whales are warm-blooded animals with skeletal, vascular, alimentary, respiratory, sensory, and reproductive features fundamentally the same as those in other mammals despite their superficial resemblance to fish.

Ⓐ mysterious

Ⓑ exterior

Ⓒ climaxing

Ⓓ interactive

14 Every summer, bears from all over southern Alaska congregate along the McNeil River.

Ⓐ scatter

Ⓑ mass

Ⓒ fly

Ⓓ swim

15 The accident caused lethal exposure to numerous people in the immediate vicinity as well as neighboring countries.

Ⓐ description

Ⓑ development

Ⓒ neighborhood

Ⓓ heartland

16 The Environmental Protection Agency considered only health, and not cost or technological feasibility, when determining what safe levels of exposure to toxic air pollutants were.

Ⓐ possibility

Ⓑ benefit

Ⓒ hazard

Ⓓ weakness

Index

정답 및 해석

PART 1 ★ Chapter01

UNIT 01 Check-up Quiz   p.12

1 **contemporary** 그의 작품은 19세기 당시의 삶에 대한 서술이었다.
2 **afforded** 양털 이불이 제공해 주는 따뜻함 때문에 추운 지방에서는 양
털 이불이 사용되었다. 3 **annually** 전국에서 가장 주목할만한 로데오 경
기는 여전히 Wyoming주에서 매년 개최된다. 4 **ascribes** 그 서사시들은
Homer의 작품이라고 전해지고 있지만, 그에 대해서는 거의 알려진 것이 없
다. 5 **imprints** 중국에서 쌀의 흔적이 발견되었기 때문에 전문가들은 쌀
의 기원지가 아시아라고 믿는다. 6 **apace with** 도시 중심가 상업 지역
은 도시 자체만큼 전반적으로 빠르게 성장하지는 않았다. 7 **cradle** 나일
강은 세계에서 가장 긴 강으로 문명의 요람이다. 8 **Undoubtedly** 의
심할 바 없이 사냥감들은 인류식단의 주요 구성물이었다. 9 **cunning** 원
시인류는 똑똑한 사냥꾼이긴 했지만, 여전히 일부 동물들에 대해서는 위협감
을 느끼고 있었다. 10 **enigmatic** 비록 관련된 화석 증거들이 많이 있지
만, 네안데르탈인의 출현은 여전히 수수께끼로 남아있다. 11 **abundant**
일부 여성들은 해안가 더 가까운 곳에 풍부하게 있었던 조개들을 수집하는 일
을 전문적으로 담당하였다. 12 **account for** 자기에 유약을 바르는 방식
이 다양했기 때문에, 도자기의 색상이 매우 다양하게 나타날 수 있었다. 13
cast 초기 문명들은 주형에 주조 가능한 합금인 청동을 발명하여 도구와
무기를 만들었다. 14 **artifacts** 고고학자들은 모든 증거를 면밀히 조사
한 후, 그 유물들의 전반적인 연대를 결정하였다. 15 **accommodate**
그 서로 붙어있는 아파트 형태의 집들은 여러 가정을 수용할 수 있었다. 16
adorned 과거에는 남성, 여성 그리고 아이들이 구슬로 자신들을 꾸몄다.
17 **abruptly** 너무 갑자기 끝이 나서 사람들은 그 연극을 좋아하지 않았
다. 18 **acclaimed** 그 발레리나는 멋진 공연으로 박수 갈채를 받았다.
19 **bears** 대안 역사는 공상 과학 소설뿐만 아니라 역사 소설과도 어느정
도 관련성이 있다. 20 **by chance** 그 등장 인물은 운이 좋아 부를 획득
한 것이지, 부지런해서 그런 것은 아니었다. 21 **abandoned** 시간이 지
나면서 몇몇 의식들은 폐지되었지만, 이후 신화라 불리게 된 이야기들은 지속
되어서 예술과 극의 소재를 제공해주었다. 22 **abstractions** 많은 조각
가들은 미니멀리즘의 추상적 개념들을 거부하고 있다. 23 **agile** 곡예사
들은 뛰어날 정도로 민첩해야만 한다. 24 **surmount** 그녀는 장애물을 극
복해 낼 수 있었다. 25 **aesthetically** 풍자극은 미적인 만족감을 주는
예술작품이기 때문에 읽혀지고 있다. 26 **akin** 그녀의 소설 속 세상은 일상
생활 속에서 사람들이 겪는 실제의 삶과 놀랍도록 유사하다. 27 **diverse**
예술 작품은 그 형태가 다양하여, 조각, 그림 그리고 사진을 포함한다. 28
acquisition 사회적 상호작용 이론가들은 아이들의 언어 습득에 성인들
이 중요한 역할을 한다는 점을 믿는다. 29 **outgoing** 사교적인 사람들은
친절하며 외향적이다. 30 **nuisance** 전쟁이 끝난 후 그 도둑은 소 도둑질
을 하게 되었는데, 그 일은 노상강도보다 더 귀찮은 일이었다.

UNIT 02 Check-up Quiz   p.16

1 **levied** 사치품 소비자들에 대하여 새로운 소비세가 부과되었다. 2
barriers 개척시대 당시 Allegheny 산맥은 교통의 주요 장애물이었다. 3
beverages 인공 향이 사용 가능하게 되자, 음료부터 향기 나는 중고차
까지 다양한 제품들이 출시될 수 있었다. 4 **bragged** 휴양지 소유주들
은 자신들의 우수한 휴양지 내 시설에 대해 종종 자랑했다. 5 **breeds** 성
공은 성공을 부르는 법, 첫 번째 거래가 성사되자, 그는 다른 거래들도 성사
시킬 수 있었다. 6 **speculators** 투기꾼에 의한 과도한 투자는 통제
할 수 없는 경제적 성장을 이끌어낼 수 있다. 7 **culminated** 경제 위기
는 1873년 공황 시 정점에 이르렀는데, 이 때 선두 투자 은행이 파산하였다.
8 **propel** 1600년대까지 식민지 선박 제조업자들이 조선업에서의 강력한
경쟁자가 되었으며, 막대한 대서양 횡단 무역을 추진하는데 일조하였다. 9
Auctions 경매는 이따금씩 열리는 교역의 또 다른 인기 있는 형태였다.
10 **urbanization** 도시화의 과정은 기술의 발전으로 인하여 더욱 자극
되었다. 11 **calamities** 적십자는 홍수, 지진 그리고 허리케인과 같은 재
난 상황이 발생하는 경우 구호 활동을 한다. 12 **infamous** James는 악
명 높은 범법자로, 은행 강도와 총기 사용으로 유명했다. 13 **notified** 당
신이 어떤 사고와 관련되는 경우, 누구에게 먼저 통지해야 할 것인가? 14
misery 신문 기자이자 사진 작가인 Jacob Riis는 New York 빈민가
의 비참한 상황을 드러내주었다. 15 **acute** 사회적 변화에 대한 대중들
의 날카로운 인식은 19세기 대중 언론의 급속한 성장과 관련이 있었다. 16
asserted 노예 소유주들은 자신들의 작물이 경제에 엄청난 혜택을 주며,
땅을 경작하기 위해서는 노예가 필요하다고 주장했다. 17 **adversity** 그
원주민들은 역경을 극복해 낼 수 있는 강인한 사람들이었다. 18 **retrieval**
기억 형성은 세 가지 과정, 즉 부호화 과정, 저장 과정, 그리고 복구과정과 관
련이 있다. 19 **assembly** 모든 대표들은 국회 및 위원회의 입법 회기 때
문에 수도로 모였다. 20 **bill** 어떤 법안이 국회에서 통과되더라도, 대통령
이 서명하기 전에는 법으로 성립된 것이 아니다. 21 **crafted** TV 뉴스의
많은 정치적 활동들은 정치가와 그들의 대중 관계를 담당하는 정치적 고문들
에 의해 만들어지고 있다. 22 **adept** 그는 정치가, 이익단체 그리고 정부
기관들을 틀림없이 능숙하게 다룰 수 있다. 23 **enacted** 시장 규제는 종
종 부패한 정부가 유착 기업, 혹은 관련 있는 정치가들에게 혜택을 줄 목적으
로 법제화된다. 24 **eligible** 미국에서는 18세 때 선거권이 주어진다. 25
conclusive 각각의 정황들은 거의 의미가 없을 수도 있지만, 연속적이고
전체적인 정황은 직접 증거만큼이나 결정적일 수 있다. 26 **verbal** 일반적
으로 꿈은 시각적 및 언어적 이미지 모두에 의해서 구성된다. 27 **able** 대학
의 학장은 뛰어난 학자일 뿐만 아니라, 동시에 유능한 행정가여야 한다. 28
adheres 그 아이는 항상 선생님의 규칙을 따른다. 29 **banned** 일부
사람들은, 너무 위험하기 때문에, 권투와 같이 폭력적인 경기가 금지되어야 한
다고 생각한다. 30 **blunt** 그 희생자는 곤봉 혹은 기타 둔기에 의해 충격을
받은 것이 확실했다.

1 **cognizant** 과학자는 결과를 왜곡할 수 있는 편견에 대하여 항상 인식하고 경계해야 한다. 2 **cohesive** 결합력으로 인하여 물기둥은 흩어지지 않고 높은 높이로 끌어올려질 수 있다. 3 **confirm** 관찰 결과가 과학자들의 예측을 확인시켜 준다면, 그것은 그들의 이론을 지지하게 될 것이다. 4 **warp** 판자는 젖으면 휠 수 있다. 5 **discharged** 상어는 먹이에서 나오는 미세한 전기 신호를 감지할 수 있다. 6 **alert** 불개미는 경고 페로몬을 이용하여 일개미가 긴급 상황에 대한 경계태세를 취할 수 있도록 한다. 7 **chambers** 수많은 연결 통로들이 서로 다른 방들을 모두 연결해주었다. 8 **classified** 원숭이는 영장류로 분류된다. 9 **claws** 다른 고양이들과는 달리, 치타는 자신의 손톱을 완전히 세우지 못한다. 10 **aromatic** 적어도 50여 개의 향기를 내는 합성물들이 난초 과에 존재한다는 사실이 분석되었다. 11 **demonstrated** 일부 식물들이 물이 거의 없는 상태에서 어떻게 살아남을 수 있는가가 많은 실험을 통해 밝혀졌다. 12 **landmarks** 일부 전문가들은 철새들이 강이나 산맥 같은 경계 표식을 따라 자신의 길을 찾는다고 주장해 왔다. 13 **bloom** 대부분의 꽃은 봄에 개화한다. 14 **venomous** 미국에서 방울뱀은 가장 일반적인 독사이다. 15 **botanical** 미국에서 가장 아름다운 식물원 중의 하나는 South Carolina에 위치한, 야생적이고 아름다운 Magnolia Gardens이다. 16 **ambidextrous** 전 인구 중 오른손 잡이는 80~90%, 왼손 잡이는 5~15%에 이르며, 나머지 소수는 양손 잡이로 알려져 있다. 17 **advent** 베트남전이 시작되자 미 공군은 동남아시아 정글 상공의 비행에 도움을 줄 수 있는 시스템을 필요로 하였다. 18 **alien** 지구 핵의 상태는 우주보다 더 먼 외계의 세계에 가깝다. 19 **boulders** 토양에서 발견되는 광물질 입자들은 아주 작은 진흙 입자에서 거대한 둥근 바위까지, 그 크기가 다양하다. 20 **stable** 노면은 고속 도로의 안정적인 토대를 제공한다. 21 **permeable** 일부 경우, 우물은 침투성이 있는 암석 층으로부터 물을 뽑아 낼 것이다. 22 **eject** 간헐천은 주기적으로 뜨거운 물기둥을 공기 중으로 분출한다. 23 **hemmed** 오대호는 서쪽으로는 Sierra Nevada 산맥에 동쪽으로는 Rocky 산맥에 의해 둘러 쌓여 있으며, 바다로 흐르지는 않는다. 24 **core** 그 소행성들의 성분은 지구 철의 핵 성분과 유사한 것으로 생각되고 있다. 25 **hampered** 악천후로 인하여 구명선을 찾으려는 구조원들은 날씨의 방해를 받았다. 26 **synthesize** 동물 세포들은 단순한 화합물로부터 일부 복잡한 분자물질들을 합성해 낼 수 없다는 점을 인식하는 것이 중요하다. 27 **delicate** 지구는 생명체에 필요한 까다로운 온도 조건을 위반할 정도로 태양으로부터 멀지도, 가깝지도 않은 위치에 있다. 28 **fueled** 태양은 그 중심부 주변에서 수소를 헬륨으로 전환시키는 열핵 반응에 의해 에너지를 공급받는다. 29 **shrink** 지금으로부터 약 50억년 후에는 태양의 중심부가 수축되어 더 뜨겁게 될 것이다. 30 **efficiency** 심지어 대체에너지를 지지하는 사람들도 탄소 방출을 감소시킬 수 있는 가장 손쉬운 방법은 효율성에 보다 초점을 맞추는 것이라고 생각한다.

1 **appeal** 철이 매력적인 이유는 낮은 가격, 견고함, 그리고 불에 대한 내구성 때문이다. 2 **bind** 호텔은 미국을 연결하는데 도움을 주는 몇몇 최초의 시설이었다. 3 **sway** 고층 건물들은 높은 바람에 약간 흔들릴 것이

다. 4 **beneficial** 일부 박테리아는 먹이를 분해하여 식물의 성장을 자극하기 때문에 유익하다. 5 **alludes** "지그재그"란 말은 기하학적인 장식을 의미한다. 6 **altered** 지구가 개발됨에 따라 다양한 화학적 반응에 의해 오염인자들의 농도가 변화되었다. 7 **appreciation** 종의 손실에 대한 우려와 함께, 생물 다양성의 중요성에 대한 점진적인 평가가 이루어지고 있다. 8 **barren** 한 쪽에는 대규모 원시림이 있고 반대 쪽에는 나무를 찾아 볼 수 없는 메마른 땅이 존재하는걸 볼 수 있다. 9 **comparatively** 운하 건설의 최초의 시도는 사기업에 의해 이루어졌으며, 비교적 소규모로만 이루어졌다. 10 **clues** 그 동물이 어떻게 죽었는지 아무런 실마리도 없었다. 11 **voluminous** 그 생태학자는 그 분야의 다른 전문가들과 수많은 서신 교환 및 수 차례의 토의를 하였다. 12 **thrives** 다른 곡물과 달리 보리는 높은 고도에서도 잘 자라기 때문에 많은 지역에서 재배될 수 있다. 13 **facilitated** 국회의 금전적 지원으로 수소 기술 연구가 촉진되었다. 14 **boundary** Superior 호수는 미국과 캐나다의 자연 경계를 이룬다. 15 **Advocates** 유기농 식품을 지지하는 사람들은 유기농 식품이 그렇지 않은 식품보다 안전하고 영양분이 더 많다고 주장한다. 16 **cope with** 일반적으로 인간의 신체는 극도의 더위 및 추위에 대처할 수 없다. 17 **crucial** 확실히 근육은 인체에 꼭 필요하다. 18 **inhibit** 항생제는 박테리아의 성장을 억제한다. 19 **illusions** 착시 현상은 인식 작용에 착각을 일으킴으로써 눈을 속인다. 20 **specimen** 많은 의학 실험은 혈액 표본을 필요로 한다. 21 **breakthrough** 그 새로운 백신은 바이러스와의 싸움에서 중요하고도 획기적인 사건이었다. 22 **codified** 1500년대까지 유럽에서는 인간의 신체에 관한 지식들이 수집되어 책으로 편찬되었다. 23 **anatomy** Thomas Eakins는 화가가 되기 위해 공부할 때, 그림뿐만 아니라 해부학도 공부했다. 24 **acrid** 고무를 태우면 역한 냄새가 나는 연기가 생성된다. 25 **corpse** 일반적으로 부패하는 개미의 시체는 일개미들에 의하여 개미집에서 끌어내어 진다. 26 **finite** 많은 사람들은 지구의 석유 공급량이 유한하다는 점과 에너지가 언젠가는 고갈될 것이라는 점에 대하여 두려워하고 있다. 27 **ignites** 공기에 노출되면 인은 즉시 점화되어 하얀색 연기를 내며 탄다. 28 **manipulate** 조종사는 이륙하고, 방향과 속도를 바꾸고, 착륙하기 위해서 제어 장치를 조작해야만 한다. 29 **drainage** 그 지역은 효과적인 하수 시스템을 갖춘, 오랜 역사의 지하 시설을 가지고 있다. 30 **ventilated** 현재 대부분의 헛간들은 단열되고, 환기되며, 전시 시설들이 갖추어져 있다.

Chapter 01 Review Test

p.28

1. Ⓑ	2. Ⓓ	3. Ⓐ	4. Ⓒ
5. Ⓓ	6. Ⓒ	7. Ⓓ	8. Ⓐ
9. Ⓒ	10. Ⓓ	11. Ⓑ	12. Ⓑ
13. Ⓓ	14. Ⓒ	15. Ⓐ	16. Ⓓ

1 그로테스크 양식과 고딕 양식이 결합된 Flannery O'Connor의 소설은 적나라하고 잔인한 희극과 격렬한 비극의 관점에서 당시 남부에서의 삶을 다루고 있다. 2 하지만 이 요인들은 출산에 매우 가까운 시기에 임신한 어룡들이 어떻게 특정지역에 모이게 되었는가라는 흥미로운 질문에 대해서는 설명을 해주지 못한다. 3 갑사기 그 장면은 공장 노동자들이 일하러 가는 도중 서로를 밀치고 있는 장면으로 바뀌었다. 4 한 연구가는 6개의 각기 다른 문화를 가진 아기들과 그 어머니들을 관찰했는데, 모든 어머니들이 단순화된 구문과 짧은

발성 그리고 뜻이 통하지 않는 소리를 사용했으며, 또한 특정 소리를 '아기 말'로 바꾸어 쓴다는 사실을 발견했다. 5 악명을 덜 떨치는 포식동물 가운데 하나가 화려한 색을 자랑하는 불가사리인데, 이것은 식물, 산호, 그리고 기타 어패류를 먹고 산다. 6 Academy and Institute의 회원은 상금에 대한 자격이 없다. 7 그 과정은 매우 빠르게 상당한 양의 얼음 결정을 만들 수 있는데, 이 얼음 중 일부는 서로 달라붙어서 얼음 결정체의 집합체, 즉 눈 결정체를 만들게 된다. 8 그들은 핵 폐기물 처리나 적절한 봉인 방법에 대해서는 전혀 훈련을 받지 않았으며, 자신들의 몸이 어느 정도의 치명적인 방사능에 노출되고 있는지에 관해서 인식하지 못했고, 또한 이에 대해 정부로부터 아무런 이야기도 듣지 못했다. 9 실제로, 이러한 화석들에 대한 훌륭한 보존이 없었다면, 그 이상한 생물들은 공룡으로 분류되었을 수도 있다. 10 종종 굴 입구 쪽에서 발견되는 꽃발게는 4인치 정도의 손톱을 가지고 있어서 짝짓기 상대를 고를 때와 신체 방어를 할 때 사용한다. 11 독사의 송곳니와 마찬가지로 오리너구리는 한 쌍의 독이 든 송곳니로써 자신들의 새끼들을 보호한다. 12 많은 대도시들은 도시 소음의 수준을 낮추기 위해 여러 조치들을 취하고 있다; 소음 문제는 초음속 제트 비행기의 출현으로 보다 많은 관심을 받게 되었다. 13 효율성에 관한 Taylor 사상의 핵심은 어떠한 일을 하는 "유일한 최선의 방법"은 주의 깊은 과학적 분석을 통하여 발견될 수 있다는 점이었다. 14 이러한 생산성의 급증 현상 뒤에 감춰진 가장 중요한 요인은 북부 농부들이 노동 절약적인 설비를 광범위하게 채택한 점이었다. 15 일반적으로 식물학자들은 식물을 출판물에서의 유사한 식물과 비교하거나 표본으로 보관되는 견본들과 비교한다. 16 증기선은 이런 새로운 형태의 동력을 이용한 최초의 교통수단으로서, 주요한 강이나 수로를 따라 미국의 성장과 산업의 발전에 촉진제 역할을 했다.

다. 15 **adversaries** 징키스칸은 성인기가 되자 그와 그의 가족들을 살해하거나 노예로 삼으려고 했던 다양한 적들과 수많은 전투를 겪어야 했다. 16 **afterlife** 죽음은 현 생의 제약으로부터 사후세계로의 해방을 의미하기 때문에 새로운 시작이라고 언급되기도 한다. 17 **composed** 어떤 영화들에는 명확히 그 영화를 위해 작곡된 음악이 포함되어 있다. 18 **costumes** 그들은 가면과 의복을 착용하고 종종 다른 사람, 동물, 혹은 초자연적인 존재들을 인격화시켜 나타냈다. 19 **overall** 책의 목차는 독자들에게 그 책이 무엇에 관한 것인지 전체적인 내용에 대한 개념을 제공해준다. 20 **assimilated** 이민자들은 새로운 국가에 빠르게 동화되었고 그 국가의 언어와 관습을 배웠다. 21 **assumption** 다수의 전문가들은 극이 다양한 의식에서 비롯되었다고 가정한다. 22 **attachments** 감정적인 애착은 실제 중요한 방식으로 사람들의 결정에 영향을 미친다. 23 **carried out** 미 흑인 그래픽 예술가들은 시각 미술을 증대 및 진전시키는데 지속적인 노력을 기울였다. 24 **coined** 'beat'라는 용어는 Herbert Huncke에 의해 만들어졌는데, 그는 이 말을 '피곤한' 혹은 '빈곤한'의 동의어로 의도했다. 25 **aristocracy** 그는 귀족이었으나 금전적으로는 가난했다. 26 **bland** 중요한 문제는 그런 엄격한 구조가 오페라를 김빠지게 만들고 때로는 뻔한 것으로 만들었다는 점이다. 27 **emphasize** 어머니들은 아이들과 의사소통을 할 때 얼굴 표정을 과장해서 나타내고, 모음을 보다 길게 발음하며, 특정 단어를 강조한다. 28 **dialect** 그들은 지역 방언을 연구했으며, 특정 지역에서의 삶에 초점을 맞춘 소설을 썼다. 29 **come up with** 경제 상황으로 인하여 기업들은 비용을 절감시킬 수 있는 혁신적인 방안을 고안해내도록 요구 받고 있다. 30 **current** "민속 음악"이라는 용어는 수백 년 넘게 사용되고 있다.

PART 1 ★ Chapter 02

UNIT 05 Check-up Quiz　　　p.30

1 **daring** Richard Bird와 그의 조종사 Floyd Bennett은 1926년 5월 북극으로 향하는 대담한 비행에 착수했다. 2 **depressed** 임대료 통제 정책은 인위적으로 장기 수익의 가장 중요한 결정요인, 즉 임대료를 억제시키고 있다. 3 **disaster** 경작이 실패 했을 때, 그것은 많은 사람들의 목숨을 앗아간 재앙이었다. 4 **domain** 조용하게, 그러나 빠르게 그 제국은 자신의 영역을 넓히고 있었다. 5 **decipher** 그들은 그 평판들을 해독할 수 있었는데, 그 이유는 학자들이 10년 전 최초로 해석에 성공했던 셈족어가 적혀져 있었기 때문이었다. 6 **ascending** Pueblo 건축가들은 절벽을 오를 수 있는 돌계단을 이용하여 공공 도로 시스템을 설계하였다. 7 **avid** 미국의 대통령인 Theodore Roosevelt는 자연보호의 신념을 지닌 열렬한 환경보호론자였다. 8 **restricted** 발자국 화석에 대한 연구는 수백 만년 전의 표본에만 한정되는 것은 아니다. 9 **roughly** 19세기 나머지 기간 동안 인구는 한 세대마다 대략 2배씩 증가했다. 10 **settled** 신석기 농부들의 일상생활이 안정화되면서 마을과 궁극적으로는 도시의 진화가 이루어졌다. 11 **attire** 몇 주 전 그는 자신의 취임식에서 정장을 입을 것이라고 말했다. 12 **components** 시간의 척도는 eon, era, 그리고 period의 세가지 구성 요소로 나누어진다. 13 **considerable** 그 책은 당시 존재했던 유일한 다른 사용지침서를 뛰어넘는 상당히 발전된 책이었다. 14 **Thanks to** 일에 대한 끊임없는 압박감 때문에, 그는 자신의 사업을 그만두기로 결심했

UNIT 06 Check-up Quiz　　　p.34

1 **sparked** 경제 호황으로 부동산 개발이 폭발적으로 이루어졌다. 2 **devastated** 전쟁으로 국가가 황폐해진 후 모든 것이 복구되는데 수년이 걸렸다. 3 **encouraged** 주 정부는 두 가지 별개의 방식으로 기업의 내부 개선이 이루어지도록 자극했다. 4 **effect** 1800년대 초 미국에서는 각 주 정부들이 연방 정부 보다 경제에 더 큰 영향을 미쳤다. 5 **end** 이러한 목적, 즉 경제의 안정을 회복하기 위하여, 정부는 몇 가지 조치를 취하려 했다. 6 **tolls** 운하는 통행료를 통하여 수지가 맞게 됨으로써, 급속도로 투자가들의 기대에 부합되었다. 7 **warranted** 모든 사람들이 무엇이 일어나고 있는지 알고 있었기 때문에 그 이상의 설명은 필요하지 않았다. 8 **phases** 전면적인 케인즈주의적 정책은 모든 경제 국면에서 정부에게 일정한 역할을 부여하는 것이다. 9 **fragrances** 천연 조미료와 향료는 종종 값이 비싸고 공급량이 한정되어 있다. 10 **sheer** 1870년대의 십 년 동안 순전히 신문사의 숫자만 2배가 되었다. 11 **significant** 1964년의 민권 법은 흑인들에게 특히 중요한 법이었다. 12 **concern** 2명 혹은 그 이상의 소유주를 가지고 있는 기업체는 동업 회사라고 지칭된다. 13 **sparse** 인구가 적은 곳에서는 흑사병도 자연스럽게 세력을 잃고 일년 내에 사라질 것이었다. 14 **undertaken** Erie 운하 건설은 당시 그 누구도 해보지 못했던 가장 거대한 공사 중의 하나였다. 15 **catastrophic** 지진 해일은 수많은 사람들의 목숨을 빼앗고 집과 건물들을 파괴시키는 재앙이 될 수 있다. 16 **coincided with** Boston의 급속한 성장은 그곳 이민자들의 대규모 유입과 동시에 일어났다. 17 **alleviate** 친척들과 친구들로 구성된 네트워크는 자녀 양육의 부담을 상당부분 덜어 줄 수 있다. 18 **antagonistic** 대부

분의 농장 소유주들은 도시의 발전에 적대적이었다. 19 **declared** 미국은 2차 대전 중 전쟁을 선포하고 유럽 전선에 병력을 급파했다. 20 **deemed** 미 대통령은 필요한 것으로 간주되는 주류에 대한 금지 규정 등을 만들 수 있다. 21 **equality** 1957년 Ralph Abernathy는 흑인들의 인종적 평등을 달성하기 위한 조직을 설립했다. 22 **collapse** 로마 제국은 막대한 영토로 인하여 점차 방어하기 어려워졌는데, 이러한 사실은 476년 결국 붕괴로 이어지는 발판이 되었다. 23 **barred** 그 정당은 이민자들의 공직 입후보가 금지되어야 한다고 주장했다. 24 **succinct** 그는 New York시의 빈민가 및 주택 문제에 관한 간결하고도 사실적인 글을 썼다. 25 **constrict** 전문가들은 성장이 지속되지 못할 것이며, 경직된 노동 시장은 경제를 수축시킬 것이라고 전망했다. 26 **allegiances** 일부 인디언들은 프랑스 예수회 신부들에게는 충성한 반면, 영국 군인들에게는 보다 의심스러운 태도를 보였다. 27 **appealing** 가장 매력적인 출판에 대한 투자는 스테디 셀러인 작은 책에서 이루어졌다. 28 **suit** 개혁가들은 교육 프로그램이 주민들의 욕구를 만족시킬 수 있어야 한다고 주장했다. 29 **cite** 연구 논문을 작성할 때 작성자는 그들이 인용하는 출처를 언급해야만 한다. 30 **flaw** 보석의 흠은 그 가치를 떨어뜨린다.

1 **dispersing** 흰 색 빛이 다양한 파장으로 구성되어 있다는 사실은 빛을 프리즘을 통해 분산시켜 봄으로써 알 수 있다. 2 **emerged** 그 종은 바다에서 나타나 육지로 이동했다. 3 **emit** 네온과 같은 특정 기체들은 전류에 노출되면 빛을 방출한다. 4 **vertical** 비록 공기가 수평적으로 그리고 수직적으로도 이동하지만, '바람'이라는 용어는 수평적 운동에만 적용된다. 5 **exhilarating** 우주 왕복선에 탑승하는 것은 유쾌한 경험이 될 수 있다. 6 **dense** 정글은 그 안에 자라는 막대한 양의 식물들로 인하여 매우 울창하다. 7 **determine** 캐나다 연구가들은 일종의 벌레인 선충류의 생애를 결정하는 일련의 유전자들을 밝혀냈다. 8 **dissenting** 이 고대 동물에 대한 우리의 이해는 전문가들 사이의 많은 이견과 더불어 서서히 증가했다 9 **edible** 셀러리는 깃털 같은 잎으로 덮여있고 긴 줄기를 지니고 있는 먹을 수 있는 식물인데, 차가운 날씨에서 가장 잘 자란다. 10 **Entire** 수확 전후로 균류가 침투하게 되면 전체 작물이 황폐화될 수 있다. 11 **fatal** 인동덩굴은 하얀색 혹은 노란색의 치명적인 꽃잎을 가지고 있는 관목이다. 12 **succumb** 대부분의 새들은 겨울에 남쪽으로 이동하지 않는다면 가혹한 날씨에 굴복하여 죽게 될 것이다. 13 **crave** 몇몇 곤충들은 개미를 깨끗이 해주거나 개미들이 찾고 있는 화학 물질을 제공함으로써 그들을 도울 수 있다. 14 **upright** 캥거루는 똑바로 서있거나 점프할 때 자신들의 길고 강력한 꼬리를 이용하여 균형을 맞춘다. 15 **ventured** 많은 갑각류 동물들은 바다에서 살지만, 일부는 민물에서도 살며, 소수는 위험을 무릅쓰고 육지로 나아가기도 한다. 16 **brood** 그 어미 오리는 새끼들을 연못으로 인도했다. 17 **bring about** 지렁이는 토양을 기름지게 하고 보다 비옥하게 함으로써 토양의 변화를 일으킨다. 18 **carry** 일부 지각은 해저를, 다른 지각은 대륙을 떠받치고 있는데, 이 둘을 모두 떠받치고 있는 지각도 있다. 19 **comprise** 지구는 핵, 맨틀, 그리고 지각의 3개의 층으로 구성된다. 20 **uncharted** 해저는 심지어 오늘날에도 대부분 탐사되지 않고 지도에 표시되어 있지 않은 거대한 미개척 영역이다. 21 **dot** 구릉 지대라고 불리는 가파르고 둥근 언덕은 Indiana 남부에 산재하고 있다. 22 **imaginary** 적도는 지구 중심을 둘러싸는 가상의 선이다. 23 **receptacles** 오대호

의 울퉁불퉁한 계곡은 습기를 언제든지 내 보낼 수 있는 저장소 역할을 한다. 24 **diminished** 허리케인의 힘은 일단 육지 위로 올라오면 곧바로 감소하게 되는데, 그 이유는 물 에너지에서 멀어지기 때문이다. 25 **balmy** 카리브 해에 위치해 있는데 Virgin Islands는 온화한 기후를 보인다. 26 **desperately** 달과 화성은 지구에서 절박하게 필요한 천연자원의 미래 공급처가 될 수 있다. 27 **flamed** 목성은 자체적인 빛을 내는 별로써 불탔었을 것이다. 28 **sustainable** 지속 가능한 인간의 정착에 절대적으로 필요한 것은 바로 물이다. 29 **terrains** 달은 두 개의 주요한 지형으로 분류될 수 있는데, maria와 terrace가 그것이다. 30 **extinguished** 주야로 쉬지 않고 2주 동안 작업한 끝에 폭발로 인한 화재는 드디어 진화되었다.

1 **confine** 도공들은 일반적으로 장식용 도자기와 가정용 도자기 둘 중 하나에 한정해서 생산을 할 수 있었다. 2 **dwellings** New England에서는 소수의 집들만 돌로 지어졌으나, 유일하게도 Pennsylvania와 인접 지역에서는 석재가 주거 시설에 널리 사용되었다. 3 **fasten** 승객들은 비행기가 이륙하기 전에 안전 벨트를 반드시 착용해야만 한다. 4 **raze** 철거용 볼은 건물을 파괴하는데 사용된다. 5 **annihilate** 인간은 자신과 자연과의 균형에 손상을 가할 수 있을 뿐만 아니라, 여러 종들을 전멸시킬 수 있는 힘을 가지고 있다. 6 **clumsy** 육지에서 물개는 우둔해 보이지만, 보통 사람보다 빠른 속도로 단거리를 달릴 수 있다. 7 **concealed** 연구자들은 지하에서 그 모습을 숨기고 있는 단층에 의하여 도시가 위협받고 있다고 주장한다. 8 **critical** 생물 다양성은 중대한 환경 보존 이슈로서 널리 인식 되고 있다. 9 **demise** 자금의 부족으로 그 프로그램은 소멸되었다. 10 **depleted** 지구에서 유기체의 시체들은 재활용되는데, 이러한 사실은, 그렇지 않으면 토양과 물의 영양분은 곧 고갈될 것이기 때문에, 다행스러운 일이다. 11 **sequence** 개미가 단계별로 이루어져야 할 일들을 직병렬 순서로 수행한다는 사실 역시 흥미롭다. 12 **turbulent** 작은 포유류들은 나무의 가장 위 부분에 위치한 노출되고 격렬한 환경에서 고생을 하게 된다. 13 **typify** 고산지대는 티베트와 네팔지형에서 전형적으로 나타난다. 14 **unprecedented** 세계의 선진국들은 전례 없는 비율로 귀중한 자원을 소모시키고 있다. 15 **feverish** 미 남북 전쟁은 중유 물품을 공급하기 위한 활발한 제조 활동을 이끌어 냈는데, 특히 북부에서 그러하였다. 16 **permanent** 과음은 두뇌에 영구적인 손상을 입힐 수도 있다. 17 **maintain** 소비자들이 유기농 식품을 건강을 유지시켜 주고 기존 식품보다 더 뛰어난 영양분을 제공해 준다고 믿는 다면, 이는 잘못된 판단이다. 18 **screened** 지금은 모든 혈액에 대해 HIV와 기타 바이러스 검사를 철저히 한다. 19 **strides** 이들 연구로부터 환자들을 치료하는 데 있어서의 위대한 진보가 이루어졌다. 20 **surpass** 차후 25년 이내에 인간에 대한 중요도 면에서 내과 의학이 외과 의학을 능가할 것이라고 보도되었다. 21 **unsubstantiated** 천연 비타민이 합성 비타민보다 더 우수하다는, 근거 없는 여러 보고서들이 존재한다. 22 **ward** 일부 식물들은 동물들을 쫓아내는 독성 연기를 방출함으로써 동물들의 접근을 막을 수 있다. 23 **articulated** 각각의 소리는 발음하기 전에 생각되고 분석된다. 24 **element** 비록 수소가 우주에서 가장 흔한 원소이긴 하지만, 지구상에서는 직접적으로 구할 수 없다. 25 **fabrics** 유사한 선질의 인공 섬유가 널리 사용되고 있지만, 천연 실크는 그 가치를 높게 인정 받고 있다. 26 **serve as** 페로몬은 같은 종의 개체들 간 사용되는, 화학 신호로서 기능하는 물질이

다. **27 brittle** 강철은 주철만큼 약하지 않기 때문에 쉽게 부러지지 않는다.
28 vibrations 진동이 공기를 통해 귓바퀴에 닿을 때 소리가 들리게 된다.
29 dazzling 산 정상의 눈은 밝은 아침 햇빛을 받으면 눈부시게 빛난다.
30 device 주행 거리계는 거리를 측정하는 장치이다.

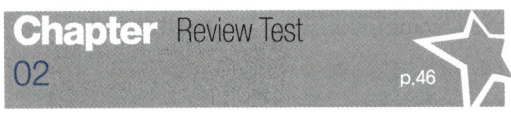

Chapter Review Test
02
p.46

1. Ⓑ	2. Ⓐ	3. Ⓒ	4. Ⓑ
5. Ⓐ	6. Ⓓ	7. Ⓑ	8. Ⓑ
9. Ⓒ	10. Ⓒ	11. Ⓑ	12. Ⓑ
13. Ⓒ	14. Ⓐ	15. Ⓓ	16. Ⓑ

1 이러한 초소들이 세워짐으로써 새로운 도로가 생겨났고, 거주민들이 정착할 수 있었으며, 또한 대담한 모험과 원정에 대한 안전 역시 보장되었다. **2** 미국 비농업인구의 수와 비율은 남북전쟁 이후의 반세기 동안 빠르게 확대되었는데, 가장 극적인 증가 중 일부는 운송, 제조 그리고 무역 영역에서 일어났다. **3** 구슬은 몸에 지닐 수 있는 특성 이외에도, 보석 혹은 의류의 장식품으로서 수집품의 특성을 가지고 있으며, 내구성이 있고, 다양하게 활용될 수 있으며, 종종 현재의 시장에서뿐만 아니라 본래의 문화적 맥락에 있어서도 귀중한 것이다. **4** 북쪽에 머무르는 동안에는 성장기가 빠르게 진행되기 때문에, 그 새들은 원하는 결과를 얻기 위해서 상당한 양의 기술을 연마해야만 했다. **5** Mimbre 사람들은 자신들의 신화와 전설, 역사를 서술하기 위해 인간과 동물의 형상을 합쳐서 표현했는데, 그 결과 학자들이 아직도 해독 못하는 우스운 장면들이 연출되었다. **6** 영국식 행동방식을 강하게 고수하였던 초기 북미 영국 식민지의 보수주의는 New England에서의 가구 제작에 주요한 영향을 미쳤다. **7** Atacama는 비그늘이라고 불리는 현상때문에 강수량이 적다. **8** 남부 및 동부 유럽 이민자들의 대규모 이동은 정규 교육의 막대한 팽창에 기여하면서 이와 동시에 일어났다. **9** 뉴딜은 Franklin D Roosevelt에 의해 채택된 가장 중요한 프로그램이었는데 이 정책은 대공황의 피해를 경감시키는데 도움이 되었다. **10** 솟아 오르는 물이 지하와 지표를 연결하는 좁은 수로로 수축되어 들어가게 되면, 이 물은 간헐천의 일부가 된다. **11** 60 종 이상의 곡물이 존재하는데, 비록 모두 먹을 수 있지만, 몇몇 종류만 인간이 소화할 수 있다. **12** 마찬가지로 이러한 상자들은, 성장하는 배아에게 치명적으로 높은 온도를 예방하기 위해, 직사광선으로부터 보호되야 한다. **13** Stuyvesant와 곧 잇따랐던 1870년대 후반 및 1880년대 초반 기타 초기 아파트 건물들의 근본적인 문제는 근 건물들이 New York의 전형적인 빌딩 구역에 제한되어 있었다는 점이었다. **14** 발달된 빠른 이동 방법을 갖고 있지 않은 동물들은 위장을 해서 약탈자로부터 숨거나 밤에 먹이를 잡아먹는 짐승이 된다. **15** 대량 멸종의 가장 잘 알려진 사례 중의 하나는 6천 5백만 전 일어난 공룡과 기타 생물들의 멸종이다. **16** 새로운 시대의 철도 역 설계자들은 철의 잠재적인 능력을 연구했는데, 철은 중세시대 교회와 성당의 거대한 아치형 구조물들을 능가하는 길이로 거대한 지역을 커버하였다.

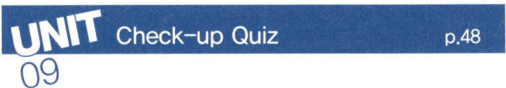

PART 1 ★ Chapter 03

UNIT 09 Check-up Quiz
p.48

1 outlaw Jesse는 무법자이고 노상 강도였으며, 범죄자였다. **2 enable** 그 경제적 지원은 사람들이 스스로 자립할 수 있을 때까지만 지속되는 것이었다. **3 fundamental** 헌법에 구현된 근본적인 이상은 경시되어서는 안 된다. **4 ignorant** 문제를 해결하기 위해 제시된 방법은 상황을 모르는 비평가들에 의해 낭비적이고 위험한 것으로서 비난을 받았다. **5 transportation** 18세기 후반 증기기관을 이용한 이동이 마침내 실용적인 교통수단으로 되었다. **6 behold** 증기선은 크기도 컸지만, 정교하고 심지어 호화롭기까지 한 구조와 외관으로 인하여 강에서 큰 구경거리가 되었음이 틀림없다. **7 mobility** 그 부대의 기동성은 전쟁에서 최고의 자산이었다. **8 Moreover** 게다가 심지어 같은 재료라도 다른 장소의 구성원에 의해 다르게 이용되면, 작품의 양식은 다양하게 나타난다. **9 chores** 최초의 도자기들은 집안 일에 사용되었으며 예술 작품으로서 만들어지지는 않았다. **10 Partitioned** 통나무집이 거주용 단순 오두막집을 대체함에 따라 통나무집의 독립된 방들은 하나의 새로운 양식이 되었다. **11 paramount** 전통은 지고한 것이어서, 대다수의 부족들은 변화에 주저했다. **12 durability** 도자기 제작은 쉽지 않은 일이었기 때문에 자기의 내구성은 부족들에게 중요한 것이었다. **13 establish** 로데오 카우보이 연합회는 1936년 설립되어 스포츠로서의 로데오 기준과 규칙을 제정했다. **14 ethnic** Harlem 르네상스는 사실주의와 인종적 자각, 그리고 미국 정신을 혼합시켰다. **15 assortment** 다양한 뼈들이 그 지점에서 발견되어, 고대 문화에 대한 학자들의 이해가 증진될 수 있었다. **16 Clarity** 명료성과 구성이 오페라 세리아의 기초를 이루었다. **17 witnessed** 1905년 그는 예술품을 거래하기 위해 파리로 갔는데, 바로 그곳에서 그는 후에 입체파의 형성기를 목격하였다. **18 devote** 때때로 일반 시민들도 이타적인 인도주의적 봉사에 자신들의 전 삶을 바친다. **19 enforce** 이러한 이미지는 그 인물이 얼마나 불쌍하고 바보스러운지를 강하게 나타낼 수 있도록 의도되었다. **20 essence** 민속 음악의 본질은 그것을 만든 사람들의 인간성을 어떠한 방식으로 반영해 내는 가이다. **21 climax** 아리아는 대개 클라이맥스로 따라나오며 배우들의 감정이나 내적 갈등을 드러낸다. **22 composite** 일부 사람들은 Iliad나 Odyssey가 한 명의 시인에 의해서 쓰여진 것이 아니라 몇몇 사람이 쓴 글이 혼합되어 있는 작품이라고 주장하고 있다. **23 encompass** "art deco"란 용어는 1920년대와 1930년대의 세 개의 구별되는 하지만 관련 있는 디자인 경향을 포함하는 의미가 되었다. **24 deliberate** 그 화가는 자신의 풍경화에서 각각의 꽃에 색을 칠하는 신중한 작업을 시작했다 **25 husbandry** 축산업의 출현으로 과학에서 심리학까지 인간의 모든 발전의 측면에서 진보가 이루어졌다. **26 hallmark** 재즈 음악의 한 특성은 최고의 음악가들이 공연 중 너무나 쉽게 실시하는 즉흥 연주 방식이었다. **27 gestures** 모든 문화에서 제스처는 의사소통의 한 형태로 사용되고 있다. **28 discipline** 모든 과학 분야는 일상 용어를 부적절한 것으로 간주하기 때문에 자체적인 특별한 언어를 개발해내는 경향이 있는데, 심리학 역시 예외는 아니다. **29 gala** 많은 사람들이 새해를 축제로 경축한다. **30 immersing** Daguerre는 또한 소금물에 이미지를 담금으로써 이미지가 영구적이 될 수 있음을 발견하였다.

UNIT 10 Check-up Quiz p.52

1 engaged in 1800년대 초 미국 노동력의 80%가 넘는 사람들이 농업에 종사하고 있었다. **2 exclusive** 저작권은 책이나 연극과 같은 창작물들을 복제, 판매 혹은 이행할 독점적인 권리이다. **3 halt** 2차 대전이 시작되어 아시아뿐만 아니라 유럽의 모든 상용 항공기 서비스가 즉각적으로 중단되었다. **4 precious** 한 때 소금은 너무나 귀중한 것이어서 일부 문화권에서는 화폐의 한 형태로 사용되었다. **5 prosper** Boston과 같은 미 식민지 항구들은 영국 및 West Indies와의 무역으로 번영할 수 있었다. **6 sluggish** 일부 경제학자들은 감세 정책이 정체된 경제 상황을 움직이기 위한 최선의 방법이라고 주장한다. **7 sound** 정부 채권과 우량주는 안정적인 투자 대상이다. **8 wares** 과거에는 많은 영업 사원들이 방문 판매로 제품을 판매하려고 했다. **9 pervasive** 그 사상의 영향력이 너무나 널리 퍼졌기 때문에, 그것의 이론적 접근법은 학계에서 Chicago 학파로서 알려지게 되었다. **10 nursing** 암 사자들은 새끼를 돌보는 동안에는 발정기에 들 수 없고 임신할 수 없다. **11 proceeded** 도시에서의 부동산 분양은 인구 성장보다 더 빠른 속도로 진행되었다. **12 donated** 1899년 Mary Elizabeth Brown은 자신이 소장한 대략 200개 이상의 악기들을 박물관에 기증하였다. **13 remarkably** 이 때 그 도시 인구가 급속하게 증가하기 시작했는데, 주로 일자리를 찾아 도시로 유입된 인구 때문이었다. **14 gregarious** 사회성이 활발한 사람은 고독을 멀리 한다. **15 confer** 가족 내에서는 전통 문화의 패턴에 따라 한 명 혹은 양쪽 부모 들이 주도권을 갖는다. **16 constitute** 군인이 불법적인 행위를 하라는 명령을 거부한 경우 반역죄가 성립하지는 않는다. **17 linear** 보통 무비판적으로 수용되고 있는 이 주제는, 다시 한번, '과학을 산업적 목적으로 이용하는 것이 일직선상의 절차이다'라는 가정을 이끌어 내었다. **18 bias** 19세기와 20세기를 통해 미 농부들은 거대 도시에 대한 선입관을 가지고 있었다. **19 exempt** 일부 부모들은 자신의 아이들을 정부 규제가 적용되지 않는 사립학교로 보내고자 마음먹게 되었다. **20 negligible** 비록 그 사고는 심각한 것으로 보였지만, 사소한 피해만이 발생했다. **21 imposed** 정부는 전시 기간 중 국민에 대해 엄격한 통제를 했다. **22 reckless** 운전자들은 무모한 운전으로 벌금을 물 수 있다. **23 bounds** 교육의 한계는 없다. **24 atheist** Allen은 이신론적인 사상을 옹호했던, 거리낌 없는 무신론자였다. **25 detect** 그 실험의 목적은 동물들의 자의식 존재 여부를 확인하기 위하여 동물들의 의식을 탐지해내는 것이었다. **26 milestone** Gallup의 실험 보고서는 동물의 마음을 이해하는 점에 있어서 획기적인 사건이었다. **27 overthrew** 로마 시민들이 통치계급인 Etruscan인들을 축출한 후 B.C 509년 로마 공화국이 구성되었다. **28 overtaxed** 공교육 시스템이 과중한 부담을 지고 있다는 점이 곧 밝혀졌다. **29 headquartered** Washington Post지와 New York Times지가 공동으로 소유하고 있는 International Herald Tribune 신문은 파리에 본사를 두고 있다. **30 zealous** 비록 그는 허약한 아이였지만, Theodore Roosevelt는 결국 성실한 노력의 덕을 찬양하는 열성적인 활동가가 되었다.

UNIT 11 Check-up Quiz p.56

1 formulated 문제에 대하여 몇몇 가능한 해결 방안들이 공식화되고 있다. **2 incorporated** 가설들이 확정되면, 그것들은 이론으로 통합된다. **3 strands** 로프는 적어도 0.15 인치의 직경을 가진 줄로서, 실을 꼬아서 만든 3개 혹은 그 이상의 가닥으로 이루어져 있다. **4 cells** 그 후에 그가 만든 수소 연료 전지는 전지를 만드는 데 든 비용을 정당화시킬 수 있을 만큼 충분한 에너지를 생산하지 못했다. **5 flourished** 또한 튤립은 Pennsylvania에서도 잘 자랐다. **6 frigid** 추운 겨울에는 먹이가 귀하기 때문에 생존을 위해서는 보다 먹이가 풍부한 곳으로 이동해야만 했다. **7 instances** 많은 경우에 있어서 표본의 직경은 1/10 밀리미터 이하이다. **8 gap** 솔잣새는 혀를 비틀어서 나무 열매의 구멍에 집어넣은 다음 씨앗을 빼낸다. **9 fused** 난초의 암술과 수술은 서로 융합되어 하나의 구조로 되어있다. **10 lumps** 수세기가 지남에 따라 송진 덩어리들은 여러 층의 토양으로 덮였다. **11 sheds** 이러한 발견은, 피할 수 없는 노화와 죽음에 대한 새로운 설명을 제시하고 있다. **12 heart** 전형적으로 혜성의 중심부는 고체상태이며, 이것의 크기는 직경 10 킬로미터 이상이 될 수도 있다. **13 startling** 벌새와 펭귄의 차이는 막대한 것이지만, 박쥐와 고래의 차이만큼 놀라운 것은 아니다. **14 sterile** 일반적으로 개미 군락은 여왕개미, 생식력이 없는 암컷 일개미와 수캐미로 구성된다. **15 canopy** 나무의 꼭대기 부근에는 적절한 크기의, 나무를 타는 포유 동물들이 상당히 많이 있다. **16 convert** "잠열"이라는 용어는 액체 상태의 물을 수증기로 바꾸는데 사용되는 에너지를 지칭한다. **17 demolished** 1980년 Saint Helens 화산이 분출했을 때 화산 주위의 거대한 양의 얼음 들판이 파괴되었다. **18 overcome** 좁은 돌출된 부위에 둥지를 지으면 특이한 문제점이 나타나는데, 그 새의 행동은 이러한 문제를 극복할 수 있도록 적응해 왔다. **19 texture** 토양의 결은 손으로 토양의 모양을 물리적으로 변화시킴으로써 확인해 볼 수 있다. **20 initiated** 또한 산악 지형은 습한 공기를 끌어올림으로써 눈을 내리게 할 수 있다. **21 drenched** 장기간에 걸쳐서 비가 오지는 않지만, 때때로 사막은 격렬한 폭풍우에 의해 적셔진다. **22 adjunct** 북미에서는 농업 용지 정리 작업에 대한 부산물로서 포타슘 생산이 이루어졌다. **23 uneven** 본질적으로 바람은 지구의 고르지 못한 공기의 분포를 균형 잡아 주는 자연적인 방법이다. **24 tepid** 허리케인이 동쪽으로 멕시코 만의 미온 해역으로 이동하면 인류에게 최대의 위험을 가하게 된다. **25 sporadically** 작은 풀들이 바위와 돌 사이에서 산발적으로 자라나는 동안, 이끼류들이 바위에 붙어서 성장하게 된다. **26 obvious** 어떤 두 개의 혜성도 동일하게 보이지는 않지만 기본적으로 같은 특성이 있는데, 그 특성 중 눈에 띄는 하나가 바로 코마를 갖는 다는 점이다. **27 plunged** 혜성이 목성의 대기권에 진입하여 목성과 충돌했을 때, 천문학자들은 가능한 면밀하게 이를 지켜보고 있었다. **28 suitable** 그 행성에서 적정 양의 물이 발견된다면, 보나 쉽게 식민지가 건설될 수 있을 것이다. **29 treks** GPS 수신장치는 대다수 신차 디자인의 표준이 되고 있으며, 황무지에서 장거리 여행을 하는 사냥꾼 혹은 어부들의 애용 품이 되었다. **30 perils** 일반적으로 허리케인의 위험성이라고 하면 강풍이 연상되지만, 가장 파괴적인 요소는 허리케인이 육지를 강타할 때 동반하는 폭풍 해일이다.

UNIT 12 Check-up Quiz p.60

1 elaborate 1600년대 신대륙에 도착한 초기 미 이주민들은 정교한 가구에 대한 재료를 거의 찾지 못했거나 혹은 그에 대한 흥미를 가지고 있지 않았다. **2 erected** 그러한 양식의 많은 건물들이 정부 프로그램을 통하여 전국적으로 건설되었다. **3 rectangular** 직사각형의 벽 안에는 상설 주택이 건설되어, 짚으로 된 기존의 Manhattanities의 주거 형태를 대체하게 되었다. **4 unifying** 모든 공원과 광장들은 주요 도로를 보완해 주는 것으로서 의도되었고, 주요 도로들은 전체 시스템을 하나로 묶는 요소로서 간주되었

다. **5 aptly** 그 도로는, 적절하게도, 곧 미국의 "대도시를 연결시켜주는 복도"라 불려지게 되었다. **6 eliminated** 아무런 이유 없이, 일부 종들은 소멸하고 다른 종들은 생존할 수 있다. **7 aquatic** 설치류는 다양한 서식처에서 사는데, 일부는 육상에서, 일부는 수중에서 서식한다. **8 efficient** 믿거나 말거나 간에, 디젤은 에너지가 대단히 풍부하며 효율성이 아주 높다. **9 habitats** Lopez와 Tinbergen은 자연 서식지에서의 다양한 동물들의 행동을 지켜보면서 생존에 유리한 행동 패턴들을 관찰하였다. **10 ensures** 그 행동은 새끼들이 어미 곁에 있게끔 해주고 위험으로부터 보호 받도록 확실히 해준다. **11 stressed** 미 식민지 사회에 있어서 산림의 중요성은 강조될 필요가 없을 정도로 중요했다. **12 striking** 아마도 나비의 다양성의 가장 독특한 측면은 열대지방과 온대지방의 종의 풍부함이 놀랍도록 차이가 난다는 점이다. **13 pliable** 백금은 구리보다 단단하고 금과 거의 같은 정도로 휜다. **14 teemed with** 한 때 미국 동해안에는 물고기들이 떼로 넘쳐났고, 일부 무리는 폭이 1마일 가량에 이를 정도로 많았다. **15 obtained** 비타민 C는 시큼한 과일에서 얻어진다. **16 nutritional** 만일 기본적인 영양학적 욕구가 충족되면 비타민 보충제를 복용할 필요는 없다. **17 deter** 생물학적으로 해충을 억제하는 또 다른 방법은 해충을 자연적으로 억제시켜준다고 알려진 다양한 식물들을 정원에 두는 것이다. **18 portable** 말을 더듬는 사람들은 자신이 말한 내용을 한 박자 늦게 들려주는 휴대장치를 가지고 다닌다. **19 populate** 골격근은 다른 근육보다 인체에서 차지하는 부분이 크다. **20 preceded** 때로는 증상이 일어나기 전에 가시적인 졸음 현상이 선행되기도 하지만 그 증상의 대부분은 갑자기 일어난다. **21 prescribed** 한방 요법에서는 뜨거운 액체 상태로 복용할 수 있도록 의사들이 특별한 약재를 처방한다. **22 reaction** 열을 흡수하는 화학 반응은 흡열 반응이라 불린다. **23 respiratory** 평활근에 해당하는 근육은 숨쉬기를 도와주는 호흡 조직에서 찾아볼 수 있다. **24 at odds** 과학자, 의사 그리고 심리학자들은 뇌가 어떻게 작동하는지에 대해 의견을 달리하고 있다. **25 ingredients** 특정 조건 하에서 이 두 성분이 함께 섞이면, 그 결과는 치명적이 될 수도 있다. **26 noxious** 공업 단지 건설의 한 결과는 대기 중 독성 화학 물질의 농도가 증가된 것이었다. **27 subject** 식물은 상당히 다양한 공생 생물들의 공격과 감염에 취약하기 때문에, 잠재적인 기생 생물들을 격퇴하기 위한 다양한 메커니즘을 진화시켜왔다. **28 proteins** 혈액 세포가 발열원이라고 불리는 단백질을 방출하면, 체온이 올라가게 된다. **29 artificial** 천연 잔디는 돔 형태의 경기장에서 자라지 않기 때문에, 경기장에는 인공 잔디가 사용된다. **30 harness** 댐은 강의 수력을 이용할 수 있지만, 그 아름다움을 파괴시킬 수도 있다.

Chapter Review Test 03

p.64

1.	Ⓑ	2.	Ⓐ	3.	Ⓓ	4.	Ⓓ
5.	Ⓒ	6.	Ⓓ	7.	Ⓑ	8.	Ⓐ
9.	Ⓒ	10.	Ⓐ	11.	Ⓐ	12.	Ⓐ
13.	Ⓐ	14.	Ⓒ	15.	Ⓑ	16.	Ⓐ

1 철로와 전보 시스템의 발전은 운송과 통신의 속도, 부피, 그리고 규칙성에 있어서 의미 있는 발전을 이루어 냈는데, 이로 인하여 상품의 생산과 유통에서의 근본적인 변화가 이루어 질 수 있었다. **2** Flank Lloyd Wright 스타일의 특성은 건축 분야에 있어서 현대성의 정수와 자연의 본질을 혼합하는 그 자신의 능력에 놓여 있었다. **3** 전세계의 많은 국가들이 노예제를 폐지 또는 포기했지만, 세계에서 가장 위대한 민주국가인 미국에서는 유독 흑인들이 노예 상태를 벗어나지 못했다. **4** 화학 제품 산업은 보다 생태학적으로 안전한 몇몇 제초제를 내놓고 있다. **5** 목재의 공급은 이점들을 가져다 주었지만, 또한 부정적인 영향도 미쳤다. **6** 일부 종들은 매우 분명한 의사소통을 하는 것처럼 보이지만, 그 의사 소통의 매개체는 인간이 연구하고 평가하기에 어려운 것이다. 그 이유는 이런 페로몬들을 탐지하고 분석해 내는 측면에 있어서는 기술적인 어려움이 존재하기 때문이다. **7** 비타민 복용으로 실제 얻을 수 있는 효과 보다 과장되어 있는, 비타민 효능에 대한 무모한 주장이 제기되었다. **8** Anasazi인들은 전통적인 도자기 제작 기술을 발전시켰으며, 여러 방을 지닌 복잡한 주거 형태를 절벽에 깎아 만들어내면서 수세기에 걸쳐 번성했다. **9** 이러한 식물들은 추운 긴 겨울 동안 살아남을 수 있는 능력이 있으며, 짧은 여름의 성장 기간 동안에는 빠르게 성장할 수 있다. **10** 해수면의 지속적인 상승으로 보다 많은 얼음들이 바다로 내던져지면서 해수면은 더욱 상승했다. **11** 어린이는 생물학적으로 특정 적합한 행동을 습득할 준비가 되어있지만, 적절한 자극을 제공해 주는 환경적 지원이 필요하다. **12** 북미 식민지에서의 기술은 유럽의 기술과 현저하게 다르지는 않았지만, 한 가지 측면에서, 식민지 주민들은 막대한 경제적인 이점을 누렸다. **13** Arizona주 Phoenix의 Papago 공원 내 Hole in the Rock라 불리는 장소로부터 얻은 증거는, 그 곳이 Hohokam이라고 알려진 원시인들에 의해 사용되었던, 일종의 관측소라는 점을 알려준다. **14** 생태학자들은 계획이 이루어진 다음에 개발이 이루어져야 한다고 주장하고 있으며, 환경적 필요성 및 장기적인 사회적 수요와 부합하는 주요 토지와 자원이 이용될 경우에는 지역적 차원의 계획이 먼저 마련되어야 한다고 주장한다. **15** 비록 매립지에 토양과 다양한 식물들을 채워 넣음으로써 인공 녹지를 조성하는 방법이 차후 개발될 여지는 있겠지만, 확실히 이들 방법 중 어느 것도 완벽하게 만족스러운 것은 없다. **16** 선장들은 선박의 통제권을 쥔 사람으로서, 그 거대한 배와 강력한 증기 기관을 다루고 조작했다.

PART 1 ★ Chapter 04

UNIT 13 Check-up Quiz
p.66

1 implications 식민지 시기의 Pennsylvania의 제철업자들은 쇠와 혁명을 만들어냈는데, 이 모두는 산업적, 정치적 의미를 지니고 있는 것이었다. **2 accompanied** 음악의 형태들은 종종 역사상의 감정과 클라이맥스를 부여해주는 이야기를 수반했다. **3 Dexterous** 도끼, 올가미, 그리고 낚시 줄을 능숙하게 다루었던 이 사람들은 새로운 것들을 개발해냈고 통나무집을 최초로 만들었으며 미 원주민 부족과도 마주치게 되었다. **4 prevent** 신선한 육류의 이용성은 매우 제한되어 있었다; 부패를 막을 새로운 방법이 없었던 것이다. **5 unrestricted** 가축 무리는 더 이상 평원에서 자유롭게 풀을 뜯어 먹을 수 없게 되었고, 울타리는 농부들과 목장 주인들간의 갈등을 일으켰다. **6 administered** 국립 해양 보호 프로그램은 국가의 해양부에서 관리한다. **7 migrate** 이 즈음 인류의 초기 무리는 동쪽과 서쪽으로 이동하기 시작했다. **8 Funeral** 인류 역사에서 장례 의식은 항상 중요한 역할을 해왔다. **9 innovative** 석기의 기능에 관한 한가지 혁신적인 접근법은 석기 도구에 나타나 있는 손상 정도와 마모 정도를 연구하는 것과 관

련이 있다. **10 framed** 행태학자들이 제기한 의문과 그들이 사용한 방법은 어떻게 사람들이 행동하는가를 이해하는데 도움이 되도록 이루어져 있었다. **11 recalled** 일부 고고학자들은 그들이 유적을 마침내 찾게 되었을 때 느꼈던 복잡한 감정을 회상했다. **12 excavating** Nineveh 남부 도시 국가를 발굴하고 있었던 고고학자들은 1890년대가 되어서야 수메르인들의 글자로만 새겨져 있는 여러 평판들을 발견할 수 있었다. **13 isolated** 민속음악을 만들어낼 수 있는 가장 이상적인 장소는 고립된 시골 지역이다. **14 fashion** 북부 California의 인디언들은 바구니 제작에 뛰어났는데, 그들은 갈대와 풀, 그리고 뿌리를 이용하여 어떤 종류와 어떤 크기라도 작품들을 만들어낼 수 있었다. **15 coffin** 클라이맥스는 축제의 끝부분에 오며, 이 때 시신은 관에 넣어지고 최종 안치 장소로 옮겨지게 된다. **16 conducted** 최근 일부 인류학자들은 인종학에 있어서의 흥미로운 사례 연구를 진행했다. **17 evoke** 시의 목적이 독자에게 무언가를 알려주는 것일 필요는 없다 오히려 감각적이고 미적으로 만족감을 느끼도록 감정을 불러 일으키는 것이어야 한다. **18 genius** 오늘날 그의 업적은 역사가 사이에서 잘 알려져 있지는 않지만, 일부 사가들은 그를 뛰어난 직관력을 지닌 천재라고 부르고 있다. **19 imitate** 그 화가의 스타일을 모방하도록 훈련 받았던 수많은 보조화가들이 색을 칠했다. **20 exerted** 발에 부과되어 있는 압력과 평균 87 센티미터에 달하는 보폭의 길이는 인류가 천천히 걸었다는 점을 나타내었다. **21 deserving** 매년 수여되는 상금은 다양한 영역에서의 자격 있는 예술가들에게 수여된다. **22 noted** 다른 연구자들은 어머니들이 수개월 된 아기들에게 말할 때 말의 음높이와 크기, 그리고 강도를 과장한다는 점에 주목했다. **23 infinite** 소설 The Library of Babel에서 Borges는 가능한 모든 문서를 포함하고 있는 무한한 도서관을 묘사하고 있다. **24 culmination** 그의 죽음은 수 년 간의 고난과 고통, 아픔의 절정이었다. **25 consciously** 격렬한 재즈를 연주할 때, 음악가는 엄격한 박자규칙으로부터 의도적으로 벗어나, 곡의 기초 리듬을 강조해 주고 느슨한 구절 감각을 만들어낸다. **26 idiosyncratic** 처음에 Cummings의 시는 특이한 구두법 및 인쇄법으로 혹평을 받았으나, 점차적으로 서정적인 측면을 인정받게 되었다. **27 elastic** 소리는 탄성이 있는 매체, 즉 공기, 토양 혹은 물을 매개로 이동하여 인간의 귀에 들려지는 모든 교란이다. **28 discriminations** 아기들은 지각적인 식별력을 갖춤으로써 세상과 소통하게 되는데, 이러한 점은 청각에 의하여 언어를 습득할 때 필요하다. **29 flamboyant** 1960년대의 남자 의상은 색상과 섬유에 있어서 혁명적인 변화를 맞이하여, 20세기에 처음으로 화려해지기 시작했다. **30 embrace** 이러한 예술가들의 일부는 소도시에서의 삶을 진정으로 감싸 안고, 대도시에서의 삶, 이른바 "세련된 사회"에서의 삶을 거부하였다.

Seasoned 숙련 노동자들은 초보 노동자들보다 고용자들에게 가치를 높게 받는다. **8 soared** 남부의 농민들이 자신들의 농경지를 면 농장으로 바꾸면서 면 생산량이 치솟게 되었다. **9 extraordinary** 19세기 미 도시에서는 새로운 이민자들과 기존 미국 정착자들이 혼재하여 살게 되었는데, 이는 특이한 현상이었다. **10 magnify** 19세기의 급속한 산업화와 지리적 이동의 증가는 여성에게 특별한 의미를 갖는데, 이는 이들 변화가 사회적 지위를 확대시키는 경향이 있었기 때문이다. **11 makeup** 인구가 증가할 수록 인구의 구성 또한 변화하였다. **12 merchandise** 사람들은 시장에서 가축을 사고 거래했으며, 필요한 물품을 얻을 수 있었다. **13 metropolises** 1930년경 미국에는 10개의 거대한 대도시들이 있었다. **14 corruption** 대다수의 사람들은 작은 마을에 살았고, 도시를 부패, 범죄 그리고 도덕적 타락의 중심지로 믿었다. **15 descent** 일부 문화들은 어머니 쪽 조상을 따라 올라가는데, 이것을 모계 혈통이라고 한다. **16 circulation** 실제로 주간지의 발행 부수는 같은 기간의 신문의 발행 부수를 초과했다. **17 competitiveness** 가정은 극도의 경쟁과 어지러울 정도의 사회적 변화의 맥락에서 초기에 지녔던 여러 기능들을 잃게 되었다. **18 disdain** 기업을 우선시하고 일반인들을 경멸했던 Hamilton과의 논쟁은 미 최초의 정당 제도를 형성하는데 기여했다. **19 constraints** 시간 제한으로 피실험자들은 제 시간 내에 답안을 마칠 수 없었다. **20 budget** 군은 최소한의 예산만 배정받았다. **21 particulars** 그 연구는 일반 대중에 대해 정확히 들어맞는 상세한 사실들을 드러내주었다. **22 step in** 시 위원회는 그 지역 개발에 개입하여 이를 중단시켜야 했다. **23 pleaded** 1977년 Richard Helms는 칠레에서의 CIA 활동에 대한 부정확한 증언을 한 점에 대하여 유죄 변론을 했다. **24 attuned** 새로운 종류의 신문이 이 시기에 나타났는데, 이 신문은 새로운 미국의 정신과 욕구에 보다 부합되는 것이었다. **25 disgust** 8 마리의 비둘기에게 행복, 분노, 놀람, 혐오의 감정이 나타나 있는 사람들의 얼굴 사진이 보여졌다. **26 assessment** 하나는 위험에 대한 의식적이고 이성적인 판단이며, 다른 하나는 무의식적인 본능적 반응이다. **27 chance** 낯선 사람과의 우연한 대화는 대화자에게 다른 종교에 대한 자신의 무지함을 드러나게 해준다. **28 integral** 교육은 입학하기 훨씬 이전부터 시작되는 평생 동안의 과정으로서, 개인의 전 생애에 걸친 필수적인 부분이 되어야 한다. **29 palatial** Miami 해변은 연중 인기 있는 휴양지로, 황금빛 모래사장에 늘어서 있는 호텔, 궁전 같은 건물들, 그리고 휴양 시설로 유명하다. **30 adoption** 1923년 그는 수정 헌법의 채택을 촉구하는 정치적 운동을 시작했는데, 이 수정 헌법은 여성에게 동등한 권리를 명령히는 내용을 담고 있었다.

UNIT 14 Check-up Quiz   p.70

1 precipitous 자산 가치의 급격한 하락은 수많은 개인 투자가들을 몰락시킨 점 이외에도 은행 및 기타 금융기관들을 긴장시키게 했다. **2 confronted** 남북 전쟁이 끝났을 때, 남부와 북부 사람들은 모두 혼란스러운 상황에 직면했다. **3 tedious** 로봇과 자동화 기계의 사용으로 일부 지루한 공장의 업무들이 사라지고 있다. **4 transition** 미국 경제는 거대한 변화를 겪었고 노동의 본질은 영구적으로 바뀌게 되었다. **5 virtually** Boston을 둘러싼 토지는 늘 열악한 경작지였으며 18세기 중반에는 그 지역의 목재가 사실상 모두 벌목되었다. **6 courteously** 서비스 부분에서 일하는 노동자들은 가능한 공손하게 행동하도록 훈련 받아야 한다. **7**

UNIT 15 Check-up Quiz   p.74

1 minute 쿼크는 물질의 기본 단위라고 생각되고 있는 미세한 입자이다. **2 cross-sectional** 로프의 힘은 그 단면의 면적에 직접적으로 비례한다. **3 spiked** 그 결과 역사상 가장 끔찍한 핵 폭발이 일어나서 주변 지역의 방사능 수치가 치솟았다. **4 literally** 이 동물들은 익룡, 문자 그대로 "날개 달린 용"이었다. **5 merely** 물떼새의 둥지는 단지 모래 혹은 흙을 모아놓은 것이다. **6 random** 털갈이는, 결코 임의적이지 않은 방식으로, 최적의 시기와 그 내구성을 고려하는, 강력한 진화론적인 힘에 의해 이루어진다. **7 rear** 캐나다 대서양 해안가의 절벽을 이용하여 짝짓기를 하고 알을 낳고 새끼를 기르는 바닷새 중 일반적인 것이 바다오리이다. **8 recruit** 아르헨티나 개미는 외부의 곤충들과 싸울 때 그들의 서식지로부터 거대한 군사를 모

을 수 있다. **9 refuge** 습지는 많은 종류의 조류, 파충류, 포유류 그리고 양서류 동물들에게 은신처를 제공해 준다. **10 respiration** 식물의 호흡 과정은 복잡한 화학적 반응의 연속이다. **11 robust** 그 새는 커다랗고 단단한 부리를 가지고 있지만, 이 점이 그 새의 가장 특징적인 모습은 아니다. **12 rotting** 양쪽 동물 모두 흙과 썩어가고 있는 식물들 위에서 살며 먹이를 찾으러 다녔다. **13 scramble** 그 동물의 작은 크기는 숲의 윗 부분에서 곤충, 꽃, 혹은 과일을 찾기 위해 크고 작은 나무 가지 사이로 오르는 것을 용이하게 해준다. **14 conspicuous** 많은 등반가들은 가능한 눈에 잘 띄기 위하여 오렌지색 혹은 기타 밝은 색의 옷을 입는다. **15 seeped** 수백만 년 전 지구 역사상의 점신세에, Balt해 분지에서 자란 소나무에서 맑은 송진이 스며 나왔다. **16 dubious** 그들은 보충 프로그램이 비용이 많이 들고 그 가치가 의심스러웠기 때문에 그 계획에 반대했다. **17 edges** 부싯돌은 날카로운 날에 쉽게 조각나기 때문에, 원시시대 사람들은 부싯돌을 이용하여 도구와 무기를 만들었다. **18 seismic** 지진파가 이동하는 방식은 지구의 내부가 균일하지 않다는 점을 보여준다. **19 sorted out** 토양의 질을 측정하기 위하여 모래, 실트 그리고 진흙 입자들이 그 크기와 무게에 의하여 분류된다. **20 squeeze** 새로운 기술로 보다 많은 석유를 추출할 수 있는 정유회사의 능력이 석유의 과잉생산을 이끌었다. **21 tangled** 그 때부터 150만개의 척추동물과 250만개의 무척추동물로부터 나온 100톤이 넘는 화석들이 발견되고 있는데, 이 화석들은 빽빽하게 서로 엉켜진 덩어리의 형태로 되어 있었다. **22 consistency** 해저의 단단함에 따라 트렌처에서 어떤 종류의 폭발 형태를 사용할지를 결정한다. **23 hazardous** 독성 물질을 다루는 작업은 위험한 일이다. **24 major** 은하계는 우주의 주요한 구성 단위이다. **25 subtle** 이용할 수 있는 날씨 데이터가 충분히 상세하지 않기 때문에, 폭풍우에 앞서는 미묘한 날씨 변화를 컴퓨터로 식별할 수 없다. **26 primeval** 15년 이상 천문학자들은 그러한 원시 은하계를 찾으려 했으나, 많은 이들이 몇 번의 천문 조사에서 아무것도 발견하지 못하자 이를 포기해 버렸다. **27 graphic** 지구의 자전을 연구하는 부서의 장인 Dennis McCarthy 박사는 색다르고 보다 생생한 방법으로 1초의 의미를 설명했다. **28 solitary** 스스로 중요한 발견을 이루어내는 일인 단위의 과학자는 서로 협동하는 과학 팀으로 대체되고 있다. **29 molecules** 물질에 대한 분자이론이 개발되었는데, 분자이론은 모든 물질을 아주 작고 눈에 보이지 않는 실체, 즉 분자로 구성되어있다고 간주한다. **30 realm** 16세기 후반 눈으로 볼 수 있는 현미경의 발명으로 이전에는 미지의 영역이었던 단세포 동식물들이 연구되기 시작했다.

UNIT 16 Check-up Quiz p.78

1 installed 1931년 최초의 철도용 냉방 시스템이 Baltimore와 Ohio 철도에 설치되었다. **2 spawns** 하나의 발명은 많은 다른 발명들을 낳는다. **3 subsequent** 현대 건축가들은 현대의 삶에 산업화가 끼친 차후의 영향을 무시하고 있다. **4 stiffened** George Washington 다리가 건설되기 전까지, 근대적인 현수교들은 교통량과 바람에 견디기 위해 강철 트러스트와 빔으로 고정되어 있었다. **5 boroughs** New York 시의 상업적 중심지인 Manhattan은 다리와 터널로서 다른 구역과 연결되어 있다. **6 obligates** 1973년 멸종위기동물보호법은 멸종위기에 처한 모든 동물들을 보호할 의무를 정부에게 지우고 있다. **7 extinction** 역사가 시작된 이래로 다른 종들을 멸종으로 이끌어낸 것은 아마도 인간이었을 것이다. **8 menace** 대머리 독수리들은 스포츠용으로, 그리고 이들이 가축을 위협한다고 생각되기 때문에 사냥되었다. **9 innate** 과학자들은 선천적으로 잡초를 없애는 능

력을 지는 생물체들, 주로 곤충과 미생물들을 연구하고 있다. **10 key** 집단성은 개별적 행동을 능가하는 여러 중요한 이점들을 가지고 있다. **11 preponderance** 신대륙의 나비들이 수적으로 우세한 편인데, 이는 아마도 나비가 가장 친숙한 종들이기 때문일 것이다. **12 profound** 부적절한 정책이 하이티의 발전에 심대한 영향을 주어 하이티는 서반구에서 가장 가난한 나라가 되었다. **13 reveals** 지구 역사상 멸종이 계속 일어나고 있음은 화석 기록을 통해 알 수 있다. **14 evading** 많은 어종은 끊임없이 서로 몰래 다가가기도 하고 피하기도 한다. **15 bloodcurdling** 특히 인간이나 대다수 다른 어종에게 더욱 등골이 오싹한 예로는 상어를 들 수 있다. **16 puzzled over** 과거에 의사들과 심리학자들은 그 질병의 원인을 두고 고민했다. **17 skyrocketing** 많은 제약 회사들이 비타민 판매가 급증하고 있다는 것을 알아낸 것을 불과 이전 10년 전이었다. **18 solely** 이침 요법은 오로지 귀와 귀에 있는 수많은 경혈점만 다룬다. **19 nervous** 척추동물의 신경계는 머리 쪽에서 끝이 나는, 속이 빈 척추 신경 인대를 그 특징으로 한다. **20 onslaught** 이러한 습격에 직면하여 생물들은 자신의 신체를 외부의 다른 유기물들로부터 보호하기 위한 다양한 방어 메커니즘을 진화시켜왔다. **21 ratio** 실험에서는 헬륨과 수소의 핵 비율이 거의 같은 상태로 남아있었다. **22 cautious** 노동자들이 독성 물질을 다룰 때는 매우 조심하여야 한다. **23 psychological** 대체 요법들은 심리적 질환뿐만 아니라 생리적 질환을 예방하는 방법으로서 놀라운 효과를 나타낼 수 있다. **24 aversion** 밀실 공포증을 겪고 있는 사람은 폐쇄된 공간에 대한 공포를 가지고 있다. **25 outraged** 환자는 살아났지만 그 일로 인해 당시 종교적 논란이 일었고 더 이상 실험은 진행되지 않았다. **26 overlap** 사람이 외쪽 뇌를 주로 쓰는가 오른쪽 뇌를 주로 쓰는가에 대해 큰 관심이 없는 하나의 이유는 이들 뇌 영역 사이에 중첩되는 활동이 많기 때문이다. **27 odor** 각각의 개미집들은 위치, 역사 그리고 인근 음식 공급처에 따라 자신 만의 고유한 냄새를 갖고 있다. **28 petroleum** 송유관은 막대한 양의 천연 가스와 액체 석유를 전송한다. **29 wholesome** 순수한 곡물과 신선한 과일 및 야채는 건강에 좋은 식품이다. **30 murky** 물 속이 탁할 때 스쿠버 다이버는 앞을 보기 힘들다.

Chapter 04 Review Test p.82

1. Ⓑ	2. Ⓒ	3. Ⓓ	4. Ⓒ
5. Ⓑ	6. Ⓐ	7. Ⓐ	8. Ⓒ
9. Ⓒ	10. Ⓐ	11. Ⓓ	12. Ⓒ
13. Ⓑ	14. Ⓓ	15. Ⓐ	16. Ⓑ

1 많은 연구자들은 복잡한 행동이 제한된 시간 내에 학습되는 것인지를 알아내기 위하여 많은 연구를 진행하고 있다. **2** 이 도공들은 또한 당시 유행했던 중국 백자를 모방하려고 시도하던 도중 새로운 유약 기술을 발견하게 되었다. **3** 미 남서부 Pueblo 인디언들의 선사시대 주거 방식인 암굴 주거는 건축 발전의 정점이라 할 수 있다 최근의 건물도 손으로 자른 석재(건설 주요 자재)와 회반죽 벽돌을 사용한 당시의 방식을 능가하지 못한다. **4** 컴퓨터 시대에는 과거 계산원들이나 점원들이 얼마나 지루해 했는가를 상상하는 것이 어렵다. **5** 16세기 이래로 튤립은 오토만 제국 정원의 필수적인 부분이 되었고, 또한 그 이후에는 유럽적 삶의 일부분이 되었다. **6** 눈은 결빙 형태로 지표면으로 떨어지는 수많은 미세한 눈 결정으로 이루어져있다. **7** 일부 생태학자들은 비록

한 때 다소 임의적으로 일정 지역이 개발되는 일이 가능했을 지라도, 이제는 전체 사회의 복지를 고려하면, 그러한 개발이 너무나 많은 위험성을 지니고 있다고 믿는다. **8** 그 새들은 또한 포식동물이나 거친 폭풍, 홍수의 위험을 느낄 때면 나무 안에 몸을 숨긴다. **9** 세가락갈매기는 둥지의 가장자리에서 배변을 하는데, 이러한 행동이 자신의 위치를 눈에 잘 띄도록 만든다. **10** 지구 주위를 도는 달은 태양과 반대로 서쪽에서 동쪽으로 이동하기 때문에, 관찰자가 남쪽을 바라보고 있을 경우 달의 그림자는 왼쪽 가장자리에서 나타나기 시작한다. **11** 거대한 혜성이 비교적 작고 눈에 잘 띄지 않는 얼음과 먼지로부터 시작되었다는 가장 생생한 증거는 1986년 Halley 혜성의 핵을 탐사했던 European Giotto 탐사전이 찍은 근접 촬영 사진이다. **12** 달 정착지가 너무 위험한 한 가지 주된 이유는 달과 화성의 대조적인 환경 때문이다. **13** 언어 습득은, 모국어든 외국어든 간에, 사람이 언어를 배우는 과정을 가리킨다. **14** 북미에서 멸종된 북미 카메리드는 아시아에서 낙타로 진화했다. **15** 이 이론을 지지하는 언어학자들은 1차 언어 습득과 관련된 능숙하고도 깊이 있는 아이들의 언어 학습 능력이 일반적으로 12세 전후로 중단될 것이라고 주장한다. **16** 인구가 밀집된 Ohio, Pennsylvania, Illinois 그리고 Michigan은 대통령 선거 후보자에게 중요한 주들이다.

다운 경치들을 그릴 수 있었다. **18 outstanding** Mark Twain은 미국의 가장 뛰어난 사실주의 작가가 되었다. **19 epoch** 1850년은 미 예술사의 새로운 시작으로 간주될 수 있는 한 해이다. **20 status** 1778년 미 혁명이 발발할 당시, 예술가들의 지위는 이미 변화를 겪고 있었다. **21 executed** 또다시 정통 초상화는 부유한 자들에 의해 요청되어 전문가들이 담당하는 하나의 사치품이 되었다. **22 flattering** 그 별명은 그의 비위를 맞추기 위해 의도된 것은 아니었으나, 꽤 적절한 것이어서, 당사자가 화를 내지는 않았다. **23 forefront** 계몽주의는 유럽에서 인간의 이성을 사고의 중심에 두었던 시기이다. **24 dubbed** 시간이 흐르면서 막간극 양식은 인기를 끌었고 결국 따로 무대에 별도로 올려져 오페라 부파라고 불리게 되었다. **25 exponents** Art Nouveau에 뛰어난 대표적 인물들이 프랑스에서 다수 배출되었기 때문에, 많은 예술가들이 프랑스에서 이 양식을 배우려 했다. **26 extolled** 영국에서뿐만 아니라 미국에서도 개혁가들이 수제품의 미덕을 찬양하여, 그 가격이 상승하게 되었다. **27 mimic** 그 나무는 구약 성서의 예언자 Joshua가 팔을 들어 약속의 땅으로 넘어오는 사람들에게 손을 흔드는 모습을 흉내 내고 있는 듯이 보였다. **28 intuitive** 화자의 어조는 직관적인 동정이나 반감, 무관심, 피로, 근심, 혹은 심지어 흥분 정도도 반영할 수 있다. **29 Caustic** 혹평은 사람들을 화나게 만들 수 있기 때문에 다른 사람 앞에서 말할 때는 주의할 필요가 있다. **30 skeptical** 그들은 그 계획에 회의적이었다; 험하고 인적이 드문 사막, 산, 그리고 반 건조 기후의 평원에 철로를 개설하는 것이 수익을 낼 수는 없었다.

PART 2 ★ Chapter 05

UNIT 17 Check-up Quiz
p.86

1 recorded 1820년 무렵 그 도시의 인구는 10,000명 이상이었고, 1880년경에는 백만이 넘는 도시로 기록되었다. **2 seized** 많은 서아프리카인들은 붙잡힌 후, 본인의 의사와 상관없이, 노예로 팔려갔다. **3 concrete** 좋은 작가는 자신의 일반화를 구체적인 사례로써 뒷받침한다. **4 provisional** 2월 7일, 7개 주는 미 합중국 임시 헌법을 채택하였다. **5 traverse** 그 선박들은 주축국과 맞설 수 있도록 미군과 다른 국가의 군대를 멀리까지 실어 나를 수 있었다. **6 boosted** (음악적인) 격렬함을 통해, 군 위문단은 여흥을 제공해주었고 사기를 진작시켰다. **7 employing** 수를 세는 최초의 방법은 일부 사람들에 의해 사용된 일대일 대응 방식을 이용하는 계산법이었다. **8 exposed** 털로 덮여진 매머드와 기타 동물들이 주기적으로 Siberia 툰드라 지대에서 나타났다. **9 favored** 먼저 그러한 사냥꾼들이 커다란 포식 동물들과 싸워서 포식 동물들을 몰아냈다면, 매년 보다 많은 새끼 동물들이 살아남아서 점차적으로 선호되는 종들의 개체수가 증가되었을 것이다. **10 glazing** 가마는 자기에 광을 입히기 위해 사용되는데, 이 때는 화덕이 2개 필요하다. **11 indispensable** 시초부터 음악은 사람들이 꼭 들어야하는 부수 요소이다. **12 legacy** 제국은 오래가지 못했지만, 그 유산은 널리 퍼지게 되었다. **13 inscribed** 다수의 다른 평판들에는 이전에는 알려지지 않았던, 따라서 해석될 수 없었던 또 다른 언어가 새겨져 있었다. **14 majestic** 이 고원은 장엄하지만 험악하지는 않다. **15 conjectured** Anasazi인들은 가뭄 때문에 자신들의 거주지를 버렸다고 추측된다. **16 disguised** 민속 음악과 달리 대중 음악은 원곡이 변할 수 없으며, 따라서 그 소유권이 주로 사회가 아닌, 작곡가에게 속하게 된다. **17 excursions** 그 미술 모임의 활동에는 또한 Hudson 강을 따라 가는 조직화된 스케치 여행을 포함하고 있었는데, 이 여행에서 화가들은 놀랍도록 아름

UNIT 18 Check-up Quiz
p.90

1 stemmed from 인상적인 산출량 증가는 노동자가 제품을 만드는 방식에서 나왔다. **2 commerce** 국제 상관래의 성장으로 세계 경제는 보다 상호의존적으로 되었다. **3 savage** 석유 산업은 극심한 경쟁을 겪었는데, 1870년대에는 많은 석유 산업체들이 파산했다. **4 sleek** Pan Am사는 19세기의 재빠르고 날렵한 클리퍼라는 쾌속 범선의 이름을 따서 그 비행기의 이름을 붙였다. **5 recession** 경기 침체기에는 경제적 상황들이, 비교적 단시간 지속되는 경기 후퇴기 보다, 더욱 악화된다. **6 tranquil** Concord의 평온한 New England시에서 제작된 Concord 마차는 미 서부시대를 상징하는 것으로 유명해졌다. **7 stock** 기업들은 주식의 판매로써 종종 자금을 마련한다. **8 verge** 안타깝게도, 1930년대 말까지는 미국 흰 두루미가 거의 멸종 직전에 이르렀기 때문에, 살아남기 위해서는 보호가 필요했다. **9 denounced** Knight와 Viner는 경제적 제국주의를 비난했는데, 경제적 제국주의는 모든 사회 세력을 경제적으로 설명될 수 있는 것으로 간주한다. **10 era** 시대에 상관없이 도시가 매력적으로 보이는 이유 중에는 시골 사람들이 갖고 있는 주요 심리학적인 요인들이 포함되는데, 이는 수많은 사람들이 도시 중심부로 몰리는 이유와 같은 것이다. **11 exceeded** 1872년 단 2개의 일간 신문만이 100,000부의 발행 부수를 주장했으나, 1892년경에는 그 외의 7개의 신문이 앞선 발행 부수를 뛰어넘었다. **12 forward-looking** 얼음은 호텔, 술집, 그리고 병원에서 사용되었고, 일부 선경지명이 있는 도시의 상인들이 신선한 육류, 어류 그리고 버터를 거래할 때도 사용되었다. **13 functional** New York만이 거대한 도시 인근 지역인 Midwestern에 쉽게 접근할 수 있는 기능적인 도로 연결 망을 가지고 있었다. **14 burdensome** 동시에, 전쟁세도 덜 부담스러운 수준으로 감소해야만 했다. **15 inadequate** 베이비 붐은 1950년대와 60년대에 구시대적이고 부적절했던 학교 교육 시스템에 큰 영향을 미쳤다. **16 intensive** 심지어

집중적인 대규모 연구 개발이 이루어지고 있는 현 시대에 조차 기업과 대학의 상호 관련성은 종종 잘못 이해되고 있다. **17 touted** Freud 지지자들은 개인의 잠재의식이 행동에 영향을 미친다고 주장했고, 행태학자들은 외부적인 보상과 처벌을 보다 강조했다. **18 congestion** 자신의 우편물을 찾기 위해 개인들이 만들어내는 혼란함과 혼잡성 그 자체가 우편의 사용을 저하시키는 충분한 요인이 되었다. **19 secession** 전쟁으로 인하여 남부는 연합에서 분리되었다. **20 position** Mary Goddard는 현재 연방 업무를 담당했던 최초의 여성으로 생각되고 있다. **21 prevalent** 그 영화는 20세기 초반에 미국에 만연했던 이상주의를 나타내고 있다. **22 supervision** 인간 게놈 프로젝트는 놀랍게도 에너지 부의 관할 하에 있다. **23 symbolize** 국기에 나타나는 이미지는, 그것이 없다면 많은 단어가 필요할지도 모르는, 정치적인 이상을 상징적으로 나타낼 수 있다. **24 revised** 입법자들은 거부권이 행사된 법안을 단순 개정한 후 다시 통과시켰는데, 이는 대중적인 지지에도 불구하고 대통령이 거부권을 행사한 점에 대하여 대담하게 맞서는 행동이었다. **25 curb** 정부는 세금 사기가 근절되기를 희망하면서, 세금 처리 절차를 덜 혼란스럽도록 단순화하고 있다. **26 authorized** 국가 노사 관계 위원회는 고용주 혹은 피고용자 입장에서 불공정한 노동 관행을 주장한 경우 이를 조사할 권한이 있다. **27 essential** 비록 작업표의 형태에 있어서 몇몇 변화들이 있었지만, 그것들은 모두 본질적인 측면에서는 서로 유사하다. **28 encounter** 과거 뱀을 만났던 기억이 있으면 뱀에 대한 인상이 더욱 강력하게 된다. **29 Illegible** 읽기 힘든 글씨가 나약한 성격을 나타내지는 않는데, 이러한 점은 George Washington의 필체를 보면 바로 알 수 있다. **30 expertise** 새로운 에너지 정책은 정치와 무관한 과학 및 기술적 전문지식에 의하여 개발되고 운영되어야 한다.

오른손 잡이용으로 조정되어 있다. **15 freeing** 빙하 아래에 존재하는 높은 수압은, 얼음과 바위 간의 마찰력을 뛰어넘어 빙하를 밀어냄으로써, 빙하를 들어 올릴 수도 있다. **16 hazy** 지진을 예상하는 일은 정말 막막한 일이다. **17 nutrients** 댐이 건설된 이후로는 양분이 많은 퇴적물이 감소함에 따라 물고기도 적어졌다. **18 residue** 물을 따라내서 증발 시키면 잔여 진흙이 남겨지게 되는데, 이 때 그 무게를 측정할 수 있다. **19 sagging** 각 진흙은 휘거나 녹지 않고 자신의 형태를 유지하면서 어느 정도의 열을 견디어 낼 수 있다. **20 segment** 해저 케이블 부설 선은 옆으로 움직여 이 과정을 반복한 후 측면 부에 케이블을 깔게 된다. **21 segregated** 한 가지 수수께끼는 미 Western 지방의 두 종류의 화산 분출물, 즉 석영과 마그마가 서로 섞이지 않고 분리되어 있다는 점이다 즉 석영 층이 마그마 층 위에 있는 것이다. **22 convoluted** 지표면의 감긴 듯한 습곡과 갈라져 있는 지질학적 구조는 지진파 에너지를 흡수하는 경향이 있다. **23 worth** 홍수는 매년 수백만 달러에 이르는 재산 손실을 일으킨다. **24 spot** 북미 대륙의 지리학적 중심부는 North Dakota에 있는 Balta 근처의 한 지점이다. **25 adjacent** 기상학은, 지표면 근처가 아닌, 대기에서 보다 높은 고도에 위치한 공기의 흐름을 연구한다. **26 retain** 달의 중력장은 너무 약해서 대기를 보유할 수 없기 때문에, 달에는 공기가 없다. **27 faint** 천문학자들은 사진과 망원경을 이용하여 모든 밝은 별들과 많은 희미한 별들의 움직임을 연구한다. **28 glimpsed** 이러한 진주 실처럼 빛났던 혜성의 행렬은 목성과의 최후의 충돌이 있기 단지 몇 달 전에 처음으로 어렴풋이 보였다. **29 mutate** 방사능은 암이 발병할 위험성을 높이고 DNA를 부정적으로 변화시켜 돌연변이를 일으키기 때문에 특히 인간에게 위험하다. **30 observations** 과학자는 실험을 계획하고 계산을 수행하며 가설을 검증하기 위해 관찰을 한다.

UNIT 19 Check-up Quiz p.94

1 optical 새 X-레이 현미경은 광학 현미경의 해상도를 훨씬 뛰어넘는다. **2 panel** 경 비행기의 계기판은 조종사가 반드시 주시해야 하는, 최소한 12개의 장치들로 이루어져있다. **3 perseverance** 연구가들의 발견은 30년 이상의 인내와 땀에 기반하고 있었다. **4 self-consistent** 비록 자명한 것이었지만, 플로지스톤 이론은 플로지스톤이 가상의, 심지어는 신비롭기까지 한, 특성을 지니고 있다고 주장한 점에서 터무니 없었다. **5 scarce** 대부분 단세포 박테리아인 원생대의 희귀한 화석들은 빙하 작용에 대한 증거를 거의 제공해 주지 못한다. **6 assure** 둥지를 만드는데 필요한 재료는, 극한 온도를 견디고 알들이 부드럽고 안전한 쉴 장소를 확보하기 위해, 충분히 공급되어야 한다. **7 conceded** Darwin은 화석 기록이 없다는 점이 자기 이론의 타당성에 대한 반박 근거로서 이용될 것이라는 점을 인정하였다. **8 principal** Darwin은 대단한 인물로서 진화론의 주요 창시자였다. **9 puncture** 식물의 겉 표면에는 종종 모상체라도 불리는 가시 같은 털이 있는데, 이것은 곤충이 그 껍질을 벗겨내는 것을 방지하며 유충을 찔러서 구멍을 내어 죽일 수 있다. **10 reproductive** 이 물고기들은 번식력이 생길 때까지 자랄 기회를 갖지 못한다. **11 repertoire** 물떼새는 노출되고 방어가 되지 않는 알들 및 새끼들을 위하여 잠재적인 침입자들의 주위를 흩뜨리기 위한 효과적인 속임수 레퍼토리를 가지고 있다. **12 deft** 원칙적으로 큰 부리 솔잣새는 커다란 솔방울에서 씨앗을 빼먹는데 뛰어난 반면 작은 부리 솔잣새는 작고 껍질이 얇은 솔방울로부터 씨앗을 제거하는 데 보다 능숙하다. **13 squirts** 해삼은 공격을 받으면 모든 내장 기관들을 물속으로 분출시킨다. **14 geared** 오른손 잡이가 우세하게 된 결과로서 대부분의 소비 물품들이

UNIT 20 Check-up Quiz p.98

1 follies 하지만 그 예술가들의 업적은 파리의 엘리트 예술가들에 의하여 비싸고 추한 어리 석은 행동이라고 조롱을 받았다. **2 regardless of** 도공들은 자신의 작업장이, 정착지 중심부와의 관련성과 상관없이, 진흙이 매장된 곳 가까이에 위치해 있는 것이 편리하다고 느꼈다. **3 renovation** 그 건물의 리노베이션은 이전에 평가했던 것보다 더 걸릴 것이다. **4 spacious** 마침내 20세기 초 넓은 공간의 건물들이 등장하면서 일렬로 늘어서 있던 빌딩들의 조명 문제를 극복했다. **5 centripetal** 따라서 사회 생활은 중심 지역 위주로 이루어졌다; 즉 마을이라고 하는 공동체의 중심지 주위에 집중되어 있었다. **6 competed** 개체수가 확대됨에 따라 같은 환경 영역을 두고 다른 종의 동물들이 경쟁했을 것이다. **7 periodic** 이러한 주기적인 멸종은 지구 궤도와 혜성의 구름층이 교차하기 때문에 일어난 것일 수도 있다. **8 perched** Alaska에서 독수리들은 물고기 덫에 앉아서 연어를 낚아채기 때문에 1917년에서 1952년 사이에는 사냥꾼들이 100,000마리 이상의 독수리들을 사냥할 수 있었다. **9 conversion** 적어도 5천년 전 유럽에서는 사막화가 시작되고 야생지가 목초지로 전환되기 시작했다. **10 jolting** 이러한 환경에서 종의 높은 멸종 속도는 놀라운 것이다. **11 magnitude** 하지만 어떤 것도 인간이 물리적, 화학적 세계를 변화시키고 환경을 파괴한, 그 규모와 속도에 상응하지 못한다. **12 perish** 한 종이 더 이상 변화하는 환경에 적응하지 못하면 멸종될 수 있다. **13 poultry** 오리는 다른 종류의 가금류보다 전염병에 더 강하다. **14 choking** 석유와 그로 인해 생기는 오염 물질은 지구상에 있는 생명체의 삶을 질식시키고 있다. **15 combustion** 석유는 인간이 내연기관을 사용하기 전에도 수백만 년

동안 지구 깊은 곳에 존재했었다. **16 tempting** 많은 사람들이 초콜릿에 유혹을 받는다는 사실은 초콜릿 산업이 막대한 이윤을 얻고 있다는 점을 반증해주는 것이다. **17 When it comes to** 시력에 관해서는 눈의 모든 구성요소가 중요하다. **18 impulses** 심장근은 뇌나 ANS로부터의 충격이 없이도 계속해서 혈액을 공급한다. **19 In retrospect** 회고해 보면, 비타민과 미네랄 요법은 건강 상의 위기가 왔을 때는 훨씬 효과적이지 않았다. **20 infections** 전쟁 당시 많은 군인들이 고통을 받았던 균상종에 대한 치료약을 개발할 필요성이 그의 연구를 자극했다. **21 challenging** 여전히 뇌는 많은 부분이 알려지지 않은 채, 가장 흥미롭고 매력적인 의학의 한 분야로 남아 있다. **22 bolstering** 기는 면역력을 증강시킬 뿐만 아니라 인간에게 힘과 에너지를 주는데 필수적이다. **23 conjunction** 때로는 한약을 침술과 병행하면 효과가 증가된다. **24 cerebral** 대부분의 간질에 있어서 대뇌의 전기적 활동, 즉 뇌파는 매우 비정상적인 리듬을 나타낸다. **25 vessel** Erlenmeyer 플라스크는 화학실험실에서 사용되는 유리로 된 용기이다. **26 neutralize** 곤충들은 특정 식물들이 만들어낸 독성 물질들을 중화시키고 변형시킬 수 있다. **27 nucleus** 원자 질량의 대부분은 핵으로 이루어지는데 핵에는 중성자와 양성자가 있다. **28 alchemists** 몇 세기를 통하여 중세 시대 연금술사들의 꿈은 납과 다른 물질들을 금으로 변화시키는 방법을 알아내는 것이었다. **29 renowned** 전기 불빛 발명은 그를 가장 유명하게 만든 것이다. **30 defective** 전기 장치는 결함이 있는 전지로 인하여 오작동될 수 있다.

Chapter 05 Review Test

p.102

1. ⓓ	2. Ⓐ	3. Ⓑ	4. ⓒ
5. ⓒ	6. Ⓐ	7. ⓓ	8. Ⓑ
9. Ⓐ	10. ⓒ	11. Ⓑ	12. Ⓑ
13. ⓓ	14. Ⓑ	15. ⓓ	16. Ⓑ

1 수심 30 미터의 바다에서 잠수부는 약 4 기압의 압력에 노출된다. **2** 신경계의 배아 빌딩 연구는 성인 형태학이 이해에 필수 불가결한 것이다. **3** 계산 방식의 발전 과정은 대게 추측되고 있을 뿐이다. **4** Pulitzer 상은 뛰어난 언론인, 소설가, 시인 그리고 기타 작가들에게 수여된다. **5** 많은 제약 회사들은 신속히 의사들에게 비타민 샘플을 제공해 주었고 다양한 건강 상태에 대한 보충제로서의 그 효과를 선전했다. **6** 1947년 새로운 항공 시대가 열렸는데, 1947년은 Chunk Yaeger가 최초로 음속을 뛰어넘는 비행에 성공한 해였다. **7** 영국의 섬에서 발견된 그 새의 전체 개체수는 66을 넘지 않았고, 유럽 전체에서도 321에 머물렀다. **8** Lincoln의 당선으로 South Carolina의 연합 탈퇴는 자명한 결과가 되었다. **9** 모자는 패션 아이템 뿐만 아니라 사회적 지위나 직업을 상징적으로 나타낼 수 있다. **10** 대중 교통은 3가지 근본적인 방법으로 미국 도시의 사회적, 그리고 경제적 구조를 바꾸어 놓았다. **11** 경제의 산업화와 관료주의화는, 자격증과 전문지식을 강조하는 현상과 맞물려, 학교 교육을 경제적 및 사회적 이동의 차원에서 보다 중요하게 만들었다. **12** 하얗고 부드러운 사막 평원은 운석을 찾아내는 데 완벽한 배경이 되는데, 운석은 보통 어두운 임갈색 혹은 검은색을 띠기 때문이다. **13** 예컨대, 오대호 인접 지역은, 지역적 규모에 따른 다양한 과정을 통해, 호수가 만들어내는 독특한 폭풍우를 경험하게 된다. **14** 만약 지구가 태양에서 너무 가깝거나 멀어서 영구히 거주 가능 지역 바깥의 궤도로만 움직인다면 대다수 생명체는 사라지게 될 것이

확실하다. **15** 현대의 모든 가금류들의 조상이 붉은 야생 닭이라는 점은 널리 인정되고 있다. **16** 비타민이 건강에 필수적인 성분으로 인식됨에 따라, 효과적인 치료법이 없어 보이는 질병 및 상태도 비타민 치료에 반응할 수 있다는 그럴듯한 주장이 제기되었다.

PART 2 ★ Chapter 06

UNIT 21 Check-up Quiz

p.104

1 settle 그 장소는 연장자들이 모여서 축제를 계획하고, 의식을 위한 춤을 추며, Pueblo 족의 일들을 처리하고 어린 세대들에게 부족의 가르침을 전달하는 성역으로서 기능했다. **2 oral** 대부분의 아프리카 문화는 구비문화라고 하는 것에 기본을 두고 있었다. **3 peak** 1957년을 정점으로 이후 캐나다의 출산율은 감소하기 시작했다. **4 initially** 재즈의 특성은, 초기에 "hot"이라고 불려지고 이후에는 "swing"으로 불려진, 리듬감 있는 격정적인 연주이다. **5 scope** 경기 침체가 어느 정도 지속될 것인지에 대한 예측이 은행이 채택할 수 있는 조치의 범위에 영향을 미치게 될 것이다. **6 tenuous** 애널리스트들은 석유 가격의 안정성이 희박하다고 했지만, 작년 석유 가격은 거의 변하지 않았다. **7 staunch** 여성 단체의 충실한 회원들은 투표권을 획득을 위한 싸움을 포기하지 않았다. **8 oversee** 고인들이 세상에 남겨둔 사람들의 삶을 지켜보고 인도하기 전에 정성 어린 장례식이 선행되어야 했다. **9 mercy** 상대방이 그가 보낸 밀사를 죽이거나 항복하기를 거부하는 경우, 몽골인들은 무자비한 모습을 보였다. **10 mandated** 1938년 공정노동 기준법은 1940년부터 최대 주 40시간의 노동이 이루어지도록 했다. **11 marginal** 그의 부족은 가난한 편에 속했으며 광활한 고비 사막의 북부 자원이 빈약한 지역에서 살고 있었다. **12 meticulously** 과거에는 오늘날만큼 세심하게 기록이 이루어지지 않았다. **13 nomads** 원주민들은 아마도 이 초기 유목민의 후손으로 남아시아에서 배를 타고 좁은 해협을 건너거나 대륙교를 건너갔을 것이다. **14 ornament** 거의 모든 가정용 및 장식용 물품들은 Rockingham 제품으로 구입이 가능하였다. **15 engulfed** 그 후 10년간 징기스칸이 몽골 부족을 모두 통일할 때까지 격렬한 내전이 이어졌다. **16 eternal** 사람의 본질은 영원한 것이어서 그 사람을 다음 단계의 삶으로 떠나 보내기 위해 제대로 된 장례식을 치를 때까지는 이승에 그대로 남게 된다. **17 primary** 사회의 우선적인 관심사들을 드러내 주는 것 이외에도, 한 사회의 예술의 내용은 그 문화권의 사회적 계층 관계를 반영해 낼 수 있다. **18 prized** Art Nouveau 양식은 당시에도 널리 퍼졌으며 오늘날에도 매우 귀중한 것으로 여겨지고 있다. **19 foremost** 최초의 자연주의 작가 Theodore Dreiser는 이해하거나 통제할 수 없는 힘에 의하여 인간이 내던져지는 어두운 세계를 적나라하게 표현하였다. **20 stereotypes** 그 버라이어티 쇼에서는 흑인분장을 한 백인 배우들이 나와서 인종적인 고정 관념을 강조했다. **21 identical** 이러한 종류의 글은 역사상 특정 시점에 이르기까지 우리의 세상과 일치하는 상상 속의 세상을 그리고 있다. **22 representative** 대부분의 이러한 지도자들은 개혁가, 혹은 여성의 권리를 위해 싸우는 활동가 옥은 직기들이었고, 대다수의 평범한 여성을 대표하지는 않았다. **23 district** New York시의 Harlem이라고 알려진 지역이 Harlem Renaissance 운동의 중심이 되었다. **24 fabricate** Dreiser

는 작가란, 낭만을 꾸며내는 것이 아니라, 인간사에 대한 진실을 말해야 한다고 생각했다. **25 faded** "railroad novel"이라는 새로운 장르를 만들어냈다고 평가되는 이러한 작가들은 현재 대부분 잊혀졌고, 그들의 이름은 기억 속에서 사라지게 되었다. **26 feuding** West Side Story는 Shakespeare의 연극에서 나타나는 Montague 가문과 Capulet 가문을, 원한 관계에 놓여 있는 갱단인 Jet 가문과 Shark 가문으로 바꾸어 놓았다. **27 originated** '에티켓'이란 말은 17세기 프랑스에서 유래된 것이지만 오늘날에는 영어에서도 일상적으로 쓰이고 있다. **28 regarding** 시간에 대한 중요성은 각 사회가 시간에 관해 가지고 있는 수많은 속담이나 표현을 통해 보여질 수 있다. **29 distinct** 모든 Pomo인 바구니 제작자들은 15에서 20개 정도 되는 다양한 패턴으로 바구니를 생산하는 방식을 알고 있었는데, 이 패턴들은 여러 가지 방법으로 혼합될 수도 있었다. **30 lamented** 철학사가들은 전통 가치를 부식시키는 점에서 비즈니스의 새로운 광기가 담당하는 역할에 대해 애통해했다.

할 수 있는 단어보다는 기억할 수 있는 영상을 포함하고 있다는 사실을 의미한다. **24 urges** League of Women Voters 단체는 모든 시민들이 투표하기를 촉구했다. **25 deploy** 그 장군은 적이 통치하고 있는 마을로 자신의 군대를 보내는 것을 꺼려했다. **26 backlash** 그 후 1920년대에 격렬한 반발이 생겼다 미국은 영국과 프랑스에게 속아 참전을 하게 되었다고 많은 사람들이 말했다. **27 evidenced** 감정의 건강 상태는 목소리에 의해 입증될 수 있다 자유롭고 멜로디가 있는 음성은 행복을, 수축되고 거친 음성은 분노를, 무뚝뚝하고 노곤한 음성은 우울함을 나타낸다. **28 concentrate** 성인들은 때때로 아이들이 모든 것에 대해 호기심을 갖는 것을 집중력 부족 현상으로 잘못 생각한다. **29 means** 점차적으로 학교는 이민자들을 미 사회로 통합시키는, 가장 중요한 수단으로 여겨지게 되었다. **30 compulsory** 안전벨트의 사용은 여러 주에서 의무적인 것이다; 착용하지 않으면 벌금을 물 수 있다.

UNIT 22 Check-up Quiz
p.108

1 commodity 옥수수, 면, 설탕, 그리고 기타 많은 물품들이 상품 시장에서 구입되고 판매된다. **2 convenient** 자동 입출금 기는 하루 24시간 동안 은행 업무를 볼 수 있게 해주는 편리한 수단이다. **3 monetary** 캐나다는 1878년 통화 단위로서 달러를 채택했다. **4 notion** 1930년대 대공황 시기에는 취직을 증대시키기 위한 일자리 나누기 운동의 개념이 등장했다. **5 furnace** 공장의 용광로는 최대한의 고열로 가열되어야 한다. **6 prolific** 다작하는 작가였던 Oliver Evans는 1782년 수력에 의해 가동되는 매우 자동화되고 노동 절약적이었던 제분소를 건설했다. **7 routine** 종이 가방의 대량 생산으로 그 비용이 급격히 절감되자, 종이 가방은 거의 모든 구매 행위에서 일상적인 것이 되었다. **8 monotonous** 공장 업무가 보다 지루하고 단조로웠지만, 한편으로는 보다 효과적이어서 대량 생산을 가능하게 해주었다. **9 posture** 정부는 관세 장벽을 마련하였고 대륙 철도를 건설하는데 대부 및 보조금을 제공해 주었으며, 사기업에 대해서도 표면적으로만 비개입의 입장을 고수하고 있었다. **10 accommodating** 정부는 도움을 줄 수 없으면 아무것도 아니다. **11 contented** 대부분의 다른 도시들은 미래 성장의 규제 계획에 만족하고 있다. **12 distinguished** 최초로 1870년 인구 조사에서 공식적으로 "도시" 인구와 "시골" 인구가 구분되었다. **13 justified** 노예 소유주들은 노예제가 당연한 일이며 세계적으로 아프리카 흑인들의 지위는 노예라고 주장하여 노예 제도를 정당화했다. **14 obliged** 노예 주인은 어린이, 노인, 병자를 포함해서 생산성이 없는 흑인들까지 돌보아 주어야만 했다. **15 outbreak** 1775년 미 독립전쟁이 일어나기 15년 전에 이십만 명이 넘는 이민자들이 북미 해안가에 도착했다. **16 overwhelming** 새 연극은 너무나 성공적이어서 연극 표에 대한 요구가 대단했다. **17 packed** 대도시들은 사실상 겹쳐 살아야 할 만큼 사람들로 넘쳐 났다. **18 sprawling** Los Angeles는 400 평방 마일이 넘는 사막을 가로 질러 뻗쳐 있는, 집중화되어 있지 않은 대도시이다. **19 counter** 사막화를 방지하기 위해 현재 사용되고 있는 한 가지 방법은 콩과 식물을 심는 것이다. **20 senator** 미 상원 의원으로 재직하기 위해서는 최소한 30세 이상이 되어야 한다. **21 temporary** Memphis시는 남북 전쟁 당시 중요한 북부 군의 군사적 중심지였고 1862년에는 주 임시 수도로써 기능했다. **22 property** 그 법에 따라 토지를 소유하게 된 245,000명 중에서 25% 이하의 사람들이 그 재산에 대한 최종 권리를 얻게 되었다. **23 Campaigning** TV 유세는 우리의 정치적 세계가 점차적으로 기억

UNIT 23 Check-up Quiz
p.112

1 outlining Charles Townes와 Arthur Schawlow는 가시 광선의 파장을 증대시키는데 필요한 조건을 개략적으로 설명하는 장문의 논문을 썼다. **2 interchangeable** 탄산 칼슘과 탄산 소다는 다른 어떤 용도로도 서로 바꾸어 쓸 수 없는 것이지만, 유리 및 비누 제작에서는 서로 바꾸어 쓸 수 있다. **3 mutual** 모든 알로사우러스는 상호 보호와 영양을 위해 협력했던 것으로 보인다. **4 latent** 열대 사이클론의 주요 에너지 원은 수증기가 압축될 때 방출되는 잠열이다. **5 ooze** 비나 물 같은 강수가 핵 폐기물 웅덩이 안으로 곧장 흘러 들어가 섞인 다음 주변 환경으로 스며나올 수 있다. **6 herbivores** 식물들은 종종 초식동물로부터 자신을 보호하는 많은 방법들을 가지고 있다. **7 hostile** 심 해서는 인간에게 적대적인 환경이다. **8 crawl** 3피트의 문어는 직경이 1인치도 되지 않는 구멍도 기어서 통과할 수 있다. **9 intervention** 일반적인 빛은 원자 혹은 분자가, 외부적인 방해 없이, 스스로 초과되는 에너지를 제거할 때 즉각적으로 방출 된다. **10 nocturnal** 대부분의 쥐는 야행성이지만 아프리카 들쥐는 낮 시간 동안에도 활발하게 활동한다. **11 abyss** 깊은 바다의 어두운 심해에서 유일한 빛은 발광성 물고기들에 의해 만들어진다. **12 palatable** 그물눈청어는 북대서양 대구류에 속하는 작은 어류로, 인간의 입맛에는 맞지 않는다. **13 fine-tuning** 조류 세계에 있어서 부리 모양은 진화적인 미세 조정의 주요 사례가 된다. **14 grumbled** 다음 해 그의 편지는 자신의 가축들이 모두 죽는다는 불평이 쓰여져 있었다. **15 sole** 페로몬은 곤충들이 사용하는 의사소통의 지배적인 매개물이지만, 유일한 수단은 아니다. **16 spanning** 물떼새의 가장 유명한 술책은 날개가 부러진 척하는 것인데, 이것은 실제 부상 흉내를 내는 연속적인 행동으로서, 그 범위가 약간 불편한 행동에서 완전히 무기력해지는 행동까지에 이른다. **17 invade** 지구 내부의 녹아 있는 물질들이 뿜어져 나오면 표면 층에 침투되거나 혹은 표면 위로 흐르게 된다. **18 intervals** 하지만, 10년에서 100년의 간격으로, 이러한 빙하는 평소보다 100배 더 빠른 속도로 이동한다. **19 intricate** 간헐천은 복잡한 연결망에 의하여 극도로 뜨거운 암석에 연결되어 있다. **20 intrusion** 때때로 사람들이 삼각주 안으로 들어가게 되면, 자연의 균형은 깨지게 된다. **21 margins** 새로운 해양 지각은, 지각의 보다 깊은 층에서 흘러나온 물질에 의해 각 판의 하나 혹은 그 이상의 가장 자리를 따라 형성된다. **22 modifying** 비는 많은 화학 합성물들을 용해시키고, 이동시키고, 침전시키며, 지구의 모습을 끊임없이 변경시킨다. **23 deductions** 엄격히 말하면

"참된" 자연 과학은 사실로 이루어지는 것이지, 추론으로 이루어지는 것은 아니다. **24 damp** Florida는 습한 기후로 여름에는 특히 덥고 습하다. **25 recede** 빙하기 말에 빙하들은 물러나기 시작했다. **26 rudimentary** 19세기 초반, 냉동 과학에 필수적이었던, 열에 관한 물리학적 지식은 초보적인 것이었다. **27 altitudes** 보다 높은 고도에서 입자가 냉각되고, 그 입자가 지닌 습기는 비 혹은 눈으로 강하된다. **28 revolve** 수성과 목성을 제외한 태양계 내의 모든 행성들은 행성 주위를 공전하는 위성을 가지고 있다. **29 devour** 블랙홀은 항성을 포함해서 그것이 지나치는 모든 것을 집어삼키는 거대한 중력장을 말한다. **30 dominated** 인접한 Virgo 은하로부터 보이는 빛은 파충류가 동물 세계를 지배했을 때 만들어진 것이다.

UNIT 24 Check-up Quiz p.116

1 presumably Thasos 섬 지방의 도자기 제작소는 많은 유형의 도자기와 함께 지붕 기와를 제작했는데, 아마도 지역적 수요를 충족시키기 위해서였을 것이다. **2 picturesque** 매력적인 가게와 식당이 있는 Old Town은 Albuquerque에서 가장 아름다운 지역이다. **3 predecessors** 18세기의 집은 이전 집들보다 훨씬 개선된 내부를 갖추고 있었다. **4 recommendations** 그 계획은 대학 관리들에게 깊은 인상을 주었고, 곧 추천된 내용의 많은 부분이 실행되었다. **5 convivial** 미 호텔들은 기타 미국의 행사들을 가능하게 했을 뿐만 아니라 즐겁고 쾌활한 것으로 만들어 놓았다. **6 pursue** 포식자들은 명백히 잡기 쉬운 먹이를 놓치는 경우가 거의 없다. **7 raided** 하이티에서는 심지어 보호를 받는 몇 안 되는 곳에서도 소중한 나무가 약탈되고 있다. **8 wary** 중고차를 살 때는 신중해야만 한다; 엔진 상태가 좋은지 확인하라. **9 exposure** 적도 근처의 사람들은 강렬한 태양 빛에 노출됨으로써 수 세대에 걸쳐 모두 어두운 피부를 갖게 되었다. **10 generated** 불완전하고 완성되지 않은 분류법에 의해 만들어진 실수들은 최소화 될 것이라고 믿어지고 있다. **11 pungent** 일부 향료들은 음식에 매운 맛을 낸다. **12 render** 급격한 생태학적 변화는 생물에게 환경을 적대적인 것으로 만들 수 있다. **13 inhabit** 알려진 종의 절반 정도가 우림 지대에 서식한다는 사실은 그렇게 놀랍게 보이지는 않는다. **14 genesis** 생명체가 바다에서 육지로 이동한 사실은 생명의 발생만큼이나 진화론으로 설명하기가 어려운 난제였다. **15 crunch** 하이브리드 자동차는 미국에 석유 위기가 닥쳤던 70년대 초반부터 여러 가지 형태로서 존재해 왔다. **16 impair** 술은 운전 능력을 저해시킬 수 있다. **17 potent** 합성 헤로인의 일종인 모르핀은 효과가 뛰어난 진통제이다. **18 curative** 일부 사람들은 특정 광물의 결정이 치유력을 갖고 있다고 믿는다. **19 density** 뼈와 근육의 밀도뿐만 아니라 구조 역시 유전자에 의해 미리 결정이 된다. **20 elongated** 실제 안구는 타원형으로, 앞쪽에서 뒤쪽까지 세로로 길게 되어있다. **21 enthusiastic** 일부 전문가들은 그 약에 열광한 반면 다른 전문가들은 그것이 단지 몇 달 동안만 효과가 있다고 주장했다. **22 circulatory** 한약은 순환계와 같은 인체의 물리적 시스템에 침술보다 더 직접적인 효과를 보인다. **23 Concomitant** 기증된 난자를 이용하는 경우가 증가함으로써, 두 번 이상의 출산 경험이 있는 40대 이상의 여성 비율도 또한 증가하고 있다. **24 crux** 한의사들은 단순히 증상만 제거하기 보다는 질병의 원인을 치료하고자 하는데, 이것은 여러 사람들이 서양 의학 기술의 핵심적인 결함이라고 주장하는 부분이다. **25 resistant** 세라믹은 금속보다 더 단단하고 가벼우며 열에 보다 강하다. **26 impurities** 에메랄드는 그 안의 티타늄과 크로미늄의 불순물 때문에 아름다운 초록색 빛깔을 띤다. **27**

modulate 시각적 혹은 청각적 수단에 의한 의사 소통과 비교해 볼 때, 생물들의 화학적 신호를 조정할 수 있는 능력은 제한되어 있다. **28 alloys** 가볍지만 알루미늄 합금은 매우 강하다. **29 tolerate** 사막의 커다란 동물들의 또 다른 전략은, 사막에 적응하지 못하는 동물들에게는 치명적일 수도 있는 수준까지, 체내의 수분 손실을 견디어 내는 것이다. **30 expelling** 해면은 표면의 작은 구멍을 통해 물을 빨아드려서 양분을 걸러낸 후 보다 큰 구멍으로 물을 배출시킴으로써 먹이를 먹는다.

Chapter 06 Review Test p.120

1. ⓒ	2. ⓒ	3. Ⓐ	4. ⓒ
5. ⓒ	6. ⓒ	7. Ⓑ	8. Ⓓ
9. Ⓐ	10. Ⓓ	11. Ⓑ	12. Ⓐ
13. Ⓑ	14. Ⓓ	15. ⓒ	16. Ⓐ

1 1790년대 이래로 북미 기업가들은 사외 근무 시스템의 범위를 넓혀서 공정을 보다 효율적으로 만들었는데, 이 시스템은 노동자들에게 순차적으로 해당 원료를 제공하여 각 노동자가 생산 과정의 한 단계만을 전담하도록 만드는 것이었다. **2** 진흙의 점도는 중요했다; 진흙은 주의 깊게 두드려졌으며 질감이 고르게 나타나도록 물과 섞였다. **3** 초기 인간 신체가 발전할 시기에는 콜레스테롤이 단백질을 이끌어 내어 뼈, 척수, 내장 기관 그리고 피부가 형성된다. **4** 양쪽 모두 이스라엘의 견고한 후원국들이었던 미국과 네덜란드는 통상 금지 정책의 주요 대상국이 되어 막대한 경제적 타격을 입게 되었다. **5** 오늘날 대부분의 천문학자들은 우주를 구성하는 별 무리가 서로 반대 방향으로 더 멀어져 가고 있다는 주장을 인정한다. **6** 미국은 세기 초 도시에 사는 인구가 5%도 되지 않는, 압도적인 전원 국가였다. **7** 1960년대 이전 지질학자들은 활화산과 강력한 지진이 왜 그 지역에 집중되어있었는가를 설명하지 못했다. **8** 1920년경 대부분의 주에서는 14세 혹은 그 이상 나이에서의 학교 교육이 의무적인 것이었다. **9** 명성을 유지하는 것과 별도로 American Academy and Institute of Arts and Letters의 유일한 목적은 문학과 음악 그리고 미술에 있어서의 관심을 만들어 내고, 지원하며 유지하는 것이다. **10** 북미 대륙에 유럽인들이 도착하기 전 미 원주민들은 수천 개가 넘는 언어를 사용하고 있었다 대부분의 언어는 상호간에 의사소통이 되지 않았다. **11** 날개를 다듬고 끊임없이 관심을 갖지만, 새 깃털의 놀랍도록 복잡한 구조는, 불가피하게, 마모된다. **12** 과학자들은 Newton의 중력의 법칙을 수정해서, 별 사이의 거리 정도 되는 먼 거리에 대해서는 중력이 끌어당기기 보다는 밀쳐내는 특성을 지닌다는 이론을 제시했다. **13** 걷기 동안에는 바다가 뒤로 물러나면서 알로사우러스는 먹이를 따라 이동해야 했다. **14** 그들은 단기간 내 먹을 수 있는 모든 음식을 먹어 치워서, 아마 아사로 멸종할 수도 있을 것이다. **15** 동시에 유행병 학자들은 어린 시절 심각한 박테리아 성 감염을 겪었던 사람들이 알레르기나 천식을 경험하게 될 가능성이 더 적다는 점에 주목했다 게다가 대가족에 태어난 아이들이 훨씬 알레르기에 덜 손상되었다. **16** 컴퓨터에 부착된 모뎀은 디지털 데이터를 전송 주파수를 조정하기 위한 아날로그 신호로 전환한다.

PART 2 ★ Chapter07

irrelevant 특히 소리 자체에 많은 중요성을 부여했던 작가들 때문에, 단어의 의미는 단어 자체와 사실상 관련이 없는 것으로 되었다.

UNIT 25 Check-up Quiz p.122

1 **vanished** 미개척지가 사라짐에 따라, 거대한 공장과 넓은 농경지가 두드러지게 나타났다. 2 **longings** 튤립의 구근은 유럽에서 미국으로 이동되어, 영국 정착민들과 네덜란드 정착민들의 고향에 대한 갈망을 해소시켜 주었다. 3 **meteoric** 많은 환경적 요인이 L.A.의 빠른 성장에 기여했다. 4 **novel** 서구 증기선에 표준이 되었던 엔진은 이전과는 구별되는, 새로운 디자인이었다. 5 **obsolete** 얼음 산업은, 냉장고에 의해 쓸모 없어질 때까지, 도시 거주민들에게 얼음을 제공했다. 6 **coerce** 이탈리아의 경우에도 러시아는 히틀러가 러시아와 싸우도록 강요했던 소수의 이탈리아 군대와 맞닥뜨렸을 뿐이다. 7 **conquered** 그는 말을 타고 활을 쏘는 유목민을 이끌고 그 이전 그리고 그 이후의 어떤 지도자보다도 광활한 영역을 정복했다. 8 **consumed** 인간들이 음식을 'home base'라 불리는 중심부로 가져와서 서로 공유하고 소비했던 점은 명백하다. 9 **disputes** 마을 족장은 토지 분쟁 문제와 종교적인 일들을 다루었다. 10 **plateau** Mesa Verde는 Colorado와 Utah, New Mexico, 그리고 Arizona 주가 합쳐지는 Four Corners 근처의 고원에 위치해 있다. 11 **pores** 화석은 종종 밀도가 높은데, 뼈에서의 구멍과 기타 공간들이 주위 퇴적물로부터 만들어진 광물질로 채워지기 때문이다. 12 **sacred** 가족의 신성한 물품들은 가장 나이가 많은 여성의 통제하에 관리되었다. 13 **staples** 다른 재료들이 때때로 사용되기는 했지만, 이러한 네 재료는 가장 섬세한 바구니를 만드는 데 있어서 주요 원료였다. 14 **stories** 가장 큰 Pueblo족은 5층짜리 집과 500개 이상의 방을 가지고 있었다. 15 **exalted** 수공업자들의 은 접시들과 은 그릇들은 자신들의 고귀한 신분을 반영해 주었고, 또한 그들의 고객의 탁월함을 입증해 주는 것이었다. 16 **foes** 인간은 적대세력과 가난, 그리고 역병으로 이루어진 가혹하고 위험한 환경에서 안보의 수단을 얻기 위한 하나의 방편으로 사회를 조직한다. 17 **realization** 풍자극은 자기 만족에서 꺼내어, 우리가 의심 없이 받아드리고 있는 많은 가치들이 실은 잘못된 것이라는, 기분 좋게 놀라운 자각을 이끌어낸다. 18 **securing** 그 단체는 Manhattan의 Liberty Society Building에서 전시 공간을 확보하는 것 이외에도 수채화 교육을 위한 작은 학교를 설립했다. 19 **ensconced** 열쇠는 입구 매트 아래에 숨겨져 있었다. 20 **marked** 번창했던, 그리고 본질적으로 중간 계급으로 이루어져 있었던 공화국의 시민들은 초상화에 대한 뚜렷한 기호를 나타내었다. 21 **medium** 미적인 원칙에는 또한 매개물이 일정 정도의 아름다움과 표현력을 가지고 있어야 한다는 점이 암시되어 있다. 22 **monopolized** 보다 이전 화가들은 종종 독학으로 풍경화 소재에 국한된 그림 연습을 했다. 23 **optimistic** 그 시의 결말은, Smith의 시에서 보였던 암울하고 비관적인 결말과는 달리, 희망적이다. 24 **tantrums** 버릇 없는 아이들은 뜻대로 되지 않을 경우 갑작스럽게 화를 낸다. 25 **flushed** "Regionalism"이라고 알려진 예술 운동은 미국에서 경기침체가 발생했을 때 시작되었지만, 실제로는 1930년대 이전에 이미 싹트고 있었다. 26 **improvisation** 오페라 세리아는 상상과 즉흥 연주를 피하고 대개 그리스 이야기인 익숙한 줄거리를 선호했다. 27 **strict** 많은 부모들은 아이들이 볼 수 있는 쇼에 대해, 그리고 TV 시청 시간에 대해 엄격한 제한을 가하고 있다. 28 **utterances** 아이들이 알아차리는 소리는 종종 말의 끝부분에 있는 단어들일 것이다. 29 **fidelity** 가장 중요한 것은 모든 화가들이, 일정 정도의 신념을 가지고, 미국에서 제일 인기있는 풍경화가의 기법과 구성에 부합하는 방식을 유지했다는 점이다. 30

UNIT 26 Check-up Quiz p.126

1 **durable** 경제학자들은 내구재를 최소 4개월 이상 지속되는 상품으로 정의한다. 2 **indifferent** 주주들은 주주총회에 너무도 무관심해서 투표를 하지 않을 수 있다 따라서 경영진을 대리인으로 위임하여 투표가 이루어진다. 3 **expendable** 새로운 기술로 자신들의 노동이 값싸게 혹은 불필요하게 되자, 일부 노동자들은 일자리를 잃게 되었다. 4 **insurance** 수많은 보험 회사들이 Connecticut주 Hartford에 자신의 본사를 두고 있다. 5 **kinfolk** 도시의 핵가족들은 친척보다 가까운 이웃에 더 많이 의지한다. 6 **lucrative** 심지어 오늘날에도 북아메리카 상용 항공 분야는 세계에서 가장 수익성이 좋은 시장에 속한다. 7 **appraise** 보석상은 때때로 보증 목적을 위해 보석 감정을 요청 받는다. 8 **out of date** 차후 개혁들이 이전의 명제들을 상당히 구시대적인 것으로 만들고 있다. 9 **barns** 다른 예술가들은 집이나 헛간에서 가족 혹은 도제들의 도움에 의지하면서 작업을 했다. 10 **collective** 표현적 리더쉽은 사회 집단 구성원들의 집단적인 행복을 강조하는 리더쉽이다. 11 **compact** 도시 거주자들은 또한 다른 즐거움을 발전시켰는데, 이 즐거움은 밀집한 사회에서만 가능한 것들이었다. 12 **affluent** 장학금은 유복하지 못한 가정 출신의 학생들이 대학에 들어올 수 있도록 해준다. 13 **ponderous** 이 무거운 기계들은 곡식을 수확, 탈곡, 포장해주었는데, 이 모든 과정들은 동시에 이루어졌다. 14 **Proponents** 이 개혁의 지지자들은 공동 소유로 인하여 이 시설에 대한 광범위한 접근성이 확실히 증대될 것이라고 주장했다. 15 **deformity** 동물들의 새끼는 부상이나 신체적 기형을 가진 채 내어날 수 있다. 16 **reaped** 도시 빈민층은 가정 용품들의 발전으로 인한 혜택을 거의 받지 못했다. 17 **brunt** 미국은 전쟁 중 태평양 전투에 정면으로 맞섰다. 18 **censorship** 그 나라에서는 정부의 검열 때문에 그러한 영화를 보기가 힘들다. 19 **pledged** 공화당은 서부 개척에 동참하는 주민들에게 무료로 토지를 제공할 수 있게 하는 법의 제정을 약속하였다. 20 **cozy** 1754년 전, 영국과 북미 식민지들은 우호적인 관계에 있었지만, 그 후 그들은 긴장 국면에 놓이게 되었다. 21 **outspoken** Roger Williams는 Rhode Island 식민지의 설립자였으며, 종교적 및 정치적 자유를 거리낌 없이 주장했던 인물이었다. 22 **penalized** 오늘날 대부분의 주요 도시에서는 재활용이 의무적인 것이어서 이를 위반하는 사람들은 5백 달까지의 벌금을 물 수도 있다. 23 **polled** 1990년의 한 조사는 여론 조사에 응답한 80% 이상이 "하느님"을 믿는다고 밝혔다. 24 **promote** 과거 대통령들이 자신의 이익뿐만 아니라 미국 국가의 이익까지 도모하기 위해 사용했던 법령이 있다. 25 **prospect** 19세기 미국인들은 국가 경제의 전례 없는 변화가 사회적 혼란을 가져올 것이라는 전망에 사로잡혀 있었다. 26 **spatial** Los Angeles는 자동차 시대의 산물이었다; 그 도시의 특이한 공간적 구조는 자가용 소유의 확대 현상에 기인한 것이었다. 27 **observe** 두려움이 인간의 신체에 미치는 영향은 오랫동안 조사되어왔으나, 두뇌에 미치는 영향은 조사되지 않았다. 28 **Circumstantial** 정황 증거는 직접적인 사실의 관찰로부터 도출되는 증거가 아니다. 29 **backbone** 1771년 기업인 Mark Bird가 Pennsylvania에서 용광로를 설치했을 때 제철업은 미 산업의 중추가 되어 있었다. 30 **plague** 그 역병은 해상무역, 즉 선박을 통해 지중해 시실리 섬으로 번져 유럽으로의 전파의 발판을 마련했다.

1 **ample** 과거 화성 표면에는 물이 존재했고, 화성이 따뜻해지면 앞으로 물이 다시 생기리라는 증거도 많다. 2 **penetrate** 물이 깨끗할 수록 태양빛이 더 깊이 투과된다. 3 **preliminary** 새로운 비행기 모델이 설계 초기 단계에서 완전한 생산 단계까지 이르는 기간은 약 4년이다. 4 **Gravitation** 중력 때문에 달이 지구 주위를 궤도를 그리며 돌 수 있다. 5 **horizontal** 보다 많은 공기가 수직 이동 보다는 이러한 수평 이동에 관련이 있다. 6 **induce** 과학자들은 여러 화학물질들을 주사형 현미경의 끝에 부착시켜 정확한 위치에서 화학적 반응이 유발되기를 바라고 있다. 7 **injection** 연료 분사 엔진은 실린더 안으로 연료를 분사하기 위해 기화기 대신 연료 분사 장치를 이용한다. 8 **Traits** 머리카락 색깔과 눈 색깔과 같은 특성은 유전적으로 부모로부터 물려받은 특성이다. 9 **courtship** 부리를 치는 것은 황새들에게 있어 일반적인 구애의 수단이며, 부리를 딱딱거리는 것은 올빼미들의 일반적인 위협 방법이다. 10 **jeopardy** 침팬지 무리가 흩어져서 서로에게서 고립되면 침팬지 고유의 유전적 구성은 위험에 처하게 된다. 11 **lairs** 공룡은 알을 낳는 보금자리나 굴을 가지고 있었다. 12 **from afar** 난초는 멀리 떨어진 수분 매개자를 유인하기 위하여 적절한 호기심을 일으키는 형태, 색깔 그리고 향을 이용한다. 13 **depart from** 사막의 포유 동물들은 일정한 체온을 유지하는 평범한 포유류의 특성과는 거리가 멀다. 14 **mature** 다 자란 미국 흰 두루미는 몸 전체가 희고 키가 5피트에 날개 폭이 8피트 정도 되기 때문에 눈에 띄는 특징을 가지고 있다. 15 **heretofore** 학자들은 그 발견이, 이전에는 신비로웠던 과정에 대하여, 귀중한 단서들을 제공해 줄 것이라고 확신하고 있다. 16 **pounces** 호랑이는 먹이 감을 탐지하면, 몸을 웅크려 천천히 다가가서는 갑자기 달려든다. 17 **immunity** 인간의 면역 체계는 방어적인 반응을 하며, 면역은 질병이 없이도 자극될 수 있다. 18 **rapidity** 마지막 수치는 수계의 주요 저수지로서의 바다의 중요성을 나타내고 있을 뿐만 아니라, 대륙에서의 물 이동의 속도도 나타내고 있다. 19 **rigid** 지구의 가장 바깥 부분을 형성하고 있는 딱딱하고 단단한 판은 그 두께가 약 100킬로미터에 이른다. 20 **tapped** 지열 에너지는 잠재적으로 고갈되지 않는 에너지 원으로서, 수세기 동안 인류에 의해 개발되고 있지만, 최근까지도 작은 규모로만 이루어지고 있다. 21 **grinding** 산업용 다이아몬드는 그 단단함 때문에, 절단, 연마 그리고 드릴링에 사용된다. 22 **groundwater** 많은 사회들은 물을 공급받기 위하여 우물로부터 얻는 지하수에 의존한다. 23 **inaccessible** 한 세기 전만 하더라도 심해저는 완전히 접근할 수 없는 곳이었다. 24 **infringe** 자녀를 염려하는 많은 부모들은 GPS 혁명을 반기겠지만, 다른 이들은 이것이 정부가 시민의 사생활을 침해하는 또 다른 방법은 아닌지 벌써부터 궁금해하고 있다. 25 **delta** 아마존 강에는 세계에서 가장 큰 삼각주가 있으며, 중국의 황화 강은 최대 규모의 퇴적물류를 자랑하는데 이것은 삼각주 형성에 매우 중요한 요인이다. 26 **sturdy** 얼음으로 막힌 수역에서는 얼음을 깨고 나아가야 하기 때문에, 쇄빙선은 매우 견고한 선박이어야만 한다. 27 **instantaneously** 통신 위성은 전세계의 데이터를 저렴하게 그리고 즉각적으로 전송할 수 있다. 28 **phenomena** 장관인 오로라 빛의 등장은, 북쪽과 남쪽 자극 주위의 하늘에 나타나는 것으로서, 한 때는 신비스러운 현상으로 여겨졌다. 29 **oompile** 현대 컴퓨터들은 거대한 양의 날씨 정보들을 빠르게 종합하여 분석한다. 30 **vast** 현재 대부분의 달 분화구에 대해서는 달 표면에 고체 물질들이 부딪쳐서 형성된 것이라는 점이 알려져 있다.

1 **combine** 열섬 효과에 의해 도시 지역의 여러 특성들이 결합되면 주위 온도의 인위적인 상승이 이루어진다. 2 **projections** 해치 돔은 쉽게 부착할 수 있는 어떠한 돌출 부분도 없이 매끄럽게 설계되었다. 3 **meager** Seattle의 공원 개발은 매우 제한된 것이었고 자금도 빈약했다. 4 **Murals** 벽화는 시각적 이미지를 통해 서사적인 이야기를 말해 준다. 5 **deck** Empire State Building의 전망대는 몇몇 영화에서 등장되어 주목을 받았다. 6 **unique** 어떤 특이한 생물학적 특성 때문에 개미가 5천 만년이 넘는 기간 동안 주목할 만하게 다양화되고 중단 없는 성공을 이루어냈을까? 7 **ultimately** 다른 종이 환경에 더 잘 적응하면 경쟁이 일어나서 궁극적으로는 또 다른 종의 멸종을 이끌어 낼 수 있다. 8 **rare** 미국인들은 훌륭한 조각을 원하는 드문 경우에 외국인 조각가에게 의존했다. 9 **ecosystems** 인간은 자신이 사는 세상과 생태계를 파괴하는 데 전문가가 되었다. 10 **measure** 객관적인 측정법이 없기 때문에 추정 값의 범위는 넓다. 11 **equivalent** 연구에 따르면 플러그인 하이브리드 자동차의 연료 탱크를 충전시키는 데는 갤런 당 1달러 정도가 든다. 12 **eschewing** 우리는 하이브리드 이외의 자동차를 피하고 보다 환경 친화적인 플러그인 하이브리드를 선택해 환경 보존의 책임을 다하여야 한다. 13 **eternity** 그 동물들은 곧 인간의 탐욕 때문에 영원히 사라지는 또 다른 동물이 될 것이다. 14 **custodian** 그러므로, 해양과 인체 모두 박테리아의 양을 조절하는 일종의 통제 장치를 두고 있는 셈이다. 15 **debilitating** 만약 박테리아 수가 증가해서 통제할 수 없게 되면, 신체 시스템을 장악하여 파괴하고 쇠약하게 만든다. 16 **flora** 이 계획들은 멸종 위험에 처한 동물군뿐만 아니라 식물군을 보호하기 위해 세워졌다. 17 **aggravated** 그 치료법은 병을 악화시킬 뿐이었다. 18 **circulate** 심장은 같은 양의 혈액을 순환시키기 위해서 보다 강력하게 박동해야 한다. 19 **blockage** 이 경락은 다양한 이유로 막히거나 방해 받을 수도 있다. 20 **clot** 이것은 심각한 문제를 일으킬 수 있다 피 덩어리인 응혈이 생기게 되는 것이다. 21 **compatible** 수혈 시에는 환자에게 그 사람의 혈액형과 거부 반응을 일으키지 않는 혈액을 수혈해야 한다. 22 **besieged** 사람들은 거의 매일 "노화 방지" 식품, 새로운 비타민, 그리고 기타 놀라운 음식물들에 의해 둘러싸여 있다. 23 **intoxication** 카페인 섭취를 급격히 증가시키면 카페인 중독이 일어나기 쉽다. 24 **chronic** 종종 만성 질환은 치료되지 않거나 치료되지 못하는 것이지만, 반드시 그런 것만은 아니다. 25 **filtered** 상업적으로 꿀은 안정되고 깨끗해지도록 가열된 후 걸러진다. 26 **detonated** 다이너마이트는 보통 뇌관이라 불리는 장치로 폭파된다. 27 **duplicated** 과학에서 실험의 결과는 다른 실험에서 다시 한번 더 반복되기 전까지는 일반적으로 인정받지 못한다. 28 **amenable** 우리는 대부분의 다른 물질들 보다 여러 열 성형에 보다 적합하다. 29 **pupa** 8에서 10일 후, 번데기에서 성인 나방이 나타난다. 30 **brilliant** Robert Goddard는 로켓 공학 분야에 있어서 뛰어난 선구자였다.

1. ⓒ	2. ⓐ	3. ⓒ	4. ⓑ
5. ⓐ	6. ⓒ	7. ⓐ	8. ⓓ
9. ⓑ	10. ⓓ	11. ⓒ	12. ⓑ
13. ⓐ	14. ⓒ	15. ⓐ	16. ⓓ

1 수소 차량에 대해 알고 있었던 극소수의 사람들은 그것을 신기한 물건으로만 보았기 때문에, 더 많은 수소 차량을 생산하려고 서두르지는 않았다. 2 Bessemer 과정은 한 때 가장 일반적인 제철방식이었지만, 오늘날에는 폐기된 것으로 간주된다. 3 이 초록색 옥수수는 끓여지고 건조된 후 껍질이 벗겨지게 되는데, 일부는 바로 소비되기 위해 보관되고 나머지는 동물 가죽으로 만들어진 자루에 저장된다. 4 물론 쟁점은 더 오래된 화석이 어딘가에 있을 수 있다는 점과 아프리카 지역이 인류의 근원지라는 100% 확신을 가질 수는 없다는 점이다. 5 도자기 제작 기법은 그리스 시대 이전부터 발전해 왔지만, 눈에 띄는 양식의 발전은 그 형태와 장식 부문에서 먼저 나타났다. 6 모든 예술가들과 마찬가지로, 재즈 음악가들도 자신의 스타일을 만들기 위해 노력했는데, 즉흥연주나 변주는 재즈 음악가들이 자신의 개성을 나타낼 주요한 기회가 되었다. 7 유리는 가볍고 액체를 통과시키지 않고, 바로 닦여질 수 있고 재사용되며, 깨지기는 쉽지만 내구성이 강하고 또한 종종 아름답기까지 하다. 8 2차 집단은 학교 친구들 혹은 직장 동료들간의 집단과 같이 그 관계가 형식적이거나 특정 사회적 상황에 근거한 대 집단이다. 9 질량도 없고 전하도 지니지 않지만, 중성자는 지구와 같은 고체 물체를 관통할 수 있다. 10 만약 지구 옆을 통과하는 거대한 중력장이 지구의 궤도에 영향을 미친다면 그런 위험한 일이 일어날 수도 있다. 11 분노와 두려움에 대한 성향은 당연히 유전적 특성이지만, 두려움의 특정 형태는 개인의 환경과 더 많은 관련이 있다. 12 세 가락갈매기는, 적 공격으로부터 안전하게 되면, 방어에 대한 안도감을 느끼고, 육지에 둥지를 튼 갈매기처럼 포식자에 대해 반응을 보이지 않는다. 13 비행은 어느 정도 딱딱한 항공역학적인 설계 원칙들을 요구하지만, 새, 박쥐, 그리고 곤충들은 모두 공중을 정복했다. 14 Clipper는 1969년 Boeing사가 747을 선보여 새 디자인으로 대체될 때까지, 단연 크기 면에서 독보적인 존재였다. 15 케인즈 주의는 국가의 통화 공급량에 대한 제한을 선호하고, 세금과 정부 지출에 의한 수단으로 직접적인 규제를 선호했는데, 이와 달리 통화주의는 직접적인 정부의 통제를 반대했다. 16 수십 년 동안 만성 피로 증후군에 시달려온 사람들은 의사, 고용주, 친구 심지어 가족들에게까지 자신들의 증상이 결코 미약한 수준이 아님을 설득하기 위해 애써왔다.

대부분의 가정에서 아이스 박스는 일상 용품이 되었고, 1920년대와 30년대 상업 냉장고가 이를 대체하기 전까지는 여전히 애용되었다. 4 **hollow** 그들은 이 구비문화를 계속하면서 그들 내부에 빈, 그리고 사라져버린 무언가를 채울 수 있었다. 5 **intent** 법의 의도에도 불구하고, 투기꾼들은 종종 거대한 토지를 획득할 수 있었다. 6 **subterranean** 세 개의 인디안 부락에서는 분리된 지하의 방이 종교적인 의식을 위해 그 사용이 유보되었다. 7 **derived from** 그 도자기의 이름은 South Yorkshire에서 제작된 영국 도자기와의 유사성에서 기원하는 것으로 생각되고 있다. 8 **Besides** 과도한 사냥 이외에도, 최소한 세 개의 요인이 그 멸종에 영향을 미쳤다. 9 **blends** Toraja족의 장례 전통에는 애니미즘 신앙과 서양 기독교의 영향이 혼재되어 있다. 10 **casual** 구어는 일반적으로 문어보다 더 비형식적이다. 11 **butt** 이러한 소위 'couch potato'는 농담의 대상이 되거나 "지적이지" 않은 존재로 간주되고 있다. 12 **supernatural** 돌 혹은 나무에 초자연적인 힘이 있다는 믿음이 조각가로 하여금 그러한 재료에 민감하게 반응하도록 만들었다. 13 **supposedly** 네덜란드인들이 그 지역의 상권을 장악하게 되었을 당시에는 아마도 영국 제품이 밀수입되고 있었을 것이다. 14 **supreme** 그 인류학자는 모든 인간에게는 최상의 신이 존재한다는 점을 이해할 수 있는 능력이 있다고 주장했다. 15 **forge** 징기스칸은 자신의 부족들을 세계 최고의 위대한 전사들로 만들 수 있었다. 16 **hearths** 대부분의 초기 도자기들은 개방된 화로에서 구워졌다. 17 **shield** 자물쇠와 열쇠구멍 가리개는 – 후자는 금속 열쇠로부터 목재부분을 보호하기 위한 것이었는데 – 종종 수입되곤 했다. 18 **sketching** 때때로 가족 구성원들의 그림을 그리기 시작한 재능 있는 남녀들이 지역적 명성을 얻게 되었다. 19 **outnumber** 가장 큰 음악적 확장과 실험은 타악기와 관련되어 있는데, 타악기는 현악기와 관악기보다 수적으로 더 많다. 20 **overtaken** 세기가 바뀔 무렵, Art Nouveau 사상은 당시 존재했었던 기능주의라고 알려진 새로운 학파에 의해서 결국 추월되었다. 21 **pessimistic** 대부분의 사람들은 일정 정도의 비관적인 전망과 낙관적인 전망을 모두 갖고 있다. 22 **prevailed** 1870년대 이후 많은 중요한 작가들은 미 독립 전쟁 직후 유행하던 낭만주의를 배격했다. 23 **prominent** New York 내 거주하는 42명의 저명한 예술가들이 The American Society of Painters in Water Colors란 단체를 설립했다. 24 **inception** 1600년경 이탈리아에서 시작된 이후로 오페라는 많은 변화와 유행을 겪었다. 25 **insanity** 그녀의 세계는 폭력과 광기, 좌절된 사랑 그리고 무기력한 외로움의 세계였다. 26 **acculturations** 이러한 음악적 문화변용의 중요한 결과는 "blue note"를 지닌 소위 블루스 음계의 발전이었다. 27 **self-sacrificing** Arizona의 Hopi 사람들은 희생적인 개인이 이상적인 존재로 되는 조화로운 관계의 가족 제도와 종교 제도를 강조했다. 28 **snap** 철조망이 일반적으로 사용되기 전에는 울타리가 종종 빽빽한 선들로 만들어졌는데, 이는 수축 작용으로 추운 날씨에는 부러질 수 있었다. 29 **fed** 미늘을 만들어 낼 선은 측면에서 기계로 들어가게 되고, 날카로운 부분을 만들어 내기 위하여 이 선은 대각선으로 잘려지게 된다. 30 **hull** 클리퍼선은 날카로운 선수를 가지고 있어서 물살을 쉽게 가를 수 있었으며 좁은 선체를 가지고 있었기 때문에 부드럽게 운항할 수 있었다.

PART 2 ★ Chapter 08

1 **fragile** 그의 섬유는 짧고 약했지만, 그는 거미줄만큼이나 얇은 유리 섬유가 유연하고 또한 직물로 만들어질 수 있으리라 예상했다. 2 **grueling** 26마일의 Boston 마라톤은 사람을 기진맥진하게 만드는 경주이다. 3 **fixture**

1 **prudent** 신중한 투자가는 결코 불필요한 금전적 위험을 무릅쓰면 안 된다. 2 **Raw** 원료는 가공품보다 경제적 가치가 낮다. 3 **cling** 산업 발전

에 있어서 19세기 이전 식민지들은 영국에 뒤쳐져 있었다. 이는 식민지에 목재가 공급됨으로써 목탄을 이용한 제철방식이 지속적으로 이루어졌기 때문이다. **4 domesticated** 수많은 사람들은 자신이 재배하는 곡물과 가축으로 기르는 동물들에 의존하기 시작했다. **5 eager** 도시에 집중된 값싼 노동력과 열망하는 소비자들을 이용하면서, 이 새로운 기술은 가장 큰 도시에 공장이 들어설 수 있게 하였다. **6 reconstruction** 남부의 절망적인 상황으로 인하여 북부에서도 재건이 이루어져야 한다는 점이 간과되었다. **7 entrepreneurs** 북미 기업가들은 업무를 재조정하고 공장을 건설함으로써 생산성을 증대시켰다. **8 busts** 다소 규칙적인 경제적 호황과 불황의 연속을 경제 주기라고 한다. **9 buttressed** 농촌에서 도시로의 인구 유입과 그러한 유입에 의한 노동력의 증가는 새로 이주한 수많은 이주민들에 의하여 또다시 보강되었다. **10 clamped** 1789년 그는 절단기가 움직이는 슬라이드에 고정되는 기계를 발명했는데, 이 슬라이드는 손 크랭크에 의해서 정확하게 앞으로 나아갈 수 있었다. **11 avail** 노동력이 군대에 빠져나가고 곡물 가격이 증가함에 따라, 북부의 농부들은 새로운 노동 절약적인 설비를 이용해야 했다. **12 rational** 이성적으로는 그냥 막대기라는 생각이 들지만 본능적으로는 그것이 뱀일 수도 있다는 생각이 든다. **13 resolve** 그들은 재빨리 유머로써 심각한 순간을 모면했고, 조직을 분열시킬 위험이 있는 안건들을 해결하려고 노력했다. **14 afterthought** 초창기의 아동용 책에서는 삽화가 부수적인 부분일 뿐이었다. **15 stimulated** 농업 혁명은 많은 농촌 사람들로 하여금 도시에서의 새로운 삶을 추구하도록 자극했다. **16 superb** 그 도시에는 탁월한 철도 연결망이 있었을 뿐만 아니라 훌륭한 천연 항구 역시 존재하고 있었다. **17 tenements** 도시 빈민가 건물에는 종종 하수구, 쓰레기 수거장, 혹은 가스 및 전기선이 없었으며, 주택에는 수돗물과 중앙 난방시설이 결여되어 있었다. **18 determinant** 경제가 베이비 붐을 설명해주는 가장 중요한 결정 요인이었다. **19 diluted** 그 결과로써 이 DNA는, 각 세대마다 50%씩 희석되는 일반적인 DNA보다 훨씬 천천히 바뀐다. **20 uniformly** 공정하기 위해서 법은 모든 사람들에게 똑같이 적용되어야만 한다. **21 inspection** 일반적으로 부패하기 쉬운 무역 상품은 국가 감시 하에 놓여 있다. **22 jury** 아직까지 많은 미국인들은 배심제가 그들의 민주주의의 핵심이라고 생각한다. **23 legislative** 국회 의원들은 입법적 사안을 처리하기 위해 대부분의 시간을 Washington에서 보내야 한다. **24 mock** 그는 다음 주 법대에서 열리는 모의 재판에 배심원으로서 참석해달라는 요청을 받았다. **25 conspiracy** John F Kennedy의 죽음에 대한 세부적인 측면들은 가장 철저한 음모 이론가들조차 알아내지 못하고 있다. **26 demographic** 오늘날 많은 선진국에서 가장 빠르게 증가하고 있는 인구층은 노인들이다. **27 characteristics** 이러한 이유들로 Chicago는 지역적인 불리한 특성에도 불구하고 대도시가 될 수 있었다. **28 assigned** 그 연구에서는 각각의 고려할 부문에 대하여 상대적인 중요성을 나타내는 수치가 할당되어 있다. **29 sponsored** 성인 이민자들을 위한 수업은 공공 학교, 기업, 노조, 교회, 사회 복지관 그리고 기타 기관들이 후원했다. **30 dismayed** 일부 방문객들은 끝없이 펼쳐져 있는 도시에 당황했고, Los Angeles를 도시를 모방한 작은 교외 지역들이 뭉쳐져 있는 도시에 불과하다고 느꼈다.

UNIT 31 Check-up Quiz p.148

1 candidate 화성은 탐사와 정착에 더욱 성공적인 후보지가 될 수 있을 것이다. **2 cushioning** 하지만 놀라운 점은 충격파를 흡수하는 공기 저

항의 능력이다. **3 bewildering** 그 행성에 대해 망원경으로 관찰을 해보면 지형이 어지럽게 배열되어 있음을 알 수 있다. **4 quantify** 과학자들은 태양 에너지의 비율을 측정하기 위해 노력해 왔다. **5 refrigerate** 화초 재배자 들은 잘려진 꽃의 신선한 외형을 유지하기 위해 종종 냉장 보관한다. **6 condense** 대기 중 증기로 저장되어 있는 수분은 압축되어 다시 액체로 될 것이며, 그 에너지는 대기 중으로 방출될 것이다. **7 constituents** 헬륨 핵은 또한 지구에 닿는 우주 광선의 구성 성분인 것으로 또한 발견되었다. **8 diffuses** 질소는 조직 세포에서 혈액으로, 다시 혈액에서 폐로 발산된다. **9 friction** 대기의 상부에 위치한 공기는 마찰력에 의해 유성을 태울 정도로 밀도가 높다. **10 wandered** 일부 쥐들은 박스 주위를 돌아다녔고, 자신들이 노출된다는 점에 대해서는 신경 쓰지 않는 것처럼 보였다. **11 ferocious** 창 꼬치는 사나운 포식자로, 때때로 열대 수역의 "호랑이"라 불린다. **12 humidity** 앵무새가 야생에서 알을 품을 때 둥지의 온도와 습도는 자연적으로 조절된다. **13 instill** 이러한 과정을 통해 환경보호론자들은 미국 흰 두루미들에게 자연스런 이동 감각을 키워주고 있다. **14 intact** 완전 무결한 상태로 발견된 거대한 공룡 화석은 흥미진진해 보이지만, 고생물학자에게 그것은 짐승 한 마리가 어떤 이유론가 죽었다는 증거일 뿐이다. **15 intake** 지방 섭취에 있어서 한 가지 고려해야 할 사항이 포화 지방과 불포화 지방의 비율이다. **16 expenditure** 신체의 각 활동은, 심지어 생각만 하는 경우일 지라도, 에너지 소비를 필요로 한다. **17 incubators** 그 알들은 인공부화기에 놓여진 후 부화되었고, 전문가들에 의해 지속적인 관리를 받으며 양육되었다. **18 ingested** 꽃의 꿀은 일벌에 의해 수집되어 소화 기관 내 특별한 주머니 속에서 벌꿀로 전환된다. **19 insulation** 지방은 추위에 대한 단열 기능, 내장 기관에 대한 완충 보호 기능을 맡는다. **20 jostled** 결국 거대한 암석들은 이리저리 부딪쳐서 모래 알갱이 정도의 크기로 부서진다. **21 submerged** Eskimo가 아시아에서 넘어오기 전에 이미 Bering 육로가 물에 잠겼기 때문에, 그들은 배를 타고 넘어 왔음에 틀림없다. **22 decomposes** 바위는 점차적으로 분해되면서 진흙이 된다. **23 deposited** 강물이 넘쳐 나면 때로 굵은 모래 퇴적층이 강둑에 침전되어 자연 제방이 만들어지기도 한다. **24 finer** 식탁용 소금은 암염보다 더 미세하다. **25 eroded** 암석이 바람과 물에 의해 침식이 되면, 침식 작용을 받는 대부분의 암석은 일정 시점에서 물로 흘러 들어가게 되어, 결국 거대한 강으로 유입된다. **26 gives way to** 약 2,900 킬로미터의 깊이를 넘어서면, 커다란 변화가 일어나고 맨틀 대신 핵이 나타난다. **27 labyrinth** Rainer 산의 얼음으로 가득 찬 2개의 분화구에 있는 농굴에는 총 길이가 약 1,5 마일에 이르는 미로 같은 터널과 아치형 동굴이 있다. **28 glowing** 외기권에서 보면 오로라는 지구의 각 자극 주위에 감싸인 채로, 어렴풋이 빛나는 벨트처럼 보인다. **29 inflow** 한번 시작된 후 계속 눈이 내리기 위해서는 핵에 수분을 공급하기 위한 지속적인 수분의 유입이 이루어져야 한다. **30 evaporate** 건조한 사막 기후에서는 비와 녹은 눈이 빠르게 증발한다.

UNIT 32 Check-up Quiz p.152

1 outlook 도시 계획 위원회는 다음 회기 년도의 자금 전망이 낙관적이라고 말했다; 즉 세수입의 증가를 기대하고 있는 것이다. **2 inviting** Hunt의 매력적인 외관에도 불구하고 거주 공간은 이상하게 배치되어 있었다. **3 loop** Chicago의 상업적 중심부인 Loop 지역은 직사각형 형태의 고가 철도 연결망으로 둘러 쌓여 있다. **4 magnificent** 비록 가장 높은 빌딩은 아니었지만, 그 빌딩의 역사와 전망대에서의 경치는 수십 년 동안 그 빌딩의

인기가 지속될 수 있도록 해주었다. **5 draw on** 공공 도서관은 모든 사회 성원들이 이용할 수 있는 자원이다. **6 toxic** 그녀의 책 Silent Spring에서 Rachel Carson은 살충제 및 살충제가 동물에게 끼치는 독성 효과에 대해 언급했다. **7 cosmic** 공룡의 멸종은 기후와 관련되거나 아니면 우주와 관련된 일부 물리적인 사건에 의해 야기되었다. **8 drastically** 사막의 날씨는 단 하루 동안에도 급격하게 변할 수 있다. **9 bleak** 엄청난 인구와 희망 없는 미래로 인하여 많은 하이티인들은 더 나은 삶에 대한 기대로 몰래 국경을 빠져나가 도미니카 공화국으로 가고 있다. **10 comparably** 많은 비교되는 다른 종들에 비해 까마귀는 덜 알려져 있다. **11 conserve** 특히 겨울에는 새들에게 그들의 귀중한 음식을 보존하는 것이 중요하다. **12 decline** 20세기 초 그 새의 수가 감소한 데는 두 가지 주된 요인이 있다. **13 deficient** 만약에 한가지라도 없거나 부족하면 전체 시스템이 위험에 놓일 수 있다. **14 mitigating** 열섬 효과를 완화시키는 한 가지 방법은, 햇빛을 흡수하지 않고 반사하는 건축 재료로 주택, 도로 포장, 그리고 고속도로 건설하는 것이다. **15 discrepancy** 두 나라는 서로 다른 방식으로 산림을 관리했고, 그 결과 현재와 같은 차이가 생겼다. **16 exhaled** 허파 내의 압력이 증가하면, 공기는 호흡을 통해 빠져 나가게 된다. **17 abuse** 그 치료법은 식이 질환이나 약물 중독을 치료하는 데 탁월하다. **18 came about** 열차 전복 사고는 기술자의 나태함의 결과로 일어났다. **19 methodically** Hazen은 방법론상 많은 토양 샘플을 거리고 배양한 후, 그녀의 동료에게 보냈다. **20 ironic** 콜레스테롤이 없다면 인간의 신체는 제대로 기능할 수 없다는 점은 다소 아이러니컬하다. **21 holistic** 많은 사람들이 단순히 빠른 치료책을 찾기 보다는 신체와 건강에 더욱 전인적으로 접근하는 방법을 취하고 있다. **22 imbibed** 전통적으로 한약은 면역력을 기르기 위해 복용된다. **23 tissue** 체내 신진 대사의 흔한 부산물인 산소의 유리기는 조직 세포의 손상을 일으킬 수 있다. **24 alternative** 천연가스는 휘발유에 대한 탁월한 대체 연료가 된다. **25 ceased** 우주가 생성된 지 얼마 되지 않았을 때, 헬륨 생성은 효과적으로 중지되었다. **26 concise** 1800년경 최초로 고안된 화학 기호들은 화합물에 대해 간단하고 즉각 알아볼 수 있는 설명을 제공해 주었다. **27 tarnishing** 금속 산업에서는 금속이 열 가공 동안 녹슬지 않도록 산소가 사용된다. **28 homology** 상사와 상동의 개념은 정의 내리기 보다는 예를 드는 것이 보다 쉽다. **29 pectoral** 어류의 가슴지느러미, 조류의 날개, 그리고 포유류의 앞 발은 서로 대응되는 구조이다. **30 afflictions** 앞으로 뇌 연구를 통해 이식할 수 있는 마이크로칩이 만들어지면, 밀더듬증 환자가 겪는 고통이 영원히 치료될 수도 있을 것이다.

Chapter Review Test 08 p.156

1. ⓒ	2. ⒟	3. ⓒ	4. ⒜
5. ⒟	6. ⒟	7. ⒜	8. ⓒ
9. ⒜	10. ⒝	11. ⒝	12. ⒜
13. ⒟	14. ⓒ	15. ⒟	16. ⒝

1 이 입법의 의도는, 국립 공원으로 지정된 육지에 부여되는 정도의 보호를 해안가 해양 생물 서식지에도 제공하는 것이다. **2** 일련의 지하실과 석회암이 용해되어 형성된 좁은 통로로 이루어진 Mammoth 동굴에는 5개의 분리된 층이 있었다. **3** 오르간, 크래비코드, 하프시코드는 건반악기의 주요 악기가 되었

고, 이 악기들은 18세기 말 피아노로 대체되기까지 최고의 지위를 누렸다. **4** 영국 철학자 Herbert Spencer와 미국 경제학자 William Graham Summer의 사회 진화론이 당시 널리 유행했었다. **5** 부유하고 사회적으로 저명한 이주민들은 영국식 퀼트를 만들었는데, 이 퀼트는 같은 색상과 같은 질감의 커다란 천을 잘라내어 만드는 것이었다. **6** 현재 기상학자들과 컴퓨터 공학자들은 공동 연구로써 날씨에 관한 원 데이터를 단어, 상징, 그리고 그림으로 생생히 나타낼 수 있는 컴퓨터 프로그램을 만들고 있다. **7** 대부분의 국립공원은 자체적인 모순을 가지고 있다: 비록 대중들이 자연에 대한 관심을 가짐으로써 국립공원이 그러한 관광업에 의존하고 있지만, 야생의 보존은 일반인들이 야생을 훼손하지 않음으로써 이루어지기 때문이다. **8** 배심원들은 정부의 관리가 아니다. 배심원이 된다는 것은 개인 자격으로 행해지는 시민의 의무로서, 오히려 투표 행위와 유사하다. **9** 18세기 Antonie Lavoisier는 연소에 대한 다른 이론을 제안하게 되었는데, 이 이론은 – 현재 산소라고 알려져 있는 – 공기의 한 구성 성분을 연소에 이용하는 것이었다. **10** 키가 큰 나무는 번개를 끌어당기지만 전기를 잘 전도하지 못한다. 하지만 강철로 된 빌딩과 차량은 전기가 땅으로 흘러가도록 좋은 통로를 제공하고 전기도 잘 차단한다. **11** 그것은 해수면이 보다 높아지고 그 반도의 나머지 부분이 잠기게 됨에 따라 수십 만 년 전에 대륙에서 떨어져 나온 해안이다. **12** 질흙의 비율이 높은 토양에 있어서 미세한 입자들은 물에 부어진 후 밑으로 떨어지는 속도를 기반으로 측정된다. **13** 정치가가 선거 운동 중 약 1시간 반에서 2시간 정도 진행하는 유세 연설은 뉴스에서의 30초 광고와 10초 영상 어록에 그 자리를 내어 주게 되었다. **14** 특정 대화에서 듣는 사람의 이해력, 흥미 혹은 감정을 어떻게 인식하느냐에 따라 화자는 격양 혹은 낙담할 수 있으며, 이로 인해 발표의 어조가 급격히 변화할 수 있다. **15** 원인이 분명히 밝혀지진 않았지만, 세포와 조직이 정상 보다 빨리 자라고 비정상적인 모양이나 크기를 가지며 정상적인 기능이 중단될 때를 암이라고 한다. **16** 초록은 학술 논문의 요약 본 형태이다 많은 언론 기관들은 초록 본을 발행하여 독자들이 논문 전체를 읽을 가치가 있는지 판단할 수 있도록 한다.

PART 3 ★ Chapter 09

UNIT 33 Check-up Quiz p.160

1 enthusiasm 종교적 열광만큼 인간이 두려워하는 것은 없는 듯 보였다. **2 eradicate** 암시장을 근절시키려고 한 정부의 시도는 오히려 성공하지 못하였다. **3 trend** 대중 문화의 한 세대는 약 2년 정도로 측정되고, 트렌드는 몇 주간 지속되는 것으로 볼 수 있다. **4 progressive** 진보 운동은 우산 개념으로, 1900년대 초반 나타났던 개혁 운동들 일부를 통칭한다. **5 crisscross** 짐마차와 대형 마차들은 도로가 아직 놓이지 않았던 West 지방 어디에서나 지속적으로 운행되었다. **6 designate** 대통령은 고대 유물법에 의하여 자신의 권한으로서 토지를 국정 기념물로 지정할 수 있었다. **7 attained** 그 원주민들은 비농업 인구로 구성된 조직 중에서 가장 복잡한 사회 조직을 이루고 있었다. **8 attributes** Arizona 주의 Hole in the Rock은 물리적 특성으로 인하여 자연 달력 혹은 시계로서 사용된다. **9 surmise** 이러한 주거시설은 보호차원에서 지어진 것이라고 추측할 수도 있으나, Anasazi인들에게는 알려진 적대 세력이 없다. **10**

synonymous 그들은 산업혁명을 인간의 노동이 기계의 노동으로 대체되는 기계화와 실제적으로 동일한 것으로 보았다. **11 henceforth** 1926년 그는 그때부터 토요일에는 하루 종일 자신의 공장을 가동하지 않겠다고 발표했다. **12 immutable** 이러한 기준이 다양한 곳에서 변형되었다는 사실은 그 기준이 불변의 것은 아니라는 점을 나타낸다. **13 imperative** 사회가 점진적으로 발전함에 따라, 보다 복잡한 계산법이 절실하게 요구되었다. **14 incised** 일부 자기들은 새겨지거나 찍혀진 문양으로 장식되어 있었다. **15 incur** 그 이유는 주로 비용 탓인데, 장례식 때문에 가족 구성원들은 엄청난 비용을 지불해야 할 것이다. **16 iridescent** 그러한 스타일 중 선호되었던 문양은 매장되었던 고대 유리에 나타나는 무지개 빛을 모방한 것이었다. **17 fate** 일부 작가들은 잔인하고 무자비한 환경이 인간의 운명을 결정짓는 그러한 세상을 그려냈다. **18 proclivity** 격정적인 연주를 할 수 있는 소질이 재즈 음악가와 다른 연주자들을 구별시켜주는 특징이다. **19 undergoing** 주변 지역은 막대한 경제적 인구학적 성장을 겪고 있었다. **20 revered** 19세기 후반 영국 사회 비평가인 John Ruskin과 William Morris에의해 시작된 그 운동은 기술을 예술의 한 형태로써 존중했다. **21 rotates** 위원회 회원들은 매년 돌아가면서 지정되기 때문에, 새로운 목소리와 의견들이 끊임없이 경청된다. **22 myriad** 일련의 기술적 향상으로 마침내 수많은 음을 낼 수 있는 악기가 생산되었다. **23 norm** 오페라의 구조가 정석에서 벗어나는 적은 없었다. **24 preoccupation** 중세 시대의 예술을 검증 해보면 중세가 얼마나 신학적 교리에 몰두하고 있었는지를 알 수 있다. **25 rage** 18세기 후반 초상화가 대유행이 되어서 Raphaelle Peale은 당시 자신의 정물화를 구입할 사람을 찾지 못했다. **26 refreshing** 풍자극은 독자들이 그 신선한 자극을 인정하기 때문에 살아남는 장르로, 독자 자신들이 진부한 사상의 세계에 살고 있다는 점을 날카롭게 상기시켜준다. **27 exuberant** 자아상은 자신감 있는, 수줍어하는, 공격적인 혹은 활기 있는 목소리 톤에 의해 나타날 수 있다. **28 delivery** 무료 우편 배달 서비스는 처음에는 도시에 한정되었기 때문에, 이러한 집 배달 서비스는 곧 도시 생활의 한 특성이 되었다. **29 insulting** 미 남북 전쟁 이후에 남부군의 지도자였던 Jefferson Davis는 북부에서 불려진 모욕적인 노래의 대상이 되었다. **30 formidable** 미국의 북서 해안은 특이하게 엄청난 Cascade 산맥에 의해 특징 지워진다.

1 prior 고용주들은 입사 지원자가 그 분야에 대해 미리 경험을 쌓았을 것을 요구한다. **2 output** 제조 상의 기술 혁신은 산출량 및 삶의 기준을, 전례 없는 폭으로, 증대시켰다. **3 capacity** 캐나다의 경제적 중심인 Ontario는 캐나다 생산 능력의 40% 이상을 차지한다. **4 cohesion** 여객기는 일종의 국제적 통합에 기여했다고 볼 수 있는데, 이는 해양 횡단 항공 여행으로 인해 가능한 것이기도 했다. **5 colossal** Lincoln 기념관은 6번째 대통령의 거대한 조각을 그 특징으로 하고 있다. **6 cramped** 낮은 수입의 사람들을 일반적으로 부유층이 사는 지역보다 인구가 밀집한 지역에 살아야 한다. **7 defunct** 시는 존재하지 않는 기업과의 계약에 서명할 수는 없다. **8 dictated** 도시 인근 지역의 상태는 도시의 성장 속도를 말해 준다. **9 astounding** Ladies' Home Journal의 발행부수는 700,000부라는 놀라운 수치에 이르렀다. **10 turmoil** 14세기 유럽에서 발생했던 사회적, 종교적 혼란에는 여러 가지 중요한 원인이 있었다. **11 valid** 일부 사회에서는 부계와 모계가 똑같이 법적인 효력을 갖는다. **12 vigilance** 이 때부터 첫 번째 그린 콩이 수확될 때까지, 작물은 노동력과 감시를 필요로 하였다. **13 exorbitant** 개혁가들은 사적으로 소유된 기업이 필수 서비스에 대해 터무니 없는 가격을 책정할 것이라고 주장했다. **14 exponential** Boston을 제외하고 도시들은 18세기를 통하여 급격한 도약을 통해 성장했다. **15 filthy** 지저분한 생활 환경은 흑사병이 유럽 전역을 그렇게 휩쓸고 지나갈 수 있었던 주원인이었다. **16 foothold** 주 5일 근무는 과거 영국을 시작으로 확대되었다. **17 foreshowed** 주요 변화의 조짐은 1860년대 후반 예견되었다. **18 ghastly** 유럽에서 역병의 무시무시하고 끔찍한 공격이 시작된 시기는 14세기 중반이었다. **19 go along with** 만약 그 부서가 세수입을 증대시킨다면, 대통령은 보다 많은 인력을 고용하자는 결정에 찬성할 것이다. **20 grants** 많은 대학들은 연방 정부를 위한 연구에 있어서 보조금을 지급받는다. **21 heralded** 미 독립 선언문은 서명자의 이름을 포함하고 있기 때문에, 모든 13개의 식민지들이 지지했다는 점을 알려준다. **22 discourse** 이전 세대의 전통적인 정치적 담론을 구성하고 있었던 많은 부분들은 사라지게 되었다. **23 emissaries** 영국이 식민지의 항복을 요구하는 밀사를 보냈을 때, 그 지도자는 싸우기를 원했다. **24 entanglements** 초대 대통령은 외국과의 분규를 피하려 했는데, 처음 100년 동안은 그런대로 꽤 잘 해 나갔다. **25 facilitation** 연방 정부의 목적은 서부 개척과 토착 산업의 발전을 촉진시키는 것이었다. **26 fatigued** 사람들은 상쾌할 때 보다 피곤할 때 더 많은 실수를 저지른다. **27 insatiable** 창의성 유형에 많은 심리학자들이 공통적인 것으로 동의하고 있는 한 가지 특성은 그칠 줄 모르는 호기심이다. **28 antecedent** 책은 판지 형태 혹은 종이 덮개에 실을 꼬매 붙인 형태로 보통 간단하게 묶여져 있었는데, 이것이 오늘날 종이표지책의 기원이 되었다. **29 blundered** 그 항공회사는 실수를 저질렀다 그는 Atlanta로 갔고, 그의 화물은 Montreal로 간 것이다. **30 ideal** 많은 사람들은 하와이의 기후가 이상적인 기후에 가깝다고 생각한다.

1 postpones NASA는 때때로 악천후 혹은 기술적인 문제로 인하여 우주선 발사를 연기힌다. **2 Atmosphere** 대기는 우주 방사선으로부터 인간과 다른 모든 생명체를 막아주기 때문에 반드시 필요하다. **3 axis** 자전축이 기울어져 있기 때문에 지구의 남반구와 북반구에서는 다양한 계절이 나타난다. **4 bypassed** 달의 비교적 가혹한 환경으로 인하여 달이 (탐사 대상에서) 피해져야 한다는 주장이 제기되고 있다. **5 related** 과학에서 이론이란 관찰을 통해 확인된 서로 관련 있는 현상들에 대한 합리적인 설명이다. **6 capsize** 작은 배들은 주의 깊게 다루어 지지 않을 경우, 쉽게 전복될 수 있다. **7 Abrasion** 일상 생활로 인한 마모는 구슬의 표면적 특성을 변화시킨다. **8 atoms** 물리학자들은 19세기 초반 이래로 모든 물질이 극도로 작은 입자, 즉 원자로 이루어진다는 점을 알았다. **9 aurora** 오로라의 빛깔은 오로라를 방출하는 원자에 따라 다르다. **10 keen** 코뿔소는 시력이 나쁘지만 예리한 후각을 가지고 있다. **11 gigantic** 익룡 중 일부는, 공룡과 마찬가지로 거대한 몸집을 갖게 되었다. **12 grasp** 개미 사회와 인간 사회 간의 두 가지 주된 차이점은 파악하기가 더 쉽다. **13 groundbreaking** 영장류 동물학자 Louis Leakey와 Jane Goodall의 획기적인 연구에 따르면, 침팬지가 단순히 원숭이의 일종에 불과하지는 않은 듯 하다. **14 hibernation** 짝짓기, 이동 그리고 동면과 같은 동물들의 일부 활동들은 1년 주기로 이루어진다. **15 hue** 그 새의 머리는 빨간색과 검정색으로 되어

있고 눈은 진한 금색을 띄고 있다. **16 fertilize** 수개미는 한 가지 일만 하는데, 바로 여왕 개미의 알을 수정시키는 일이다. **17 lacerate** 잡초는 목장 인부들 혹은 말들의 살을 찢을 수 있는, 날카롭고 가시가 있는 잎들을 가지고 있다. **18 littered** 높이 솟아 있는 참나무 아래에는 다람쥐들이 먹다 버린 수많은 도토리들로 어지럽혀 있었다. **19 huddling** 굴뚝새, 칼새, 갈색 나무발바리와 같이, 한 가지에 모이는 습성을 가진 몇몇 새들은 은신의 효과를 강화시킨다. **20 nostrils** 바다 수달은 해양 생활에 잘 적응되어 있으며, 물 속에서는 닫혀지는 귀와 콧구멍을 가지고 있다. **21 summit** Hood 산의 눈 덮인 정상은 Oregon주의 가장 높은 지점이다. **22 igneous** 심지어 오늘날에도 전체 지각의 96% 정도는 화성암이다. **23 crack** 만약 바위에 틈이 있다면, 대수층에서 표면으로 이어지는 틈으로 물이 위로 밀려나가게 된다. **24 facets** 다이아몬드는 보다 많은 면을 가질 수록 더 빛이 난다. **25 expedition** Jefferson 대통령이 지원한 Lewis와 Clark의 원정은 1812년 전쟁 전에 이루어졌던 고원 및 북서부 지방에 대한 가장 중요한 조사였다. **26 entombed** 비록 수백만 년 된 바위에 묻혀져 있지만, 많은 화석들은 유기물의 잔해로 이루어져있다. **27 flecks** Oklahoma 북서쪽에 위치한 Glass 산맥은 석고로 된 반점으로 덮혀 있는데, 이 반점들은 햇빛을 받으면 반짝인다. **28 oscillation** 번갈아 해수면이 오르고 내리는 주간 조수 간만의 진폭에 있어서는 조수간만 기준으로 1일에 한 번의 만조와 한 번의 간조가 있다 **29 consecutive** 가장 건조한 사막은 극건조 사막이라 불려지는데, 이 사막에서는 최소 12개월 연속으로 비가 내리지 않는다. **30 embedded** 운석이 대륙에 떨어졌을 때 운석은 움직이는 빙원에 묻혔다.

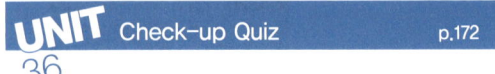
UNIT 36 Check-up Quiz

p.172

1 harmonizing Frank Lloyd Wright는 건물과 그 주변 환경을 조화시키는 매우 독창적인 방법으로 유명하다. **2 intimacy** 미 농부들은 도시 사람들만큼이나 마을의 친밀함을 느끼지 않는다. **3 impetus** Boston에서는 벽돌집이 일반적이었는데, 그 이유는 화재의 위험성 때문에 보다 내구성 있는 건축 재료의 사용이 촉진되었기 때문이다. **4 edifice** 1790년대에 건설되고 현재는 백악관이라 불리는 Executive Mansion은 Washington, D.C.의 가장 오래된 건물이다. **5 foliage** Art deco는, 있는 그대로 표현하는 형식이 아닌, 추상적이고 반복되는 패턴으로 그 형식을 정형화시켰다. **6 archaic** 사실 하이브리드 기술은 배터리 기술만큼이나 오래된 것이었다. **7 bark** 나무의 껍질은 오래될 수록 두꺼워 진다. **8 Emissions** 새 디젤유는 가스 버너보다 대기 중에 30%나 적은 이산화탄소를 배출한다. **9 encroach** 아프리카 인구가 폭발적으로 증가하고 침팬지의 서식지를 침해하면서 침팬지들이 질병에 감염되어 앓다가 죽게 된다. **10 entrenched** 이러한 자원과 기술력의 결합은 인간의 삶에 너무도 확고하게 자리를 잡고 있다. **11 environs** 박테리아는 그 수가 엄청나기 때문에 서식지를 지배하면서 건전한 균형이 유지되도록 한다. **12 impede** 잡초는 수로를 막히게 하고 야생 생물의 서식지를 파괴시키며 농업에 방해가 된다. **13 epic** 그물눈청어의 감소는 엄청난 생태계 변동을 야기하기 때문에, 이는 안타까운 일이 된다. **14 forage** 새 무리들은 낮 동안 서로 흩어진 수 넓은 지역을 따라 먹이를 찾아 돌아다닐 것이다. **15 fraction** 지구 상에 존재했던 모든 생명체 중 극히 일부만 화석으로 보존되고 있다. **16 laymen** 의사와 일반인들은 뇌의 오른쪽 반구와 왼쪽 반구가 마치 서로 다른 특정한 기능을 하는 것처럼 이야기한다. **17 ailment** 탄저균은 일반적으로 양과 소들에게 감염되는 질병이지만, 인간에게도 전염될 수 있다. **18 nausea** 바이러스성 간

염의 정확한 초기 증상은 복통, 구역질 그리고 종종 오한을 수반하는 열이다. **19 perspiration** 다량의 땀 손실이 일어나는 상황에서 일하는 사람은 열손실을 겪을 수 있다. **20 pharmaceuticals** 오늘날 수많은 사람들은 매일 약을 복용함으로써 스트레스가 감소되는 놀라운 효과를 보고 있다고 주장한다. **21 pulsates** 기는 인간의 신체에 흐르는 일종의 힘이다. **22 rectified** 연구 조사에 따르면 급속한 체중 감소는 특정 음식들의 단백질을 적절히 섭취함으로써 치료될 수 있다. **23 spinal** 척추는 주요 기능이 감각 기관 혹은 운동 근육으로 분류된다는 점에서 뇌와 비슷하다. **24 stamina** 어떤 차는 정력을 증강시키고 소화도 촉진시켜 준다. **25 correlate** 그 크기와 상관없는 바이러스의 기능 중 하나는 심각한 질병을 일으킬 수 있다는 점이다. **26 corrosive** 화학 원소인 염소는 부식 성이 있고, 초록색을 띈 노란색 기체로 뚜렷한 향을 가지고 있으며, 무게는 공기보다 2.5배 더 나간다. **27 Detergents** 세제는 먼저 섬유에서 먼지 입자들을 제거함으로써 의류를 세탁하고 이후 먼지 입자가 씻겨져 나가도록 물 표면에 뜨게 한다. **28 tart** 신 과일은 구연산 때문에 시큼한 맛이 난다. **29 haphazard** 처음에는 실험 결과가 아무런 규칙이 없는 것처럼 보였지만, 마침내 일정한 패턴이 드러났다. **30 tampered** 만약 포장이 명백히 누가 만져본 것 같이 되어 있으면, 절대로 그 음식 혹은 약품을 구입해서는 안 된다.

Chapter 09 Review Test

p.176

1. Ⓐ	2. Ⓓ	3. Ⓓ	4. Ⓑ
5. Ⓒ	6. Ⓓ	7. Ⓐ	8. Ⓐ
9. Ⓒ	10. Ⓒ	11. Ⓑ	12. Ⓑ
13. Ⓑ	14. Ⓐ	15. Ⓒ	16. Ⓑ

1 1950년대의 경제적 상황이 인구수를 증가시키는데 도움을 주었지만, 그러한 증가는 조기 결혼과 평균적인 가족 규모의 증대로 인해 가능한 것이었다. **2** 목성은 핵 반응을 일으키는 발화점만큼의 뜨거운 내부 온도를 가지고 있었을 것이다. **3** 산업 혁명의 시작과 함께 주 6일 10시간에서 12시간 노동이 표준이 되었다. **4** 봄 새들의 풍성한 노랫소리와 비교해 볼 때, 늦은 여름의 숲은 꽤 조용하게 느껴진다. **5** 도구, 수레를 끄는 동물, 마차, 우물, 담장을 마련하는 비용과 가장 간단한 주거를 건설하는 비용은 아마도 1,000 달러에 이를 것인데, 이것은 결코 쉽게 마련할 수 없는 금액이다. **6** 또 다른 인구 증가 현상은 1957년 이전 높은 출산율이 진행되던 시기에 태어난 아이들로 인해 발생하게 되는 것이었다. **7** 최초의 승객들은 오늘날의 화폐가치로 환산했을 때 만 달러 정도의 항공료를 지불했는데, 이 금액은 지금은 존재하지 않는 콩코드기의 항공료에 맞먹는 금액이었다. **8** Donald Appleyard의 선구적인 연구는 한 지역의 갑작스러운 교통량 증가가, 범죄의 갑작스러운 증가와 마찬가지로, 사람들에게 영향을 미칠 수 있다는 놀라운 결과를 밝혀냈다. **9** 일부 백인들은 교회 지역을 가난한 흑인과 시 교육의 저하에 따른 소동이 없는 평화로운 피난처라고 인식했다. **10** 특정 여성주의자들은 여성이 종사하는 활동들을 기록함으로써 날카로운 역사관을 나타냈다. **11** 그 줄기는 한번의 수정으로도 수많은 씨앗들이 수정될 수 있도록 고안되었다. **12** 과학자들은, Everest 산의 높이를 계산하기 위한 시스템을 사용하기 위하여, 그 정상에 인공 위성의 신호를 받을 수 있는 특별한 수신기를 장착할 필요가 있다. **13** 강화 콘크리트는 그 안에 들어가 있는 금속 막대기에 의해 강화된 콘크리트이다. **14** 다층 구조의 거대한 건물들은 각 층에 일련의 테라스를 만들면서 층들을 계속 쌓는 방법으로 지어졌기 때문에, 지구라트와 유사한 외형을 지니고 있었다. **15** 비록

둥그런 춤을 추는 것이 방향에 대해서는 어떠한 정보도 주지 않지만, 꽃의 꿀을 맛봄으로써 꿀을 찾는 벌들은, 근처 돌아다니는 벌들의 도움을 받아, 냄새를 확인할 수 있다. **16** 이러한 동굴은 파도의 거대한 압력과 파도에 의해 실려온 모래 및 자갈의 침식 능력을 입증해 주고 있다.

PART 3 ★ Chapter 10

UNIT 37 Check-up Quiz   p.178

1 forts 군사적인 용도 이외에도 19세기의 요새들은 미 West 지방에 수많은 다른 혜택을 제공해주었다. **2 imposing** 미 First Bank는 1790년대에 지어진 위압적인 스타일의 건물로 여전히 존재하고 있다. **3 retract** 일단 결정이 되면 기념물의 제정을 철회하거나 중지시키기 위해 할 수 있는 것이 거의 없다. **4 apparent** 사회가 환경을 바라보는 방식은 때때로 예술 작품 재료의 선택과 사용에서 명백하게 드러난다. **5 unearthed** 우연한 시기에 다양한 장소에서 수메르 언어로 작성된 다량의 평판들이 발굴되었다. **6 utmost** 선사시대 도기를 만드는 데 사용되었던 진흙은 예외 없이 극도로 주의하여 선택된 것이었다. **7 luster** 도자기의 독특한 색과 빛은 가마 온도를 기술적으로 조절함으로써 나타난 결과였다. **8 mundane** 인간은 신성한 것과 세속적인 것 사이에서 영원히 망설이는 존재이다. **9 ornate** 이 도구들은, 정교한 가시와 뾰족한 끝을 가진 매우 화려한 것이었다. **10 procuring** 씨앗과 과일로 식단이 보완될 때 조차도 사냥은 음식을 조달하기 위한 불안정한 한 방법이었다. **11 rambling** Anasazi인들은 땅 위에 집을 짓고 함께 모여 다층의 주거 단지를 돌아다니기 시작했다. **12 rebuke** 싸움, 괴롭힘 혹은 다른 사람들을 짓밟으려는 시도는 사회로부터 즉각적인 비난을 일으킨다. **13 sufficient** 그들은 자신의 그림에 사인을 함으로써 전문 예술가로서의 이미지를 유지할 수 있는 충분한 후원을 받을 수 있었다. **14 sellings** 그 박물관은 자연 환경에서의 동물 전시뿐만 아니라 Peale과 그의 가족들의 그림들을 전시하고 있는 것이 그 특징이다. **15 solemn** 진지한 영화에 생음악을 덧붙이는 것은 곧 부적절한 것으로 판명되었다. **16 contrasting** 새로운 취향은 뚜렷한 윤곽과 복잡한 표면의 대비가 만들어내는 극적인 효과를 요구했다. **17 struggle** Hudson River 학파는 구세대와 신세대 예술가들 간의 갈등의 산물로써 1870년대에 등장한 것으로 보인다. **18 prodigious** 그녀의 작품 활동은 대단한 것이어서, 20년이 채 되지 않아 거의 30여권의 책이 출시되었다. **19 protrude** 그 화가는 가시가 튀어나와 있는, 굽은 등을 지닌 실물 크기 여성의 그림으로 주목 받고 있다. **20 score** 가장 유명한 악보는 D. W. Griffith의 영화를 위해 작곡되고 편곡되었던 곡인 Birth of a Nation이었다. **21 spontaneous** 음악은 오페라에서 더 큰 역할을 하기 시작했고, 자연스러워졌으며, 종종 등장 인물의 감정을 나타내 주었다. **22 criteria** 일부 단체는 종종 계급, 교육 정도, 그리고 피부색깔을 포함한 복잡한 기준을 통해 그 회원 자격을 정했다. **23 In vain** 진시에는 보급선이 필수적인 것이었는데, 보급선 없이는 모든 것이 무의미했기 때문이었다. **24 ragged** 그 유리 섬유는 무르고, 거칠었으며 10 피트 이상으로 길지 않았다. **25 in proportion to** 고압 엔진은 마력 대비 매우 가벼운 편이었고, 이전 엔진보다 가벼웠으며, 수리 비용도 적게 들었다. **26 obsessed** Evans는 곧 생산의 기계화 가능성 및 증기력의 이용 가능성에 대해 골몰하게 되었다. **27 option** 이동 속도 때문에 증기선은 사람의 이동뿐만 아니라 화물을 운반하기에도 제일 매력적이고 실용적인 수단이 되었다. **28 ridges** 거리는 350 마일 이상이었으며 가로질러야 하는 산등성이와 뚫고 들어가야 하는 야생 숲과 늪이 존재하고 있었다. **29 resort to** 나무꾼이 상자를 조립할 때 못이나 아교에 의존하지 않고 신중히 목재를 끼워 맞추는 일을 상상하는 것은 유쾌한 일이다. **30 aided** 습지대의 환경이 박테리아 부패를 최소 수준으로 유지해주었기 때문에 동식물의 보존에 많은 도움이 되었다.

UNIT 38 Check-up Quiz   p.182

1 wage 의회는 시간 당 가장 적은 보수를 받는 노동자들이 받을 수 있는 최저 임금을 설정한다. **2 Communal** 대중 폭동이 그 나라의 여러 지역에서 발생했다. **3 boomed** Ohio 주 Toledo의 유리 공장들은 Michael Owens가 유리병을 대량 생산하는 과정을 고안해 낸 이후 번창하게 되었다. **4 ploys** 현 상황에서 그녀는 몇몇 책략 중 하나를 사용하여 자신의 적을 속일지 모른다. **5 follow suit** 영국이 코크 제련법을 개발한 후 미 식민지들은 이를 따라 하지 않았는데, 그 이유는 이들이 많은 양의 목재를 보유하고 있었기 때문이었다. **6 fomented** 그 사건은 영국과 영국 식민지 간의 분열을 조장하는 주요 이슈였다. **7 implement** 쟁기는 흙을 파내어 작물을 심기 위한 땅을 일구는데 사용되는 농기구이다. **8 jolts** 그 마차의 울퉁불퉁한 몸체와 완충 장치는 거친 도로로부터 나오는 급격한 충격을 처리할 수 있었다. **9 altogether** 오늘날 과학, 기술 그리고 산업의 상호 관계를 한 마디로 요약하면, 완전히 정확한 것은 아니지만, "연구 개발"(R&D)이다. **10 assassinated** 로마 공화국의 복원을 원했던 집단이 기원전 44년 Caesar를 암살했다. **11 optimal** 작업 계획표 절차를 옹호하는 사람들은 작업 계획표 절차가 최적의, 즉 최선의 결정을 낳는다고 믿는다. **12 hygiene** 도시의 거리는 시민들오 가득차 있었고, 위생은 14세기 유럽 사람들의 우선 순위에서 뒷자리에 있었다. **13 influx** 세계 2차 대전 동안 흑인들의 도시 유입은 증가하였는데, 이는 흑인들이 군수 산업에서 일자리를 찾으려 했기 때문이었다. **14 ingenuity** 공원의 일부 기능들은 일반 시민들의 창의적인 제안이 직접적으로 반영된 결과였다. **15 instability** 그 재정비 계획은 물리적인 팽창을 촉진시키고, 도시 생활의 고유한 불안전성을 증가시킬 것이었다. **16 gulf** 다리를 놓을 수 없을 것 같은 불화가 남편과 아내 사이에서 생겨났다. **17 intriguing** 도시 생활의 번잡함과 도시의 사회적 교류는 고립된 시골에서 자란 이들에게 특히 매력적인 것이었다. **18 cooperation** 우주 정거장의 본래 목적은 미국과 소련의 협력을 증대시키기 위한 것이었다. **19 accused** 미국에서는 범죄로 기소된 모든 사람들에게 배심원에 의해 재판을 받을 권리가 부여된다. **20 eloquently** Jennings Bryan만큼 설득력 있게 말하는 미국 정치인은 거의 없었다. **21 feeble** 국가 정부는 미약한 감세 정책을 시도하였다. **22 intertwined** 미 헌법은 종교 숭배와 정부 활동이 서로 연관되지 않아야 한다는 점을 명백히 하고 있다. **23 nominated** 대법원 재직 전 변호사였던 Belva Lockwood는 1884년 미 대선 후보에 지명된 최초의 여성이었다. **24 decreed** 대통령은 더 이상 어떤 돈도 미사일 방어에 사용되지는 않을 것이라고 포고했다. **25 fairs** 그 박람회는 외부로부터 만들어진 수제품을, 구매의사가 있는 도시 소비자들에게 가져다 주는 하나의 방편이 되었다. **26 bonds** 투자 은행업은 정부 채권뿐만 아니라 기업의 주식과 채권도 취급한다. **27 condemned** Martin Luther가 16세기에 종교적인 불법 행위자

로 비난을 받고 있었을 당시, 그는 극심한 정신적, 육체적 고통을 겪고 있었다. **28 nurture** 다른 이론들은 아이들이 환경, 즉 선천성이 아니라 후천성에 의해서 정의된다고 주장한다. **29 statutorily** "설립 허가장"이라는 명칭은 학교들이 충족시키리라 기대되는 법정 이행 계약서를 지칭한다. **30 intruding** 확실히 인쇄된 글자는, 이전 기간에는 서로 단절되어 있었던 미국 사회 내로, 침투하고 있었다.

UNIT 39 Check-up Quiz
p.186

1 fickle 허리케인의 특성이 변덕스럽기 때문에 그 타격을 입는 주민들은 보다 큰 피해를 입게 된다. **2 celestial** 천체의 궤도는 보통 타원형 모양이다. **3 staggering** 그 과정은 수백 년 혹은 수천 년에 걸쳐서 완성될 수 있으며, 그 비용도 예측하기가 어렵다. **4 contradicted** 중력을 일종의 인력으로 바라보는 Newton의 사상은, 이것은 우주가 정적이라는 세계관과 배치되는 것이었는데, 변하지 않았다. **5 craters** 달 표면의 거친 특성은 주로 분화구가 많기 때문에 나타난 것이다. **6 retreated** 약 800년 전에 Alaska의 Hubbard 빙하는 바다 쪽으로 전진한 후 물러났다가 500년 후 다시 앞으로 나아갔다. **7 interstitial** 일부 화석 뼈들은 외부 광물질로 채워진 빈 틈을 가지고 있다. **8 misconception** 모든 사막이 뜨겁다는 생각은 일반적인 오해이다. **9 granular** 새로운 눈이 내려서 기존 눈에 묻히게 되면, 눈 알갱이로 이루어진 층들은 눈은 더욱 촘촘해진다. **10 Hemisphere** 논리적으로 북반구에서는 북풍은 보다 차가운 날씨를 몰고 오고, 남풍은 보다 따뜻한 날씨를 몰고 온다. **11 ornamental** 관상용 식물은 주로 그 아름다움 때문에 길러진다. **12 estimated** 그 큰 참나무들은 각각 2 천에서 8천 개의 도토리를 만들어냈을 것이라고 한 교수가 추측했다. **13 disproportionately** 불균형하게도 인간은 오른손 잡이가 많다. **14 stashed** 개미의 서식지에는 여왕개미와 따로 숨겨둔 비상 식량과 같은 중요한 재산들이 있다. **15 forerunner** 전문가들은 거대한 티라노사우루스 렉스의 선조인 알로사우러스라는 종의 연구에 초점을 맞추었다. **16 fragrant** 백합은 매력적이고 향기로운 꽃이다. **17 Dehydration** 탈수 증상은 수분 섭취에 의해 보충되는 양 이상으로 보다 많은 물이 발한 혹은 설사로 인해 빠져나갈 때 발생한다. **18 obedient** 그들은 야생동물이기 때문에 유순하게 길들여지는 애완 동물이 되지는 못한다. **19 impinge** Florida의 주변 식물들의 무성함이 사막의 관목들에게 영향을 끼치지는 못한다. **20 omnivorous** 침팬지는 잡식성이라 양분을 얻기 위해 고기, 식물, 열매를 먹는다. **21 pandemonium** 침팬지의 도구 사용 능력은 과학계에 거의 대혼란을 가져왔다. **22 transmitted** 오솔길과 도로, 산길 덕분에 여행이 더 쉬워졌고, 지도의 탄생으로 인하여 이러한 지식들이 다른 사람들에게도 전달되었다. **23 bound** 각각의 얼음 결정이 얼음 수정의 집합체로 굳어지는 과정을 통하여 빙하의 얼음이 생성된다. **24 ore** 광물은 일련의 폭파로 인해 분쇄된다. **25 bunch** 극 지방에서는 지구의 지력선과 태양풍의 자력선이 서로 모이게 된다. **26 acronym** 'laser'라는 단어는 'Light Amplification by the Stimulated Emission of Radiation'의 앞 글자를 따서 만들어진 말이다. **27 conflicting** Jules Verne가 1864년 Journey to the Center of the Earth를 썼을 당시 지구의 내부의 성질에 대해서는 많은 대립되는 이론들이 존재하고 있었다. **28 outfit** 해저 케이블 부설선에 있는 선원들은 트렌처를 다시 수면까지 끌어올려서 매설 장치를 부착할 것이다. **29 percolating** 뼈에 쌓인 모든 광물질들은 그것을 걸러내는 물의 작용에 의하여, 용해 작용으로 재결정화된다. **30 insurmountable** 그렇게

낡은 네트워크로부터 신속하게 날씨에 관한 원 데이터를 수집하고 처리하는 것은 극복할 수 없는 난관이었다.

UNIT 40 Check-up Quiz
p.190

1 commissioned 많은 지역에서는 아파트와 호텔들이 생겨나는 동안, 도시의 사회적 지도층들은 저택을 의뢰했다. **2 engaged** 1903년 Washington 대학의 운영위원회 위원들은 실외 환경 디자인 전문 조경 건축 회사와 고용 계약을 체결했다. **3 frenetic** 호텔은 공동체를 위한 열광적인 요청이었을 뿐만 아니라 사회가 만들어 낸 것인 동시에 사회를 만들어 내는 것이었다. **4 hurled** 사람들을 끌어 모은 호화로운 특급 열차와 마찬가지로, 승객용 터미널은 철도의 낭만을 부각시켰다. **5 suspension** George Washington 다리는 New York 시와 New Jersey의 Fort Lee사이에 놓여져 있는 현수교이다. **6 arbitrary** 식물원 건설에 있어서 일부 자의적이고 잇속만을 챙기려는 결정들이 이루어졌다. **7 fringe** 지역 생태계와 해양 생태계의 육지 인접 지역에서 가장 일반적인 문제는 서식지의 파괴이다. **8 germinate** 이러한 반쪽 도토리들은, 이 중 다수는 씨앗을 포함하고 있는데, 이후 발아할 수도 있다. **9 hacked** 걱정스러운 점은 동물들의 서식지가 하루하루 계속해서 잘려나가고 있다는 것이다. **10 herbicides** 제초제는 효과적이지만, 일부는 특히 잘못 사용될 경우, 심각한 문제를 일으킨다. **11 scurrying** 그 오리들은 그녀 주위로 급히 달려감으로써 반응을 나타냈다. **12 inclinations** 각각의 새들은 상당히 각기 다른 관심과 성향, 전략을 가지고 있다. **13 infrastructure** 그들은 수소 분리와 수소 공급처 인프라 개발을 돕기 위해 또 다른 회사를 설립했다. **14 ironed out** 이러한 기본적인 문제들이 해결되기 전까지는, 수소가 주요 에너지원이 될 수는 없을 것이다. **15 lurking** 하지만 바다 속에는 보이지 않게 숨어있는 또 다른 포식자가 존재하는데, 그것은 바로 박테리아이다. **16 stimulants** 때로는 의사가 흥분제를 처방하기도 하지만 이런 약들은 중독성이 있기 때문에 극단적인 경우가 아니라면 피한다. **17 stroke** 만약 혈전이 뇌로 들어가게 되면 뇌졸중을 일으키거나 사망에 이르게 할 수 있다. **18 stuttering** 말더듬증에 관한 최신 이론은 말을 하는 동안 뇌가 어떻게 작용하는지에 집중한다. **19 subconscious** 전문가들은 말을 더듬는 사람들이 자신이 말을 더듬는 것을 직접 듣긴 하지만, 잠재 의식 수준의 이해만을 갖고 듣는다고 믿는다. **20 transfusions** 아시다시피, 한 사람의 피를 다른 사람에게 주는 수혈은 오늘날 흔한 일이다. **21 transplanted** 면역 체계는 외부 침입자들과 외부 세포로 인식되는 이식 세포를 알아차린 후 행동을 취하게 된다. **22 equilibrium** 질병은 신체 시스템이 불균형 상태에 있을 때 일어날 수 있다. **23 outage** 1979년 New York의 정전 사태로 도시의 절반은 몇 시간 동안 전기를 공급받지 못했다. **24 infinitesimal** 바이러스는 너무나 작아서 전자 현미경으로만 볼 수 있다. **25 inert** 이 기체에는 헬륨, 네온, 아르곤 등이 있는데 이것들은 다른 원소와의 결합이 대단히 어렵기 때문에 불활성 기체라고 한다. **26 integrity** 서식지의 냄새는 개미로 하여금 침입자를 확인하고 서식지의 무결함을 유지하도록 해준다. **27 malleable** 그 혼합물은 가열되면 부드럽고 늘릴 수 있게 되어, 다양한 모양과 크기로 만들어질 수 있다. **28 fortuitously** 1948년 휴가 때 Hazen은 Virginia주 Fauquier에 있는 한 목장의 주위에서 우연히 한 줌의 토양을 수집하게 되었다. **29 prows** 자신들을 적절히 확인시키기 위하여 바이킹 전투 선들의 뱃머리는 조각상으로 장식되거나 화려한 색깔로 칠해져 있었다. **30 counterparts** 전기 부품 값이 하락함에 따라서 디지털 카메라가 기존의 카메라를 대체할 가능성이 크다.

Chapter 10 Review Test

p.194

1. ⓒ	2. ⓑ	3. ⓐ	4. ⓑ
5. ⓒ	6. ⓐ	7. ⓒ	8. ⓑ
9. ⓐ	10. ⓑ	11. ⓑ	12. ⓑ
13. ⓓ	14. ⓒ	15. ⓐ	16. ⓑ

1 박물관의 가장 인기 있는 전시물은 멸종된 거대한 코끼리인 마스토돈의 뼈인데, 이것은 Peale이 1801년 뉴욕의 한 농장에서 발굴한 것이었다. 2 1700년대 후반이 되자 계몽주의의 영향이 힘을 잃기 시작했다. 3 석기 제품은 19세기를 지나면서 매우 장식적이 되었다. 4 Abraham Lincoln은 엄숙함과 위엄의 이미지를 나타낸 것 이외에도 날카로운 유머감각을 가지고 있었다. 5 장붓구멍은 끌로 파내어 잘려진 나무 구멍이다 반면 장부는 이 장붓구멍에 들어맞기 위하여 또 다른 나무 조각으로부터 만들어진 튀어나와 있는 은촉이다. 6 이러한 상황을 고려해볼 때, 일반사람들은 마을 약제사를 후원하기로 결정했는데, 이 약제사는 효과 없는 약물 치료물품을 팔던 인근 식료품 상인이었다. 7 팬 아메리칸 항공은 클리퍼스라고 하는 비행기 함대를 구성하여 광활한 해양을 가로지른 첫 상용 항공사가 되었다. 8 1960년대는 항상 베트남 전쟁, 히피, 그리고 John F Kennedy의 암살 사건으로 기억될 것이다. 9 이러한 많은 과학적 발명품들은 거의 모든 분야에 걸쳐 생산성의 새로운 기준을 만들어 냈다. 10 Bill the Kid는 Southwest 국경 지방에서 가장 유명하고 매력적이었던 총잡이 무법자였다. 11 별들은 구형일 수 있지만, 모든 천체 물체들이 구형은 아니다. 12 호수가 형성되는 또 다른 방식은 화산 활동에 의한 것이다. 세계의 많은 지역에서 활동을 멈춘 화산의 분화구에는 작은 호수들이 있다. 13 심하게 탈수된 사람은 한 번에 원상으로 돌아올 정도로 많은 물을 마실 수는 없는데, 부분적으로 그 이유는 인간의 위가 충분히 크지 않기 때문이다. 14 Fessenden은 음성 전송의 가능성을 탐구하기 위해 전파 탐지기로 실험을 시작했다. 15 심지어 먼지 한 톨도 은판 사진술을 쓸모 없게 만드는 흠집을 부드러운 표면에 만들어 낼 수 있기 때문에, 완전히 매끄럽게 될 때까지, 그들은 광범위하게 문질러 댔다. 16 화석 뼈를 다루는 사람이라면 이것이 현대의 뼈와 똑같지 않다는 것을 알 수 있는데, 가장 다른 점은 이 뼈가 훨씬 더 무겁다는 점이다.

PART 3 ★ Chapter 11

UNIT 41 Check-up Quiz

p.196

1 **veiled** 결국 의식의 신비스러움을 설명하거나 감추는 이야기들이 나타났다. 2 **worldly** 정성 어린 장례식은 또한 개인이 속세에서 누렸던 중요성과 부유함으로 신을 감동시키는 데 충요하나. 3 **relented** 그는 마음을 누그러뜨릴 수도 있었지만 공격을 감행하기로 했다. 4 **sanitation** Sacramento의 한 지역에서는 건물 지하의 쓰레기장이 발굴되었는데, 이는 당시 위생법에 반하는 것이었다. 5 **scorched** 이 목재는 때때로 탈 수도 있었지만, 불기둥 앞에 놓여져 불이 붙기에는 충분히 안전한 위치에 있었

다. 6 **stalked** 여러 설명에 따르면, 징기스칸은 이복 형에게 몰래 다가가서 살해한 것으로 되어있다. 7 **stringent** 고고학자들은 자신들이 발견한 것들을 수 차례에 걸쳐, 그리고 엄격하게 테스트한다고 주장했다. 8 **subjugated** Nazi에 정복당한 민족들은 때로는 급료 없이, 혹은 아주 적은 대가만을 받고 노동을 했다. 9 **lavish** 대부분의 문화권에서는 경축일을 기념하기 위해 후한 식사를 제공하는 것이 전통이다. 10 **vital** 식민지 시대에 항해용 선박은 경제에 매우 중요한 것이었다. 11 **supplant** 현대의 독재자들은 자신들의 정부가 종교를 정치적 신조로 대체할 수 있도록 예술을 이용하고 있다. 12 **frustrations** 표현주의 희곡은 작가의 내면적인 좌절감을 반영함으로써, 종종 현대 심리학에 의해 영향을 받았음을 보여준다. 13 **traces** 또 다른 이론은 극장의 기원을 이야기에 대한 인간의 관심에서 찾는다. 14 **vividly** 자신의 소설 The Red Badge of Courage에서 Stephen Crane은 남북 전쟁의 전투를 생생하게 묘사하고 있다. 15 **accomplished** 뛰어난 색소폰 연주자이자 작곡가인 John Coltrane은 1950년대 초반 큰 밴드에서의 연주로 자신의 일을 시작했다. 16 **subjected** 노래가 복잡한 처리 과정에 놓이게 되면, 그 원곡은 추적하기가 불가능해 진다. 17 **unadorned** 많은 초기의 재즈 밴드들은 대중 음악을 출시된 형태 그대로 연주했다. 18 **inflections** 아기는 올라가는 억양과 떨어지는 억양으로 발음되는 음절의 차이를 감지해 낼 수 있다. 19 **varied** 미국 초기에는 우편 요금이 영수증에 의해 지불되었으며 거리에 따라 요금도 다양했다. 20 **applied** 이 용어는 통상적으로, 두꺼운 의류와 겨울용 퀼트 페티코트에서 사용되는 모직과 리넨 섬유에 적용되었다. 21 **periphery** 야생 동물 보호 지역은 100개 이상이 카리브해 주변에 존재한다. 22 **persisted** 장이 서는 날과 함께 년간 2회 열리는 정기 장 제도는 Philadelphia에서 지속되었다. 23 **indigenous** 호주 원주민들은 영국 정착민들에 의해 Aborigine이라고 불려졌다. 24 **submission** 징기스칸은 종종 미리 밀사를 보내 항복을 요구하곤 했다. 25 **thereby** 전형적으로 비 서구 음악은 서구 음악에 비해 보다 세밀하게 두 음간의 음정을 구분한다. 따라서 같은 음정에서도 많은 구별되는 음조, 즉 마이크로톤을 만들어낸다. 26 **agents** 유기물들이 원소들에 의해 파괴되지 않고 풍화작용과 침식작용으로부터 보호 받기 위해서는 땅에 빨리 묻혀야 한다. 27 **trickle** 기후는 건조하지만, 깊게 패인 계곡 아래에서는 작은 시냇물들이 흐르고 있다. 28 **perishable** 농촌 사람들은 냉장고가 일반적으로 사용되기 이전에는 부패하기 쉬운 음식을 신선하게 유지시키기 위해서 종종 우물이나 냇가의 저장시설을 이용했다. 29 **preside** Kennedy 대통령은 오후 4시에 국가 안보 위원회를 주재할 예정이었다. 30 **anonymous** 당시 예술가들을 나타내는 용어는 그들의 지위를 암시해준다: "화공"이란 말은 보통 1760년대까지 초상화를 그리는 무명의 화가들에게 적용되었다.

UNIT 42 Check-up Quiz

p.200

1 **yields** 비료는 농부들의 생산량을 증대시킬 수 있다. 2 **allotting** 배급제는 희소한 자원을 나누어주는 시스템이다. 3 **discriminate** 성, 종교 혹은 인종에 기반하여 대학이 차별을 자행 하는 것은 위법이다. 4 **lull** 부모들은 종종 아이들을 재우기 위해 노래를 불러 달랜다. 5 **lured** 많은 성인들이 안정된 고용 약속에 의하여 도시로 유인되었다. 6 **mason** 건축 자재인 석재가 지역적으로 쉽게 구해지는 곳에서는 석공이 납세자 명단에 반드시 들어있었다. 7 **merger** 합병은 한 기업이 다른 기업의 자산을 구입했을 때 이루어진다. 8 **minted** 미국의 1달러 은화와 50센트 은화 모두 1794년 최

초로 주조되었는데, 한 쪽 면에는 자유의 여신상이, 다른 한 쪽에는 독수리의 형상이 새겨져 있었다. **9 ratify** 법과 마찬가지로 의회 선언도 작성 후 승인을 받아야 한다. **10 reverse** 오늘날에는 노화 과정을 억제하거나 되돌릴 수 있는 인간형을 소망하는 사람들이 많다. **11 irrigation** 관개 용수가 발견되는 경우, 그 지역의 농업적 잠재력은 막대한 것이었다. **12 lineage** 같은 혈통의 구성원들이 혈연 관계에 있다는 것은 언제라도 증명할 수 있다. **13 divulge** 범죄로 기소된 사람은 자신의 유죄를 입증하는 어떠한 정보도 강제로 밝히도록 강요 받을 수 없다. **14 monarchies** 부계 혈통 방식은 군주제에서 누가 왕좌를 물려받을 것인지 결정하는 문제에 빈번히 사용되었다. **15 municipal** 상하수도 시스템은 보통 시 정부에 의해서 운영되었다. **16 potential** 부동산 개발업자들은 50년 만에 Chicago에 800,000개의 건물이 들어설 수 있는 부지를 마련하였다. **17 precarious** 도시에서 보다 안전하고 보수가 높은 일자리를 얻기 위하여 수많은 사람들이 불안정한 농촌 생활을 포기했다. **18 notoriety** 그는 워터게이트 사건에서 Nixon 대통령의 주 변호사로서 악명을 얻었다. **19 prejudice** 인종적 및 종교적 편견은 종종 정치에 영향을 미친다. **20 split** 미 남북 전쟁을 이끈 것은 1861년 남부 11개 주의 연방 탈퇴였다. **21 appliances** 전기 토스트기는 주방용으로 개발된 최초의 기구였다. **22 loomed** 남북 전쟁 이후 북부 및 1861년 남부 양쪽에서 재정상의 문제가 크게 부각되었다. **23 dramatically** 비판가들은 도시화가 많은 문제점을 일으키고 도시에서의 삶의 질을 극적으로 저하시켰다고 주장했다. **24 snippets** 정치인들은 단편적인 지식으로 자신의 주장만을 할뿐, 논쟁을 하려고 하지는 않는다. **25 superintendent** 그녀는 연방 정부에서 여성 간호사들을 감독하는 직책을 맡았다. **26 pertinent** 인간이 관심을 갖는 주제에 대하여 적절한 질문을 하고, 적절하고 정당한 답변을 찾아내며, 허위의 혹은 관련 없는 답변들을 거부할 수 있는 것은 하나의 능력이다. **27 triggers** 실제이던 상상이던, 근처에서 위험을 인식하게 되면 인체에 여러 가지 반응들이 일어난다. **28 cursive** 아이들은 블록체 대문자 글자에서 흘림체로 서체가 바뀌었다. **29 ranks** 전사자 수가 더 많긴 했지만, 2차 대전시 러시아의 분투는 미국 다음이었다. **30 preoccupied** 사람들은 더욱 더 자신의 삶에만 몰두하게 되었다.

UNIT 43 Check-up Quiz p.204

1 descend 산림 소방대원은 산불을 진압하기 위해 먼 곳에서 낙하산을 타고 불에 뛰어내리는 소방관들이다. **2 inexorable** 빙하의 형성 과정은 느리지만 멈추지는 않는다. **3 docket** 달은 이미 미 항공우주국의 향후 20년 내 추가 탐사를 위한 곳으로 그 검토 목록에 올라 있다. **4 commenced** 우주 시대는 Sputnik호가 소련에 의해 발사되었던 1957년 10월에 시작되었다. **5 entities** 하지만 목록에 있는 어떠한 형태도 우주에 존재하는 가장 큰 천체를 설명하지는 못한다. **6 extracted** 수소는 물에서 추출하여 연료로 쓸 수 있다. **7 rear** 고양이는 몸의 전면은 시계 방향으로, 뒤 쪽과 꼬리 부분은 시계 반대 방향으로 돌기 때문에 전체적인 회전은 0이 된다. **8 intense** 레이저는 인조 루비를 이용하여 빛을 집중시킨 후, 극도로 강렬한 고 에너지빔으로 만든다. **9 plates** 판의 운동 속도를 측정할 수는 있지만, 언제 지진이 일어나리라는 것은 예측할 수 없다. **10 kinetic** 각 조각들이 시속 60 킬로미터로 대기에 부딪힐 때, 막대한 운동 에너지는 열 에너지로 전환된다. **11 lubricant** 빙하 밑에서 녹은 물이 흐르게 되면, 빙하를 바다 쪽으로 빠르게 흐르게 하는 윤활유 작용이 일어날 수 있다. **12**

extend 식물의 꼭대기에서 뿌리까지 뻗어져 있는 식물 내부를 통해 이동한 물은 수분 증발을 보충한다. **13 casts off** 해삼은 공격을 받으면 촉수와 같은 부착 기관들을 잘라내어 버린다. **14 colonies** 개미 군락에 있어서 어떤 종류의 개미들은 고도로 분화된 신분으로 나누어 진다. **15 Porous** 초크와 사암과 같이 구멍이 많은 암석들은 그 속으로 물을 통과시킨다. **16 discards** 그 새는 부리와 혀를 사용하여 씨의 단단한 껍질을 깨어 제거한 후, 안에 있는 영양 물질을 삼킨다. **17 counteracted** 뿌리가 커서 식물의 보호가 강화된다는 사실은, 반대로 그 결과 포식자들을 유인하게 되어 지상에서의 위험성이 증가한다는 점에서 상쇄된다. **18 parasites** 한 종이 다른 종에 가장 직접적으로 의존하는 형태는 기생 생물에서 존재한다. **19 peculiar** 모든 새들은 날개를 가지고 있지만, 날개는 새들만의 특징은 아니다. **20 predators** 어류만이 그물눈청어의 포식자가 아니라 새들 역시 그물눈청어를 먹이로 삼는다. **21 dwindled** 보다 많은 토지가 개발됨에 따라 공터의 양의 줄어들고 있다. **22 applications** GPS는 응용범위가 넓다. **23 primates** 그들의 놀라운 연구에 따르면, 이 영장류는 정신적인 특징뿐만 아니라 고도로 발달된 여러 가지 신체적인 특성까지 지닌 것으로 밝혀졌다. **24 pry** 다람쥐는 도토리의 위 부분을 비틀어 벗겨내고, 껍질을 깨물어 그 안의 가운데 부분을 먹는다. **25 benign** 초기 원생대 이후 일정 기간 동안은 기후가 꽤 온화했던 것으로 보인다. **26 Hydraulic** 수력 엘리베이터는 여전이 일부 오래된 건물에서 사용되고 있지만, 새로 건설된 거의 모든 건물에는 전기 엘리베이터가 설치되어 있다. **27 discrete** 난초는, 특정 수분 전달자에게만 적응함으로써 개별 개체로서 종의 생존을 보장하면서, 야생에서의 무분별한 이종교배의 위험을 피해왔다. **28 quarrying** 최신 채석 방법 중 하나는 돌을 분사 토치로 잘라내는 것이다. **29 scuffed** 동굴은 보통 위에서 떨어지는 탄산에 의해 형성되지만, 그 동굴은 밑에서 올라오는 강력한 산에 의해 부식되어 생겨난 것이다. **30 sediment** 삼각주는 수 세기에 걸쳐 형성되기도 하는데, 퇴적물의 양이 많으면 섬이 형성되기도 한다.

UNIT 44 Check-up Quiz p.208

1 adjoining 보다 위 층에 위치한 그들의 방들은 인접한 방과 연결된 문으로 그리고 천장에 있는 구멍을 통해서 들어갈 수 있었다. **2 clustered** 모텔들은 미 40번 도로와 66도로와 같은 대륙간 고속 도로를 따라 밀집해 있었다. **3 lug** 자른 지 얼마 되지 않은 목재는 자루 막대로 사용되었고 열에 강하였다. **4 sumptuous** 감당할 여력이 있었던 사람들은 보다 호사스럽고 한 가구만을 위한 주택들이 결집되는 것에 대하여 상당히 만족해 했다. **5 motifs** 석공들은 석판에 해골과 뼈 형태로 된 자신들의 주제와 죽음을 상징하는 종교적 우상을 새겼다. **6 aerial** 하이티와 도미니카 공화국의 국경을 공중에서 내려다보면 놀라운 광경이 눈에 띈다. **7 Marring** 잡초의 보다 미약한 영향은 우리의 정원을 훼손시키는 것이다. **8 pneumatic** 압축된 공기는 공기압 식 공구를 작동시키는 동력을 공급해 준다. **9 paucity** 아프리카의 많은 지역에서는 인구의 폭발적인 증가와 주택 부족 현상 때문에 개발업자들이 정글을 파괴하고 있다. **10 perpetuation** 미국 흰 두루미의 지속적인 생존을 위해 미국 흰 두루미와 환경보호론자 모두가 극복해야 할 두 번째 장애물은 이 철새의 이동 문제이다. **11 pesky** 다람쥐는 떡갈나무 숲을 확산시키고 경작하는 동물인가, 아니면 성가신 씨앗 도둑일 뿐인가? **12 pillaged** 일단 알이 둥지에서 약탈되면 미래 세대는 훨씬 더 큰 위험에 놓인다. **13 pollutant** 미래에는 특정 조건 하에서 심지어 수증기도 공기 오염 물질로 간주될 수 있을 것이다. **14 proliferate** 세계 대다수 지역에

서 이들 종은 세력을 확장시키며 증식해 나갈 것이다. **15 purification** 인간이 만들어 낸 것은 순환 과정 상 일시적으로 자연적인 정화시스템에 과도한 부담이 될 수 있다. **16 fractures** 우리는 골절이나 피부 및 근육 상처와 같은 손상들을 치유할 수 있다. **17 cranial** 말초 신경계는 두개골, 척추 그리고 자율 신경계의 통제를 담당한다. **18 dissections** 초기 해부학 연구는 정부 당국이 시체 절단을 허가하지 않음으로써, 그리고 냉장 기술이 미약했기 때문에 어려움을 겪었다. **19 veins** 콜레스테롤은 신체의 동맥과 정맥에 과다한 잔여물로서 쌓이는 경향이 있다. **20 championed** 수년 동안 의사들은 콜레스테롤이 위험한 물질이라는 견해를 지지했다. **21 acupuncture** 침술과 한약은 오늘날 서양에서 가장 인기 있는 대체 요법 중 하나이다. **22 appendages** 그 근육은 사지나 부속기관의 실제적인 신체 움직임을 담당한다. **23 artery** 폐 동맥은 혈액을 오른쪽 심장에서 허파로 운반한다. **24 complication** 당뇨의 고통스러운 합병증은, 신체의 신경계에 영양분을 전달하고 유지시켜주는 호르몬이 감소 생산됨으로써 나타날 수 있다. **25 microbes** 어류의 수가 남획과 같은 요인들에 의해 고갈됨에 따라 바닷말과 같은 미생물이 증가하면서 연약한 해양 생태계가 위협받고 있다. **26 resin** 호박은 단단하고 노란 갈색의 물질로, 수백 만년 전에 살았던 소나무의 송진으로부터 만들어진 것이다. **27 saturated** 모든 지방에는 포화 지방산과 불포화 지방산이 결합되어 있다. **28 trebles** 아기의 몸무게는 생후 4개월 말 2배로 되며, 1살 무렵에는 3배가 된다. **29 summon** 초음파 호각은, 인간은 듣지 못하지만 개에게는 들리기 때문에, 개들을 부를 때 사용된다. **30 helical** Franklin은 X-ray 결정학이라는 기술을 이용하여 DNA가 나선형 모양을 가지고 있다는 점을 밝혀냈다.

Chapter 11 Review Test
p.212

1.	ⓒ	2.	ⓓ	3.	ⓐ	4.	ⓐ
5.	ⓓ	6.	ⓑ	7.	ⓓ	8.	ⓐ
9.	ⓑ	10.	ⓐ	11.	ⓒ	12.	ⓐ
13.	ⓓ	14.	ⓐ	15.	ⓑ	16.	ⓒ

1 오르간, 크래비코드, 하프시코드는 건반악기의 주요 악기가 되었다 이 악기들은 18세기 말 피아노로 대체되기까지 최고의 지위를 누렸다. **2** 화석은 만년 이상 된 고대 식물 및 동물의 잔해나 흔적을 말한다. **3** 비록 그 메커니즘은 상당히 다양하지만, 모든 주요 동물들은 "외부" 세포들의 존재를 감지하고 이에 반응할 수 있다. **4** 이런 식의 아마추어 족보가 흥미로울 수도 있지만, 혈통은 한 사람의 사회적 지위에 훨씬 더 중요한 위치를 차지했었다. **5** 침팬지는 자생지가 아프리카로, 그 곳에는 수관 층이 있어 보금자리, 먹이, 보호장치를 제공해 준다. **6** 그 부지는 직사각형의 건물을 수용할 수는 있었지만, 대규모의 아파트들이 필요로 하는 빛이 잘 들고 합리적으로 배열된 방을 갖출 수는 없었다. **7** 화성이 장기적인 최종 목적지로 떠오르는 가운데, 달 정착의 위험성과 그 어려움이 너무 극심하고 불필요한 것은 아닌지에 대하여 진지한 의문이 제기되고 있다. **8** 합리적 의사결정에 있어서는 각 결정에 영향을 받게 될 관련 고려 사항들이 목록화되며, 각 고려 사항의 결과에 대한 상대적인 중요성이 결정된다. **9** 1969년 소설 Portnoy's Complaint는 청소년들의 정욕과 성인들의 성에 대한 솔직하고 대담한 묘사로 큰 반향을 일으키긴 했지만, 비판적인 찬사를 받았다. **10** 이러한 발견은 노화 과정에 대한 새로운 사실을 알려주었는데, 이는 궁극적으로 노화와 죽음이라는 번지지 않는 과정을 연기시킬 수도 있을 것이다. **11** 해저 시추선은 해양 표면 위에서 위치를 고정시킬 수 있었고, 해저로부터 침전물과 암석의 표본들을 추출하면서 매우 깊은 수역을 시추할 수 있었다. **12** Erie 운하의 성공에 고무되어 Ohio주와 Indiana주가 Erie호와 Ohio강 사이에 연결 수로를 설치하게 되었을 때 New York 운하 시스템의 범위는 보다 확장되었다. **13** 진드기와 옴 같은 기생충들은 거의 눈에 보이지 않지만, 장충은 6~7 피트 길이까지 성장할 수 있다. **14** 각각의 석기는 고기를 자르거나 말리는 특별한 방법을 필요로 하는 각자의 특성을 가지고 있었다. **15** 양성 종양은, 비록 그 위치나 크기로 인해 정상적인 신체 작용이 방해 받게 된다면 그럴 수 있지만, 보통 사망으로는 이르지 않는다. **16** 가장 단순한 형태는 개미 군락 내의 호흡으로부터 나오는 이산화탄소인데, 이 화학 물질은 개미가 서로 모이도록 촉진하는 페로몬으로 기능한다.

PART 3 ★ Chapter 12

UNIT 45 Check-up Quiz
p.214

1 maritime 북 태평양 해안의 미 원주민들은 매우 복잡한 해안 문화를 만들어냈다. **2 jolly** 명랑한 인물인 Falstaff는 Shakespeare가 만들어낸 가장 희극적인 인물 중 하나이다. **3 shunned** Shaker 교도들은 엄격한 종교 집단으로 모든 종류의 쾌락을 멀리한다. **4 envision** 사냥 전 사냥꾼은 이동하는 동물들을 그리고 연구했으며, 성공적인 사냥이 이루어지는 광경을 머리 속에 그리곤 했다. **5 depicted** Joel Chandler Harris와 Ellen Glasgow는 그들의 소설에서 남부의 삶을 묘사했다. **6 tremendously** 대공황 당시 경제는 막대한 피해를 입었다. **7 vigorous** 보건 위원회는 New York 주거지의 위생을 최고의 상태로 만들기 위한 적극적인 조치를 취했다. **8 vocalize** Malcolm X 행진은 Harlem가의 개발에 대해 불만족을 표출하는 하나의 수단으로 종종 이용되고 있다. **9 puzzling** 소설 속의 탐정인 Sherlock Holmes는 수많은 난해한 범죄를 해결했다. **10 ushering** 1839년 은판 사진기법이 미국에 소개되어 사진의 시대가 열렸다. **11 complement** 영화 감독은 화면에서의 연기를 보완하기 위해 음악을 사용한다. **12 eerie** 작가 H. P. Lovecraft는 초자연적인 현상에 대한 많은 기묘한 이야기들을 썼다. **13 entice** Vance Packard의 책, The Hidden Persuaders는 소비자를 유혹하기 위해 광고업자들이 이용하는 전술을 다루고 있다. **14 jargons** 기술상의 전문용어들은, 종종 단어의 정의를 퇴색시키고 문법 규칙을 어기면서, 어법의 변화를 가속화시키고 있다. **15 roll back** 1979년 Santa Monica의 시 정부는 토지소유자들에게 1978년 책정된 수준까지 임대료를 삭감하라고 명령했다. **16 maintenance** 임대료는 기존 주택의 효과적인 관리를 증진시키고 새로운 주택의 건설을 자극했다. **17 kilns** 고열로 구어지는 자기를 만들기 위해 보다 더 커다란 화덕이 지어졌다. **18 carve** 조각가들은 망치와 정을 사용하여 석재로 조각상을 조각한다. **19 rehearse** 음악가는 공연 전 예행 연습을 해야 한다. **20 time-wise** 철도가 시간적으로 더 정확해지고 그 운행 간격이 효율적으로 단축됨에 따라, 철도는 다시간내에 미국의 주요 교통 수단이 되었다. **21 mythology** 6세기와 7세기에의 도공들은 신화에 나타나는 일화와 고대 그리스의 영웅담을 표현했다. **22 deteriorate** 불에 구운 진흙은 시간이 지나도 질이 떨어지지 않는다. **23 homage** 이집트와 그리스에서는

성직자들이 당시 유행했던 3개의 서체를 사용하여 자신들의 서약을 기록했다. **24 carcasses** 초기 석기 도구의 중요한 기능 중에 하나는 거대한 동물의 시체에서 영양분이 풍부한 음식, 즉 고기와 골수 부분을 추출해내는 것이었다. **25 tactics** 그것은 미국과 러시아 사령관의 전술 때문이기도 했는데, 미군 사령관은 인명을 구하는 데 더 관심을 두었다. **26 cathartic** 노예들은 노래와 구비문학을 통해 어떤 의미에 있어서는 자유로울 수 있었는데, 이것은 그들에게 카타르시스를 제공해 주었다. **27 logistical** 자국 군대와 다른 여러 나라의 군대를 모두 지원하기 위해서는 물류상 엄청난 노력이 필요했다. **28 spectacular** D.W. Griffith는 장엄한 장면의 영화를 만든 최초의 감독으로, 엄청난 규모의 영화들을 제작했다. **29 unravel** 그 도자기의 역사, 제조, 문화적 맥락, 경제적 역할 그리고 장식적인 사용은 모두 해명되기를 바라는 점들이다. **30 obscure** Ezra Pound의 시는, 너무나 많은 애매모호한 언급들이 있어서, 때때로 이해하기 어렵다.

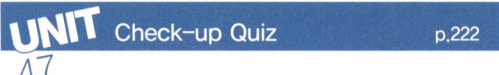

UNIT 46 Check-up Quiz p.218

1 preached 대공황 이전 고전 경제학은 자유방임주의를 전도하고 있었다. **2 abounded** 모든 종류의 소나무들이 풍부했으며, 서쪽으로 진출한 사람들은 또한 새로운 산림들과 마주하게 되었다. **3 accelerated** 1825년 Erie 운하의 개통은 오대호 지역의 상업 발달을 가속화시켰다. **4 pastoral** 일부 수렵 채취자들은 기존의 전원적인 방식과 유목민의 삶을 지속해 나갔다. **5 plush** 그 숙박 시설은 결코 호화롭지 않았다. **6 shrewd** 기민한 여성 사업가인 Oprah는 방송에 특정 제품을 언급함으로써 시장에서의 유행을 만들어내는데 기여했다. **7 stabilize** 국제 통화 기금은 무역 성장을 방해하지 않으면서 환율을 안정시키기 위해 설립되었다. **8 rejuvenate** 음악은 환자를 활기 있게 해주거나 위안을 줄 수 있다. **9 vying** 1880년대 New York과 Chicago 간 5개의 철도가 교통에 있어서 경쟁관계에 있었다. **10 abolish** 1864년 미 하원은 노예제를 폐지하기 위한 헌법 수정안에 대해 논의하기 시작했다. **11 precursor** 새로운 가전 기구였던 아이스 박스는 현대 냉장고의 전신이었다. **12 uncanny** Abraham Maslow는 당대 가장 위대한 사상가들과 어깨를 나란히 할 수 있을 정도의 막대한 지성을 소유하고 있었다. **13 reciprocal** 상호적인 관계 덕분에 모든 사람이 생존 수단을 확보할 수 있었다. **14 replicate** 연구자들은 가능한 정밀하게 발굴된 표본을 복제할 수 있는 도구들을 만든다. **15 revolt** 영아살해에 대해 수많은 사람들이 불쾌감을 감추지 못하지만, 적어도 동물계 내에서는 그 자체적인 목적이 있다. **16 gratified** 그는 기본 욕구가 채워진 개인들의 성과와 그렇지 못한 사람들의 성과가 다르다는 점을 관찰했다. **17 sired** 일부 종에 있어서는 암컷 무리를 지배하게 된 수컷이 다른 수컷에 의해 태어난 새끼들을 전부 죽이기도 한다. **18 upheavals** 현 정당들이 사회적 대이변에 좌절한 이들을 대변하지 못하자 정치적 불만족이 생겨났다. **19 aspirations** 정치적 포부 이외에도, 그는 Green Mountain Boys라고 알려진 단체의 지도자로서 활동하였다. **20 coordinate** 정당은 당원들의 선거 운동을 조정하는 데 도움을 준다. **21 unions** 1886년 많은 국가 차원의 노동 조합들이 Samuel Gompers의 지도하에 미 노조 연합을 결성했다. **22 autocratic** 자신의 국민을 잘 돌보는 독재자는 때때로 이로운 독재자라고 불려진다. **23 lucid** Julius Caesar는 정치적 재능으로 유명할 뿐만 아니라 명료하고 유익한 글로도 잘 알려져 있다. **24 morale** USO는 미 군을 즐겁게 해주고 사기를 진작시키는 서비스 기관이다. **25 substantially** 커피, 차, 그리고 초콜릿 같은 제품들의 광고가 신문에 실리게 되자, 그 광고 효과는 실

질적으로 증가하였다. **26 dogma** 동물 실험들을 통하여 인간만이 감정을 가지고 있다는 행태주의적 교리는 의구심을 받게 되었다. **27 endow** Massachusetts는 MIT 공대에 많은 기금을 기부했다. **28 inevitably** 교육자들의 초점은, 불가피하게, 보다 낮은 학년으로 기울어졌으며, 또다시 기본적인 학문적 소양과 학습에 맞춰지게 되었다. **29 wharf** 최대 규모의 회사들은 많은 노동자들을 해고할 수 밖에 없었으며, 많은 선박들 역시 부두에서 정박하고 있을 뿐이었다. **30 arable** 토지는 생산 과정에서 이용될 수 있는 모든 천연자원, 즉 경작지, 산림 그리고 기타 등을 뜻한다.

UNIT 47 Check-up Quiz p.222

1 arid Arizona 남부는 건조 기후이며, 약간의 사막이 존재한다. **2 precipitation** 사막은 연간 강수량이 25 센티미터 이하인 지역이다. **3 rim** 개기 월식 때는 달의 남쪽 가장자리를 따라 밝은 테두리가 있는 것처럼 보인다. **4 incinerated** 그 소행성 충돌로 폭발이 일어났는데, 이 폭발은 각 얼음 덩어리가 타면서 급격히 확대되었다. **5 inhospitable** 우주 탐사선과 우주비행사들이 수집한 확실한 증거에 의하면, 화성은 사람이 살 수 없는 행성이다. **6 intensity** 거주 가능 지역은, 태양의 강도를 가진 항성으로부터 7천 5백만 마일에서 1억 4천만 마일 이내의 지역이다. **7 lethal** 화성에는 오존층이 없어서 태양의 치명적인 빛을 차단하지 못한다. **8 ambient** 환경 보호국에서 작성한 보고서에 따르면, 주변 대기의 납 성분 수치가 유아에게 심각한 위험이 되고 있다. **9 acidic** 비는 오염되지 않은 대기 중에서라도 약간 산성을 띈다. **10 ominous** 천둥을 몰고 다니는 먹구름은 상당히 불길한 것으로 보인다. **11 radiation** 원자로에서는 연기와 함께 해로운 방사선이 계속해서 대기와 수중으로 뿜어져 나온다. **12 resonance** 전기 기타의 음은 기타 몸체의 공명에 의해서가 아니라, 전기적 증폭에 의해서 생겨난다. **13 aggression** 이러한 군체 내에서는, 서식지가 다른 개미들 간 공격 성향이 거의 나타나지 않는다. **14 speculated** 전문가들은 건기와 우기의 주기가 있었을 것으로 추측한다. **15 bizarre** 진흙을 먹는 별난 동물에 대해 그 밖에 말해질 수 있는 것은, 이 동물이 거의 끊임없이 밤낮으로 먹는다는 것이다. **16 carnivores** 우리가 공룡에 대해 갖고 있는 이미지는 브론토사우루스처럼 몸집이 대단히 큰 초식동물에 대한 것이거나 티라노사우루스 렉스같은 육식동물에 대한 것이거나 둘 중의 하나이다. **17 torque** 어떠한 신체도 회전력 없이는 돌 수 없는 반면, 고양이와 같이 유연한 신체는 즉시 그 방향을 바꿀 수 있다. **18 scale** 산에 오르는 등반가들에게 가장 인기 있는 봉우리인 하나는 Yosemite 국립 공원에 위치한 티 Capitan이다. **19 scavengers** 독수리와 마찬가지로 콘도르도 청소 동물인데, 이 말은 그들이 이미 죽어 있는 동물들을 먹는다는 의미이다. **20 blistering** 그 곳의 기후는 연 강수량이 50 인치가 넘긴 하지만 척박한 편이다. **21 untamed** 하와이의 다양한 야생 화산 지역 및 원시 해변가는 여러 야생성을 즐기는 많은 관광객들을 불러 모으고 있다. **22 accessible** 강은 또한 둑을 따라 존재하는 진흙을 드러나게 하며, 비탈진 쪽에서의 침식 작용으로 인해 진흙에 접근하기가 보다 쉬워질 수 있다. **23 apparatuses** 비록 정교한 장치들이 사용되고 있지만, 화산은 여전히 신비스러운 대상으로 남아있다. **24 sieve** 진흙은 너무 작아서 정확하게 체로 걸러질 수 없다. **25 scourge** 잡초는 수많은 씨앗을 급속히 퍼뜨릴 수 있는 능력이 있기 때문에, 곧 초원의 재앙이 되었다. **26 skimmed** 거품은 붙어 있는 광물질과 함께 표면으로 올라간 후, 걷어 내어졌다. **27 trench** 트렌처는 케이블 부설을 위해 참호를 파고 올바른 위치에 케이블을 설치한 후 마지막으로 매립하는 복잡한 기계이다.

28 thrusters 트렌처의 뒤 쪽에는 수중에서 추진력을 내는 팬 추진 장치 10개가 있다. **29 accumulated** 이러한 저수지에 물이 축적되었던 시기는 여러 번 존재했었던 것으로 보인다. **30 homogeneous** 철도는 지역적 특성과 지역주의를 제거하면서, 미 국민들을 동질적으로 만들었다.

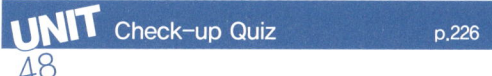

UNIT 48 Check-up Quiz   p.226

1 reoriented 철도는 북미 지역의 환경을 다시 만들었으며, 북미 지역 사람들의 행동을 재정립시켰다. **2 deciduous** 이 해충들은 낙엽 성 떡갈나무와 같은 관상목들의 잎을 떨어지게 만든다. **3 expedient** 그는 메시지를 보낼 보다 편리한 방법이 틀림없이 존재한다고 느꼈다. **4 stake** 19세기 미 호텔 관리인들은 지역 사회에 막대한 이해관계를 갖고 그 사회를 번영시키기 위해 영향력을 행사했다. **5 adverse** 페니실린은 그것에 알레르기를 갖고 있는 사람에게 부작용을 일으킬 수 있다. **6 replenish** 공급량을 충전할 손쉬운 수소 공급처가 없다. **7 resilient** 포식동물들은 바다에서 약한 물고기를 제거함으로써, 강한 물고기의 수를 늘리고 이들 종의 복원력을 보다 강화시킨다. **8 sanctuary** 한 지역을 해양 생물 보호 구역으로 지정하는 것은, 국립 공원이 그러한 것처럼, 보호 구역임을 나타낸다. **9 sedentary** 진디는 그 군집성과 이동하지 않는 특성 때문에 포식자의 위험에 특히 취약하다. **10 stagnant** 흐르지 않는 물 한 컵에는 수많은 미생물들이 포함되어 있을 수 있다. **11 suffocate** 만약 그 박테리아가 통제되지 않는다면, 그것들은 사실상 바다를 질식시킬 수도 있다. **12 nemesis** 그는 AIDS가 우리의 공동의 적이라고 믿는다. **13 hatched** 암컷 바다 거북은 2000 킬로미터에 이르는 거리를 헤엄쳐서 자신들이 태어났던 해안가로 다시 돌아온다. **14 surrender** 군은 국가의 산림을 보호하는 임무를 맡고 반항하는 불법 벌목꾼은 사살하라는 명령을 받았다. **15 symbiotic** 공생 관계는 종이 다른 두 개의 유기체가 "함께 일하고" 그 관계로부터 서로 이득을 얻을 때를 의미한다. **16 Glucose** 포도당은 소화될 필요가 없기 때문에 직접 혈액 속으로 주입될 수 있다. **17 prosthetic** 보첨 다리는 휠체어나 목발의 도움 없이도 사람이 걸을 수 있게 해준다. **18 amnesia** 뇌에 경미한 손상이 일어나는 경우, 기익싱실증이 일시적으로 나타날 수 있다. **19 Analgesics** 진통제는 고통을 경감시키고 열을 내리는 데 사용된다. **20 antibiotics** 균류는 임상 의학에서 사용되는 가장 강력한 여러 항생제의 성분으로 쓰인다. **21 Hypnosis** 최면술은 때때로 금연을 돕는 수단으로서 이용된다. **22 insomnia** 불면증의 원인은 스트레스, 우울, 과다한 근심 등 주로 심리적인 것이다. **23 terminology** 정확한 전문 용어를 사용하지 않고 말하면, 뇌의 오른쪽 반구는 신체의 왼쪽 부분을 통제한다. **24 ulcers** 궤양이 있는 사람은 순한 음식을 먹어야 한다. **25 secreted** 페로몬은 신체의 외부로 분비되어, 다른 개체들로 하여금 특정 반응을 일으키게 한다. **26 volatility** 화학적 신호는 화학물의 휘발성에 따라 지속될 수 있다. **27 welding** 용접기에는 2개의 가스 탱크가 연결되어 있는데, 하나는 산소로 가득 차 있고, 다른 하나에는 아세틸렌이 채워져 있다. **28 streamlined** 문제는 장거리를 빠른 속도로 날 수 있는, 유선형 모양의 날개를 만드는 것이었다. **29 revolutionized** 철광석을 제련하는데 목탄 대신 코크스가 사용되면서, 18세기 초반 쇠 생산은 대변혁을 맞이하게 되었다. **30 serene** 그 건축가들은 자연적이고 평온한 환경의 필요성을 강조했는데, 이러한 환경에서는 바쁜 도시 거주민들도 때때로 도시에서 해방될 수 있었다.

Chapter 12 Review Test   p.230

1. ⓒ	2. ⓓ	3. ⓐ	4. ⓒ
5. ⓑ	6. ⓓ	7. ⓓ	8. ⓓ
9. ⓑ	10. ⓒ	11. ⓑ	12. ⓐ
13. ⓐ	14. ⓓ	15. ⓐ	16. ⓐ

1 그의 소설 속 등장 인물들은 현실 속 실제 사람들을 나타내기 위해 사용되었고, 그는 가능한 적나라한 방법으로 인간의 나약한 현실을 나타내는데 관심을 갖고 있었다. **2** 밝고 활기찬 소리를 내는 하프시코드는 당시 소규모 오케스트라의 베이스 악기를 지원해주었던, 선호되는 악기였다. **3** 특별한 전문 용어의 목적은 심리학자가 아닌 사람들을 당황케 만들려는 것이 아니다; 오히려 심리학자들로 하여금 그들이 이야기하고 논의하는 현상을 정확하게 파악하게끔 해주는 것이다. **4** 지구와 같은 행성들의 표면은 망원경과 우주 탐사선으로 볼 수 있는 반면, 목성형 행성들의 중심부는 두꺼운 가스층으로 인해 명확히 보이지 않는다. **5** 후보자 개인의 정치적 견해에 초점을 맞춤으로써, TV는 현안 보다 개인의 성격에 시민들의 관심을 증대시켰다. **6** 1885년경 상당한 간접 증거들로 인하여 염색체, 즉 세포핵에 있는 짙은 색의 나선형 형체가 세포 유전에 대한 정보를 지니고 있음이 밝혀졌다. **7** 따라서 Whistler는, 음악을 순수한 형태로 나열하는 것과 같이, 그림들을 나열하는 것을 선호하였는데, 이로써 그는 추상 미술의 선구자가 되었다. **8** 모든 비행기는 4가지 힘, 즉 양력, 중력, 추진력, 그리고 제동력을 조정하는 능력을 갖고 있기 때문에 날 수 있다. **9** 여러 분교를 가지고 있는 Texas 대학은 미국에서 가장 많이 기부를 받는 대학 중 하나이다. **10** 북미의 오대호는, 빙하작용에 의해 더 깊이 파이고 빙하 퇴적물이 가장자리 부분에 쌓이게 된 고대의 강 계곡이나 저지대에 자리 잡고 있다. **11** 강수가 핵 폐기물에 미치는 다른 효과는 훨씬 더 즉각적이고 위험하다. **12** 변압기와 전선과 같은 어떠한 종류의 전자기 에너지 장치도 유해한 방사 물질을 생산해낼 수 있다. **13** 절벽에 둥지를 트는 것의 장점은 여우로부터 안전하게 된다는 점인데, 여우는 가파른 바위를 오를 수가 없다 그리고 까마귀와 기타 갈매기들로부터도 안전해지는데, 이들은 알을 훔치기 위해 좁은 바위에 내려 앉기가 힘들다. **14** 석회암은 산호와 같은 해양 동물들의 시체가 얕은 바다에서 점차적으로 축적되어 만들어진 암석이다. **15** 공기 오염 인자에 대한 유용한 정의는 인간, 동식물 혹은 다른 물질들에 악영향을 미칠 정도의 양으로, 직간접적으로 인간에 의해 대기로 들어간 합성물질이다. **16** 자원을 보충할 방법이 없는 고립된 문화권에서는, 이미 Malthus의 재앙이 일어나고 있다.

PART 4 ★ Chapter 13

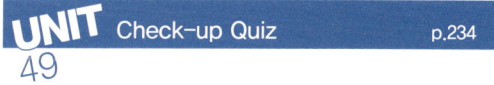

UNIT 49 Check-up Quiz   p.234

1 subsidizes 어떤 상은 전도 유망한 미국인 작가에게 로마 방문의 경비를 보조해 준다. **2 utter** 이 영화는 인간의 기본적인 욕구 충족을 위해 의도된 기계에 직면하여 인간이 느끼게 되는 전적인 무력함을 나타내고 있다.

3 article Pomo인들은 (도자기 제작 상의) 기본 꼬기 방식으로 네 개의 기법들을 이용했는데, 종종 한 작품에서 한 개 이상의 기법이 동시에 사용되기도 했다. **4 convergence** 다양한 사회적 및 지리적 배경을 가지고 있는 예술가들이 모임으로써 새로운 사상이 생겨나기 시작했다. **5 hilarious** Shirley Jackson의 때로는 으스스하고 때로는 유쾌한 소설들은, 발간되었을 당시, 비평가들에 의하여 무시되었었다. **6 jester** 이 우스꽝스러운 옷은 어릿광대 또는 심지어 여자 같은 느낌을 줄 것이다. **7 puppet** 인도네시아 음악에 기반을 둔 음악은 그 지역 그림자 인형극에서 사용되었다. **8 memoir** 회고록은 범위에 있어서 제약이 있으며, 통상 자서전 보다는 짧은 편이다. **9 obscenity** 또한 William S. Burroughs의 소설 Naked Lunch 역시 영향력이 있었는데, 이 소설은 음란 죄 관련 소송에서도 승소했다. **10 prosaic** 아기들에게 있어서 언어는, 성인들이 느끼는 평범한 의미에 이르는 과정이 아니라, 감각을 일깨워주는 하나의 기쁨이 된다. **11 auditory** 인간의 목소리에 대한 아기들의 반응은 다른 청각 자극에 대한 반응과는 차이가 있을 것이다. **12 utensil** 포크는 적어도 20세기 이후 식기 도구로 사용되고 있다. **13 cumbersome** 수고스러운 과정의 일부로 구덩이가 만들어졌고, 그 구덩이를 가로지르는 판자가 설치되었다. **14 strategic** 고려해야 할 또 다른 사항은 전략적 폭격 작전이었다. **15 coarse** 이집트 인들은 기원전 1600년 조잡한 형태의 섬유를 제작했는데, 이 섬유는 기원전 1375년까지 이집트의 도자기를 장식하는 용도로 사용되었다. **16 infiltrated** 군인들은 어둠을 틈타서 적 방어 시설로 침투했다. **17 niches** 그 고고학적 지점에는 제사 물품을 두었던 장소와 중앙의 화덕 자리가 있었다. **18 eccentricity** 극작가인 Oscar Wilde는 재치와 의상, 취향, 그리고 매너에서의 엉뚱함으로 자신을 부각시켰다. **19 rote** John Dewey는 아이들이 틀에 박힌 수업을 받아서는 안 된다고 강력하게 주장했다. **20 shards** 다양한 층에서 다양한 파편들을 발굴함으로써 고고학자들은 문화의 발전 단계의 시기를 손쉽게 알아낼 수 있다. **21 chronicled** 그 책은 알코올 중독을 극복한 작가의 이야기를 시간 순서에 따라 생생하게 설명했다. **22 libations** 그 축제 기간 동안에는 많은 양의 음식과 제주를 먹고 마시게 된다. **23 figurines** 그 고고학적 지점에는 품질이 떨어지는 다수의 작은 입상들과, 쉽고 비용이 저렴한 방식으로 대량 제작된 채색 도기들이 있었다. **24 conventional** 유럽이 재즈에 미친 영향은 트럼펫, 현악기 그리고 피아노와 같은 악기의 사용에서 찾아볼 수 있다. **25 betrayed** Arthur Miller의 걸작인 Death of Salesman은 자기 자신의 공허한 가치에 배신감을 느끼는 한 영업사원의 비극적인 이야기를 그리고 있다. **26 sentiments** Modern Times는 자신들이 과도하게 기계화된 세상에 있다고 느끼는 다수의 정서를 정확하게 반영하고 있다. **27 dilapidated** 이 화가들은 너무도 평범했기 때문에 흥미로웠던 대상들 즉, 문닫은 주유소, 버스를 기다리는 노인, 황폐화된 간판을 일반적으로 선택했다. **28 aviation** Charles Lindbergh의 최초의 대서양 횡단 비행은 항공 분야, 특히 상업 항공 분야의 새로운 지평을 열었다. **29 plucked** 하프는 그 기원이 고대로 거슬러 올라가는 현악기로, 손가락으로 현을 튕겨서 연주한다. **30 decode** 이집트 숫자를 판독하기 위해서는 숫자들을 나열한 후 분류하여 다시 합쳐야 한다.

UNIT 50 Check-up Quiz p.238

1 pivotal 증기 엔진의 발전은 공장 시스템의 확산에 주축적인 역할을 담당하였다. **2 barter** 통화가 사용되기 전에는 상품을 직접 상품과 교환하는 물물교환 시스템이 사용되었다. **3 lay off** Brindley 회사는 매출액 감소

로 직원의 10%를 해고시켜야 했다. **4 reprieve** 공장은 또한 농부들에게 농사의 고된 일과 금전적으로 예측하기 힘든 농사의 특성으로부터 일시적인 구제방안을 제공했다. **5 juggernauts** 그것들은 하늘을 누비는 거대한 항공기로 당시로서는 단연 최대 규모의 상용항공기였다. **6 per capita** 1950년 미국의 1인당 소득은 연 1,500 달러였다. **7 arduous** 등산은 힘든 스포츠이다. **8 frivolous** 그는 자신의 상사가 그에게 사소한 일을 시켰기 때문에 당황스러워했다. **9 consistent** 연구가 수십 년 동안 지속되고 있지만, 일관된 증거는 밝혀지지 않고 있다. **10 subdue** 진압용 방패와 경찰봉으로 무장한 경찰들이 흥분한 축구 팬들을 진압하기 위해 전화를 받고 달려왔다. **11 patented** 1867년 미국에서 특허를 받은 철조망은 미 농업의 발전에 중요한 역할을 담당하였다. **12 strain** 두 번째 종류는 폐렴 흑사병으로 선페스트의 변종이라 할 수 있다. **13 abortion** 중국과 같이 한 자녀 낳기 정책을 실시하는 사회에서는 남아 선호 사상이 낙태의 강력한 이유가 된다. **14 census** 1970년 미 인구조사에 의하면 Louisiana의 프랑스어 인구는 미국에서 가장 집약적으로 모여있는 언어 소수민족 중 하나였다. **15 locale** 경보 장치에 대한 정보는 그것이 사용되는 장소에 적혀있다. **16 ovulating** 발정기 동안 암컷들은 배란을 해서 임신을 할 수 있는 상태가 된다. **17 put down** 지도자들은 서로 다른 집단들을 진정시킴으로써 국가 내의 폭동을 누그러뜨렸다. **18 falter** 앞서서 출발했지만, 그는 결승선 근처에서 비틀거리기 시작했다. **19 federal** 캐나다의 연방 정부 시스템은 미국의 시스템과 유사하다. **20 electorate** 1867년 영국의 선거법 개정법안은 일반 노동자들에게 선거권을 부여함으로써 유권자를 2배 이상으로 증가시켰다. **21 hierarchical** 그들 군대의 엄격함 및 위계 질서 때문에, 그들은 미국에서 가장 큰 원주민 사회가 되었다. **22 amendments** 미 헌법 상 최초의 10개의 수정 법은 권리 장전이라고 알려져 있다. **23 ammunition** 다수의 프랑스인들은 음식에서 무기까지 모든 것을 인디언들에게 제공해 주었다. **24 bladder** 장과 방광도 사고를 당할 경우에는, 내용물 때문에 몸에 감염이 있을 수 있기 때문에, 내용물을 비울 준비를 한다. **25 ruthless** 해적인 Blackbeard는 가혹하고 무자비한 인물로서 악명을 높였다. **26 incest** 사실상 모든 문화에 근친상간을 금하는 규정이 있는 반면, 무엇이 근친상간인지는, 일단 핵가족 구성원의 범위를 넘어서게 되면, 분명치 않다. **27 inaugural** 딕시 클리퍼 항공기의 최초 대서양 횡단 비행에서 22명의 승객들은 플러시 천으로 된 소파와 넉넉한 공간을 즐길 수 있었다. **28 soothed** 공동 작업 후의 음식, 술 그리고 축하연은 긴장을 풀어 주었으며, 지친 근육을 이완시켜 주었다. **29 interdisciplinary** 인지 과학은 학문간 연계 분야로 심리학, 언어학, 그리고 생물학이 연계되어 있다. **30 dignified** 농업은 연구 부서들의 업적에 의해 고상한 것으로 되기 전까지는 과학으로 간주되지 조차 못했다.

UNIT 51 Check-up Quiz p.242

1 hexagonal 눈송이는 다양한 아름다운 형태를 지니고 있는데, 보통은 육각형 모양을 띈다. **2 torrential** 허리케인이 동반하는 폭우나 강풍은 폭풍 해일에 영향을 미친다. **3 luminous** 망원경으로 볼 수 있는 가장 밝은 빛을 내는 물체는 아마도 백억 광년 떨어져 있을 것이다. **4 spiral** 은하수는 나선 모양의 은하계로, 평면 원반 모양에 중앙 핵 부분에서 뻗어 나온 2개의 나선형 가지가 있다. **5 tentacles** 대왕오징어는 8개의 짧은 팔과 두 개의 긴 촉수를 가지고 있다. **6 sinuous** 마리아의 거대한 원형 지역은 이상하게 보였으며, 마리아 지역 내에서 굽이진 지형들이 관찰되었다. **7**

rupture 이러한 공기 부피의 변화는 허파를 부풀려서 심지어는 터지게 할 수도 있다. **8 tension** 물이 잎 표면에서 사라지면, 서로 밀어내는 힘, 즉 장력이 잎 표면에 만들어 진다. **9 translucent** 반투명 물질을 통해 볼 수는 없지만, 빛은 그 물질을 통과할 수 있다. **10 borealis** 사진으로 북극광의 아름다움을 담아내는 것은 거의 불가능하다. **11 reactor** 1986년 4월 체르노빌 원자력 발전소의 원자로 4호기가 원자폭탄의 400배나 되는 강력한 폭발을 일으켰다. **12 oval** 배 나무는 사과 나무의 잎보다 더 부드럽고 더 선명한, 단순하고 타원 모양의 잎을 가지고 있다. **13 gyrations** 고양이의 공중 회전은 너무 빨라서 인간의 눈에 보이지 않기 때문에 그 과정이 잘 알려져 있지 않다. **14 anomaly** 우리가 자연을 지배하고 있다면, 그리고 기술이 모두 강력한 것이라면, AIDS는 우리에게 무언가를 말해주고 있음에 틀림없는 끔찍한 예외이다. **15 antlers** 사슴은 주로 뿔을 이용하여 짝짓기를 위한 혹은 무리의 지도자가 되기 위한 싸움을 한다. **16 epidermis** 식물의 외부 표면은, 표피와 상피에 덮여져 있는 것 이외에도, 종종 뾰족한 털들을 가지고 있다. **17 conifer** 가장 높은 나무 중 하나인 그 침엽수는 특이하게도 낮은 근압을 가지고 있다. **18 piqued** 비록 이 충격적인 사건의 과학적 중요성은 막대하지만, 그것은 특히 일반 대중들의 호기심과 관심을 자극했다. **19 phosphorescent** 심해 구 바닥의 완전한 어둠 속에서 사는 어류들은 믿을 수 없을 정도로 민감한 눈과 인광성 기관들을 진화시켜왔다. **20 vascular** 유관 식물이 보다 발전된 형태로 간주되는 석송은 종종 습한 지역에 산다. **21 pollinate** 일부 꿀벌들은 수분 능력 때문에 양육되는데, 이 벌들은 과실 생산이 증대되도록 식물의 수정 작용을 보장해준다. **22 unfurls** 물은 햇빛을 가로지르는 무지개 색깔로 햇빛에 펼쳐진다. **23 aquifer** 간헐천 물이 분출되기 위한 첫 번째 조건은 대수층에 물이 존재해야 한다는 점이다. **24 cartographer** 지도 제작자의 일은 지표면을 대축적 지도에 나타내는 것이다. **25 fault** 버클리의 캘리포니아 대학을 최초로 건축한 사람들은 단층 위에다가 캠퍼스를 건설했다. **26 parole** GPS는 심지어 일일 휴가나 가석방으로 풀려나는 범죄자들의 위치 파악에도 이용된다. **27 ensued** 1906년 San Francisco의 많은 부분이 지진과 그 이후 일어난 잇단 화재로 황폐화되었다. **28 impending** 위험 지역과 임박한 화산 폭발을 감지할 수 있는 능력이 향상되었음에도 불구하고 보다 많은 이들이 일정 위험에 직면하고 있다. **29 overcast** 태양의 자외선은 구름을 뚫기 때문에 구름 낀 날에도 햇빛에 의한 화상을 입을 수 있다. **30 gauge** 잠재적 증발량이라고 알려진 그 기준값은 일상적인 증발 및 식물에 의해 일어나는 증발로 인한 수분 손실을 합한 값이다.

saline 염분이 있는 지하 수면이 지표면 2미터 내로 올라오게 되면, 표면에서는 증발이 일어나 염도가 짙어진다. **10 seemingly** 왜 거대하고 겉으로 보기에는 성공적이었던 매머드가 사라졌을까? **11 bogs** 많은 동물들은 식물들이 과다하게 자라났던 습지에 갇히게 되었다. **12 propagation** 우리의 문제는 증발된 수분의 양이 아니라 산업과 자동차로 인한 이산화 탄소 및 온실 효과 가스의 방출이 확산되고 있다는 점이다. **13 groom** 원숭이는 매우 사회적인 동물이다 한 가지 좋은 사례는 그들이 서로에게 몸단장을 시켜준다는 점이다. **14 cetaceans** 고래류의 동물은 매우 지능적이라고 널리 알려져 있다. **15 antigen** 혈액은 표면에 일종의 단백질인 항원을 가지고 있다. **16 capillary** 산소와 영양분들은 혈액으로부터 모세 혈관 벽을 따라 신체의 조직 세포에 도달한다. **17 canines** 앞니는 음식을 씹을 때, 송곳니는 찢을 때, 어금니는 빻을 때 사용된다. **18 incisors** 유아에게 나타나는 첫 번째 치아는 일반적으로 아래쪽 앞니이다. **19 diaphragm** 호흡에 필요한 에너지는 늑간 근육과 횡격막으로부터 나온다. **20 iris** 홍채는 카메라의 조리개와 비슷한 역할을 하는 눈의 조리개이다. **21 neurosis** 정신병은 심각한 정신 장애로 신경증보다 심각한 것이다. **22 pneumonia** 폐의 감염인 폐렴의 증상은 고열, 흉부 통증, 호흡 곤란, 그리고 기침을 포함한다. **23 pupil** 동공은 눈으로 들어오는 빛의 양을 조절한다. **24 paralysis** 비록 신경 염에 있어서 완전한 마비가 발생하는 경우는 드물지만, 근육들이 일부 쇠약해지는 현상은 일반적인 것이다. **25 arthritis** Isadora Martinez는 관절염을 겪고 있는 사람들이 쉽게 무릎을 구부릴 수 있도록 무릎 이식 물질을 발명했다. **26 viable** 19세기 동안 여러 기술적 발전들이 이루어졌는데, 이 중 주목할 만한 것으로서 Bessemer의 쇠를 철로 전환시키는 기술은 원료를 더욱 상업적으로 이용 가능할 수 있도록 만들었다. **27 Carbohydrates** 인간과 동물에게는 당과 전분과 같은 탄수화물이 중요한 에너지 원이다. **28 Viscosity** 점성도는 액체 흐름의 상대적인 어려움 혹은 쉬움을 나타내는 측정값이다. **29 pavilion** Philadelphia의 역사적 건물인 독립 기념관에 있었던 자유의 종은 1976년 별도의 유리 건축물 안으로 옮겨졌다. **30 prodigy** Edison은 12살의 어린 나이에 최초의 발명 작업을 시작함으로써 신동으로 불리게 되었다.

Chapter 13 Review Test

p.250

1. Ⓑ	2. Ⓓ	3. Ⓐ	4. Ⓓ
5. Ⓐ	6. Ⓓ	7. Ⓑ	8. Ⓐ
9. Ⓒ	10. Ⓐ	11. Ⓑ	12. Ⓑ
13. Ⓑ	14. Ⓓ	15. Ⓑ	16. Ⓒ

1 국회 위원회 의장은 정부의 보조금이 없이 그렇게 불투명한 모험은 아무도 시도하지 않을 것이라고 강하게 주장했다. **2** 비록 합성 나일론이 주로 섬유용으로 만들어지지만, 로프, 절연체, 유리섬유, 그리고 기타 가정 용구를 만들기 위해서도 제조된다. **3** 이러한 성가신 제도가 존재했던 시기에 영리적인 우편 기업이 발전하게 되었다는 점은 놀라운 일이 아니다. **4** 그 퀼트들은 맨 아래 층에는 보다 거친 재료로 이루어진 층을 가지고 있었고, 맨 위층에는 양털 혹은 유약이 칠해진 무직 섬유로 이루어져 있었는데, 이 섬유는 남색, 초록색, 혹은 갈색으로 염색된 긴 모직물로 된, 부드럽고 빽빽한 털실로 이루어져 있었다. **5** 고고학자들에게 도자기 파편을 수집하는 일은 고대 문화권들의 발전 수준을 확인해 줄 수 있는 가장 손쉬운 방법 중의 하나였다. **6** 곧 신석기 사회가 복

UNIT
UNIT 52 Check-up Quiz p.246

1 minuscule 그의 꿈을 실현하기 위해 그는 5천만 달러를 빌렸는데, 이 금액은 오늘날 기준으로 볼 때 매우 적은 금액이다. **2 ledges** 굴뚝 안에는 서로를 가로질러 있는 두 개의 선반이 설치되었다. **3 tendons** 근육 섬유 세포들은 힘줄에 의하여 뼈에 붙어 있다. **4 electron** 양성자는 양전하를, 전자는 음전하를 띤다. **5 scaffolding** Guggenheim 미술관을 거의 3년 동안이나 덮고 있었던 비계가 건설 노동자들에 의해 해체되고 있다. **6 terrestrial** 지구 상의 생명체의 다양성에 대한 많은 글들이 작성되었다. **7 thwarting** 해양 포식자들은 박테리아의 성장을 방해하고 먹이 사슬의 취약한 연결 고리를 감소시켜서 해양의 균형을 유지함으로써 매우 중요한 역할을 한다. **8 parched** 한 과학자에 따르면 불에 탄 대부분의 나무들은 50에서 500 킬로헤르쯔까지의 범위로 자신들의 상황을 서로 알려준다. **9**

잡해짐에 따라, 기록을 유지할 필요성 및 이후 경험과 지식, 그리고 신념을 시간대 별로 서술하기 위한 필요성에서, 쓰기가 발전되었다. **7** 1950년대 초반 여성 과학자들은 종종 남성 과학자들의 그늘에서 일하도록 강요 받았기 때문에, 과학사에 있어서 Franklin의 주요 업적은 부수적인 것으로 취급되어 그 가치를 인정받지 못하였다. **8** 잉여 농산물들은 다른 상품과 교환되기 위해 물물교환되었다. **9** 추상적이거나 양식화되거나 혹은 사실적으로 다루어지던 간에, 사실상 모든 예술과 기술 디자인의 일관된 주제는 자연이다. **10** 현대의 기준에서 볼 때, 초기 광고는 오늘날처럼 전면이 화려하게 장식된 종이가 아니라 상당히 작고 차분한 것이었는데, 그렇다 하더라도 이 들 중 일부는 신문 앞 페이지를 장식했다. **11** 해외 원정에서는 승리했지만, 내부의 지지를 이끌어 내는 노력이 이에 미치지 못하자, 로마 공화국은 안으로부터 쇠약해지기 시작했다. **12** 가장 많은 피해를 끼치고 생명을 위협하는 대부분의 날씨 현상, 즉 폭우, 심한 폭풍우, 토네이도는 빠르게 시작되어 갑자기 충격을 준 후 빠르게 사라진다. **13** 송진은 시간과 압력에 의해 단단해져서 호박이라고 불리는 화석이 된다 호박은 무르며, 노란빛을 띤 갈색의 반투명한 물질이다. **14** 20세기에는 전자 현미경을 이용하여 바이러스와 미세한 표면 구조를 직접적으로 관찰할 수 있게 되었다. **15** 또 다른 유리의 특성은 차가운 물질에서 뜨겁고 연성이 있는 액체로 변화할 때 나타나는, 점성도가 변하는 방식이다. **16** 프랑스 태생의 Robert Laurent는 미국에서 교육을 받은 신동이었다.

견디어왔다는 사실은, 오래 전 멸종한 동물들의 유전 물질이 발견될 수도 있을 것이라는 희망을 과학자들에게 선사해 주었다. **17** **limbo** 그 원주민들은 장례식을 통해서만 죽은 가족의 어중간한 상태를 깰 수 있다고 생각한다. **18** **hominids** 초기 인류의 발자국에서 많은 것을 알아낼 수 있다. **19** **vault** 시신은 수평으로 된 납골당에 넣어져서 돌이나 나무로 둘러 쌓인다. **20** **freakish** 기묘한 재능을 지는 트럼펫 연주자였던 Louis Armstrong은 늘 가장 영향력 있는 재즈 연주가로 기억될 것이다. **21** **characterized** 그녀의 작품은 몇 마디 말로써 규정될 수 없다. **22** **glorify** 예술은 특정 통치자들을 찬양하지는 않았다. **23** **delineates** 지역 소설은 어떻게 환경이 거주민들에게 영향을 미치는가를 보여주기 위해 특정 지역 사람들의 삶을 서술한다. **24** **embarked** Dadaist들은 공격적인 혹은 폭력적인 예술 및 문학 작품을 만들어 대중들에게 충격을 빠르게 함으로써 자신들의 개혁 운동을 시작했다. **25** **rekindled** 1912년 그녀가 Virginia 대학 여름 학기의 예술 수업에 참석하면서 O'Keeffe의 창의력이 다시 불붙게 되었다. **26** **relegated** 그 쇼는 합법적인 무대에서 쫓겨나 술집과 바로 밀려나는 신세가 되었다. **27** **came of age** 또한 식민지 시기의 구리 세공업은 18세기 초 확립되어 북부 도시에서 번성하게 되었다. **28** **in regards to** Poe의 작품을 읽을 때는, 특히 세부적인 내용들이 다 존재하는 이유가 있기 때문에, 특별히 신경 써서 읽어야 한다. **29** **impostor** 그 인물은 바보 같아 보이거나 심지어는 사기꾼 같은 느낌을 강하게 준다 즉 부는 소유했지만 본질적으로는 광대이며 가짜라는 느낌을 주는 것이다. **30** **lyrics** Louis Armstrong은 가사 대신 리듬만 있고 뜻은 통하지 않는 말을 하는 스캣 스타일로 노래를 한 최초의 음악가 중 한 명이었다.

PART 4 ★ Chapter 14

UNIT 53 Check-up Quiz p.252

1 **caliber** 그 배우들은 일류 배우이거나 그냥 아르바이트 풋내기일 수도 있다. **2** **cardinal** 현악기의 일종인 류트 연주자에게 가장 중요한 규칙은 모든 음이 가능한 오래 지속되어야 한다는 것이다. **3** **hisses** 주변 환경의 소리와 전기 장치에서 나오는 히스는 하나의 음악으로 합성될 수 있다. **4** **luminosity** 그의 작품들은 네덜란드 거장들의 작품과 동일한 밝기 및 세심한 주의력을 나타내고 있다. **5** **lurid** 1940년대 종이 표지의 소설들은 종종 독자들의 주의를 끌기 위해 눈에 띄는 표지로 장식되어 있었다. **6** **choreography** 1925년경 발레의 안무법을 기록할 수 있는 정확하고 편리한 시스템이 개발되었다. **7** **punctuality** 당신은 시간 엄수에 대해 다양한 태도를 가진 많은 사람들을 반드시 마주칠 수 있을 것이다. **8** **babble** 4개월에서 8개월 사이에 유아는 의미 없는 음절들을 재잘거리기 시작한다. **9** **clichés** 미 언어의 "시간은 돈이다", "시간은 아무도 기다려주지 않는다" 등의 일부 표현들은 너무 흔해서 진부한 표현이 되었다. **10** **sprout** 증기선 덕분에 수많은 마을과 기업들이 강을 따라 급속히 성장하기 시작했다. **11** **supplements** 화물 마차, 역마차, 그리고 증기선 운행은 최초의 열차 이용객들을 위한 보충적인 역할을 담당하게 되었다. **12** **treacherous** 초기의 노예 노래들은 그들에게 불안정한 노예의 굴레에서 탈출할 수 있는 일종의 탈출구였다. **13** **discretion** 기념물은 대통령의 자유재량으로 이루어진다. **14** **feudal** 비록 봉건제에 기반하고 있었지만, Pennsylvania 식민지는 진보적인 정치적, 사회적 전망으로 명성을 얻게 되었다. **15** **mutiny** 선상 반란은 복종과 규율 체계가 붕괴되었다는 점을 의미한다. **16** **detectable** 탐지 가능한 정도의 양으로 DNA가 4만년을

UNIT 54 Check-up Quiz p.256

1 **spearheaded** Taylor는 20세기 초 효율성 운동을 이끈 미국인 기술자였다. **2** **haul** 농장 여성들은 우물 혹은 양수기가 있는 곳으로부터, 어떤 용도로 쓰던 간에, 상당한 양의 물을 집으로 끌어 날라야만 했다. **3** **arithmetic** 읽기, 쓰기 그리고 수학은 초등 교육의 기본 교과이다. **4** **encyclopedias** 백과 사전의 출판사들은 수많은 전문가들과 광범위한 편집 직원들을 고용했다. **5** **protocol** 이러한 끊임없는 반복은, 엄격한 일정 및 노동 규약과 함께, 노동자들에게는 매우 소모적인 양상으로 나타났다. **6** **hinged on** 경제 성장은 몇 가지 경제적 요인에 달려있다. **7** **lathe** 1700년대 후반까지 금속은 선반에서 작업되지 못했기 때문에 고르게 매끈하고 둥글게 깎여지지 못했다. **8** **subsisted** 선사 시대의 많은 사람들은 수렵 채취로 살아갔다. **9** **heading** 공장 노동자와 사무 노동자의 노동은 노동의 일반적인 범주에 해당된다. **10** **disseminated** Hollywood는 미 전역의 스크린을 통해 Southern California에서의 멋진 삶에 대한 이미지를 널리 퍼뜨렸다. **11** **windfalls** 남부 지역은 현금작물로 엄청난 경제적 이득을 얻었다. **12** **linger** 일부 사람들은 식사 후 커피와 디저트를 먹으면서, 떠나지 않고 꾸물거리기를 좋아한다. **13** **ideology** 부분적으로 농부들의 도시에 대한 불신은, 농업이 최고의 직업이고 농촌 생활이 도시 생활보다 더 우수하다는 국가 이념에 의한 것이었다. **14** **litters** 많은 동물 종들은 출산 시 여러 마리의 새끼를 낳는다. **15** **puberty** 청소년기는 사춘기의 시작에서부터 감정적, 사회적, 그리고 신체적 성숙기까지 이르는 인간 발전의 전환 단계이다. **16** **chaos** 새로운 도시들은 혼란 상태로부터 도시의 질서를 이끌어내겠다고 공약한 진보적인 개혁 정책을 열정적으로 환영했다. **17** **institution** 노예제도는 수천 년간 인류 역사의 한 부분을 차지

해왔다. **18 gullible** 사기꾼들은 잘 속는 사람들을 속여서 돈을 가로채는 범죄자이다. **19 pending** 미결정 상태에 있었던 New York항 개선 계획은 회의를 통해 논의되었으나, 안타깝게도 합의에 이르지는 못했다. **20 ravaged** 현재 그 나라는 뿌리깊은 종교적 갈등으로 황폐화되고 있는 중이다. **21 epithet** 심지어 그 이름은 왜소한 것들, 지저분한 것들, 그리고 하찮은 것들에 대한 통칭이었다. **22 cabinet** 미국에서는 법무 장관이 사법부의 행정 책임을 맡는 내각 구성원이 된다. **23 credentials** Jelks 씨에 대한 그들의 의견이 무엇이던 간에, 그는 매우 인상적인 증명서를 지니고 있었다. **24 isolationism** 직접적인 위협이 없는 한 미국은 세계사의 테두리 밖에 머물러야 한다는, 고립주의로 알려진 전반적인 운동이 시작되었다. **25 arena** 그는 국제적인 사안에 있어서 미국을 국제적 권력 투쟁의 장으로 들어가게 함으로써, 전통적인 미국의 고립주의 정책을 밀쳐내었다. **26 bowel** 미국인 다섯 명 중 한 명은, 심한 경련과 변비 및 설사를 일으킬 수 있는 과민성 장 증후군을 겪고 있다. **27 variables** 작업 계획표는 복잡한 관계의 많은 변수들과 관련된 결정을 내릴 때 매우 유용할 수 있다. **28 exaltation** 2기 Chicago 학파는 신고전주의 경제학을 고수했고, 정부의 개입에 대한 케인즈주의 학파의 지지 입장을 거부했다. **29 cost-effective** 소책자와 가두 판매용 책은 대규모의 비용 효과적인 부수로 인쇄될 수 있었고, 저렴한 가격으로 판매될 수 있었다. **30 territory** 캐나다는 인구가 적지만 영토는 미국보다 약간 더 크다.

UNIT 55 Check-up Quiz

p.260

1 concentric 태양계에 있는 행성들은 동일한 평면상 배열되어 있으며, 대략 태양을 그 중심으로 하는 타원형 궤도를 갖고 있다. **2 wisp** 그 행성의 낮 기온은 영상에 이를 수도 있지만, 그 행성은 적은 대기에 덮여져 있기 때문에, 열은 다시 우주로 반사된다. **3 eclipsed** 달은 인류에게 정복되어 명성이 쇠퇴되었기 때문에 당연히 화성이 우주 탐사의 다음 단계가 되어야 한다. **4 skewed** 단단한 목재로 만들어진 부메랑은 대략 V 자 모양으로, 양 끝이 약간 기울여져 있는 형태를 갖는다. **5 constellations** 고대인들에게 12 궁도 이외에도 30개의 다른 성운들은 친숙한 것이었다. **6 tributary** Valerie 빙하라고 불리는 서쪽 지류는 매일 122 피트 정도 나아갔다. **7 velocity** 강의 유속은 경사, 깊이 그리고 강 바닥의 거친 정도에 따라 결정된다. **8 refraction** 수조에 있는 물은 굴절 작용 때문에 결코 실제 깊이만큼 깊어 보이지 않는다. **9 narcotic** 일부 의사들은 수술, 주사, 그리고 마취성 진통 치료가 적절하게 사용되고 있는 지에 대해 의구심을 갖고 있다. **10 petals** 꽃잎의 가장 주목할 만한 부분은 순형 화판, 즉 입술 꽃잎이라 불리는 부분이다. **11 hitch** 그 프로그램에는 오류가 있어서 2시간 동안 작동이 지연되었다. **12 molt** 모든 성인 새들은 일년에 적어도 한번 털갈이를 한다. **13 coronary** 콜레스테롤은 심장의 동맥에 쌓임으로써, 관상 동맥 질환을 일으킬 수 있다. **14 hypersensitive** 알레르기에 있어서, 동물의 면역 체계는 동물이 접하게 되는 일부 물질들, 즉 알레르기 항원이라 불리는 것에 과민한 반응을 일으킨다. **15 embryo** 난자는 배아가 더 이상 살 수 없을 정도로 차갑게 되면 안된다. **16 fauna** 까마귀는 아마도 가장 흔하고 쉽게 알아볼 수 있는 미국의 토종 동물 중에 하나이다. **17 intestine** 단백질 소화는 위에서 시작되고 소장에서 끝난다. **18 resilience** 작은 개미는 비길 데 없는 복원력 때문에, 이제까지 발견된 종 중 가장 성공적이고 놀라운 종 중 하나일 것이다. **19 metabolism** 실제 모든 종들은 24 시간 주기로 신진대사를 통제해 주는 생물학적 시계를 지

니고 있다. **20 crevice** 선인장은 바위틈에 사는 3 인치의 fishhook 선인장에서 30~40 피트 높이의 Saguaro 선인장에 이르기까지 다양하다. **21 grid** 차량에 사용되는 더욱 현대적인 GPS 장치에서는 심지어 도시를 나타내는 격자 눈금상에서 움직이는 자동차의 정확한 위치를 보여주기도 한다. **22 quicksand** 유사는 전세계 각지에서 발견되지만, 그것의 성분에 대해서는 최근까지도 알려진 바가 거의 없다. **23 dunes** 사구는 바람의 활동에 의해 쌓여진 흐트러진 모래로 이루어져 있다. **24 Geysers** 간헐천은 종종 화산과 비교되는데, 그 이유는 양쪽 모두 지표면 아래로부터 뜨거운 액체를 방출해 내기 때문이다. **25 incandescent** 일부 지질학자들은 지구의 내부에 매우 압력이 높고 빛이 나는, 공 형태의 가스층이 있을 것이라고 생각한다. **26 synchronizes** GPS수신기는 인공위성의 원자 시계와 같은 시각을 표시한다. **27 basalt** Yellowstone 국립 공원의 검은 흑요암 절벽은 현무암의 용암 흐름이 빙하 쪽으로 흘렀던 결과로 만들어 졌다. **28 strata** 눈의 형성 과정은 대기의 중간 부분 혹은 상부의 어느 점 아래의 층에 존재하는 눈 결정체로부터 시작된다. **29 Weathering** 풍화작용은 지각과 대기, 그리고 대기 중의 물이 상호작용하는 것과 관련된다. **30 symmetrical** 타원 은하는 뚜렷한 구조를 지니고 있는, 대칭적인 타원형이거나 구형 모양이다.

UNIT 56 Check-up Quiz

p.264

1 thaws 여름 동안 영구 동토층은 충분히 녹기 때문에 식물들이 자라고 번식할 수 있다. **2 crooked** 가파른 언덕에 이르는 구불구불한 길이 있는 San Francisco의 Lombard 거리는 세계에서 가장 구불구불한 거리로 알려져 있다. **3 hoist** 고층 건물이 지어지는 동안, 크레인은 건축 자재를 상부 층으로 올려 보내는데 사용된다. **4 opulent** 세계의 가장 호사스러운 식당들 중 다수는 고급 호텔 안에 위치해있다. **5 barge** 석탄, 곡물, 강철 그리고 기타 상품들은 내륙 수로를 통해 바지선으로 운반된다. **6 pegs** 초기 목수들은 못을 사용하지 않고 나무 쐐기를 이용하여 건축물들을 견고히 해야 했다. **7 canals** George Washington은 운하의 건설이 국가 발전에 얼마나 중요한 것인지를 깨달은 최초의 인물들 중 한 명이었다고 한다. **8 vindicated** Carson의 업적은 미 대통령 과학 자문 위원회의 1963년 보고서에서 정당한 것으로 입증되었다. **9 roamed** 한 때 수많은 들소들이 북미 평원을 돌아다녔었다. **10 pasture** 과도한 방목은 너무나 많은 가축들이 특정 목초지에서 길러질 때 일어난다. **11 pulverization** 한 지역에서 소가 풀을 뜯어먹으면 천연 식물들의 감소와 토양의 분쇄가 그 결과로서 나타난다. **12 enzyme** 실제로 효소가 작용을 하면, 효소가 없는 경우보다 수 십억 배 빠른 속도로 반응이 진행될 수 있다. **13 stasis** 나륵풀은 이로운 곤충들과 협동하여 어떤 화학 약품도 사용하지 않고 해충의 피해를 최소화시키는 안정상태를 만들어낸다. **14 mileage** 실험에 따르면 새 디젤유가 휘발유에 비해 연비가 25~45% 더 높다. **15 tusks** 매머드는 두껍고, 털이 많은 피부, 그리고 거대하고 위로 치켜 올라간 엄니를 가지고 있었다는 점에서 오늘날의 코끼리와는 차이가 있었다. **16 camouflage** 이 뱀들은 위장술을 갖고 있기 때문에 찾기가 대단히 어렵다. **17 splicing** 과다한 어획을 막기 위한 또 다른 가능한 방법이 유전자 접합인데, 이로써 어류의 번식이 수배 더 가속화될 수 있다. **18 arboretum** 수목원에서는 과학적, 교육적 목적을 위해 나무들이 배양된다. **19 infrared** 온실 효과는 태양의 적외선이 대기 속으로 보다 즉시 흡수되는 과정이다. **20 kingdom** 동물계의 구성원들은 기생 생물에 대처하기 위한 다양한 방어 매커니즘을 발전시켜왔다. **21 veterinarian** 개는 건강 상태가 좋은지 확인하기 위해 수의사에게 정

정답 및 해설

325

기적인 검진을 받아야 한다. 22 **slash and burn** 식물과 농장의 끔찍한 손실은 토착민들이 사용하는 화전 농법 때문이다. 23 **astigmatism** 난시의 증상은 상이 흐리게 보이는 것, 그리고 좀 더 극단적인 경우에는 두통이 온다. 24 **dementia** Alzheimer 병은 치매의 가장 일반적인 형태이다. 25 **hepatitis** 바이러스성 간염의 정확한 초기 증상은 복통, 구역질 그리고 종종 오한을 수반하는 열이다. 26 **plasma** 혈액은 보통 전액이나 혈장의 형태로 저장을 한다. 27 **hypersomnia** 사람들이 일반적으로 알고 있는 것과는 달리 많은 연구에서 수면 과다증은 또 다른 야행성 질환인 불면증보다 훨씬 더 흔할 수 있다는 결과가 나왔다. 28 **ligaments** 또한 그것은 뼈에 힘줄이나 인대와 연결되는 근육이다. 29 **anesthesia** 변경 지역의 의사였던 Ephraim MacDonald는 마취 없이 수술을 해야만 했다. 30 **pituitary glands** 내분비선은 갑상선과 뇌하수체와 같은 선을 지칭하기 위해 사용되는데, 이들은 생성물질을 혈액에 직접 분비한다.

Chapter Review Test 14
p.268

1. ⑩	2. ⓒ	3. ⓒ	4. ⒶA
5. ⒶA	6. ⓒ	7. ⓑB	8. ⓒ
9. ⒶA	10. ⓑB	11. ⒶA	12. ⑩
13. ⓒ	14. ⒶA	15. ⒶA	16. ⑩

1 곤충 섭취를 과일 혹은 씨앗으로 보충하는 많은 작은 포유류들에게 있어서, 나무 꼭대기 사이를 뛰어 넘지 못하는 점은 문제가 될 수 있다. 2 예컨대 이 산화 함은 0.08 ppm일 경우 건강에 알아차릴 수 있을 정도의 영향을 미칠 수 있다. 3 John Barth, Donald Barthelme, 그리고 Tomas Pynchon 등과 같은 작가에 의해 사실주의 전통이 배제되었던 기간 동안, Joy Carol Oates는 때때로 자신의 작품에 사실적인 특성을 고집함으로써 구시대적인 것으로 비춰졌다. 4 그 화가들은 작은 마을 혹은 농장에서의 일상적인 장면들을 연출했고 그 스타일은 결코 모호하지 않았다 실제로 그들은 안정적이고 유익하며, 중요한 미 전통을 구현하는 시골에서의 삶을 찬양했고 낭만적으로 그려냈다. 5 포장 마차는 1812년 이후로 Eastern Seaboard와 Ohio Valley 사이의 화물과 승객을 나르는데 이용되었다. 6 텔레비전은 정보를 유포시키는 방식과 선거 운동에 변화를 일으킴으로써 미국의 정치를 바꾸어 놓았다. 7 겨울은 종종 떠나기를 싫어했다 봄은 심한 서리에 의해 인도되었다. 8 그들은 입법 현안에 대해 상사가 잘 알고 있도록 조치하고, 청문회를 조직하며, 또한 지역 국회 의원들에게 최신 정보를 제공해줌으로써 국회의 다른 쪽에서 어떤 일이 일어나는가에 대해 알려준다. 9 인도 남부 지역을 황폐화시킨 홍수로 인하여 적어도 92명이 목숨을 잃고 수많은 사람들이 이재민이 되었다. 10 수학자들은 몇 세기에 걸쳐 현재 대수학에서 사용되는 방법들을 발전시켰다. 11 일단 이 시스템이 더 강해지고 지속되는 속도가 시속 75마일을 넘어서게 되면 이 폭풍은 진정한 허리케인으로 분류될 수 있다. 12 인간의 도움으로 그 새들은 별 어려움 없이 북쪽에서 남쪽으로 1,250 마일을 이동했다. 13 작고 섬세한 뼈들은 화석으로 되기 전에 보통 청소부 동물에 의해 흩어지거나 풍화작용에 의해 파괴된다. 14 복원할 수 없는 그리스 조각들은 복제품으로 제작되어서, 조각과 천장, 그리고 벽에 화려하고 정교한 형태들이 다시 나타났다. 15 미 대법원은 미 사법부의 명예를 위해 그를 변호할 마지막 기회를 달라는 Manton의 청원을 거절했다. 16 많은 다른 동물들과 곤충들은 위장 혹은 의사소통에 사용하기 위하여 대조적이거나 강렬한 무지개 색깔을 만들어내는 신체 기관을 지니고 있다.

PART 4 ★ Chapter 15

UNIT 57 Check-up Quiz
p.270

1 **footage** 공장 내부의 장면은 Modern Times 전체 분량의 1/3 정도만 차지한다. 2 **chisel** 신고전주의 조각가들은 나무 망치 혹은 정을 거의 잡지 않았다. 3 **snide** 비록 많은 지성인들이 TV 시청에 대해 비난을 하고 있지만, 다수의 "지식인용" 쇼들이 존재하고 있다. 4 **intonation** 성인의 강세 및 억양의 특성은 아기의 감정적인 상태와 그 행동에 영향을 미칠 수 있다. 5 **vowel** 모음이 따라오는 p, b, d, n으로 시작되는 단어들이 가장 흔하다. 6 **stationary** 일찍이 1802년, 그는 자신의 제분소에 있었던 고정 고압 증기 엔진을 사용하고 있었다. 7 **surging** 대부분의 인구 급증 현상은 자연적 증가에 기인한 것이었다. 8 **salvaged** 심지어 배가 침몰한 후에도 화물은 종종 인양된다. 9 **hinterland** Philadelphia는 거대하고 성장하는 농업 지역으로 점차적으로 중요한 마케팅 중심지가 되었다. 10 **semantics** 언어학의 중요한 분야 중의 하나는 단어의 의미를 분석하는 의미론이다. 11 **utilitarian** 도자기는 보통 실용적인 목적을 지니고 있었으며 때로는 순전히 장식적인 목적으로 만들어지기도 했다. 12 **derogatory** 과거에 그들은 Eskimo인이라고 불려졌으나, 오늘날 그 용어는 다수의 Inuit인들에 의해서 경멸적인 표현으로 간주되고 있다. 13 **polygamy** 결혼이 항상 일부일처제이지는 않았다. 일부 사람들은 일부다처제였다. 14 **Hieroglyphs** 상형문자는 종교적인 규칙들을 나타냈고, 양식화된 그림과 함께 중요한 개념들을 표현했다. 15 **etched** Rushmore 산의 기념비는 Black Hills 산맥의 가장 높은 꼭대기에 조각된 4명의 미국 대통령에 대한 거대한 조각이다. 16 **humanitarian** 그녀는 문학 작품으로 기억되고 있지만 또한 인도주의적인 활동으로도 기억되고 있다. 17 **evacuated** Buck 가족은 1927년 중국으로 돌아갔으나 중국의 내전 당시에는 일본으로 피난해 있었다. 18 **hoard** 유명한 구두쇠인 Ebenezer Scrooge는 자신의 돈을 모아두고는 결코 쓰지 않았다. 19 **consorted** 일부 식민지 도시 초상화가들은 부유한 후원자들과 교제했다. 20 **gruff** Louis Daniel Armstrong은 아름답고 정확한 트럼펫 연주와 걸걸하고 쉰 목소리의 노래로 유명하다. 21 **faction** 노예제 찬성론자들은 민주당에 합류했고, 노예제를 반대했던 사람들은 공화당원이 되었는데, Abraham Lincoln이 이들을 이끌게 되었다. 22 **morph** 그 화가들의 독특한 양식들은 당대의 사회적 사고방식과 그 사회가 새로운 방향으로 형성되고 성장하는 모습을 반영하고 있었다. 23 **fiddle** 개척지의 사람들은 일과를 마친 후, 노래를 부르고 바이올린 소리에 춤을 추거나 컨트리 댄스를 췄다. 24 **props** 지역 극장은 종종 난방시설 및 최소한도의 소도구, 그리고 무대 시설을 결여하고 있다. 25 **pretend** 그 실험에서는 아이에게 실제 존재하지 않는 생물들을 그린 그림이 주어졌다. 26 **lexicon** 최초 "couch potato"란 말이 농담으로 혹은 진담으로 쓰여졌건 간에, 그것은 오랫동안 쓰여져 왔으며 현재는 현대 사람들이 사용하는 어휘 중 일 부분이 되었다. 27 **Metaphysical** 형이상학적인 철학은 관찰 가능한 실체 속에 숨겨진 원칙, 구조, 그리고 의미들에 관심을 갖는다. 28 **template** Rainbow호는 세계를 놀라게 한 새로운 세대의 선박의 모범이 되었다. 29 **catalyzed** 대중 교통은 물리적인 확장을 가속시켰고, 사람들과 토지의 사용을 구분시켜 주었으며, 도시 생활의 고유한 불안정성을 증대시켰다. 30 **thermal** 유리 섬유는 1930년대 유리섬유의 열차단 및 절연 효과가 인정받기 전까지는 크게 부각되지 못했다.

1 **premise** Keynes의 전제는 경제 성장률이 총수요에 의존한다는 것이었다. 2 **heyday** 쾌속 범선은 1800년대 중반 전성기를 맞이했다. 3 **consensus** 그 회의는 다양한 난제들을 극복하고 합의에 이르렀다. 4 **sweatshops** 도시 건물 내에는 노동자들을 혹사시키는 공장이 있었는데, 여기서는 여러 남성과 여성 노동자들이 의류나 담배를 제조하였다. 5 **depression** 1929년 Wall Street의 붕괴로 미국의 경기 침체의 시기가 시작되었다. 6 **tariffs** 연방 정부는 사실상 근본적으로는 보호무역적인 관세 제도를 마련하였다. 7 **microcosm** Virginia주 Jamestown의 정착지는 많은 방면에 있어서 북부 식민지 경제의 축소판이었다. 8 **surplus** 행정부는 둔화되는 경기로 인해 여분의 연방 예산이 올해 정부가 예측한 바 이상으로 감소하게 될 것이라는 가능성을 시사했다. 9 **embargo** 나치의 통상 금지 정책은 곧 미국과 많은 동맹국들에게 영향을 미쳤다. 10 **laissez-faire** 그는 전통적인 연방 정책인 자유방임주의를 뒤집고 미국 산업과 상업 분야에 질서와 사회정의, 공정거래를 도입시키려 했다. 11 **tenets** 모든 교인들이 교회의 교리를 받아들이지는 않았다. 12 **pluralism** Locke는 문화적 다원주의를 제시했는데, 예술가들은 이를 통해 미국의 문화를 풍부하게 할 것이었다. 13 **decimal** 캐나다는 1867년 십진법에 기초한 화폐 제도를 도입했다. 14 **pseudo** 인종 분류법이라는 사이비 과학에 따르면, 아프리카 흑인들은 원래부터 열등하고 무지한 존재였다. 15 **breadbasket** New York과 Philadelphia의 도시 주변은 북미의 주요 농업지대가 되었다. 16 **genealogy** 오늘날 개인들은 자신의 가족사에 대해 더 알고 싶은 충동에서 종종 온라인 족보 사이트를 통해 자신의 혈통을 추적한다. 17 **miscarriages** 일부 동물에게 있어서 낙태는 자연유산이라는 자연적인 현상으로서 존재한다. 18 **commentary** James Franklin은 신문을 사회적 및 정치적 비판의 한 수단으로 바라본 최초의 편집자였다. 19 **questionnaire** 사회 과학 연구의 가장 중요한 도구 중의 하나는 적절하게 작성된 설문지이다. 20 **treaty** 패자들은 적과의 조약에 서명해야만 했다. 21 **vetoed** 대통령이 원하지 않는 경우, 법안에 대한 거부권은 두 가지 방식으로 행사될 수 있다. 22 **bracket** 안타깝게도, 그런 선택권이 모두에게 주어지는 것은 아니며, 특히 저소득층 여성들에게는 더욱 그렇다. 23 **egalitarian** Olmstead의 생각은 그 공원을 민주주의와 평등주의의 이상에 대한 상징으로 만드는 것이었다. 24 **cognition** 심리학자들이 인지라고 하는 것은 모든 정신적 상태와 활동을 포함하는 일반적인 범주이다. 25 **Ethology** 행동 생물학 이론은 1960년대 아이들에 관한 연구조사에서 적용되기 시작했지만, 현재 그 영향력은 보다 증대되어 있다. 26 **paranoia** 그 끔찍한 사건들의 기억이 너무나 강력했기 때문에, 그들은 편집증 및 다른 극적인 부작용들을 겪었다. 27 **traumatic** 자동차 사고, 강도 사건, 혹은 정신적 충격을 줄 수 있는 일들을 경험한 사람들은 외상 후 스트레스 장애를 겪을 수 있다. 28 **superseded** 플라스틱과 유리섬유는 인공 안구, 치아, 뼈와 같은 신체부위의 대체재로서 금속을 대신하고 있다. 29 **hub** Phoenix는 미국에서 9번째로 큰 도시로, Salt River 계곡의 풍부한 농업 지역의 중심지이다. 30 **anarchy** Dadaist들의 답은 혼란과 비 이성을 감싸 안는 것이었다.

정답 및 해설

1 **tilt** 계절이 나타나는 원인인 지구의 기울기는 아마도 생성 초기 거대한 물체와의 충돌 때문일 것이다. 2 **nebula** 목성은 가장 잘 보존된, 초기 태양 성운에 대한 표본이다. 3 **tug** 조수 간만은 달 중력의 끌어당기는 힘 때문에 발생한다. 4 **elliptical** 그 위성은, 지구로부터 가장 멀리 떨어져 있는 지점이 680마일에 이르는, 타원형 궤도를 따르고 있다. 5 **plasma** 그 기체는 열에 의해 전자를 잃게 되고, 각 원자는 따라서 양전하를 띄게 되는데, 이러한 형태의 기체를 플라즈마라고 한다. 6 **diffraction** 두 젊은 과학자들이 빛의 회절 현상에 대한 실험 결과를 대담하게 발표했다. 7 **spells** 고기압 셀들은 심지어 한 겨울에도 따뜻한 날씨를 가져다 줄 수 있다. 8 **imprinting** 모든 철새와 마찬가지로, 미국 흰 두루미도 각인이라고 하는 자연 본능이 있는데, 이것은 미국 흰 두루미가 눈앞에 최초로 보이는 물체를 믿고 따라다니는 것을 의미한다. 9 **gills** 그물눈청어는 입을 벌린 상태로 움직이면서 아가미로 물을 통과시킨다. 10 **herbaria** 안타깝게도 어떤 책도 잡초를 설명하지 않았으며, 미 식물 표본 집에도 그 표본이 존재하지 않았다. 11 **biodiversity** 툰드라 지역의 한가지 명백한 특성은 생물 다양성 수준이 매우 낮다는 것이다. 12 **pathological** 일부 연구가들은 왼손 잡이의 특성이 병리학상의 기원을 가지고 있는 것으로, 태어날 당시 뇌 손상에 의해 나타났을 것이라고 주장한다. 13 **vertebrates** 최초로 하늘을 날았던 척추동물은 파충류로서, 수족으로부터 뻗어있는 손가락 중 하나는 매우 길게 되어 있었다. 14 **invertebrates** 일부 해양 무 척추 동물들은 봄 혹은 초여름 동안, 깊은 수역에서 얕은 수역으로 이동한다. 15 **metamorphosis** 나비는 애벌레에서 번데기로 변하면서 변태 과정을 겪는다. 16 **superficial** 그 두 생물은 단지 외형적으로만 비슷할 뿐이었다. 17 **avalanches** 산악 지방에서 주로 나타나는 눈사태는 지진의 진동, 인간 활동, 혹은 과도한 강수에 의해서 일으켜진다. 18 **estuaries** 다른 삼각주들은 그 지역의 조수와 파력이 너무 커서 전혀 삼각주처럼 보이지 않고 오히려 하구처럼 보인다. 19 **longitude** 경도선은 북극에서 남극으로 이어져 있다. 20 **coma** 눈에 보이는 코마는 핵으로부터 빠져 나온 가스와 먼지로 형성된 거대한 구름층이다. 21 **Reclamation** 개간은 경작이 불가능한 토지를 농업에 적합한 토지로 바꾸는 성공적인 방법이다. 22 **congregate** 별과 마찬가지로 은하계도 무리를 이루려는 경향이 있다. 23 **Granite** 화강암은 거친 알갱이로 이루어진 화성암으로 각 생물 결정은 육안으로 보여질 정도의 크기로 형성된다. 24 **lava** 녹은 상태에서, 그 물질이 지각으로 흘러 들어가면 마그마라고 하고, 표면 위로 흐르면 용암이라고 부른다. 25 **asteroids** 태양계에는 240개의 달, 즉 자연적 위성이 존재하는데 이것들은 행성과 소행성 주위를 돌고 있다. 26 **bulging** 행성은 그 자전으로 인하여 극지방은 약간 평평하게, 그리고 적도 지방은 약간 불룩하게 되어 있다. 27 **scrapped** 지하철을 건설하려던 Denver의 계획은 1970년대 폐기되었다. 28 **tectonics** 지질학자들은 판 구조론의 이해로서 지표면에 대한 새로운 역사를 구성해내고 있다. 29 **Latitude** 위도 선은 적도에서 0도가 되고 북쪽으로 북극까지 올라가 북위 90도가 된다. 30 **stark** 화성은 인간에게 적합한 장소가 아니며, 지구보다는 지구의 달과 보다 더 그 환경이 유사하다 즉 건조하고, 삭막하고, 생명체가 살 수 없는 듯 보인다.

UNIT 60 Check-up Quiz
p.282

1 **vicinity** 대도시 지역은 중심부와 그 주변에 위치한 주변부로 구성된다. 2 **feasibility** 운하는 결코 완성되지 못했지만, 운하의 실현 가능성은 국가적으로 알려졌다. 3 **arch** 시장에 의해 지명된 위원회는 전사한 군인들을 기리기 위한 기념 아치를 세울 것이다. 4 **divergence** 18세기 중 후반 대다수 국내 건축은 그 선호도가 서로 나누어지는 모습을 보이고 있다. 5 **topography** 그와 그의 형제들은 공원들이 지역적인 지형에 적합해야 한다는 점을 믿었다. 6 **orders** 과학자들은 벼룩이 기타 다른 목의 곤충들과 어떤 관련이 있는지에 대해 의견을 달리하고 있다. 7 **environmentally-kind** 현재 보다 환경 친화적 연료인 그린 연료가 시장에 많이 나와 있다. 8 **adrenal** 각 신장의 위쪽에 위치한 부신선은 여러 중요한 호르몬들을 분비한다. 9 **cardiac** 이름에서 알 수 있는 것처럼 심장근은 심장을 둘러싼 근육으로 몸 전체에 혈액을 공급하는 중요한 역할을 맡고 있다. 10 **inflammation** 뇌염은 뇌에 염증이 생기는 것으로서 광견병에 의해 생길 수 있다. 11 **hyperopia** 때로는 성장하면서 안구의 모양이 바뀌어 원시가 완화되기도 한다. 12 **narcolepsy** 과학자들은 발작성 수면이 수 세대 동안 전해 내려온 유전성 질환이라고 믿고 있다. 13 **antidepressants** Alaska의 10명 중 7명 정도의 보건 전문가들은 환자들에게 항우울제를 처방한다. 14 **neutron** 중성자는 아무런 전하도 띠지 않는 중성 입자이다. 15 **photosynthesis** 녹색 식물의 광합성 과정에서는 빛 에너지가 포착되어 사용된다. 16 **genetics** 우리의 체질은 보통 유전에 의해 결정이 된다. 17 **antioxidant** 한약 가운데 한 가지 훌륭한 예가 버섯차인데, 이것은 탁월한 항산화제이다. 18 **asthma** 뜨겁고 습한 날씨는 천식을 더욱 악화시킬 수 있다. 19 **chromosomes** 유기체의 거의 모든 유전 물질들은 염색체 내에 존재한다. 20 **endocrine** 내분비계는 신경계와 밀접히 관련되어 기능한다. 21 **cornea** 각막은 이물질과 같은 물질에 맞서 눈의 내부 작용이 제대로 일어나도록 하는 보호 작용을 한다. 22 **lens** 수정체는 상이 안쪽 망막에 맺히기 전에 상의 초점을 맞춘다. 23 **myopia** 근시가 있는 사람들은 멀리 있는 것은 잘 보지 못하지만, 가까이에 있는 것들은 아주 잘 본다. 24 **measles** 홍역의 증상에는 고열, 목 주변의 갑상선 팽창, 그리고 기침이 있다. 25 **polio** 소아 마비용 백신은 Jonas Salk라는 의사에 의해서 발견되었다. 26 **receptors** 이것은 뇌의 특정 신경 세포 수용기와 관련된 유전자이다. 27 **kidneys** 신장은 혈관에서 불순물을 제거함으로써 건강을 유지하는데 매우 중요한 역할을 한다. 28 **pancreas** 호르몬인 세크레틴은 혈관을 따라 이동하여 췌장이 소화 액체를 분비하도록 자극한다. 29 **isotopes** 탄소는 탄소-12, 탄소-13, 탄소-14와 같은 동위원소가 있다. 30 **protons** 원자의 핵의 양성자 숫자는 원소마다 다양하다.

Chapter 15 Review Test
p.286

1. Ⓑ	2. Ⓐ	3. Ⓓ	4. Ⓓ
5. Ⓐ	6. Ⓑ	7. Ⓑ	8. Ⓑ
9. Ⓒ	10. Ⓑ	11. Ⓑ	12. Ⓓ
13. Ⓑ	14. Ⓑ	15. Ⓒ	16. Ⓐ

1 제조업자들은 새롭고 개선된 고정식 증기 엔진을 이용하여 자신들의 공장에 전력을 공급했다. 2 두 파벌간의 갈등의 결과 중 하나는 이전에 "미국적인", "본래의", 혹은 "New York"이라고 불리었던 학파가 1890년경에는 비평가와 대중들의 마음 속에 Hudson River 학파로 자리잡게 되었다는 점이다. 3 재산권이 재산 소유자로 하여금 부를 개발하고, 시장 원리에 기반한 자원의 효율적인 배분을 이룰 수 있게 한다는 강력한 사회적 합의가 존재한다. 4 그들의 규제는 관세를 높이는 것이었는데, 이는 국제적인 경쟁으로부터 미 산업주의자들을 보호하는데 일조했다. 5 신석기 시대 농부들은 보통 소비할 수 있는 것보다 많은 량의 식량을 생산하였는데, 이 잉여 생산물들로 인해 보다 많고 보다 건강한 인구가 나타나게 되었다. 6 기능주의의 기본적인 신조, 즉 기능이 형태를 결정 해야 한다는 점은 새로운 개념이 아니었다. 7 1992년150개국은 Rio de Janeiro에서 열린 UN 후원하의 정상 회담에서 지구 온난화에 관한 조약에 서명했다. 8 사회보장 수혜 금에는 이미 세금이 과다하게 붙어있다 예를 들면 수혜 금으로 20,000만 달러를 받는 28%의 계층에 속한 노년 부부는 세금으로 2,800달러를 지불하고 있다. 9 이러한 부분 가운데 어느 하나가 손상되어 제대로 발달하지 못하는 경우에는 시력에 문제가 생기게 된다. 10 달의 궤도는 황도 면에 대해 약간 기울어 있고 이심 율이 그다지 크지 않아 이러한 일식 혹은 월식이 매번 발생하지는 않는다 하지만 부분일식과 개기일식은 다소 빈번히 일어나는 편이다. 11 실제로 'give and take' 방식은, 과학자들이 합의를 이루기 전에 자신들의 결과물 혹은 다른 학자들의 결과물들을 서로 교환하는, 협력의 한 방법이다. 12 건조한 기후가 계속되면서 대도시 지역의 토양은 메마르게 되었고, 옥수수, 토마토, 건초, 그리고 사료의 생산이 차질을 빚게 되었다 또한 사람들이 선호하는 여름 과일 및 채소의 공급량이 감소되어 그 가격이 증가할 것이었다. 13 고래는 물고기와 겉으로는 비슷하지만, 다른 포유류와 마찬가지로 뼈대, 관, 영양분, 호흡, 감각, 생식의 구조를 가지고 있는 온혈 동물이다. 14 매년 여름 Alaska 북쪽 전역에서 온 곰들은 McNeil 강을 따라 모인다. 15 그 사고는 이웃 나라뿐만 아니라 근처의 수많은 사람들에게도 치명적인 피해를 입혔다. 16 환경부는 유독성 대기 오염 인자에 대한 허용치를 결정할 때, 단지 건강만을 생각하고 그 비용이나 기술적인 실현 가능성은 고려하지 못했다.